Praise for *Until Justice 1*

"There are several themes that emerge in this excellent book. ...
do with how African-Americans led the struggle [Kate] Masur describes, even
as racially discriminatory laws made them vulnerable—whether to the whims
of local officials exerting their discretion or to white mobs seeking legal cover
for anti-Black violence. Another concerns how the language of race and class
was, as Masur puts it, 'fungible': Even after the Civil War, legislation cracking
down on 'vagrancy' and 'vagabondage' allowed state legislatures in the former Confederacy to practice discrimination under cover of laws that seemed
'race-neutral.' . . . Masur takes care to show not only the limitations of what
was achieved at each step but also how even the smallest step could lead to
another. The people she writes about seized openings and opportunities where
they could find them, and then they used any hard-won advances to push for
more." —Jennifer Szalai, *New York Times*

"We should feel blessed that Kate Masur . . . has now turned her attention to
the long-sanitized early days of the republic with *Until Justice Be Done*. Prodi-
giously researching legislative and court records, pamphlets, petitions, and the
press. . . . Ms. Masur's monumental account focuses not only on government-
sanctioned pre-Civil War racism, but on the efforts by black activists and their
white allies to compel America to make good on the 'created equal' pledge
in the Declaration of Independence. . . . [Masur's] book should mortify any
reader who still doubts that America was in many ways built on a foundation
of white supremacy and black oppression."
—Harold Holzer, *Wall Street Journal*

"Masur's monumental account leaves no doubt that a generation of 19th-
century racial egalitarians altered history. They forced white supremacists to
change course, and they created resources used ever since by advocates in the
fight for equality." —John Fabian Witt, *Washington Post*

"Masur . . . skillfully establishes that 'America's first civil rights movement' started as far back as the late 18th century. The free states of the North and Midwest, she insightfully argues, constituted a 'post-slavery' society where resistance to anti-Black laws formed a foundation for later federal legislation and constitutional reform. . . . Masur's account speaks across time."
—Jill Watts, *New York Times Book Review*

"A clear and compelling account, Masur's book pushes us to rethink our understanding of anti-Blackness in the North and the activism that helped free Black people through the constitutional amendments that abolished slavery and granted them citizenship and equal protection under the law. . . . One aspect of Masur's book that is particularly welcome is her decision to center her narrative on the efforts of Black Americans to achieve a national consensus surrounding citizenship and civil rights."
—Kellie Carter Jackson, *Nation*

"Through her engaging prose, clear narrative framework, and ability to weave in a wide cast of characters, Masur has written a book that will fundamentally reshape the understanding of the abolitionist movement."
—Erik J. Chaput, *Providence Journal*

"A rich survey of antiracist politics. . . . Masur neither idealizes her subjects nor denigrates them for failing to live up to some heroic activist ideal. Their accomplishments were hard-fought, partial, and often precarious, yet real enough given all that their demand for equality was up against. Moreover, in helping to prepare a generation of reformers who went on to make sweeping legal change at the national level, Masur's first civil rights movement helped create the tools and lay the foundations for modern civil rights reform."
—Sean Wilentz, *New York Review of Books*

"*Until Justice Be Done* is necessary reading for any scholar of U.S. history. In addition to the book's important contributions to the historiography of activism, law, race, and the Civil War, the book offers striking methodological insights about centering Black actors in historical study, the chronology of U.S. history, the intersection between law and everyday life, and the distinction between civil and political rights, that will provoke discussion for years to come. I also hope that the work will receive a wide readership beyond academia. It is filled with interesting characters, and it frames the essential question of citizenship in a non-polemical manner that may well challenge those of various political stripes to reexamine their ideas and strategies for honoring, changing, or using the Constitution."

—Ben Davidson, *Civil War Book Review*

"Marvelous.... *Until Justice Be Done* ... is stuffed with ... fascinating revelations. It is a treasure trove for readers interested in politics, race, and law in antebellum America."   —Reuel Schiller, *JOTWELL Legal History*

"*Until Justice Be Done* pays tribute to the forgotten foundational work that must precede social change. Entrenched interests rarely concede power or privilege until required to do so, whether by law or force of arms, and even if so persuaded, rights won must be protected and defended against repeal. As we see in our own time, America is still grappling with the fact that it was born in slavery and weaned on racism."

—Brian Tanguay, *California Review of Books*

"During the George Floyd family press conference following the Chauvin conviction . . . Rev. Al Sharpton admonished the audience to remember those in the struggle for equality who had come before: 'The movement didn't start with us. We are a continuation of movements before us and they will continue until [we attain] freedom.' Kate Masur has captured many of those initial legal battles for the soul of this nation. When America finally does realize Martin Luther King's 'mighty stream' of justice, it will stretch all the way back to the headwaters of the Republic."

—Jim Swearingen, *National Book Review*

"*Until Justice Be Done* demonstrates that the fight for equality and justice is as old as the republic itself. With meticulous research, Masur lays out the history of Black Americans' struggle to be recognized as citizens—a struggle that started before the ink on the Constitution was dry. . . . While these activists' victories weren't total—many of their achievements were later reversed—their efforts laid essential groundwork for future generations, including our own. Masur's book is both instructive and inspiring as it charts the path to freedom from the 1800s to today."　　　—*BookPage*

"A stunning accomplishment. . . . Masur shows that opposition to racial inequality had much deeper roots than previously thought. . . . What makes the work so brilliant is Masur's ability to connect seemingly unrelated events in different states: from the institution of racial restrictions through poor laws to state campaigns against those restrictions to, ultimately, the push to change the entire balance of power in the federal system. . . . It is a story of heroism and hope: of a biracial movement, built brick by brick, which successfully addressed deeply rooted racial inequalities and changed the course of the country."　　　—Laura F. Edwards, Princeton University

"A truly extraordinarily book from which I learned something on almost literally every page. . . . Kate Masur has written what should be recognized as a classic, upending lots of "conventional wisdom." . . . No book published in recent years deserves more careful study by anyone seeking illumination about the American past and pondering any "lessons" of that past for our present and future."　　　—Sanford Levinson, University of Texas

"A new and utterly convincing account of the historical roots of the Civil Rights Act of 1866 and the Fourteenth Amendment. This book will forever change the way we think about the history of citizenship, civil rights, constitutional change, and the long struggle for racial justice in America. It is impossible to overstate the accomplishment here."
　　　—William J. Novak, University of Michigan

"Kate Masur's sobering and inspiring history of the 'first civil rights movement' could not be more timely."

—Steven Hahn, author of *A Nation Under Our Feet*

"[A] tour de force of scholarship and lucid analysis."

—James M. McPherson, author of *Battle Cry of Freedom*

"*Until Justice Be Done* tells the origin story of one of the most important and often-misunderstood ideas in American law and politics: racial equality before the law. It is a brilliant book."

—Dylan C. Penningroth, author of *The Claims of Kinfolk*

"In our current moment, as we imagine paths forward for American democracy, Kate Masur's revelatory book is essential reading."

—Daniel J. Sharfstein, author of *Thunder in the Mountains*

ALSO BY KATE MASUR

An Example for All the Land:
Emancipation and the Struggle Over Equality in Washington, D.C.

The World the Civil War Made
(coedited with Gregory P. Downs)

They Knew Lincoln
by John E. Washington (editor)

UNTIL
JUSTICE
BE DONE

America's First Civil Rights Movement,
from the Revolution to Reconstruction

KATE MASUR

W. W. NORTON & COMPANY
Independent Publishers Since 1923

For information about permission to reproduce selections from this book, write to Permissions,
W. W. Norton & Company, Inc., 500 Fifth Avenue, New York, NY 10110

For information about special discounts for bulk purchases, please contact
W. W. Norton Special Sales at specialsales@wwnorton.com or 800-233-4830

Manufacturing by LSC Communications Harrisonburg
Book design by Patrice Sheridan
Production manager: Julia Druskin

Library of Congress Cataloging-in-Publication Data

Names: Masur, Kate, author.
Title: Until justice be done : America's first civil rights movement, from the revolution to
    reconstruction / Kate Masur.
Other titles: America's first civil rights movement, from the revolution to reconstruction
Description: First edition. | New York : W. W. Norton & Company, [2021] | Includes
    bibliographical references and index.
Identifiers: LCCN 2020045654 | ISBN 9781324005933 (hardcover) |
    ISBN 9781324005940 (epub)
Subjects: LCSH: African Americans—Civil rights—History—19th century. | Civil rights
    movements—United States—History—19th century. | African Americans—Politics and
    government—19th century. | African Americans—Legal status, laws, etc.—History—
    19th century.
Classification: LCC E185.18 .M337 2021 | DDC 323.1196/07309034—dc23
LC record available at https://lccn.loc.gov/2020045654

ISBN 978-1-324-02184-1 pbk.

W. W. Norton & Company, Inc., 500 Fifth Avenue, New York, N.Y. 10110
www.wwnorton.com

W. W. Norton & Company Ltd., 15 Carlisle Street, London W1D 3BS

1 2 3 4 5 6 7 8 9 0

FOR PETER

CONTENTS

PREFACE

IN THE SUMMER OF 1843, a group of African American activists in Ohio—among them ministers, teachers, and laborers—convened in the state capital of Columbus with the primary goal of fighting the state's racist laws. Since the first decade of the nineteenth century, the laws of this free state had construed African Americans as a separate and threatening class of people. Ohio laws prohibited Black people from testifying in cases involving whites. The laws required African Americans to register with local authorities, which included paying fees and finding two landowners to promise that they would not become dependent on public resources. These discriminatory laws, which abridged what many considered basic civil rights, were commonly known as the "black laws."

African American men were not permitted to vote in Ohio, despite a declaration in the 1803 Ohio Constitution "that all men are born equally free and independent, and have certain natural, inherent and unalienable rights." The constitution reserved the franchise to white men, leaving Ohio's Black residents, just one percent of the total population, at the mercy of the white majority that elected the legislators who wrote the laws. If African Americans wanted state laws to change, they needed to persuade white Ohioans that their cause was just.

The result of the 1843 meeting was an address to the "citizens of Ohio," written by four men, including A. M. Sumner, a Tennessee-born barber, and George Vashon, the first African American graduate of Oberlin College. The address called on white Ohioans to recognize the injustice of their laws, insisting that the government's policy toward them was "utterly at variance" with the promises of the Declaration of Independence. State law "should constitute the bulwark of our liberties," the committee declared, and yet Ohio law was "employed as the instrument to hunt us down to degradation and shame." The group implored white Ohioans to see the world through their eyes. Their own state denied their fundamental rights, while just to the south, the slave states of Virginia and Kentucky were even worse. "Is life secure, is liberty inviolate, is the pursuit of happiness left open to us," they asked, "when . . . the hand of the ruffians can be raised against our existence with impunity; when the legislatures of adjoining states hesitate not to enact laws which militate against freedom, and the laws of our own state . . . may be construed to deprive us of the enjoyment of liberty[?]"[1]

Would the Ohio legislature allow the racist laws to remain? Or would voters change course and embrace the principle of racial equality before the law? Across the twenty-six states that then formed the United States, state legislatures enjoyed enormous authority, and laws that singled out Black residents for discriminatory treatment were widely accepted. Writing in 1846, a political season in which repeal of the Ohio black laws took center stage, the *Cincinnati Enquirer,* a Democratic newspaper, defended the laws with the argument that they were among the many kinds of regulations "which may be designed for the protection and peace of the actual settlers of a State." States were entitled to adopt policies that guarded residents against threats of fire, disease, crime, and other kinds of disorder. If the Ohio legislature believed that African Americans threatened the public peace, the *Enquirer* contended, it was within its rights to impose special regulations designed to discourage them from entering its jurisdiction and to hem them in once they arrived.[2]

The push to repeal the Ohio black laws was one revealing episode in a sustained struggle over race and equality that stretched from the nation's founding until the Civil War and beyond. Across the free states, activists forcefully insisted that laws that made explicit race-based distinctions had no place in American life. The movement began in the era of the American Revolution, when demands for citizenship and equal rights for Black Americans were part of broader revolutionary currents that emphasized the dignity and fundamental equality of all humanity. Advocates persisted in the period of retrenchment that followed, as states increasingly adopted laws that construed free Black people as an unwanted class. They made their case in antislavery societies, in the press, and in party politics, where they eventually found a home in the Republican Party. During the Civil War and Reconstruction, Republican majorities in Congress pursued the agenda of racial equality before the law that earlier generations of activists had established. Empowered by the crisis, they passed the nation's first federal civil rights law and the Fourteenth Amendment, which forever changed how Americans understood individual rights and their protection.

This sustained struggle against racist laws was America's first civil rights movement. We have often failed to see this movement because our focus was elsewhere—on the origins of the sectional crisis, the great pre–Civil War debate over slavery, or the history of northern Black communities themselves. What we have missed was a struggle for racial equality in civil rights that spanned the first eight decades of the nation's history, a movement that traveled from the margins of American politics to the center and ended up transforming the US Constitution. The movement encompassed pastors, journalists, lawyers, politicians, and countless ordinary citizens who demanded that the nation's white majority reject racist laws and join the struggle for a better, more just society. Activists mainly advanced their arguments at the state level, where most individual rights were defined and enforced. When they could find a constitutional rationale to do so, they also addressed the federal government, in Congress and in the courts. They pressed new ideas about citizenship, individual rights, and the proper scope of state power, and their arguments informed the remarkable congressional debates of the 1860s.

The movement described in this book was a coalition that encompassed people with a wide array of views. African Americans were at the forefront of the activism and conceived racial equality most expansively. For Black people, the urgency was greater than for whites, and so was the danger. It was their children who were denied education, their property that could not be defended in court if they could not testify, and their brothers who might end up in a southern jail while pursuing their livelihoods as sailors. In the decades after the American Revolution, African Americans in the free states developed activist networks that spanned cities and regions. In newspapers such as New York City's *Freedom's Journal* and Ohio's *Palladium of Liberty,* Black correspondents and editors denounced racism and advocated racial equality in all areas—not only in what contemporaries understood as basic civil rights but also in political rights and public accommodations, including railroads, steamships, and hotels. "Repeal all laws and parts of laws that make a distinction on account of color," the Ohio convention demanded in 1843, "and you will make manifest to the world your love of justice, your hatred of oppression, and your determination to preserve a strict adherence to the great principles of your fathers."

The white northerners who participated in the movement for civil rights in these decades emerged from diverse political orientations, held different beliefs and convictions, and felt varying levels of commitment to the cause. They included radical abolitionists who followed the famous leader William Lloyd Garrison beginning in the early 1830s, but their ranks extended well beyond that. In the states carved from the Northwest Territory—Ohio, Indiana, Illinois, Michigan, and Wisconsin—antislavery activists made repeal of state-level black laws central to their movement. In the Northeast, particularly in Massachusetts and New York, merchants who did business in the slave states joined committed antislavery activists in a struggle for recognition of the civil rights of northern Black sailors who worked in southern ports.

The struggle was arduous. Most white northerners were indifferent, particularly early on, and the influence of African Americans was limited by Black men's inability to vote in most places. The political-party system that characterized the antebellum era—a rivalry between the Whigs and the Democrats—did not help. Leaders of both parties were committed to suppressing the sectionally divisive issue of slavery, and questions of racial equality were almost as volatile. Activists therefore turned to a rich array of political strategies in addition to voting. They organized petition campaigns that drew thousands of women and men into the movement. They lobbied elected officials, writing to them directly or visiting in person. And they worked to shape public opinion by giving speeches and publishing newspapers and pamphlets. All these forms of activism were available, albeit in uneven ways, not just to white men but also to African Americans and white women.

The movement for racial equality in civil rights gradually found purchase in politics by organizing insurgent third parties and also by pushing to reform existing parties from within. In the mid-1850s, amid a national crisis over the expansion of slavery, the party system defined by the Whig–Democrat rivalry collapsed, and the Republican Party took form. Leaders of this new party, which was based almost entirely in the free states, embraced the movement's longstanding vision for civil rights. Some of them, including Salmon Chase of Ohio and Henry Wilson of Massachusetts, had a long history of pushing for racial equality in their home states. Others, such as Lyman Trumbull of Illinois, had played almost no role in the antebellum struggle but became reliable advocates during and after the Civil War.

The war settled the question of slavery itself, but it resolved nothing about the future of African Americans in the United States. In the war's aftermath, after some two hundred fifty years of race-based slavery, the federal government was forced to consider what a postslavery United States would look like. To which rights were newly freed people entitled? How would those rights be protected? Would the US government step in when

state and local officials curtailed people's rights and, if so, under what circumstances? This book demonstrates that the Republicans who led the
federal government in that pivotal time had years of experience with such
questions. The antebellum north had been, in its own way, a postslavery
society. At the time of the nation's founding, slavery had been legal almost
everywhere, while in the Northwest Territory, where the federal government outlawed slavery in 1787, states quickly adopted policies targeting
free Black people. Republican leaders of the Civil War generation had
witnessed—and in many cases joined—struggles to repeal racist laws and
advance the project of racial equality. Those fights gave them a vocabulary
and a set of principles that they translated into national policy during and
immediately after the war. The Civil Rights Act of 1866 declared African
Americans citizens of the United States and promised them the same civil
rights as white citizens. The Fourteenth Amendment did that and more,
promising equal protection of the law and due process of law to all persons
living under US jurisdiction. These measures were the culmination of a
decades-long movement that insisted that all people, not just white people,
were entitled to protection of their civil rights.

LIKE ITS SUCCESSOR in the twentieth century, there was nothing foreor-
dained about the success of the first civil rights movement. The positions
it took were broadly unpopular. Northern Democrats in particular moved
easily from traditional concerns about the economic dependency of formerly enslaved people to visions of Black criminality and racial inferiority.
Many white northerners who considered themselves forward-thinking on
issues of race and slavery believed that the United States was destined to
be a white nation in which free African Americans would never truly have
a place. Among them were supporters of the American Colonization Society and its decades-long drive to persuade free Black people to emigrate to
Liberia. At the same time, many white Americans viewed laws designed to
constrain and marginalize free Black people as entirely justifiable within

a broader legal and cultural tradition that encouraged state and local governments to regulate groups of people who were construed to be dependent and potentially disruptive, including paupers, vagrants, wives, and children.

The movement for racial equality confronted all these ideas about race and government while also adapting itself to the constitutional order in which it operated. The American Revolution had bequeathed to Americans the Declaration of Independence and its ringing promise that "all men are created equal." But the revolution had also given the nation the Constitution, a blueprint for governing that gave state and local governments tremendous power over the status and rights of their inhabitants. In a world that was anything but egalitarian, states were empowered to legalize a host of coercive practices designed to control and manage groups considered to be dangerous or destabilizing. Legislators wrote laws targeting the transient poor and allowing paupers and vagrants to be expelled from communities at will. They construed married women and children as dependents of their husbands and fathers, denying them rights and limiting their liberty. Most germane to the activists described in this book, they passed race-based regulations that not only legalized slavery itself but also targeted free Black people and Native Americans. People seeking to challenge such oppressions found little support in the first eight amendments to the Constitution, now known as the Bill of Rights. Although those amendments, adopted in 1791, enumerated a variety of individual rights, the prevailing view was that they were designed to limit the power of the federal government, not the states.

Movement activists made their case in constitutional terms anyway. They focused much of their energy at the state level. Sometimes they adopted the language of legal personhood; other times, the concept of citizenship. Both had constitutional foundations—personhood in the Bill of Rights, and citizenship in the Constitution's privileges and immunities clause (Article IV, Section 2). They directed their claims at courts when they could. But state courts were immensely deferential to legislatures, and getting a case about the rights of free African Americans into federal court proved exceedingly difficult. Many of the most important debates about race and civil rights, therefore, occurred in meetings, newspapers, and political venues. State legislators, activist lawyers, and everyday people all engaged with constitutional questions, some challenging and others accepting what legal authorities had to say. Congress was also a crucial site for constitutional interpretation. This was evident during the Missouri crisis of 1819–21, as well as on the several occasions when it debated legislation to enforce the privileges and immunities clause, and when, after the Civil War, it decided that the Constitution must be dramatically altered.

What brought the disparate groups of people in this movement together was a commitment to racial equality in what they often termed *civil rights*. For Americans of the early nineteenth century, civil rights were basic or fundamental rights associated with being a free person. Virginia congressman Philip P. Barbour, who later became a Supreme Court justice, described "civil rights" in 1820 as the rights of "personal liberty and the free possession and enjoyment of personal property."[3] These were rights associated with the abstract promises of "life, liberty, and property" handed down from English common law and referenced in the Declaration of Independence. Adding specificity, Barbour's contemporaries would have mentioned the rights to enter into contracts, sue and be sued, testify in court, and more generally to receive protection from the law. Most Americans of this era distinguished civil rights from political rights, which included the rights to vote, hold office, and serve on juries. The majority believed political rights were more like privileges, reserved for a subset of people charged with making decisions for the whole community. Some of the white Americans who joined the movement to secure civil rights for free African Americans wanted to go no further than that. They did not support racial equality in political rights, or they did so only reluctantly, when pushed by the force of the Civil War and the need to reconstruct the nation. That cohort was in a sense the movement's lowest common denominator, a part of the coalition that was both critically important and, at times, frustratingly timid.

———— ·•· ————

THE FIRST CIVIL RIGHTS MOVEMENT had proponents and leaders in every free state, but this book focuses on several locales that stand out for their significance in the broader struggle. The states carved from the Northwest Territory are of particular interest because it was there that the experiment with barring slavery while permitting racially discriminatory laws took hold most firmly. Ohio is especially prominent as the first state created from the Northwest Territory and the first to adopt antiblack laws. It remained the most populous Old Northwest state throughout this period and was home to the largest Black population and the most robust abolitionist movement. Ohio was also the Old Northwest state where the movement against racist laws was most successful. The history of Illinois offers a counterexample, showing how Democrats continued to mobilize to bar Black migration and deny Black citizenship in the 1850s, but also how the nascent Republican Party staked out a very different position.

Early on, Philadelphia and New York City emerged as centers of African American activism, places where abolitionists cultivated and sustained the vision of universal rights represented by the Declaration of Independence. The states of New York and Massachusetts also loom large because there, agitators together with legislators made the most consequential arguments that free African Americans were state citizens, entitled to enjoy the privileges and immunities of citizenship promised by the Constitution's Article IV, Section 2. Massachusetts activists and politicians, supporting African American sailors working in southern ports, invoked the privileges and immunities clause to insist on the right of free African Americans to move freely from one state to another. At the end of the 1830s, the Massachusetts legislature instructed the governor to use public funds to rescue Black citizens from southern jails; in the early 1840s, legislators succeeded in getting Congress involved in the issue.

Washington, DC, is essential to this story, both as the seat of the US government and because of its anomalous constitutional status. Activists often pushed the struggle for racial equality into the halls of Congress, seeking to publicize their agenda and provoke outsize reactions from southern legislators. At the same time, because the Constitution placed the District of Columbia under the "exclusive" jurisdiction of Congress, civil rights advocates frequently made it a target, especially by demanding respect for the rights of free Black northerners who traveled there. Still, efforts to bring the question of racial equality before federal authorities—Congress as well as the courts—were only marginally successful in an era in which southern slaveholders held disproportionate power in Washington.

In the free states by 1860, the movement for racial equality was on solid ground, but it was the cataclysm of the Civil War that gave Republicans an opportunity to implant their vision in federal policy. When the Republicans of 1865 and 1866 crafted the language of the Fourteenth Amendment, which explicitly limited the power of the states, they were tackling a problem they knew well. Many had long opposed racially discriminatory laws in the states and wanted to ensure that the Constitution barred such laws forever. When they included in the amendment the language of "privileges or immunities"—and referenced both state and federal citizenship—they were trying to resolve problems that had long bedeviled northerners who demanded respect for the rights of free African Americans. Yet the unprecedented federal civil rights measures also had their limits, and this book helps explain those, too. Why did Republicans resist the argument that new promises of equality should encompass sex as well as race? Why did they not address the antivagrancy laws and other race-neutral measures that targeted poor people and remained so effective in limiting the freedom and opportunities of Black Americans? And why, even after the new measures passed, did states retain such expansive powers to oppress?

The end of explicitly racist laws did not mean the end of racist law enforcement, much less the end of racism itself. That much remains terribly clear. Yet the first civil rights movement changed America. The movement advanced a vision of racial equality that, despite the ideals set forth in the Declaration of Independence, had never been pursued or widely accepted in state or federal policy. Its most enduring consequence, the Fourteenth Amendment, became a bulwark for individual rights. It is the constitutional foundation on which generations of people living in the United States have built their demands for equal protection and due process of law, and on which Americans have made claims to birthright citizenship.

The movement's accomplishments are all the more impressive if we consider the immensity of the opposition. Those who fought for racial equality in civil rights confronted deeply ingrained convictions about white racial superiority that originated in centuries of African slavery and Native dispossession. Moreover, to secure federal protections for the rights of vulnerable individuals, the movement challenged American federalism and its tradition of allowing states to determine the status and rights of their residents. In every generation, those who have waged such struggles have encountered staunch, often violent, resistance. The people portrayed in this book persevered, acting on the conviction that we are better off without racist laws than with them, and better off struggling for justice in a multiracial society than rejecting the possibility that one could exist.

UNTIL JUSTICE BE DONE

CHAPTER 1

"ON THE GROUNDS OF EXPEDIENCY AND GOOD POLICY"

Free-State Antiblack Laws in the Early Republic

JOHN BURNS WAS one of thousands of African American Virginians who made his way north across the Ohio River in the early decades after American independence. For Burns it was not a simple process. In late November 1813, he visited the clerk of Augusta County, Virginia, and secured papers certifying that he was "a freeman by birth," raised in the county, and "a man of good character." Three days later, a justice of the peace issued Burns a paper that declared the clerk's document authentic. Burns then received yet another document. It was a pass, signed by the clerk, that linked his name with his physical attributes. The pass read: "John Burns of Dark yellow complexion, about thirty years of age, five feet ten inches high, born free and by trade a shoemaker. Requested in said office this day."[1]

Twelve months later, Burns was more than three hundred miles from home. He had crossed the Allegheny Mountains and the Ohio River into the free state of Ohio. His papers would have served him on his journey, allowing him to prove that he was a free man, entitled to his liberty. In slaveholding Virginia, dark skin color or the appearance of being a person of African descent were considered prima facie evidence of enslaved status; the burden was on the person of color to produce evidence that he or she was free. What could Burns expect in Ohio? North of the Ohio River, slavery had been outlawed by the Northwest Ordinance of 1787. The Ohio Constitution of 1803 strongly disavowed slavery, but state laws passed in 1804 and 1807 required that free Black people register with county officials and, in a host of other ways, established that African Americans could not expect the same freedoms as white residents of Ohio.

Burns arrived in Chillicothe, then the state capital of Ohio, and presented his papers to the county clerk of Ross County. The law required not only that African Americans register but also that they get two landowners to pledge to pay up to $500 in expenses, should the Black registrant prove unable to support him or herself. The Ross County clerk registered Burns, even though he did not have those sureties. The clerk copied the text of Burns's papers into the record book, and with that, Burns become a legal resident of the county.

Free African Americans like John Burns, who sought to migrate from slave states to free ones, made the southern reaches of the Northwest Territory a battleground in a decades-long struggle over race and civil rights. In slaveholding states, the free Black population grew dramatically during and after the American Revolution. Maryland and Virginia in particular loosened their manumission laws, and enslaved people became free either by working to purchase themselves and family members or through the good graces of their owners. In Virginia, the US Census counted 12,866 free African Americans in 1790; ten years later, that population had increased to 20,124. But legislatures quickly moved to curtail that trend. In the 1780s and 1790s, the Virginia General Assembly passed laws that required free Black people to register with local officials and observe special curfews, barred free African Americans from testifying in cases involving whites, meted out harsher criminal penalties for Blacks than whites, and banned certain kinds of interactions between enslaved and free Black people. In

1793, Virginia became the first state to pass a law that banned free African Americans from migrating into the state.[2]

Retrenchment in the slave states coincided with growing American settlement north of the Ohio River. During the colonial period, slavery had put down roots in some areas of that immense expanse, particularly where French traders clustered in places such as Detroit and towns just east of the Mississippi River in the Illinois Country. Under American rule, however, the Northwest Ordinance of 1787 outlawed slavery in the region. Many white settlers who moved to the area were drawn there precisely because they wanted to avoid living amid human bondage. But as Virginia and the more recently settled state of Kentucky cracked down on free African Americans, white settlers north of the Ohio River increasingly feared that free Black people would choose to migrate into free territory, and they took action to discourage it.

From the outset, settlers in the Old Northwest adopted laws that imposed special regulations on free African Americans. The black laws of Ohio required migrants like John Burns to register with county officials and post bonds designed to ensure that they would not become dependent on public relief. They barred African Americans from testifying in court cases involving white people, and they allocated funds for the education of white children only. The state constitution permitted voting by white men only. Such provisions, and similar ones elsewhere in the region, reflected the possibility that jurisdictions—or, even at some future date, the nation as a whole—could reject race-based slavery but use lawmaking power to render African Americans as a suspect class, separate from and inferior to the white majority. A similar sentiment was evident in the goals of the American Colonization Society (ACS), an organization led by elite white men and founded in Washington in 1816. ACS leaders viewed the growing free Black population of the United States with concern, believing that free people of different races could not coexist as equals within a single nation. Seeking to resolve the problem as they understood it, they launched an effort to remove free African Americans from the United States.

Yet antiblack laws and the white-led colonization movement did not represent all of white opinion on the question of free African Americans' future in the free states, nor did oppression and degradation tell the whole story of African Americans' experiences on the northern side of the border with slavery. In Ohio, despite racist laws and sporadic but malignant white violence, African Americans managed to purchase land, establish communities, organize independent churches and schools, and build lives in relative freedom. There and elsewhere, African Americans resisted whites' claims that they did not belong. Together with white allies, they demanded a different vision for the United States—one in which African Americans were promised the same fundamental rights and the same legal protections as white people, where people of all races were equally entitled to life, liberty, and the pursuit of happiness.

———

ANTIBLACK LAWS IN FREE STATES such as Ohio enjoyed tremendous legitimacy and staying power. As late as the 1850s, some states in the former Northwest Territory and the Far West were still adopting new ones. The laws were racist by definition because they sorted people by race and subjected those deemed "negroes and mulattoes" to regulations that white people did not face. By the era of the American Revolution, Americans lived in a nation profoundly shaped by African slavery as well as settler colonialism, both premised on the idea that people of European origin were more entitled than others to benefit from the land and its bounty, to command labor, and to govern their communities. White Americans regularly told themselves that certain differences in background and physical appearance—in the continent where one's ancestors originated, or in skin tone and hair texture—aligned with meaningful differences in temperament or intelligence. Many hoped to create communities, states, or even an entire nation in which white people were the only ones who mattered.

But race was not the only kind of difference that was significant in this society, and many of the racist laws in Ohio and elsewhere were built atop laws designed to address challenges of poverty and dependency. These legal structures dated back to the sixteenth century and the English tradition of managing the poor. Local governments in England had responded to a rising population of mobile poor people and their demands for aid by establishing regulations designed to distinguish between those who belonged in the community and those who did not. The core idea in the English poor-law tradition was that families and communities were obliged to provide for their own dependent poor, but not for transients and strangers. The most privileged people were those with a legal "settlement." People who were legally settled in a local jurisdiction were recognized as permanent residents. If they became needy and had nowhere to turn, they might be able to draw on the public poor-relief fund. By contrast, local authorities were under no obligation to help residents who had no legal settlement. Officials could expel such people from the jurisdiction, sending them back to their place of origin. Even people considered *likely* to become a public charge could face regulation and removal.

Settlement law made no pretense of treating everyone equally. Its main orientation was not individual rights but community well-being, and in this context, persons who were perceived as economically and socially independent had far more privileges than those who were not. The ability to choose one's own legal settlement was most available to male heads of household, who in turn were expected to be responsible for dependents such as wives, children, and servants. Dependents who attempted to move on their own could be forcibly returned to the place where the husband, father, or master was a legal resident. Strangers seeking settlements in new communities had to pass certain hurdles—paying taxes, owning property, or posting security to indemnify the community against the possibility that they might become dependent on public welfare. If all went well, some might ultimately gain a settlement in a new place. The law of settlement meant that personal liberty—the ability to move freely from place to place—was unequally distributed. Male heads of households and landowners enjoyed the greatest privileges, while servants, women, children, and other dependents faced restrictions based on their status.[3]

In the British North American colonies, largely as in England, local authorities monitored who was moving into the community, and they treated potentially dependent people with special suspicion. Whether someone came into the jurisdiction from elsewhere in the colonies or from abroad mattered little in this regime of regulation. What was important to authorities was knowing who was there and trying to keep needy people, especially strangers, off the books. The American Revolution did not fundamentally change such practices. Americans brought traditional poor-law and settlement-law policies—always fluctuating but always present—into the new nation. In the words of an early historian of poor relief in the United States, "while the political and the economic legislation was revolutionary, the social followed the old and well marked grooves."[4] Enforcement continued at the town or county level, while state governments enacted statutes designed to inform local practices.

The Articles of Confederation, drafted amid the American Revolution in 1777, reflected the Anglo-American tradition of seeing the mobile poor—people often labeled "vagabonds" or "paupers"—as less than fully vested members of the community. The Articles were a precursor to the Constitution, drafted ten years later, and the goal was similar: to provide guidelines for knitting the disparate states into the "United States of America." Part of the fourth section of the Articles was designed to facilitate migration from state to state. "The better to secure and perpetuate mutual friendship and intercourse among the people of the different States in this Union," it read, "the free inhabitants of each of these States, paupers, vagabonds, and fugitives from justice excepted, shall be entitled to all privileges and immunities of free citizens in the several States." The clause used the terms *free inhabitants* and *citizens* interchangeably. As James Madison later lamented, "There is a confusion of language here which is remarkable."[5] But, in making a clear distinction between *free citizens* and those whose status was degraded, the measure reflected the idea, commonplace at the time, that paupers, vagrants, and criminals were not entitled to the same freedom of movement as other ostensibly free people. Free citizens ought to be able to travel freely among the states, the measure implied, while members of the excepted classes could not necessarily expect the "privileges and immunities" of citizenship when they moved into new jurisdictions.

The measure made no mention of race, and that was by design. During debate about the Articles of Confederation in the Second Continental Congress, delegates from South Carolina had suggested inserting the word *white* between the words *free* and *inhabitants*.[6] If they had had their way, the Articles would have promised privileges and immunities only to "free white inhabitants" of each state. Yet the Congress rebuffed their suggestion by a vote of eight states to two (with one state divided), so the provision remained as originally drafted. It suggested that free persons or citizens had certain privileges and immunities, without regard for race or color. And it rendered paupers, vagabonds, and fugitives as marginal, implying that local jurisdictions would be entirely within their rights to treat them as pariahs or even exclude them entirely. Such people might become dependent on local alms and disruptive of social harmony; they might threaten, either literally or figuratively, the health of the body politic.

In 1787, the framers of the US Constitution established a stronger federal government than the Articles of Confederation had provided. Yet the Constitution still left great power to the states. The system was complicated, and the boundaries between state and federal power, particularly when it came to interstate relations, deliberately were left vague. One starting point was reasonably clear, however. The states were in charge of issues associated with poverty and poor relief. The question of what to do about poor and needy people in the community fell under the broader umbrella of what contemporaries called the "domestic police." Alexander Hamilton called it the "mere" domestic police because the police powers seemed so mundane. He wrote in *Federalist Paper* No. 17 that even the most power-hungry leader would have no interest in commanding "those residuary authorities, which it might be judged proper to leave with the

States for local purposes." "The regulation of the *mere domestic police* of a State appears to me to hold out slender allurements to ambition," he added.[7]

Hamilton's views notwithstanding, the police powers of the states were far from diminutive in the lives of everyday people. The theory of police power was grounded not in the idea that a government's duty was to protect individual rights but, rather, in the conviction that government's most important obligation was to secure the health, safety, and general well-being of a community. States exercised their "police power" when they regulated slaughterhouses and ports; when they established rules for the sale and consumption of alcohol; or when they made provisions to encourage commerce and build infrastructure. Laws concerning paupers and vagrants, legal settlement, and the distribution of poor relief were all "police" laws, designed to ensure public peace and protect a community's coffers. In the slave states, people frequently described as police laws measures designed to prevent slave uprisings and otherwise safeguard the slave-holding order.[8] In this context, many Americans—in free states and slave states alike—viewed laws that imposed special regulations on free people of African or Native American descent as just another appropriate use of the police power.

The American Revolution did not fundamentally change American leaders' desire to create a peaceful and orderly society, but it did foster an abolitionist movement. Adopting revolutionaries' rhetoric of universal natural rights, African Americans claimed freedom and equality every way they could: by escaping from slavery during the war, filing freedom suits in local courts, and petitioning governments. Among white people, Quakers most often took the lead in the efforts to end slavery and emphasize the common humanity of all persons. Their movements saw tangible results, particularly in the northern tier of states whose economies were relatively less dependent on enslaved labor and plantation agriculture. Beginning with Vermont in 1777, states in the Northeast began to adopt abolition measures, and by 1800, six more—New Hampshire, Massachusetts,

Rhode Island, Connecticut, New York, and Pennsylvania—had passed gradual emancipation statutes or abolished slavery outright. The free Black population of these states grew dramatically in the nation's first decades as former slaves became free and newcomers arrived from elsewhere. In New England and the Mid-Atlantic states, the free African American population almost tripled between 1790 and 1810, increasing from 27,034 to 75,156. In 1804, New Jersey became the last state to join the first wave of state-level emancipations.[9]

The revolutionary era's abolitionist movement sought not only the end of race-based slavery but also the recognition of the fundamental rights of the newly freed. At the behest of abolitionist activists, states passed laws designed to protect free African Americans from kidnappers who looked for vulnerable people to steal into slavery farther south. Quaker-led organizations in New York City and Philadelphia—the New-York Manumission Society (NYMS) and the Pennsylvania Abolition Society (PAS)—provided legal defense for freedom-seekers and founded schools designed to help free African Americans flourish. Pennsylvania's Quaker-influenced emancipation law of 1780 began with an unequivocal condemnation of slavery and racial prejudice and included a provision requiring racial equality in the administration of criminal justice. In New York in the late eighteenth century, the NYMS helped rebuff efforts to restrict the rights of African Americans to vote, hold office, serve on juries, and marry white people. Indeed, the initial wave of states that undertook gradual emancipation imposed no special restrictions on African Americans' right to vote, so Black men became voters in many locales.[10]

In most states that carried out gradual emancipation, however, emancipation-related laws also revealed lawmakers' concerns about potential poverty, dependency, and criminality among the newly freed. Even before the Revolution, in northern seaboard cities, community authorities had regularly treated people of African descent as paupers or as strangers with no legal settlement, even when they were not in motion or transient. Colonial assemblies and town governments often demanded that free people of color show passes or proof of freedom when traveling.[11] Legislators who wrote gradual emancipation statutes during and after the Revolution showed similar concerns that the newly freed would become a drain on public coffers. Pennsylvania's 1780 law, for instance, created a system of registration for enslaved people and made provisions for the apprentice-ship of children whose owners relinquished them early. The law also held former slaveowners "liable" to local overseers of the poor for any expenses the overseers incurred in the upkeep of the owners' destitute former slaves.[12]

In contrast to Pennsylvania, Connecticut's Gradual Emancipation Act, passed four years later, maintained tight, settlement-based regulations on manumission. The portion of the law that provided for ending slavery began by alluding to government's mandate both to protect rights and to secure collective peace. Abolition, it said, "should be effected as soon as may be, consistent with the Rights of Individuals, and the Public Safety and Welfare." An owner wishing to manumit servants or slaves had to obtain approval from the town selectmen, who would assess whether the person, when free, was likely to become self-supporting. Slaveowners who did not go through the required approval process would be held financially responsible if a person they freed became a public charge. The law also articulated concerns about mobility of nonwhite and poor populations, requiring that "free Negroes," as well as "all Vagrants or suspected Per-sons," and all "servants" who were "Negro, Molatto, or Indian," must carry a "Ticket or Pass in Writing" that showed their status and presumably their place of settlement.[13]

In Massachusetts too, abolition was accompanied by both universal rights rhetoric and fears about poverty, crime, and dependency among free African Americans. The state's 1780 constitution forthrightly declared that "all men are born free and equal, and have certain natural, essential, and unalienable rights." On the basis of that sweeping language, the Massachu-setts Supreme Court declared in 1783 that slavery was legally dead. Then ensued several years of discussion in the general assembly about the future of slavery and free African Americans in the state. Finally, in March 1788, the assembly passed its first explicitly antislavery legislation, which barred residents from participating in the slave trade and kidnapping. The next day, it adopted a new residency law designed to address problems associated with "rogues, vagabonds, and common beggars." The residency law singled out Black people for special regulation, though it exempted subjects of Morocco, which in 1786 had become the first Muslim state to recognize American independence. According to the law, "no person being an African or Negro, other than a subject of the Emperor of Morocco or a citizen of some one of the United States," could remain in the state more than two months. Newcomers could establish their status as a "citizen" of another state by showing an official "certificate." Meanwhile, those who overstayed were subject to being "warned out"—asked to leave the jurisdiction and possibly forced to go—and, if they remained, to incarceration.[14]

Slaves and free people of African descent were not the only outsider populations that new state legislatures singled out as potentially dependent and damaging to the community. Public officials continued to pass and enforce settlement laws, and to arrest and remove people of all kinds for the crime of vagrancy. Many jurisdictions were particularly concerned about dependent immigrants from abroad. In 1785, for example, the Pennsylvania General Assembly provided for a registry of German passengers arriving at the busy port of Philadelphia. A health officer was authorized to perform inspections of the ships and empowered to send people back to their places of origin. Authorities regularly removed immigrants, and they were also empowered to bind out—or force into labor for a limited period of time—those permitted to land.[15]

In this world of intensive state and local efforts to regulate migration and settlement—efforts validated by a long tradition of policies designed to prevent the dependent poor from overwhelming local poor-relief funds— many people found it unremarkable that former slaves or racial "others" were singled out for special regulation. At the moment of manumission, freedpeople often had few resources of their own and limited opportunities to secure paid work. Yet valid concerns about the financial fortunes of people just freed from bondage readily melded with existing racial prejudices. Americans had varying views on what it meant that human beings came in varying colors, with different hair textures and physical features. Some claimed that newly freed slaves were poor merely because of their circumstances, while others insisted that enslavement and degradation were the natural destiny of people of African descent. Regardless of what they believed about the nature of race itself, however, their justifications for race-based laws entered deep currents in political and legal thought, which heightened their power. From the colonial period until the Civil War, white northerners regularly characterized free African Americans, as a group, as dependents, vagrants, or criminals who lowered the moral standards of the community. The poor-law tradition and the nation's federated structure itself, combined with antiblack racism, gave racist laws legitimacy and made them difficult to dislodge.

In the 1783 Treaty of Paris, Great Britain acknowledged that the colonists had won the American Revolution and ceded to them jurisdiction over almost 900,000 square miles of territory, extending from the Atlantic Ocean westward to the Mississippi River. The nation's legislature for most of the 1780s, the Confederation Congress, soon established rules for settlement of the area that became known as the Northwest Territory—the expanse of land, some 260,000 square miles, that lay west of the Appalachians and north of the Ohio River. The British had previously attempted to restrict white settlement in the region, hoping to avoid costly wars with Native American groups that had forged longstanding military and trading alliances with colonial powers. The US government now moved to incorporate the region into the United States and open the way for settlement. In 1785, a federal Land Ordinance established the Midwest's distinctively rectangular political geography by prescribing square townships, six miles long on each side, with straight county roads to demarcate boundaries. Two years later, Congress passed the Northwest Ordinance, which formally established the Northwest Territory and provided mechanisms for creating political institutions and eventually converting the federal territories into new states. This was the first time the US government had created a federal territory.

Consistent with the strand of revolutionary-era thought that proclaimed natural rights and human equality, the Northwest Ordinance outlawed slavery throughout the territory. "There shall be neither slavery nor involuntary servitude in the . . . territory," read Article 6, except as "punishment of crimes whereof the party shall have been duly convicted." In reality, slavery already existed there. Along the Mississippi River and in areas of the Illinois Country, from the late 1600s through the 1760s, French traders enslaved Native people as laborers and within networks of kinship. African slavery also extended into the territory, particularly along the Mississippi River, where trade routes connected the Illinois Country with New Orleans. After American independence and adoption of the Northwest Ordinance, some settlers continued to fight for slavery and long-term indentures.[16] Those efforts would ultimately prove futile, in part because so many of the white people who moved into the territory were trying to get away from slavery, not drag it along with them.

The Ohio Country—the part of the Northwest Territory that lay just west of Pennsylvania—was where settlers arrived first and in greatest numbers. The area was the site of protracted and often excruciating violence between settlers and Native groups. In an incident that shook the entire region, in March 1782 an American militia rounded up the largely Native residents of two Moravian missionary towns, Salem and Gnadenhutten, and killed ninety-six defenseless men, women, and children. After the Treaty of Paris, US officials hoped the region's Native people would, like the British, consider themselves defeated. Instead, Native leaders from different tribes coalesced into confederations to fight the Americans. In 1786, one such group warned Congress that Americans must remain south of the Ohio River and threatened to defend their territory should surveyors and settlers attempt to move north. The settlers remained undaunted. In the early 1790s, under the leadership of George Washington and the Federalist Party, the US government redoubled its efforts at conquest. After several battles in which the Indians of the Northwest Confederacy prevailed over American forces, a larger contingent of the US Army won a major victory in the 1794 Battle of Fallen Timbers, near present-day Toledo. The next year, through the Treaty of Greenville, a delegation of Native leaders ceded most of present-day Ohio to the United States while reserving the northwestern portion of the state as Indian land.[17]

As this phase of conflict between the United States and Native nations wound down, white settlers migrated into the area from points south and east, seeing vast potential for economic growth in a place where land was inexpensive, the climate temperate, and waterways abundant. Some of the earliest and wealthiest white settlers were men like territorial governor Arthur St. Clair, a military veteran and a Federalist with strong ties to President Washington. St. Clair and his closest allies hailed from Pennsylvania and the Northeast. Other early settlers migrated north across the Ohio River. Among the antislavery settlers from the slave states were ministers and congregants—Quakers, Presbyterians, Congregationalists, Baptists, and, to a lesser extent, Methodists—who opposed slavery in principle and, when they arrived in the Old Northwest, established antislavery churches and communities whose members became active in organized efforts to abolish slavery and the black laws.[18]

Ohio's political founders began the business of lawmaking in the summer of 1795, even before the Treaty of Greenville was approved. Establishing regulations for migration and settlement, Arthur St. Clair and his colleagues drew heavily on a revamped poor law that Pennsylvania had adopted in 1771, which was in turn modeled on English traditions. Like its many antecedents, Ohio's territorial poor law provided rules for establishing legal settlement. As elsewhere, men with resources were the most privileged: If they moved into an Ohio township and bought real estate or paid substantial rent, they were considered legally settled after one year of residence. Men with fewer resources could gain settlement if they paid local taxes without incident for two consecutive years or, if they were servants or apprentices, after working for someone else for one year. Indentured servants were subjected to additional constraints. Married women were in a category of their own; upon marriage, a woman's place of settlement became that of her husband. Every township had a three-man board of overseers of the poor that was authorized to levy taxes to support poor relief, hold elections for township offices, and visit and evaluate people who might not be self-supporting. The overseers of the poor made decisions about who was considered to be legally settled in the community, who was entitled to receive public aid, and who had no real right to be there and could be removed, particularly if they became needy or threatening.[19]

The 1795 Ohio poor law did not target people of African descent for special regulation, and the state's first constitution, adopted in 1803, also largely rejected racial distinctions. In the run-up to the constitutional convention, the opposing political parties—the Federalists and the Republicans—had each charged the other with conspiring to legalize slavery. In fact, leaders of neither party had such intentions. Republicans dominated the convention, where delegates debated but rejected proposals to bar Black testimony in cases involving whites, to prohibit Black office-holding, and to exempt free Blacks from the duties of poll taxes and militia service. The constitution they drafted declared slavery illegal and explicitly banned the kind of long-term indentures that white people sought when hoping to continue holding slaves despite the Northwest Ordinance's ban. The Ohio Constitution's enumeration of individual rights began with familiar language about human equality: "That all men are born equally free and independent, and have certain natural, inherent and unalienable rights, amongst which are the enjoying and defending life and liberty, acquiring, possessing and protecting property, and pursuing and obtaining happiness and safety." Still, the constitution did not distribute political privileges equally. Voting rights were restricted to white men only, a provision that prevailed in the convention by just one vote.[20]

Ohio was the first state carved from the Northwest Territory, but it was developing in relation to its neighbor, Virginia, with which it shared a long boundary defined by the Ohio River. The Northwest Ordinance's ban on slavery, together with Ohioans' unvarnished opposition to the institution, gave the river extraordinary significance as a border between slavery and freedom. The American Revolution temporarily weakened slavery in Virginia. When the war was over, however, the Virginia General Assembly moved to curtail manumissions, and the reactionary impulse intensified in the 1790s amid fears of a growing free Black population and slave rebellions in Saint-Domingue and at home. The state government increasingly sought to monitor the movement of free Black people, worried they might foment unrest among the enslaved. In 1793, it passed a law that required all free African Americans to register with town or county clerks who would record their names, sex, color, and age, and issue them certificates showing their status. That same year, Virginia lawmakers banned free people of color from moving into the state, a policy that other slave states soon emulated.[21]

Many white residents north of the Ohio River agreed that free people of African descent posed a threat to public peace and good order, a feeling strengthened by the knowledge that Virginia was making life increasingly difficult for its own free Black residents. In southern Ohio, along the river, white sentiment was decidedly mixed; some politicians and editors regularly deprecated slavery and condemned restrictions on free African Americans. Others expressed concern that Black migrants would bring crime and disorder into the state. If Ohio did not impose restrictions, they worried, the state would become an increasingly popular destination for Black migrants.[22]

Advocates of racial restrictions managed to accomplish in Ohio's first legislative session what they had failed to do in the constitutional convention. The legislature that met in 1803–4 enacted a raft of laws designed to limit the migration and settlement of free people of African descent. This was the beginning of what was commonly referred to as the Ohio "black laws." Passed in 1804, the laws erected barriers to Black migration and settlement, with enforcement located at the county level. Laws required "black or mulatto" persons seeking to "settle or reside" in the state to provide proof of their freedom to a clerk of court within two years of their arrival. All current residents who were Black or mulatto were expected to register with county clerks within five months of passage of the measure. Newcomers and current residents alike would receive certificates from clerks of court. Those certificates would also serve as labor permits, for the law stipulated that employers convicted of hiring Black people who had no certificates would be fined between ten and fifty dollars. In a measure designed with fugitive slaves in mind, the law also mandated fines for anyone who "shall employ, harbor or conceal" a Black or mulatto person who was not registered.[23] Every interaction with a county clerk required a fee, making it difficult for impoverished migrants to comply with the law, even if they wanted to do so.

Over the next few years, as Virginia placed new strictures on free Black people, the Ohio legislature moved to integrate its antiblack measures with its poor-law policies. Ohio passed its first comprehensive poor law in 1805. Echoing the territorial poor law, the new law established township-based boards of overseers of the poor charged with raising money for poor relief, visiting and evaluating needy persons, and determining who was entitled to relief and who had to be removed to their community of origin. The following year, the Virginia General Assembly tightened its policies on manumission and free Blacks with a new law requiring manumitted slaves to leave the state within a year of becoming free. In 1807, Ohio merged its black laws with the poor-law system. The new Ohio laws drastically increased the fee for registering and required that Black settlers get "two or more freehold sureties" of $500. The people who served as sureties— freeholders, meaning people who had unencumbered title to land—did not literally hand over $500 to the county clerk. Rather, the bonds were essentially a guarantee of Black migrants' "good behavior" and a promise to "pay for the support" of such migrants if they were "found unable to support themselves." The revised law also explicitly charged township overseers of

the poor with removing Black or mulatto persons found to be either unable
to support themselves or in violation of the registration laws. In essence, the
overseers of the poor, whose general charge was poor relief and enforcement
of settlement laws, now became enforcers of the black laws as well. Black
newcomers, in turn, faced two sets of overlaid and intertwined regulations:
one particular to people of African descent that required registration in the
county courts, and the other compatible with settlement laws and enforceable at the township level.[24]

Ohio's 1807 black laws included an additional and particularly unjust
provision: It forbade Black and mulatto persons from testifying in court
cases involving whites. That kind of law was increasingly typical in slaveholding states, and Ohio's adoption of it in 1807 suggests the legislature's
determination to further diminish the advantages free African Americans
would enjoy if they migrated to Ohio. Without the same right as whites to
testify in court, African Americans would have little ability to defend their
most basic rights—to enforce contracts, secure wages, or obtain justice in
criminal cases. The discriminatory testimony law became one of the most
hated parts of Ohio's black laws, a target for activists and even for the
Ohio Supreme Court, which found ways of limiting its impact. Activists
regularly held up the state constitution's declaration of rights (and also the
American Declaration of Independence) as evidence that black laws violated fundamental principles of American government.[25] But in Ohio, as
elsewhere, abstract declarations of universal rights and equality were easily
subordinated to the demands of "domestic police"—that is, to the idea that
the paramount concern of government was the safety and good health of
the community, not the rights of individuals.

———————

THE IMPULSE TO ADOPT LAWS designating free African Americans as a
separate class from whites seemed to be spreading. After Ohio, other territories and states in the Old Northwest passed antiblack provisions of their
own. As governor of Indiana Territory, William Henry Harrison pushed

Congress to permit slavery to continue despite the Northwest Ordinance, but he failed in Washington and faced increasingly organized opposition at home. Slavery remained officially prohibited, but Indiana Territory—and Illinois Territory when it was carved off from Indiana in 1809—passed antiblack regulations that echoed those of Ohio. For instance, in 1803 Indiana Territory required every newly released "servant" to have "his or her freedom recorded" and to receive a certificate that essentially served as a work permit. In 1810, the territory put township overseers of the poor in charge of ensuring that all "black or mulatto" persons under their jurisdiction found someone to post a security of $500 as indemnity against the possibility that they would become "a charge" to the county. Illinois, in turn, distinguished itself for permitting long-term indentures that resembled slavery in almost every respect.[26]

The tendency spread to Pennsylvania, which shared a long border with slaveholding Maryland and a shorter one with Virginia. Maryland banned free Black migration into the state in 1807, amid a number of other restrictive measures directed at free African Americans. From then until 1814, Pennsylvanians regularly pressed their legislature to echo the Maryland ban with one of their own. In the winter of 1813, for example, state representative Jacob Mitchell introduced a petition from Philadelphia residents complaining that people of color were "becoming nuisances." The petitioners sought a law that would oblige African Americans to register, allow them to be sold for "a term of years" if convicted of a crime, provide compensation to persons they "may have plundered," and pay the expense of their prosecution. Reflecting perennial concerns about the economic burdens imposed by the transient poor as well as the conviction that free Black people constituted a separate and uniquely challenging class, the petitioners asked that people of color be assessed a special tax to support "their own poor."[27]

Yet Pennsylvania was not Ohio. Philadelphia in particular was a meeting place for people with strong convictions in favor of abolition and racial equality. Beginning in the 1770s, a Quaker-led abolitionist movement helped make the city a hub of free-Black life. Black Philadelphians—their work infused with optimism born of the Revolution and its promises of equal rights and self-government—nurtured a lively intellectual and educational culture. They published political pamphlets and treatises and established a robust network of teachers and schools. Men and women built a host of mutual aid organizations, including the Free African Society, which worked with white Quakers to advocate the interests of Black Philadelphians. In 1794, the Free African Society gave rise to two independent Black churches: the African Episcopal Church of St. Thomas led by Absalom Jones, and Bethel Church, led by Richard Allen. A Methodist, Allen became the progenitor of an entirely new denomination, the African Methodist Episcopal (AME) Church.[28]

Nor was Philadelphia an island. The city's Black and white abolitionists cultivated ties to allies elsewhere through a host of institutions and personal connections. In the 1790s, through Quaker connections, the city became an asylum for African American refugees from North Carolina who had been freed by Quaker owners before and during the American Revolution and were in danger of being re-enslaved by state policy. African Americans in Philadelphia, Boston, New York, and other places also forged ties through the Prince Hall Masons, a Freemasonry organization inaugurated in 1775 by Prince Hall, a Boston-born Black man. The white-led New-York Manumission Society and Pennsylvania Abolition Society encouraged peers in other states to form abolitionist societies, and by 1794 they collectively formed the American Convention for Promoting the Abolition of Slavery and Improving the Condition of the African Race, an organization that met regularly to develop strategies for demanding abolition and protecting the rights of free African Americans.[29]

Black Philadelphians and their white allies urged Congress to take action to end slavery and protect the rights of free African Americans. At the end of December 1799, Richard Allen, Absalom Jones, and sixty-nine other Black Philadelphians signed a petition to Congress in which they described themselves as a "class of citizens" of the United States and part of "the People of the United States" who were members of the constitutional compact. They claimed rights as citizens and as human beings, arguing that since neither the Constitution nor the 1793 Fugitive Slave Act mentioned "Black people or slaves," therefore "as we are *men,* we may be admitted to partake of the Liberties and unalienable Rights therein held forth." They wanted Congress to take steps to protect free African Americans from kidnapping, curtail illegal aspects of the international slave trade, and "prepare the way for the oppressed to go free." The Philadelphia-based Black sailmaker and activist James Forten later wrote that this remarkable petition had spoken for "Seven hundred thousand of the human race."[30] Black Philadelphians like Forten, bolstered by the abolitionist groundswell of the late eighteenth century, pressed the nation as a whole to live up to its most vaunted promises of universal rights.

James Forten was among those who vehemently resisted efforts to bar or regulate Black migration into Pennsylvania. Born to free parents in 1766, he grew up and attended school in the radical climate of revolutionary Philadelphia. His father, a prosperous sailmaker, died when he was a boy, and he had volunteered at age fifteen for service aboard a privateer in the American Revolution. On returning to Philadelphia, Forten became a vocal participant in the city's activist community. In the early nineteenth century, faced with the possibility that their state would adopt antiblack laws like those in Ohio and elsewhere, white and Black organizations petitioned the state legislature to reject the proposal. Forten, for his part, wrote a series of public letters that were published as a pamphlet in the winter of 1813 and in the city's leading newspaper a year later.[31]

Forten's eleven-page pamphlet, entitled *Letters from a Man of Colour, on a Late Bill before the Senate of Pennsylvania,* voiced themes that became central to the struggle against racist laws in subsequent years. He reminded readers of the egalitarian promise of the Declaration of Independence and the Pennsylvania Constitution, both of which claimed that all men were created equal. That equality, he insisted, transcended perceptions of skin color, national origin, religion, or supposed level of civilization. It "embraces the Indian and the European, the Savage and the Saint, the Peruvian and the Laplander, the white Man and the African." Since all human beings were fundamentally equal in the eyes of God and the law, racial discrimination violated moral principles as well as the founding charters of the nation and his state.[32]

Moving from lofty principles to practical impact, Forten explained how the proposed Pennsylvania law would humiliate and endanger people of African descent who were simply seeking to live peacefully in the community. Imagine, for example, that he had a brother who lived "in a distant part of the Union" and came to visit because he missed his family. Under the proposed law, the brother would be forced to register within twenty-four hours or risk incarceration or even sale into hard labor for seven years. Forten explained how racially discriminatory legislation empowered officials to act on their prejudices, even to the point of inciting violence. The city register would collect the fees, he wrote, but, "Who is this Register?" "A man, and exercising an office, where ten dollars is the fee for each delinquent, will probably be a cruel man and find delinquents where they really do not exist. The poor black is left to the merciless gripe [*sic*] of an avaricious REGISTER, without an appeal, in the event, from his tyranny or oppression!"

By officially casting Black people as outsiders, Forten argued, the law would sanction white racism and serve as an invitation to mob violence. The measure would invite abuse by officials, he predicted, allowing "police officers . . . to apprehend any black, whether a vagrant or a man of reputable character, who cannot produce a Certificate that he has been registered." Authorities could use the law to foment mob behavior among whites:

> The Constable, whose antipathy generally against the black is very great, will take every opportunity of hurting his feelings!—Perhaps, he sees him at a distance, and having a mind to raise the boys in hue and cry against him, exclaims, "Halloa! Stop the Negro!" The boys, delighting in the sport,

immediately begin to hunt him, and immediately from a hundred tongues is heard the cry—*"Hoa, Negro, where is your Certificate!"*—Can any thing be done more shocking to the principles of Civil Liberty!

Forten's vision for law was clear: It must be a source of protection, not abuse, and it must operate without regard to race. Concluding one of his letters, he wrote, "The same power which protects the white man, should protect A MAN of COLOUR."[33]

The proposed antiblack law failed in Pennsylvania in 1813, and the state never adopted race-based registration laws similar to those in Ohio and elsewhere in the Old Northwest. Yet the next legislative session revealed how laws directed at the poor could substitute when explicitly racist laws seemed unacceptable. As the new session opened in early 1814, Representative Joel Barlow Sutherland introduced yet another petition from inhabitants of Philadelphia, asking for an act to prevent "the migration of people of color into this commonwealth." The petition went to committee, and Sutherland reported back weeks later, introducing on behalf of the committee a bill titled, "An act to prevent the migration of people of colour into the city and county of Philadelphia." When debate began, Representative Jacob Mitchell, who had introduced a similar bill the previous year, joined Sutherland in sponsorship of the bill. A week later, however, when it was time to discuss the bill a second time, Mitchell announced that he—together with William Duane—was offering a "substitute" for the original.[34]

The substitute bill was dramatically different from its precursor. Now the legislators defined the problem not as one of race but rather of vagrancy. The new proposal empowered the mayor and other Philadelphia officials to "commit to prison any vagrant or other idle or disorderly person living without employment, wandering about begging, having no visible means of subsistence, or being unable to give a reasonable account of himself or herself or of his or her business." Persons convicted of vagrancy would be forced to labor for various lengths of time, depending on how often they had been so convicted. In the ensuing debate, legislators mostly sought to reduce the length of sentences for vagrancy convictions. The House then officially renamed the bill. Instead of bearing a name that associated it with prejudice against persons of color, House Bill 202 was now called "An act to prevent the increase of idle and disorderly persons within this commonwealth."[35]

With that bit of alchemy, the Pennsylvania House moved from explicit racism to a more politically palatable policy that targeted people based on their perceived class status. The registration provisions and lengthy labor sentences in the original proposal were removed, making the entire law less punitive. It is clear that the legislators had sought a compromise, trying to accomplish their end of discouraging what they saw as idleness without specifically or overtly targeting people of color. The House agreed, by a vote of 49 to 29, to move ahead with this new version of the bill. Sutherland, Duane, and Mitchell—all of whom were already on record supporting measures that directly targeted persons of African descent—signed on, and the House passed the bill. The Senate was not interested, however, and it rejected the House bill at the end of the session.[36] Still, the debate had been instructive. Evidently the language of race and class were to some extent fungible. Legislators who first sought to target African Americans likely knew that authorities could use discretion when enforcing race-neutral laws regulating vagrancy and disorderly conduct, allowing them to accomplish the desired ends even if the statute itself made no reference to race.

———————

DESPITE THE LAWS meant to discourage them, African Americans continued to move into the Old Northwest. In 1800, the US Census counted just 337 African Americans in Ohio. Ten years later, their numbers had grown to 1,899; by 1820, the state's Black population had more than doubled, to 4,723. The white population was growing rapidly too, which meant that, according to the census, the state's proportion of African Americans remained virtually unchanged, moving from about .7 percent in 1800 to .8 percent in 1820. Observing that the state's racist settlement laws were not enforced, one early booster stated, "We have all the black population which unopposed immigration could give." At the very least, Ohio seemed to be more appealing than the places people left behind. The allure of migration was clear to Israel Jefferson, who migrated from Thomas Jefferson's Monticello and recalled, "When I came to Ohio I considered myself wholly free, and not till then."[37]

The state's race-based settlement laws were indeed enforced in some places, as county-level records reveal. People arrived at county clerks' offices in Ohio, traveling from places such as Virginia and Kentucky and carrying documents that explained where they came from and how they came to be free. Some people carried a copy of a slaveowner's will that showed precisely how they had been manumitted; others brought a testimonial to freedom issued by a clerk of court in a slaveholding county. Some documents represented repeated trips to a southern courthouse, revealing how personal identity was established at home and made portable in the form of a pass or free papers. Whatever the case, the clerk of court in an Ohio county transcribed the newcomer's papers in his registry, word for word, and often sketched the wax seal that typically adorned the original documents, indicating that they were official.[38]

John Burns, with his three carefully authenticated documents, represented about the most straightforward case possible. Many others were far more complicated and tenuous. A woman named Polly sought to register her freedom in Ross County in the fall of 1812, but she evidently did not have adequate proof. The Ross County clerk, based in Chillicothe, wrote to Polly's home county—Essex County, Virginia—for copies of her papers. A clerk in Essex County received the query and forwarded to Ohio copies of papers showing that seven and a half years earlier, a slaveowner had released his claims to Polly and her three children, Barbara, Joe, and Carter. A deed of manumission had been duly issued. When the documents arrived in Chillicothe, the Ross County clerk transcribed them into his book. Polly was now a legal resident and had the papers to show it.

Freedom papers could get lost, damaged, or stolen, imperiling a person's chances of safely registering. One man's papers had been badly burned in a fire and were now barely legible. His friends or patrons in Virginia wrote a note explaining about the fire and providing a legible transcript of the original. Another man had moved to Kentucky and given his papers to a white man for safekeeping. The white man misplaced the papers, so he and two others wrote a note describing the situation. Another set of papers was lost in a trunk that was stolen while en route from New Orleans. People guarded their papers vigilantly, keeping them close to their bodies, or entrusted them to people whose lives seemed stable. One set of freedom papers preserved by the Ohio History Connection bears marks of having been folded into even rectangles, small enough to fit in a pocket or a wallet.[39]

Because the documents were intended, in part, to show that a person would not burden local resources, they sometimes attested to the person's good standing in their community of origin. For instance, a document filed in Cleremont County, Ohio, certified the freedom of a man named James Rose and attested to his "good credit."[40] A note from a Kentucky white man explained that his former apprentice had served his time and was now at liberty to settle elsewhere, calling the man a "first rate work-man, orderly and peaceable in his demeanor and has acquired as good a character for a man of color as any in the State." That man—once called "Sam" but now calling himself "Sam Washington"—appeared at court in Ross County and entered his papers a month after his former boss wrote the letter.[41]

The interactions recorded in the registries suggest some of the discretion that county clerks and other authorities could exercise in such a system. Clerks had to be prepared for various kinds of irregularities, and they were entitled to make their own determinations about whether sufficient proof had been provided. They could decide whether to enforce the requirement that each registrant needed two freeholders to vouch for their independence, one of the most onerous aspects of the law for Black newcomers to the community. In John Burns's case, it seems the registrar waived that demand. The records also suggest the hardships and anxieties the system imposed on traveling African Americans. A migrant might lose her papers or have them stolen. She might encounter challenges that forced her to rely on white acquaintances for substitute documentation or a letter of endorsement. On arriving in Ohio, if she could not secure the necessary sureties, she had to hope the county clerk would exercise discretion in her favor. The journey from Virginia to Ohio was full of peril.

In fact, local authorities would have found it difficult to enforce the Ohio black laws fully or consistently. That would have meant rooting out people who had not followed the letter of the law and removing them to another jurisdiction. As an African American writer named David Blackmore pointed out in 1817, forcible removal was costly to the state. Manpower and time were required to find people who were living there illegally and force them to leave. Moreover, the border between Ohio and Virginia was porous, and the law provided no additional penalties for people who were caught resisting. If Ohio officials removed him to Virginia, Blackmore said with bravado, he could "cross the River back again in the same boat with the Officer who had transported me." And so the cycle would begin again. "To their own credit," he wrote, Ohio officials had generally refused to "be concerned in so base and unfeeling a transaction." Cincinnati authorities worried that the city was a haven for runaway slaves from Kentucky in the first decade of the nineteenth century, but they evidently did not enforce the state's racist registration law.[42]

Americans of this era did not, however, draw a clear distinction between public and private enforcement of the values their laws represented. Ohio's black laws sent a message that free African Americans were not full-fledged members of the community and that white people were not required to tolerate their presence. White Ohio residents drew on those principles when they threatened and assaulted Black neighbors in efforts to take their property, intimidate them, or run them out of the community entirely. Incidents of bullying and violence abounded. Blackmore, for instance, wrote of a Black man who had emigrated to Ohio from Pennsylvania. The man

had a wagon for sale, and some white neighbors wanted to buy it. When
the man refused to sell to them, the neighbors invoked the registration law
to drive the man off his land. He was forced to "leav[e] his growing crop of
corn &c. in the field" as "booty" for his oppressors.[43] A man named David
Barrett likewise encountered a group of white Ohioans who intimidated
him by demanding to see his pass. He had escaped slavery in Kentucky
and was traveling alone. As Barrett recounted: "One cried out 'there's a
nigger,' said another, 'I wonder if he has any authority for going through
here.' I walked on as if I would pass without noticing them. One cried out
'ha! There, have you got any pass? Where are you going?' I told them it was
none of their business. They attempted to stop me, but I ran from them
into the woods." The white men chased Barrett for several hours, but he
managed to get away.[44]

White Ohioans did not need the patina of law to show Black neighbors that they were unwelcome. That much was clear in the experiences of
a large group of freedpeople who migrated together from Virginia. When
slaveowner Samuel Gist died in 1815, he manumitted more than three
hundred enslaved people through his will. Realizing that these freedpeople could not remain in Virginia, Gist's agents contacted, among others,
white abolitionists in Philadelphia. Through Quaker channels, news of
the Gist estate traveled to Ohio, where Thomas Rotch of Stark County
explored possible destinations in Ohio or Indiana. The corresponding
secretary of a Cincinnati organization, the Western Emigrant Society,
speculated that most white people in the region "politically opposed . . .
the settlement of so large a body of blacks in the heart of the State," but
he affirmed that "there is nothing in the Constitution or laws of either
state to prevent it." He added that land purchases were open to all; state
authorities "never enquire the colour or features of a man's countenance
when he comes to purchase land either of the US. government or of individuals." Gist's agents bought two separate tracts near the Ohio River in
Brown County, Ohio, for the freedpeople, who began to make their way
north in the fall of 1818.[45]

The Virginia freedpeople received a mixed reception from white Ohioans. An inflammatory anonymous letter, written from Virginia and published in a Chillicothe newspaper, warned that "about five hundred" slaves had recently been freed and "are to be marched for Ohio, and there settled on land provided for them." The author, likely Allen Trimble, a Virginia-born state senator who was later elected Ohio governor, added that he had heard the group was "perhaps as depraved and ignorant a set of people as any of their kind." Raising the specter of public safety, the author predicted that Ohio would "suffer seriously" from the policies of Virginia and Kentucky "in driving all their free negroes upon us," and he urged that Ohio must "adopt some counteracting measure." The Chillicothe editor added further commentary, writing that "we trust our constitutions and laws are not so defective as to suffer us to be overrun by such a wretched population."[46] Neighboring whites harassed the Black settlers, and someone kidnapped a girl from the community and carried her into Kentucky, presumably to sell her into slavery. The land that had been purchased for the community turned out to be low-lying and difficult to farm. When winter came, they faced starvation.

Yet the Brown County communities had staying power. Ohio Quakers had known of the Gist freedpeople before their arrival and provided significant relief—in the form of food and other supplies—during the settlers' first bleak winter. The governors of Kentucky and Ohio cooperated to ensure that the kidnapped girl was returned, and the migrants appeared to be doing better by late spring. A year later, however, a Quaker newspaper declared that continuing aid to the Black settlers felt like a "tax on benevolence" and recommended that they "ought to be removed some way or other." Some of the African American migrants returned to Virginia and others resettled elsewhere in Ohio, but the two main communities in Brown County—popularly known as the "camps"—persisted.[47]

About fifteen years later, the English abolitionist Edward Abdy visited the communities, where his hosts related stories of great hardship. "They are still liable to the intrusion of slave-traders and marauders, who break open their doors, and subject them to outrage and insult," Abdy recounted. The racist testimony law, he emphasized, meant that a young woman who became pregnant when an employer coerced her into sex could "obtain neither reparation for herself, nor maintenance for her child. Her evidence is worthless." Still, he acknowledged, the populations of the settlements had grown considerably, and some of their white neighbors were respectful and accommodating. "Under all these difficulties, and discouragements," Abdy wrote, some of the Black settlers "had contrived to build themselves comfortable log-huts, and to bring up their children" the best way they could.[48]

James Forten, David Blackmore, Edward Abdy, and many others recognized how racist laws contributed to African Americans' vulnerability and stymied their efforts to secure their lives and livelihoods. Laws that singled out free African Americans for special, discriminatory treatment likened everyone who was Black to paupers, vagrants, and criminals—people who might be tolerated in a community but had no real claim to membership and could be removed or driven out at will. These laws were uniquely unjust, they argued, because they targeted people for their racial *status,* which they could not change, rather than for their poor *conduct,* which they ostensibly could. In their practical operation, these contemporaries understood, the laws emboldened ill-intentioned white people. Whether they registered or not, African Americans were susceptible to exploitation by employers, harassment by white neighbors, and even kidnapping into slavery. Black Ohioans could expect little protection from the law. Unable to testify in cases involving white people, they were forced to depend on their white neighbors' good graces—a highly unreliable proposition. In some places, Black Ohioans managed to establish their own villages, purchase land, and even prosper, but their precarious position persisted. John Malvin, who became a prominent Cleveland activist, recalled learning of Ohio's black laws soon after arriving in Cincinnati. "I found that every door was closed against the colored man in a free state," he wrote, "excepting the jails and penitentiaries, the doors of which were thrown wide open."[49]

THE STATE OF OHIO's official position on free African Americans—that they were unwanted sojourners rather than fully vested members of the community—represented one position in a broader national debate about the nation's racial future. After the War of 1812, leading Americans increasingly turned their attention to the question of what would become of the growing free Black population. One increasingly prominent view was that everyone would benefit if free African Americans left the United States entirely. The idea was to transport free people of African descent out of the United States, to "colonize" them in a place where they could eventually build their own nation. Scattered clergymen and political leaders floated this possibility in the late eighteenth century, but it circulated more widely in the late 1810s.

Early advocates of Black colonization provided varied explanations for why they thought free African Americans should leave the United States. Some believed different "races" were naturally inclined toward conflict and could not live side by side unless one was subordinated to the other. Others insisted that white Americans' prejudice would condemn free Black people to misery if they stayed. As with the policy of removing Native Americans from the path of white settlement, visions of Black colonization reflected the belief—widespread but not universal among white Americans—that the United States was destined to be a white nation and that it was possible, and desirable, to expel large groups of people in the effort to realize that destiny. Early colonizationists envisioned various destinations for former slaves and free-born African Americans. Great Britain had created a colony in Sierra Leone to serve as a home for free Blacks from across the empire, including many who had become free during the course of the American Revolution. Some US-based colonizationists likewise looked to West Africa, believing that a colony there could have multiple desirable effects: not just removing free African Americans from the United States but also establishing US outposts abroad and helping propagate Christianity in a supposedly benighted region.[50]

Among African Americans in the late eighteenth and early nineteenth century, there was considerable interest in leaving. The most prominent Black emigrationist was Paul Cuffe, a Massachusetts-based shipbuilder and captain. Cuffe, the child of a Ghanaian man and a Wampanoag woman, developed business and personal connections with Black and white Philadelphia abolitionists and became a practicing Quaker. He was already prosperous and well connected in 1811, when, urged by British abolitionists, he visited Sierra Leone with an eye toward establishing a trade route and perhaps encouraging Black Americans to emigrate there. On returning to the United States, he led an effort to establish Black emigration societies in cities on the Eastern Seaboard, including Boston, Philadelphia, and New York. Although few people proved willing to venture to Sierra Leone, Cuffe did transport a group of thirty-eight settlers in 1815. Cuffe and that small group of settlers were not alone. On farms and in hamlets across the country, free Black people considered taking their chances with emigration. The Black northerners who explored the idea tended to be skeptical about their future in the new republic, believing that white Americans would never accept them as equals and imagining better lives elsewhere. In 1818, an Illinois man named Abraham Camp put into words what many surely felt: The "free people of colour" in his neighborhood were ready to leave, he wrote. "We love this country and its liberties, if we could share in an equal right in them; but our freedom is partial, and we have no hope that it ever will be otherwise here; therefore we had rather be gone."[51]

Leading white advocates of colonization consolidated their movement in December 1816, forming a society for "Colonizing the Free People of Color of the United States," soon known simply as the American Colonization Society (ACS). The goal was to create a centralized movement to address what they saw as a pressing problem. Among the group's founding members were some of the country's most eminent men, including Henry Clay of Kentucky, then a US congressman, and Bushrod Washington, associate justice of the Supreme Court and George Washington's nephew. Supreme Court Chief Justice John Marshall served as president of the Virginia branch of the organization. Thomas Jefferson was not directly involved, but the ACS often invoked him and an 1811 letter in which he declared that establishing a colony in Africa was "the most desirable measure . . . for gradually drawing off" the nation's Black population. Citing the 1820 US Census, which revealed that the nation's free Black population was growing rapidly, the ACS told Congress in 1821 that free Black people "are not, and cannot be, either useful or happy among us," and it was "best, for all the parties interested, that there should be a separation."[52]

The ACS leadership worked on many fronts. The society sent two men to West Africa to investigate potential sites for a colony and lobbied Congress for help with financing. National organizers encouraged allies to form local branches to sponsor lectures, raise money, and generate publicity for the cause. After Paul Cuffe died in 1817, white colonizationists continued to invoke him in service of their argument that free African Americans should welcome the chance to depart the United States. And yet, traversing towns and cities in the free states, ACS lecturers and essayists often used deeply racist rhetoric, emphasizing that free Black people would always constitute a criminal class because their African "race" rendered them poorly adapted to live in cool climes or unable to conduct themselves as independent citizens. In this respect, the colonization movement was an extension of the impulses that spurred the black laws of Ohio and other free states. Most colonizationists believed African Americans could never be assimilated into American civil and political life. Most thought the United States was destined to be a white nation, and they fundamentally opposed—or simply could not imagine—any alternative.[53]

Free African Americans boldly rejected the ACS and its vision for the United States and, in the process, advanced an entirely different argument about their own future and that of the entire nation. Richard Allen, pastor at Bethel Church, and other members of Philadelphia's Black elite, including James Forten, author of *Letters from a Man of Colour*, initially expressed interest in departing the United States, and some were in contact with leading white colonizationists. But when Allen and other prominent pastors held a mass meeting in Bethel Church in January 1817, they discovered that Black Philadelphians disapproved en masse. Some three thousand people were present when the pastors called for a voice vote in favor of colonization, and their flock refused. The meeting in Bethel Church passed strong resolutions against the ACS and the "unmerited stigma" it cast on "the reputation of the free people of color." The meeting also expressed Black Philadelphians' determination to remain in the United States. They would stay to support their brethren in bondage, and any attempt to force them into exile "would not only be cruel, but in direct violation of those principles which have been the boast of the republic." Black Philadelphians were not alone. African American groups also protested the ACS in Richmond, Virginia, and the District of Columbia.[54]

In subsequent decades, Black activists continued to denounce the ACS, even as many grappled with the question of staying or leaving a nation that often seemed committed to denying them the most basic rights and privileges. But the 1817 protests, coming immediately on the heels of the ACS's creation, were a milestone. Theodore Wright, who became a well-known Black abolitionist and Presbyterian minister, later recalled that his father, Richard P. G. Wright, had traveled from Schenectady, New York, to Philadelphia, "under great anxiety," to learn about the protest. His father was among those who had, in that "dark period . . . lifted up their voice and said, this is my country." News of the Philadelphia protest reached southeastern Ohio, where the ACS was already making inroads. The state had at least one auxiliary in 1817, and in January 1818, the Ohio legislature passed a resolution asking Congress to support "the emancipation and colonization of the people of color of the United States."[55]

A small number of white Ohioans, many of them with Quaker ties, denounced both the ACS and the black laws. Their central contention was that free African Americans had every right to stay where they were, and that it was unjust to deny them fundamental rights, including the right of free mobility and protection of the laws. Charles Osborn, a Quaker activist and newspaper editor, publicized the Philadelphia protest against the ACS in the pages of the newspaper he published in Mount Pleasant, a town not far from the Virginia border and the home of a cluster of Quakers who had left North Carolina to escape the influence of slavery. Osborn, who himself was raised in North Carolina, had organized a manumission society in Tennessee before moving to Mount Pleasant in 1816.[56] Osborn regularly condemned the ACS in the pages of his newspaper, the *Philanthropist*. He insisted that colonization was not a way station on the road to emancipation but rather a grand detour destined for failure. In an editorial noting African Americans' opposition to the ACS, he claimed colonization would only "rivet closer the chains that already gall the sons of Africa."[57]

Those who rejected colonization in the late 1810s and early 1820s looked for other ways of imagining free African Americans' future in the United States. Theodore Wright's father had proclaimed, "This is my country." But what did advocating for African American belonging and racial equality look like in a decentralized nation, where local and state law had the greatest influence on everyone's daily lives? A good place to start was to demand repeal of racist laws in the states. In the pages of Osborn's paper, David Blackmore skewered the Ohio black laws. He began with a critique of race "prejudice," and he wrote hopefully that "many of the white people themselves" were beginning to understand that "climate, state of society, manner of living, etc., have produced the external differences which are apparent between them and us." He invoked passages of the Bible that became crucial to later abolitionists. God had "made of one blood all nations of men," he insisted. White people in Ohio must begin to believe "that we ought to do unto all men as we would wish them to do unto us."[58]

Blackmore went on to assess the Ohio black laws "on the grounds of expediency and good policy." He criticized the Ohio legislature for having "become [an] accomplice with Virginia in her cruel Slave system," noting that other states—Pennsylvania, New Jersey, New York, and the states of New England—had chosen not to adopt measures like Ohio's 1807 black laws. Blackmore dismissed the typical rationales for such laws: fears of being "overrun" by free blacks and concerns about the "cost for their maintenance." These were "immaginary evils," he insisted. Free Black people were generally poor, he acknowledged, but any thinking person could understand the reason. If African Americans had been paid for the labor of "our fore-fathers" from the time they had arrived in America, they would certainly not be in such straits. More to the point, he argued, the law opened the door to abuse and did not even serve its intended purpose of discouraging Black migration. It was merely a "scare-crow" and served to "keep out of the state the more prudent and respectable persons of our colour whilst it is almost daily violated with impunity by those who have nothing to lose."[59]

Southeastern Ohio was an incubator for institutions and ideas that soon became more widely significant. Based in nearby St. Clairsville, Benjamin Lundy, also a Quaker, helped organize the Union Humane Society in 1815. This abolitionist association fostered eight branches, provided legal defense for African Americans who were threatened by kidnappers, and worked to secure the freedom of African Americans illegally held in bondage in Ohio. The society denounced colonization and called for the removal of "disqualifications and other legal impediments which obstruct people of colour in the enjoyment of civil rights." In 1818, the Union Humane Society connected with the annual meeting of the American Convention for Promoting the Abolition of Slavery, which met in Philadelphia. Meanwhile, Lundy went to work for Osborn's newspaper, at first selecting articles to publish and then writing editorials. When Osborn stopped publishing in 1821, Lundy founded a newspaper of his own, the *Genius of Universal Emancipation,* which he moved to Baltimore in 1824 and then to Washington, DC, in 1830.[60]

Lundy insisted that abolitionists engage in the world of politics, striving to make their voices heard by petitioning, voting, and running for office. In 1821, he advanced a constitutional theory of slavery and civil rights that became increasingly prominent in subsequent decades. Lundy conceded that Congress had no authority over slavery in the states, but he insisted that the states themselves could play a powerful role in ending slavery and guaranteeing basic rights to free African Americans. He encouraged slave states to undertake "gradual though *certain* Emancipation" and to repeal laws designed to "forc[e] the free colored people away." The free states, in turn, should "all agree to receive free colored persons upon the footing of aliens, without imposing any other restraints than white persons of that description are subject to."[61]

The impulse to secure fundamental rights for African Americans in Ohio was not limited to radicals like Blackmore, Osborn, and Lundy. The legislature discussed repeal of the black laws in 1816, and the Ohio Supreme Court was also involved. In the 1810s, Kentuckians and Ohioans were already at odds over the extent to which slaveholders were permitted to employ, live with, or travel with their human chattel in Ohio. The Ohio River was easily crossed, not only by slaveholders but by enslaved people laboring for their owners or attempting to flee bondage. In 1817, the Kentucky governor formally complained to the Ohio governor about Ohioans' unwillingness to help recapture escapees.[62] That same year, in the case of *Ohio v. Carneal*, the Ohio Supreme Court considered whether an enslaved person who conducted his owner's business in Ohio could still be considered enslaved. The case involved the fate of an African American man named Richard Lunsford, whose owner, Thomas Carneal, lived in Kentucky but frequently sent Lunsford to work in Cincinnati. The parties to the lawsuit clashed over who owned Lunsford now that Carneal had died.

The Ohio court, in an opinion written by Judge John McLean, dispensed with the complexities of Carneal's will and estate and decided that Lunsford was a free man. McLean, who would later sit on the US Supreme Court and author a dissent in the 1857 *Dred Scott* case, offered a moral condemnation of slavery and drew a stark distinction between the laws of Ohio and Kentucky. In Kentucky and other slave states, he wrote, "A presumption may perhaps arise, that every black man is a slave unless the contrary appear." In Ohio, he said, "The presumption is different. Every man is supposed to be free, until his obligation to servitude is clearly shown." Lunsford was entitled to the presumption that he was free, and he could only be held in bondage if the Kentuckians could affirmatively prove their "right in his own person." The claimants had no such right, McLean and the other judges decided. Lunsford was entitled to his freedom because he had worked in Ohio, where slaveowners were not permitted to command labor from enslaved people. To permit people to work as slaves in Ohio, McLean argued, was "an evasion of the policy of the [state] constitution" that could "never be sanctioned."[63]

The Ohio court not only freed Lunsford but also elevated Ohio's sovereignty as a free state in the face of Kentucky slaveowners' habit of employing their slaves north of the river. In explicitly condemning the prima facie principle—the idea that the burden was on Black people to demonstrate that they were free—McLean insisted that freedom was *everyone's* default status in Ohio. The judge's clarion statement about the meaning of free territory echoed the famous case of *Somerset v. Stewart,* decided in 1772 by Lord Mansfield, the chief justice of the highest common-law court in England. In that case, an American slaveowner named Charles Stewart had traveled to England with James Somerset, his enslaved servant. While in England, Somerset ran away, but Stewart recaptured him and threatened to sell him to Jamaica. Abolitionists intervened, keen to use the incident as a test case. After several hearings, Mansfield determined that Stewart could not claim Somerset as a slave in England. Slavery could exist only where it was created by positive law, the judge declared, and no person could be claimed as a slave in a place where slavery has not been explicitly legalized. Judge John McLean did not mention the *Somerset* case, but later American jurists would do so as they developed the legal concept of "free soil." This was the principle, increasingly accepted by free-state residents in the antebellum decades, that slaveowners traveling in jurisdictions where human bondage was not permitted would receive no help from local law enforcement when they sought to secure their slaves.[64]

In 1821, with McLean still on the bench, the Ohio Supreme Court narrowed the reach of the state's antiblack laws, establishing a precedent that it continued to uphold until the laws were repealed. The court was asked to decide whether the 1807 state law that prohibited "black or mulatto" persons from testifying in cases involving whites should apply to a person who was "a quadroon or one fourth black." The case at issue involved the prosecution of a woman named Elizabeth George for infanticide. When prosecutors called a Black woman as a witness in the case, George's lawyer insisted that the witness should be excluded because Ohio law prohibited Black and mulatto people from testifying in cases involving whites. George's lawyer acknowledged that George herself was "a quadroon or one fourth black" but asserted that for legal purposes she was white. She was clearly not "black," he said. Nor was she mulatto, since "mulattoes" were "half bloods, or the offspring of a white and a black." Because George was more than half white, the lawyer argued, she "was to be considered as white, and entitled to all the privileges of a white." Therefore, he insisted, a Black woman could not be called to testify in her case. Lawyers for the state found this argument preposterous. They rejected the proposition that Elizabeth George should be treated as a white woman. The "white person," the prosecutor said, "in common parlance, meant one who had no mixture of black blood." He argued that there was "no instance, in any dictionary of the English language, or in any other book, where the term white person was not limited to those who were pure white."[65] Certainly, "quadroons" were not included in that hallowed category.

The court rejected the state's argument, holding that a person with mixed ancestry who was more than "half" white should be considered white before the law. Benjamin Lundy's *Genius of Universal Emancipation* praised this "important" holding that people "of an intermediate grade between whites and mulattoes, are entitled to all the rights and privileges, and subject to all the liabilities of white persons;—or, in other words, are in law, to be considered as white." As years passed, the Ohio Supreme Court continued to uphold the right of people who were considered more than half white to exercise the same rights white people did, including attending public schools, giving sworn testimony, and even voting. In an 1831 decision, the court declared itself "unwilling to extend the disabilities of the statute further than its letter requires" and dryly noted the "difficulty of defining and of ascertaining the degree of duskiness which renders a person liable to such disabilities."

In an era in which state courts rarely invalidated state laws, this was about the best that advocates for racial equality could expect from the court. In 1844, a statewide convention of Black activists praised the court for having construed the black laws "to the very LETTER," ensuring "that their devastating influence may not reach any who could escape under any exceptions." Yet, the convention noted, the state's "subordinate tribunals" did not always adhere to the standard established by the high court. Moreover, the principle did nothing for the masses of Black Ohioans who could not claim to be more than "half" white for legal purposes.[66] Still, the 1821 Elizabeth George case established that the Ohio Supreme Court was on the side of those who were reluctant to deny basic rights to people of color and who rejected the fiction of white racial purity.

———————

IN THE FIRST SEVERAL DECADES after independence, free African Americans were a significant force in American life. Their growing numbers, combined with their claims that they were entitled to remain in place and live in dignity, generated a widespread debate about their collective future in the United States. State laws that regulated or excluded free Black people were part of that debate, as was the colonization movement and its vision of a white nation. African American activists not only criticized such developments but offered an entirely different vision. As James Forten's protest suggested, antiracists had a range of powerful arguments at their disposal. They insisted that race was just one of many categories of human difference; that God had made all of humanity "of one blood"; and that the

American Revolution had committed the nation to the principle that all people were created equal.

Those broad principles could be extracted from such authoritative texts as the Bible and the Declaration of Independence, but only a small minority pushed to apply them to questions associated with race and inequality in the early United States. Those activists also had to work within the federal order established by the US Constitution. They recognized that most of the struggle against racially discriminatory policies needed to occur at the state level, because under the Constitution the states enjoyed virtually unlimited power to regulate their own "domestic police." In some situations, however, it was worthwhile to approach Congress. Antislavery activists like Lundy wanted Congress to attack slavery in places where the Constitution gave it exclusive jurisdiction—the District of Columbia and the federal territories in particular. They demanded, as Lundy put it, a "positive injunction" against the admission of new slave states, and they wanted Congress to use its power over interstate commerce to end the interstate slave trade.[67] Although Congress seemed to have little authority over the rights of individuals within the states, some people also saw in the Constitution's privileges and immunities clause—Article IV, Section 2—the possibility of pushing the question of free African Americans' civil rights onto Congress's agenda.

CHAPTER 2

"A FREE MAN OF COLOUR, AND A CITIZEN OF THIS STATE"

*The Privileges and Immunities of
Citizenship in the 1820s*

FROM BEHIND THE BARS of the Washington, DC, jail, a twenty-six-year-old Black man named Gilbert Horton told concerned visitors that he was a free-born resident of New York State. He provided extensive details about his story because his jailers had refused to listen. Most recently he had lived in New York City, he said, and his Lower East Side neighbors could attest that he was a free man, not a runaway slave. He had worked on a ship called the *Macedonian* and was discharged in Norfolk, Virginia. From there, he had made his way to Georgetown, in the District of Columbia, where he had been arrested and thrown in jail.[1]

It had happened on a late summer day in 1826, when a white man named John Edds noticed "a strange negro" and, suspecting a runaway slave, summoned a police officer. The pair questioned Horton about his business and found his account "contradictory and evasive." He could provide "no evidences of freedom," so they brought him before a justice of the peace who sent him to jail "after due investigation." The marshal of the District of Columbia, in keeping with local law, placed a notice in the *National Intelligencer,* a prominent daily newspaper. The advertisement was prosaic, indicating that Horton was committed "as a runaway" and providing details about his physical appearance: He was five feet four inches tall, "stout made," with "large full eyes," and a scar on his left arm near the elbow. Horton claimed "he was born free" near Peekskill, New York, the advertisement said. It requested that Horton's "owner or owners . . . if any" come forward immediately or Horton would be sold into slavery, "as the law directs."[2]

The *Intelligencer* ran notices like this one almost every day. Like other slaveholding jurisdictions, the District of Columbia was governed by the principle that people of African descent traveling at large were prima facie assumed to be runaway slaves. All people who appeared to be Black were subject to questioning by local officials and members of the public. To avoid incarceration, they had to show written proof of their freedom or a pass from their master. Without such documentation, they faced arrest and imprisonment. If they remained unable to prove freedom and no owner came forward to claim them as a slave, they could be sold into slavery, with the proceeds used to pay the expenses of their incarceration.

That likely would have been Gilbert Horton's fate if allies in New York had not seen the advertisement in the *Intelligencer.* On learning of his arrest and incarceration, people from Horton's home community in Westchester County, including his father, Peter Horton, rallied to his defense. William Jay, a prominent local lawyer and judge, sent word of Gilbert's incarceration to the governor of New York, DeWitt Clinton, who in turn wrote to the president of the United States, John Quincy Adams. Clinton's message was clear. Gilbert Horton was "a free man of colour, and a citizen of this state," and he was "unlawfully imprisoned in the jail of the city of Washington." The law under which he was incarcerated was surely "void and unconstitutional in its application to a citizen," the governor wrote, and therefore Horton must be released.[3]

In arguing that Horton was a citizen of New York and therefore could not be summarily arrested by authorities in the capital, Clinton took a strong position in an ongoing debate. African Americans and their white allies regularly insisted that racially discriminatory laws were unjust and out of step with the ideals of Christianity and the Declaration of Independence. What was different here was that Clinton invoked the US Constitution and its privileges and immunities clause when making the claim that Horton was entitled to his freedom—not in New York, where Clinton had considerable authority, but in an entirely different jurisdiction.

In the 1820s, the privileges and immunities clause (Article IV, Section 2) became critically important to the American debate about the rights of free African Americans, and it would remain so until passage of the Fourteenth Amendment in 1866. The clause read, "The citizens of each state shall be entitled to all privileges and immunities of citizens in the several states." It alluded to state citizens ("the citizens of each state"), but it did more than simply recognize the existence of state citizenship; it suggested that citizens of a state should enjoy some basic prerogatives when they were in other states. What those prerogatives were was not specified. Adding to the ambiguity were questions about the nature of state citizenship itself. The Articles of Confederation had used the terms *citizen* and *person* interchangeably, leading to criticism from James Madison. The framers of the Constitution had cleared up that problem by using the word *citizen* consistently throughout the clause, but the practice of eliding *persons* and *citizens* continued elsewhere. Early state constitutions, for example, sometimes made little distinction among *citizens*, *persons*, and *inhabitants*, while other times they indicated that *citizens* enjoyed special privileges such as the right to vote or to own land.[4]

In the first three decades of American nationhood, state and federal courts began to interpret the privileges and immunities clause, at least as it applied to white men. Courts generally held that the clause prohibited states from treating people from out of state differently from their own residents in what they considered matters of fundamental rights. These were what contemporaries sometimes referred to as "civil rights"—the right to move freely from state to state, enter into contracts, own property, and sue and be sued.[5] Did this principle also apply to free African Americans when they moved from one jurisdiction to another? The question remained unanswered for decades.

The first major reckoning with the clause's meaning for African Americans came in 1820–21, when Missouri political leaders presented Congress with a state constitution that barred "free negroes and mulattos" from entering. Legislators from the free states protested that the Missouri ban was unconstitutional under the privileges and immunities clause, spurring an intense debate during which many free-state legislators emphatically declared that African Americans were citizens of their states. Before the Missouri conflict, state-level lawmakers seemed to care little about defining state citizenship as such. The Missouri conflict cast citizenship in a new light, so when Governor Clinton and other New Yorkers insisted in 1826 that Gilbert Horton was a *citizen,* their claim reflected the new significance of state citizenship and the privileges and immunities clause in the national debate about racial equality. From the Missouri debates onward, advocates of racial equality continued to use the Constitution's privileges and immunities clause as a conduit for elevating demands for racial equality in civil rights from the state level, where they usually resided, into the realm of Congress or the federal courts. It was difficult to make headway in these realms, but their efforts publicized the injustice of racist laws and helped establish the foundation on which federal measures were finally built in 1866.

THE MISSOURI DEBATES OF 1820–21 thrust the privileges and immunities clause into public view in an unprecedented way, but that was not the first time people recognized the clause's potential for advancing federal-level claims to rights for free African Americans. At the end of the eighteenth century, free Black Philadelphians, with support from Quaker allies, had identified themselves as "citizens" when petitioning Congress. In 1803, a Massachusetts congressman insisted that free Black people were entitled to the "privileges and immunities" of citizenship under the Constitution, a claim that forced Congress to clarify that a measure directed against Black immigrants from the Caribbean applied only to persons of color who were not "a native, a citizen, or registered seaman of the United States." The issue arose again in 1818, when free-state congressmen rejected a proposed fugitive slave law on grounds that it did not sufficiently protect the rights of free African Americans. As Thomas Scott Williams of Connecticut put it, "In attempting . . . to secure the right of property to one class of citizens, it was unjust that the rights of another class should be put in jeopardy."[6] These skirmishes set the stage for the sustained attention Congress devoted to the question of African American citizenship during the great national debate about Missouri's admission to the Union.

The territory that became the state of Missouri had been part of the Louisiana Purchase, an immense expanse of some 830,000 square miles that the US government acquired from France in 1803. Slaveholding was widely practiced in the region, having been permitted during French, Spanish, and US territorial rule. Amid growing settlement, much of it by slaveholders, the territorial government of Missouri applied to Congress for statehood in 1818. Many Americans would have been completely unsurprised to see Congress welcome yet another slave state into the Union. In 1811, Congress had admitted the slave state of Louisiana from the Louisiana Purchase lands, and after that there had been no congressional objections to the admission of the slave states of Mississippi and Alabama. Yet Missouri's request for statehood created a crisis in Congress that lasted a year and a half and at times seemed poised to destroy the nation. In part, this was because the partisan alliances that had defined the first few decades of independence had broken down. The Federalist Party was dramatically weakened after the War of 1812, though a rump of Federalists remained in the northern states, and many were strong advocates of what they saw as explicitly "northern" interests in the American economy. The

Republicans, strongly identified with Thomas Jefferson, were in a decided majority nationwide. Yet the Republicans were also significantly divided, and one of the major fault lines was slavery.

The decline of Federalists in the slave states and the attenuation of party unity among Republicans opened the possibility that northern politicians might form cross-party coalitions to attack slavery. In states where slavery was ending, many Republicans saw the institution as antidemocratic and viewed slaveholders as a malignant aristocracy. After the War of 1812, northern Republicans were among those who challenged the proposed Illinois Constitution for not doing enough to stamp out slavery. In the 1810s, free-state Republicans also rebuffed slaveholders' demands for a draconian new fugitive slave law and condemned the abuses of the growing domestic slave trade. When Missouri applied for statehood, such Republicans were perfectly willing to align with Federalists in an effort to set the state on a course toward abolition. Led by Republican James Tallmadge Jr. of New York, northern congressmen from both parties insisted that Missouri could join the Union only if it committed to a program of gradual abolition. Southern politicians, in turn, defended Missouri's entry as a slave state. The debate spanned two congresses and generated an outpouring of antislavery sentiment in the free states. Many observers worried that the crisis might shatter the union. Finally, in the spring of 1820, Congress struck a deal that allowed Missouri to maintain slavery while also barring human bondage from any future states carved from the Louisiana Purchase lands north of the 36°30′ parallel.[7]

Yet the Missouri crisis was not over, and its often-neglected second phase consisted of a wide-ranging and transformative debate about the rights of free African Americans and the meaning of citizenship under the privileges and immunities clause. After Congress decided to admit Missouri as a slave state, the nascent state's leaders needed to submit a constitution to Congress for approval. The constitution they proposed contained a clause instructing the state legislature to pass "such laws as may be necessary to prevent free negroes and mulattos from coming to and settling in this State, under any pretext whatsoever." The Missourians likely believed they were on firm ground. In 1793, Virginia had become the first state to pass a law barring entry of free African Americans, and the legislatures of other slave states soon followed. By 1820, laws prohibiting Black migration existed in Maryland, Kentucky, South Carolina, and Georgia. Their rationales were similar to those offered in free states like Ohio. That is, state legislatures drew on their "police power" to bar entry of groups of people they considered potentially disruptive. In the case of slave states, legislators feared not only that free African Americans were impoverished or criminally inclined but also that they would foment uprisings among the enslaved population.[8] To delegates attending Missouri's 1820 constitutional convention, then, banning migration by free people of African descent would have appeared entirely consistent with policies in other slaveholding states.

Unfortunately for the Missourians, however, Congress still needed to approve their new constitution, and many northern legislators, Republican and Federalist alike, objected to the proposed ban on Black migration. Because the ban involved migration from outside the state (rather than internal state matters only), it was plausible to invoke the US Constitution's privileges and immunities clause as an authority for rejecting the Missouri Constitution. Anticipating the congressional debate, the widely read *Niles' Weekly Register* denounced the Missouri Constitution, declaring that the privileges and immunities clause was "a very plain, simple and imperative sentence" whose evident meaning was that Black citizens of the states "cannot be dispossessed of their right to locate themselves where they please." *Niles* exaggerated in asserting that the meaning of the privileges and immunities clause for African Americans was obvious. Not all states recognized African Americans as citizens, and not everyone in the United States had a "right to locate where they please." The stage was set for an intense debate about race, state sovereignty, and the meaning of the privileges and immunities clause itself.[9]

In Congress, supporters of the proposed Missouri Constitution insisted that Missouri's bar on Black migration fell squarely within the states' power over their domestic police. Senator John Holmes of Maine, a Republican and one of the few free-state legislators to defend the Missouri Constitution, emphasized that states could use "discretion, policy, [and] expediency" to determine who could enter. "It is the State law which defines who are worthy of a residence within the State," he said. Several legislators analogized directly from the poor-law tradition. In the House, Philip P. Barbour of Virginia argued that, "if vagabonds and fugitives from justice infest a State, they may certainly be expelled," and the same principle applied to free African Americans. If a state's white population believed free Blacks posed a threat to public peace, that was a legitimate reason to remove them or bar them from entry. As Republican Congressman Alexander Smyth of Virginia insisted: "[H]as not every county and parish a right to exclude paupers and vagrants? May not every city and town exclude persons having infectious diseases, although they are citizens? . . . The right of self-preservation confers this right of exclusion."[10]

In addition to defending state authority over migration and settlement, many of Missouri's advocates insisted that racial differences were natural and immutable, and that the United States was fundamentally a white nation. Barbour of Virginia, for example, argued that racist laws were founded "in the best good sense, in the preservation of public morality and of the dignity of our nature." Representative Charles Pinckney of South Carolina charged his free-state colleagues with "a total want of knowledge of the distinction which has, from time immemorial, existed in the civilized world, between the black and white race." Louis McLane of Delaware emphasized that the United States began as an "association . . . of white people—Europeans and their descendants." The nation's founders had excluded Indigenous people and Africans from the "civil and political community," he argued, and members of such groups could not be included, "unless by some positive law, or by long usage and custom."[11] Such arguments for the fundamental importance of race in the distribution of status and rights in American communities informed southerners' claims about the nature of citizenship at the state level.

There was little consistency in the way legislators talked about state citizenship during the debate. In part, this was because everyone recognized that states could define citizenship for themselves. It was also because, in the absence of formal state-level definitions of citizenship, legislators were largely making it up as they went along, theorizing from a panoply of local laws, customs, and practices. Congressman Smyth of Virginia argued that not everyone who was born in a state, or even born free in a state, "becomes a member of the political community." He suggested that free Black people were "denizens" because they were "admitted to some portion of the rights and privileges of citizens, but not to all those rights and privileges." This suggested that only white men were citizens because only white men enjoyed *all* the rights and privileges available. If that were the case, then how should legislators think of white women and minors? Congressman Barbour won praise from other slave-state legislators with the argument that "the term citizen" should be applied only to a person who was "possessed of all at least of the civil rights if not of the political, of every other person in the community, under like circumstances, of which he is not deprived for some cause personal to himself." The idea was that white women and minors should not be compared to white men because they were in different "circumstances," while free Black men and white men were in "like circumstances." Black men did not possess the same rights as white men, the argument went, and therefore they were not citizens. Representative McLane theorized that free African Americans were "perpetual inhabitants" who enjoyed certain privileges not as "a matter of right" but as "matters of grace from the local municipality." In this view, free Black people were not entitled to certain fundamental rights simply by virtue of being human. The prerogatives they did enjoy came from positive enactment of government and could be granted or taken away.[12]

The free-state legislators who rejected the Missouri Constitution embraced very different visions of citizenship, nationhood, and the meaning of racial difference. In the first place, they insisted that free Black people were citizens of most northern states and that skin color or race was not an acceptable category for discrimination, even in matters of the states' domestic police. In the House, James Strong, a New York Federalist, affirmed that states could remove paupers if "likely to become a public charge," banish criminals, or exclude people in the interest of preventing the spread of disease. And yet, he asked, "Because a State can banish a traitor does it follow that she can deport every or any harmless, unsuspected citizen?" It was inappropriate, he insisted, to banish or exclude someone who had done nothing to offend the public peace. Congressman Joseph Hemphill, a Pennsylvania Federalist, agreed that certain legal processes were required before a person could be deemed a "nuisance" and removed. "What is our general idea of a nuisance? Is it not a fact to be ascertained by legal investigation? One man may be guilty of a nuisance, while another of the same color may be innocent; and shall a whole description of people be condemned and deprived of valuable rights without a hearing?"[13] Both men conceded that states could regulate and even exclude, but they argued that such actions had to be based on evaluation of individuals' conduct, not simply on the color of their skin.

The United States was *not* fundamentally a white nation, these men also insisted. Free Black people had been part of the founders' vision of the United States. Black men had fought in the American Revolution; they had voted in many states at that time. African Americans were implicitly included in the Constitution's opening phrase, "We the People." William Eustis, a Massachusetts Republican, pointed out that Black people were among the constituents he represented in Congress. In this view, differences in race or color should be immaterial when it came to the question of citizenship and basic rights. Senator David Morril, a New Hampshire Republican, emphasized the arbitrariness of sorting people by supposed race. "Color no more comes into consideration to decide who is a citizen than size or profession," Morril said. "You may as well say a tall citizen shall not settle in Missouri, as a yellow citizen shall not." Under such a system, he asked, "where are our liberties and privileges? They are fled."[14]

As free staters pieced together their own vision of state citizenship, they generally avoided the tortured parsing of status differences among free people that many southerners had undertaken. Northerners frequently invoked ancient Rome to insist that there were just two kinds of free people in any society: citizens and aliens. If you were not one, then you were the other. In this view, white women, minors, free African Americans, and many others were citizens despite having different—and fewer—civil and political rights than most white men. Pennsylvania Federalist Congressman John Sergeant claimed that "more than half the white men in some of our States did not vote, because they were not freeholders; yet no one would deny them to be citizens of those States." The free staters' capacious vision of citizenship allowed them to claim that free African Americans were citizens even in states with racially discriminatory laws, or where Black men were denied the vote. For Representative Strong of New York, free mobility and residency were critical to the definition of state citizenship. A state citizen was a person entitled to "the right of passing, freely and unmolested, from town to town, and place to place, within the State, and the right of residing, at pleasure, in any part of the same." Yet Strong conceded that "these rights are also common to all free persons, of every age and sex, within the State, except aliens, lunatics, vagabonds, and criminals; because their possession and exercise are indispensably necessary to the social relations of life, and to the preservation of the State."[15] In this view, the basic rights of citizens were coextensive with the basic rights of most free persons. "Aliens, lunatics, vagabonds, and criminals" might not enjoy the same prerogatives, Strong acknowledged, but exclusion based on race was not permissible.

Northern legislators proceeded to insist that everyone included in their capacious definition of state citizenship was entitled to the "privileges and immunities" promised by Article IV, Section 2, and this included the right to move freely across state lines. Whereas slave state politicians tended to invoke the sovereignty of states and the states' preeminent right of self-preservation, free staters emphasized personal liberty and national cohesion. In *Federalist Paper* No. 80, Alexander Hamilton had called the privileges and immunities clause "the basis of the Union." Northerners echoed that view, emphasizing that the clause rendered the nation more than just a collection of small sovereignties and complemented the commerce clause of the Constitution (part of Article I, Section 8), which facilitated inter-state and international trade. Slave staters worried that their northern peers would obliterate the states and their traditional power over their domestic police. Morril of New Hampshire imagined nothing of the sort. He drew a strong distinction between prohibiting migration and merely regulating it. "Any State may regulate the terms upon which emigrants shall become residents; but no State has any right to exclude them. To utterly prohibit, and regulate by law the terms of inhabitancy, are materially and essentially different; and one within the municipal power of every State, the other expressly prohibited by the Constitution of the United Sates." Morril and his allies did not deny that states could impose different regulations on Blacks than on whites once people were *in* the state. They might have believed it was bad policy to do so, but they affirmed that it was within a state's purview. What they refused to countenance was entirely blocking migration. "It was the humble simple privilege of locomotion only that was now claimed for these persons," said Sergeant. "It was a right indispensable to citizenship, and it was *all* that was asked for in the present case."[16]

The second Missouri debate continued from the waning weeks of 1820 through the spring of 1821, when Congress finally arrived at a compromise. On December 12, the Senate passed a resolution to admit Missouri with the caveat that the action must not be construed as giving "the assent of Congress" to any part of the Missouri Constitution, "*if any such there be*, which contravene[d]" the privileges and immunities clause. This was entirely unsatisfactory to the northerners who insisted that the Missouri Constitution violated the US Constitution, but the Senate adopted it nonetheless. The House proceeded to reject the Senate measure and continued to argue. Southerners insisted that there was nothing wrong with the proposed Missouri Constitution and that, in any case, Congress had already tacitly admitted Missouri in the previous session. Northerners maintained that the Black exclusion clause was unconstitutional and that Congress was duty-bound to step in. The Capitol reverberated with frustration that another session of Congress had been consumed by debate about Missouri, and some legislators intimated that the conflict might lead to bloodshed. Finally, the House agreed to a compromise measure developed by Congressman Henry Clay of Kentucky. The terms were as follows: Missouri could become a state on the condition that its legislature ignore the state constitution's instruction to exclude African Americans and never use it to justify a law "by which any citizen, of either of the States in this Union, shall be excluded from the enjoyment of any of the privileges and immunities to which such citizen is entitled under the constitution of the United States."[17]

Many of the staunchest defenders of Black equality voted against the compromise, likely because they wanted Missouri to rewrite its constitution or because they simply didn't want Missouri to enter the Union as a slave state. Indeed, from their perspective there was much that the compromise failed to accomplish. Clay's compromise emphasized that after Missouri became a state, none of its rights would be impaired, including the right "to exclude from her jurisdictions persons under peculiar circumstances, (such as paupers, vagabonds, &c.,)."[18] The compromise thus affirmed the right of Missouri (or any state) to "exclude" people it deemed undesirable in conventional poor-law categories. It reinforced distinctions between "citizens" and "paupers," suggesting that insofar as state authorities construed free Black people as paupers, vagrants, drains on public resources, and so on, they might be excludable. Moreover, the compromise did not require Missouri to change its constitution, and it did not challenge a state's authority to make laws targeting Black people as a suspect class. It did not venture a definition of United States citizenship or affirm that African Americans were US citizens, nor did it define the "privileges and immunities" of state citizenship. Congress left all those matters unresolved.

All those deficiencies, however, did not make the compromise meaningless. To the contrary, the compromise recognized many of the free staters' most important arguments. Southerners had insisted that Congress must ask nothing more of Missouri and that the constitutionality of Black exclusion must be decided in the courts. Free staters had argued that Congress must act. Congress had acted. The compromise acknowledged free staters' claim that many states recognized free Black residents as citizens. The compromise also supported their argument that, under the Constitution, African Americans who were recognized as state citizens could not be prohibited from traveling to new places, just as white citizens could not. In keeping with Congress's requirement, Missouri's first post-statehood statute on Black migration stipulated that "no free negro or mulatto, *other than a citizen of some one of the United States*" could enter or settle in the state. The Illinois legislature followed Missouri's lead, passing a new black code that exempted "black or mulatto" persons who were citizens of "some one of the United States" from its requirement that Black newcomers register with freedom papers and post bonds.[19] All these measures acknowledged that some states recognized free African Americans as citizens and that those citizens were entitled to benefit from "privileges and immunities" promised by the Constitution.

The concerns that animated the second Missouri debate moved quickly into new venues. Later in 1821, the US customs collector in Norfolk sought clarification on whether a free Black Virginian was a citizen of the United States. The man was seeking the collector's approval to become a captain of a merchant vessel, a privilege that, according to federal law, was reserved for United States citizens. The customs collector put the question to the US treasury secretary, who asked the attorney general, William Wirt, for an official opinion. Wirt wholeheartedly embraced the position many southerners had taken during the Missouri debate—that the Constitution construed as US citizens "those only who enjoyed the full and equal privileges of white citizens in the State of their residence."[20] Because free Black people in Virginia did not have all the same rights as whites, Wirt claimed, they were not citizens of either the state or the United States.

In the aftermath of the Missouri debates, state governments took up questions of state citizenship in new ways. What exactly was state citizenship in the early republic? As the Missouri debates suggested, Americans used the term *citizen* regularly but without much specificity. Citizenship status was often a highly local affair, and at the local level, citizens were often people with special prerogatives—the equivalent of freeholders or burghers in other contexts. Citizenship could therefore connote respectability, and people sometimes posited "citizens" as the opposite of poor people or those who conducted themselves disreputably. The paradigmatic citizen was often a man, while "wives," no matter how upstanding, were not often seen as citizens. In this context, when Black activists and their white allies referred to free African Americans as "citizens"—which they often did—they were making an argument for African Americans' status as members of the community and, particularly in light of the colonization movement, their right to remain where they were. Because citizenship was often associated with elevated status, when African Americans claimed to be *citizens*, they were fighting back against racial stereotyping and insisting that Black people were equal to whites in their capacity for reason, virtue, and hard work. Such claims to citizenship and belonging were highly significant, but they did not clarify whom states recognized as citizens and what the rights and responsibilities of state citizenship were. In fact, most states had done little to answer such questions.[21]

The question of who was a state citizen emerged in Massachusetts soon after the Missouri debate ended. The state's representatives in Congress had been among the strongest advocates of racial equality in citizenship. And yet, as Senator William Smith of South Carolina pointed out, even Massachusetts had laws that drew distinctions based on race. Smith discussed the 1788 law that permitted local authorities to expel from the state any "African or negro" who was not a "subject of the Emperor of Morocco" or a "citizen of the United States," if the person stayed more than two months. Even in the state that called itself "the cradle in which the Revolution had been rocked," Smith chided, Black and white people were not permitted to intermarry, and Black men were barred from militia service. Meanwhile, Senator Holmes of Maine had warned that if "free blacks are citizens and may go where they will," the free states would be in grave danger from a potential influx.[22]

At least some people in Massachusetts seemed to share Holmes's concerns about an influx of Black migrants, because in the summer of 1821 a subcommittee of the Massachusetts General Assembly's lower house reported on a proposal concerning the settlement of "free Negroes and Mulattos." Noting that other states had recently passed laws severely restricting Black migration, the subcommittee predicted that if Massachusetts did nothing to protect itself, migrants would increasingly cross into the state, bringing problems of pauperism, unemployment, and crime. Expressing the tension between individual rights and a state's power to regulate undesirable populations, the committee recommended that the commonwealth adopt policies that honored the "respect for humanity and the just rights of all classes of men, by which this commonwealth has been long and greatly distinguished," but, "at the same time, protect this state from the burthen of an expensive and injurious population." As a St. Louis newspaper pointed out, this was "The Missouri Question in Massachusetts." The legislature resumed the discussion in its next session. In the meantime, Benjamin Lundy's *Genius of Universal Emancipation* condemned Massachusetts for even taking up the question. "Non-slaveholding states" ought not indulge the argument that free Blacks were "dangerous to the welfare of the community," he cautioned. Willingness even to discuss the matter would "strengthen the prejudice of the whites against the free people of color, and have a direct tendency to prevent any measures from being taken for the liberation of those held as slaves."[23]

Despite these misgivings, Lundy would likely have been pleased with the outcome of deliberations in Massachusetts. In January 1822, the subcommittee report recommended against action. It affirmed the state's authority over its domestic police, stating that it was the legislature's "duty . . . to protect the population of this Commonwealth from all dangers and injuries, whether affecting morals or health, whether introduced from foreign countries, or from the sister States of these United States."

Yet the subcommittee rejected the suggestion that the state should impose on Black people regulations that did not apply to whites. Rehearsing the history of slavery's abolition in Massachusetts, the committee stated that the 1788 law was never enforced and, in fact, was an embarrassment. It concluded that "the people of this Commonwealth have always believed negroes and mulattoes to possess the same right and capability to become citizens as white persons." Massachusetts took no action, and when the state published a new code of laws in the 1830s, the 1788 statute was gone.[24] Coming in the wake of the second Missouri debate, the state's affirmation that African Americans were citizens not only put Massachusetts on record against the racially discriminatory measures that many other states had passed. It also established the possibility that African Americans could claim prerogatives of free mobility under the Constitution's privileges and immunities clause.

After the Missouri debate, lawmakers in New York also affirmed that African Americans were state citizens, though they did so in the context of restricting Black men's right to vote. As gradual emancipation unfolded in the late eighteenth and early nineteenth centuries, Black New Yorkers developed cultural and political institutions, including churches and mutual aid societies, that became foundations of communities and cradles of political activity. Abolitionists and their allies had previously beaten back attempts to impose race-based restrictions on voting, but Black men's right to vote in New York was under attack again in the 1810s. African Americans mainly voted Federalist, the party that most consistently supported abolition and racial equality. But Federalist power had faded after the turn of the century, and New York Republicans split into rival groups, one of which—Martin Van Buren and his "Bucktail" faction—was intent on diminishing Black voters' power. In 1811 and 1815, the Bucktails prevailed over protests by their white political rivals and by African Americans, pushing the state legislature to enact laws that required Black men to produce freedom certificates before casting their ballots. In the years leading up to the Missouri debates, then, the survival of New

York's revolutionary-era regime of racial equality in public policy was very much in doubt.[25]

During the Missouri debates, New York politicians were virtually united in opposition to slavery's extension and to the Missouri Constitution's Black exclusion clause. In 1817, the state legislature passed, with bipartisan support, a new gradual emancipation act that sped up the process, promising freedom to all enslaved people in the state by July 4, 1827. During the initial crisis over Missouri, almost all of the state's twenty-seven-member congressional delegation voted against allowing Missouri to join the Union as a slave state. New York legislators also exhibited near unanimity when it came to Black citizenship itself. Amid the second Missouri crisis, one prominent state legislator argued that New York lawmakers' "first duty" was "protection of their citizens in their legitimate rights" under the US Constitution. Soon thereafter, the legislature voted 117 to 4 to instruct the state's congressional delegation to reject any new state whose constitution "den[ied] to any citizens of the existing states, the privileges and immunities of citizens of such new state."[26]

But what exactly did citizenship mean for African Americans living in New York State? It was not clear, in part because the state, like others, had never explicitly defined citizenship. New Yorkers made fateful decisions on the matter at a constitutional convention held in Albany in August 1821, several months after Congress resolved the second Missouri crisis. The Bucktails had pushed for the convention partly with a goal of eliminating property requirements for white men's right to vote. African Americans from New York City, concerned about the Bucktails' opposition to their right to vote and about Black New Yorkers' larger vulnerability to the whims of the state's white majority, petitioned the convention for a constitutional provision that would prohibit the legislature from passing laws encroaching on their right to vote. Not surprisingly, the Bucktails were moving in the opposite direction. A Bucktail delegate proposed adding the word *white* to the constitutional language about voter requirements, a change that would have fully disenfranchised the state's Black population.

Opponents mobilized to defeat the Bucktail proposal, among them Peter A. Jay, the eldest son of John Jay, a leading New York Federalist during the Revolution. The elder Jay had been a slaveowner but had worked to bring the institution to an end in New York, including helping to found the New-York Manumission Society in 1785. Almost four decades later, his son Peter placed debates about voting rights in New York in the context of the congressional struggle over Missouri. He reminded his colleagues that only ten months earlier, the New York legislature had stood up for racial equality in the "privileges and immunities" of citizenship. He urged the convention to stay the course, arguing that the convention's decision would have national implications. "Adopt the amendment now proposed," he warned, "and you will hear a shout of triumph and a hiss of scorn from the southern part of this nation."[27]

In the end, the constitutional convention restricted Black men's right to vote while also explicitly recognizing African Americans as New York citizens. Under the new constitution, white men no longer faced any property requirements for the franchise, while Black men could vote only if they owned $250 or more of freehold property. This was a major defeat for the principle of racial equality and for Black New Yorkers, who had heretofore exercised their right to vote regularly and, in some locales, were numerous enough to be politically influential. Still, the convention's affirmation that a "man of color" could be a citizen of the state mattered, particularly in the broader context of the recent Missouri debate.[28] The state had adopted the generally northern view that state citizenship was capacious and, for men, need not be associated with racial equality in voting rights. The move gave Black New Yorkers a place to start when they wanted to assert rights to "locomotion"—to travel and even settle in other states. In subsequent years, people waging the fight for racial equality in civil rights regularly invoked Massachusetts and New York as states that regarded African Americans as citizens. These states' policies, read together with the Constitution's privileges and immunities clause, troubled and contradicted those who insisted that states could exclude free African Americans at will.

GILBERT HORTON, IMPRISONED in Washington, DC, was a citizen of New York. Born around the turn of the nineteenth century, he had grown up amid New York's gradual abolition of slavery, its promises of racial equality, and its encroachments on Black men's right to vote. Horton became free not as a result of state policy but because his father, Peter Horton, spent a year working for Gilbert's owner and purchased the boy's freedom when he was five years old. Peter Horton remained in rural Peekskill, where, according to one account, he "accumulated a snug little property by his industry and economy." Meanwhile, Gilbert moved to New York City, a center for jobs and African American civic culture, where he eventually found employment on the *Macedonian*, working the coastwise trade. In the summer of 1826, Gilbert disembarked in Norfolk, Virginia. His ship proceeded onward, while Gilbert made his way to Washington.[29]

Gilbert Horton's arrival and arrest in the nation's capital set in motion a national controversy that amplified the questions of citizenship and race that defined the second Missouri debate. The District of Columbia was then a perilous place for free African Americans like Gilbert Horton who were not already residents. The capital was slaveholding territory, the land having been donated to the federal government by the slaveholding states of Maryland and Virginia. Slave traders established businesses there, serving slaveholders of the Chesapeake region seeking to profit by selling slaves into the expanding economy of the Southwest. The domestic slave trade became even more lucrative after 1808, when Congress barred Americans from participating in the international trade. By the late 1810s, antislavery people regularly represented the capital as a slave trader's emporium, drawing attention to the juxtaposition of a self-proclaimed free government convening amid the spectacle of human beings, chained together, forced to leave their families against their will and doomed to a lifetime of bondage.[30]

At the same time, the capital was a growing center for free African

Americans in the region. By the time Gilbert Horton arrived in the summer of 1826, free Black people made up almost half of the capital's African American population of roughly twelve thousand, and the proportion of free Blacks to slaves continued to rise.[31] In the District of Columbia's three separate cities—Georgetown, Alexandria, and Washington—free African Americans labored in the homes of white people, in the ports of Georgetown and Alexandria, and in businesses associated with the political life of the nation. Although they faced a web of legal restrictions, they were also able—often with the blessings of prominent whites—to live together as families and establish their own schools and churches. The threat of kidnapping remained pervasive, however, and law enforcement regularly applied the prima facie principle, presuming people of African descent to be slaves unless they could prove otherwise. This was why, when Gilbert Horton arrived at the Georgetown wharf, a white stranger felt entitled to stop him and demand his papers.

Back in New York, news of Horton's arrest galvanized former Federalists and their allies—people with connections to the administration of President John Quincy Adams who were interested in continuing to agitate slavery-related questions. Party politics on the national stage had been chaotic in the years since the Missouri crisis. The 1824 presidential election was indicative. After the disintegration of the Federalist–Republican rivalry, the election featured five contenders with different regional strengths. When the votes were tallied, Andrew Jackson of Tennessee, famed for his performance as a general in the War of 1812, had won a plurality in both the popular vote and the electoral college but not the required majority in the electoral college. The contest then moved to the House of Representatives, where Henry Clay of Kentucky, one of the five original candidates, threw his support to Adams of Massachusetts, another of the five. In what came to be known as the "corrupt bargain," Adams became president.

Many northerners viewed John Quincy Adams, son of American founder and former president John Adams, as a decidedly northern president and a welcome relief from the string of southerners who had preceded him in the White House. Not only was Adams a son of Massachusetts, but he also supported federal funding for infrastructure improvements and a tariff intended to promote American manufacturing. During the Adams presidency, Jackson and his supporters, feeling robbed of a victory to which they were entitled, sought to stymie Adams and his coalition at every turn. At the same time, Jackson and other members of the old Republican Party, including Martin Van Buren of New York, worked to rebuild the North–South sectional alliance that had characterized the party in its heyday. That effort would bear fruit in Jackson's 1828 election to the presidency and the emergence of the Democratic Party. Yet the southern resurgence in Washington did not silence those committed to condemning slavery as a great evil and defending the rights of free African Americans. To the contrary, they continued to pressure Congress to take action in places where they believed it had authority.[32]

For New Yorkers eager to make the case, Gilbert Horton's arrest offered an opportunity to revive the questions that had animated the second Missouri crisis. New York newspaper readers learned of Horton's arrest on August 15, 1826, when the New York *Daily Advertiser* published the notice run by the Washington *National Intelligencer* with commentary urging New Yorkers to secure his release. News of Horton's arrest quickly coursed through Westchester County, where Horton and his family were well known. A man named James Brown affirmed that Horton was a free man from Peekskill and that Peter Horton, Gilbert's father, was "willing to offer any testimony" to help secure his son's release. John Owen, a local lawyer, wrote immediately to Washington authorities, giving them an account of Horton's life that would have been useless had Horton provided it himself, but, when given by a respectable white man like Owen, would be treated seriously. Owen attested that he knew Horton to be a free man because Horton had been indentured, as a child, to Owen's father. He offered to provide copies of the indenture as well as an affidavit from Peter Horton if Washington authorities needed more information.[33]

William Jay soon moved to the forefront of the effort. The second son

of John Jay and brother of Peter, William had attended college at Yale and
then studied law. Physical infirmities, including near-blindness, limited his
professional prospects, so as a young man he moved to his father's rural
estate in Westchester County, where he married and lived the life of a
politically engaged country gentleman. Appointed a county judge in 1818,
he was active in agricultural reform, religious life, and temperance. He had
strongly opposed Missouri's admission as a slave state, but he had evidently
done little antislavery work until the fall of 1826, when he committed himself to freeing Gilbert Horton and drawing attention to the unjust laws of
the District of Columbia.[34]

Jay had been thinking about slavery in the nation's capital at least since
the previous spring, when Congressman Charles Miner of Pennsylvania
made an audacious proposal to end slavery there. Miner's gambit itself
originated in a longer history of antislavery activism. Since the late eighteenth century, antislavery advocates, particularly those associated with
the Pennsylvania Abolition Society (PAS), had urged Congress to abolish
slavery in places where the Constitution clearly gave it jurisdiction, including in the District of Columbia. There, according to Article I, Section 8 of
the Constitution, Congress had the power of "exclusive Legislation in all
Cases whatsoever." Benjamin Lundy, publisher of the *Genius of Universal
Emancipation*, was a crucial force in pushing abolitionists to pay attention to the nation's capital. In 1821, Lundy argued that Congress should
act against slavery by refusing to admit new slave states, terminating the
domestic and international slave trades, and abolishing slavery in "all the
territories and districts" where it had "exclusive" control. Three years later,
he moved his newspaper to Baltimore, and in the spring of 1826, he publicly urged Congressman Miner to propose the abolition of slavery in the
District of Columbia.[35]

Miner obliged in June, just as the congressional session was ending.
His proposal to abolish slavery in the national capital caused, in the words
of one observer, "great excitement" among the "Southern gentlemen" in
the chamber. Miner, who represented a Quaker-heavy district southwest

of Philadelphia, was a lawyer, newspaper editor, and friend of John Quincy Adams. He had longstanding ties to the PAS, and he surely knew his proposal was inflammatory. Suggesting that the capital would be safer and more prosperous with a mostly "free white population," he proposed that the House committee charged with overseeing the District of Columbia be instructed to consider a bill to abolish slavery gradually and restrict the slave trade in the national capital. His colleagues in the House were not interested. Miner hoped they would at least allow the proposal to "lie on the table" for further consideration, but instead they voted immediately to prohibit discussion and then proceeded to adjourn for the summer.[36]

New York antislavery people greeted Miner's resolutions with pleasure. The New-York Manumission Society sent the congressman a congratulatory message and called on the public to support him. That fall, as William Jay became involved in the Gilbert Horton case, he credited Miner for raising his awareness about slavery in the District of Columbia and the possibilities for undermining it. Jay wanted to free Horton from jail, but he also saw the moment as an opportunity to generate publicity and force debate. As he told Miner, "Every discussion in Congress in relation to slavery, no matter how great may be the majority against us, advances our cause. We shall rise more powerful from every defeat."[37]

Jay and his allies in Westchester County organized a high-profile campaign to free Horton, in the process mobilizing arguments about African American citizenship under the privileges and immunities clause. At a strategy meeting on August 30, 1826, the Westchester residents decided to ask Governor DeWitt Clinton, a Republican, to appeal to President Adams for Horton's release. They also adopted resolutions calling for the abolition of slavery in the District of Columbia. Echoing arguments northerners had made in the Missouri debates, the Westchester group claimed that, as a citizen of New York, Horton was entitled to "all the privileges and immunities of citizens in the several states" and therefore had the right to move freely to, from, and within the District of Columbia. They also insisted that he had been denied due process of law, condemning any policy that permitted "a free citizen, without evidence of crime, and without trial by jury" to be "condemned to servitude for life." The practice, they said, was "repugnant to our republican institutions, and revolting to justice and humanity." Governor Clinton took up the cause, reiterating in his letter to President Adams that Horton was entitled to the same basic rights when he traveled as when he was at home. Any law that provided that a free man like Horton could be incarcerated merely on suspicion of being a fugitive slave, Clinton insisted, must be "at least void and unconstitutional in its application to a citizen, and could never have been intended to extend further than fugitive slaves."[38]

With antislavery people already watching the nation's capital, and questions of African Americans' citizenship under the privileges and immunities clause already on the table, the saga of Horton's incarceration found purchase in northern papers. Theodore Dwight, editor of the *Daily Advertiser,* was a major force behind the effort. Dwight was a longstanding Federalist whose paper had strongly opposed Missouri's admission as a slave state. Dwight broke the news of Horton's arrest with the headline, FROM THE DECLARATION OF INDEPENDENCE, and his story began with the familiar words: "We hold these truths to be self-evident,—that all *men* are created equal; that they are endowed by their Creator with certain inalienable rights; that among them are life, *liberty*, and the pursuit of happiness." Having placed special emphasis on the word *liberty*, the *Advertiser* published the full text of the *Intelligencer*'s advertisement for Horton. "Alas!" the paper lamented, Horton was "taken up, imprisoned, and sold by the Marshal of the District of Columbia . . . for the colour of the skin, and the difference of a few degrees of latitude." Why would Americans object to such practices in places like "Russia and Turkey," he questioned, while allowing them to continue at home?[39]

Coverage in the New York *Commercial Advertiser,* edited by William Leete Stone, another former Federalist and an ally of DeWitt Clinton, helped expand the significance of Horton's arrest and incarceration. Newspapers of the era often filled their pages with items from other papers, and the *Commercial Advertiser*'s first major article on Horton—which included James Brown's letter affirming that Horton was free—circulated widely. As weeks passed, the paper published updates on Horton's status and New Yorkers' mobilization for his release. It covered the Westchester meeting and announced that the county's representative in Congress, Aaron Ward, was paying attention, as was Miner of Pennsylvania. The *Commercial Advertiser* asked New Yorkers, particularly in the metropolis, to be a "strong voice of public opinion" in favor of anything Miner might propose, including abolition in the District of Columbia. Newspapers in the Northeast and the Mid-Atlantic picked up the *Commercial Advertiser*'s stories, revealing widespread interest in Horton's fate and the larger questions his imprisonment raised. One Philadelphia paper reported that Horton's incarceration had "justly excited considerable feeling" and "place[d] in a striking light the tyranny frequently exercised over the abused African race."[40]

Responding to the critical onslaught, editors in slaveholding jurisdictions defended local laws and law enforcement in the District of Columbia. The editor of Washington's *National Intelligencer,* which had originally published the notice of Horton's arrest, was irate that a Philadelphia paper blamed "the good people of Washington" for Horton's incarceration. It might be passé to sell into slavery suspected runaways whom no slaveholder claimed, he said, but Congress was to blame, not the people, because Congress had failed to modernize the District's laws even as states had updated theirs. He was correct on that front. Among the laws in force in the capital was a 1715 Maryland law that permitted authorities to sell free people of color into slavery to pay jail fees, even if they were able to prove their freedom. The state of Maryland had repealed that law in 1818, making counties responsible for the costs associated with incarcerating alleged fugitives who turned out to be free. Yet the antiquated law persisted in the District, where Congress was in charge. If northerners wanted to see the law changed, the *Intelligencer* intoned, they must lobby their representatives in Congress. And if Congress decided that such prisoners could no longer be sold for jail fees, Congress itself should pay the costs associated with keeping alleged runaways behind bars.[41]

On the larger issue of free African Americans' rights in the District of Columbia, however, the *Intelligencer* was unyielding. Authorities had no choice but to "investigate the characters of persons unquestionably free, in order to prevent our being completely overrun by the refuse of the free colored population of the adjoining states," the editor asserted. Some free Black people "enjoy general respect" and were entitled to it. Yet all people of African descent, the *Intelligencer* said, must be "subjected to the municipal regulation, which, in fact, protects them, even more than it does the whites, from the consequences of a vicious and degraded immigration to the City."[42] The *Intelligencer*'s argument—that race-based regulations protected city residents from undesirable immigrants—was grounded in the concept of police powers. The core idea, widely accepted at the time, was that local government's responsibility to secure public peace and good order was more important than its obligation to protect the fundamental rights of individuals, particularly those who were not propertied white men.

The *Richmond Enquirer* likewise sneered at the notion that, as a citizen of New York, Horton was entitled to move freely when traveling in other jurisdictions. The paper offered a disquisition on the power of states to determine who entered and who remained within their purview, advancing its argument in the form of a series of questions directed at "the good people of Westchester":

> Must all coloured persons be at liberty to travel in the Southern States, be they free or slaves; without the States requiring the evidence of their freedom? Must each State be an open asylum for the fugitives from other States? Have the States parted with the right of regulating their own police? Have they less right to protect themselves against the most dangerous and suspicious species of population which can enter them, than the States of Europe? They demand a passport in certain cases from travelers—and yet

we have not the right to protect ourselves by exacting from the suspected person his certificate of freedom.[43]

Comparing states with nations, the *Enquirer* insisted that the states, and local authorities in the District of Columbia, were entirely within their rights when they enforced laws that required "coloured persons" to carry identification wherever they went.

———•◦•———

GILBERT HORTON HAD been in the Washington, DC, jail just over one month when he finally regained his freedom on August 28, 1826. President John Quincy Adams, responding to DeWitt Clinton's entreaty, had asked the State Department to liberate Horton. By that time, however, the US marshal for the District of Columbia had already received proof of Horton's free status (probably the materials from the Westchester lawyer John Owen) and had seen fit to let Horton go. So visible had Horton's case become—and so central was the *Commercial Advertiser* in spreading the word about it—that the *Intelligencer* informed the *Advertiser*'s editor directly of Horton's release. The *Intelligencer* ran its own notice, stating that "evidence of [Horton's] freedom" had arrived from New York.[44] Other papers in turn published the news, alerting readers that the immediate crisis was resolved. From the perspective of those who supported the existing legal regime in DC, the episode exemplified procedural fairness. The system had worked as it should; Horton had been permitted to prove his freedom, and his liberty was restored. The larger questions, of course, remained unanswered: Was it constitutional for local authorities in Washington to detain and imprison a citizen of New York merely on the basis of his race and the suspicion that he was a fugitive from slavery? Should Black citizens, like white citizens, enjoy the benefits of the Constitution's privileges and immunities clause—that is, the right to move unimpeded from one jurisdiction to another?

Antislavery people, particularly in New York, continued to highlight

Gilbert Horton's ordeal to keep those questions alive, pushing for answers that favored racial equality. The *Daily Advertiser* and the *Commercial Advertiser* kept up their publicity campaigns. The *Commercial Advertiser* published the correspondence between Clinton and Adams, and other papers again followed its lead, disseminating the New York governor's defense of Horton's rights as a citizen of New York. Both newspapers urged a fundraising campaign to help Horton hire a lawyer and file suit against Washington officials "for the double purpose of doing him justice, and trying the question of the constitutionality, or unconstitutionality of the act under which he suffered." In what sense was the District of Columbia law unconstitutional? William Leete Stone, using his platform as editor of the *Commercial Advertiser*, insisted that the Constitution guaranteed all free people the right to mobility and personal liberty within the United States. He wrote, "It is high time that it should be settled, whether a freeman can be sold into perpetual slavery in this country, without even the pretence of any criminality, but only for exercising the privilege guaranteed to him by the Constitution of the United States, of passing unmolested from State to State."[45]

In suggesting that Horton sue local authorities in Washington, Stone pursued a strategy that had characterized the work of the New-York Manumission Society and the Pennsylvania Abolition Society, which had long helped African Americans stake claims to freedom before the courts. He also reinforced a point suggested by *Niles' Weekly Register* at the outset of the second Missouri debate: that existing state laws barring or discriminating against African Americans were "proper questions for the judiciary, the rightful tribunal to appeal to." Stone recognized the District of Columbia as an auspicious place to try the question of free African Americans' rights under the privileges and immunities clause because it was such an unusual jurisdiction. After arguing the case in the US Circuit Court for the District of Columbia, which exercised both local and federal jurisdiction, the plaintiffs could appeal to the US Supreme Court, "where the specific question must be tried and determined." Other editors agreed, amplifying Stone's proposal that Horton "try the question, whether a colored man must, at the seat of government of this free republic, carry about with him . . . his certificate of origin and of freedom."[46]

Coverage and commentary by the Washington *National Intelligencer* shows how contemporaries defended racist policies by saying they were little different from measures that impinged on the liberty of poor and itinerant white men. Early in the Horton controversy, the paper asked why some people seemed to care so much about free African Americans when white people faced abuse and incarceration simply for being poor. The cruelest laws were not those that forced African Americans to carry passes and certificates of freedom, the *Intelligencer* maintained. They were the debtor laws that shoved "white people" into prison because they couldn't pay their creditors. Those very same debtor laws, the paper observed, exempted slaves, who were in the fortunate position of having no financial responsibility for themselves. Meanwhile, the paper argued, Horton's imprisonment was his own fault, for he evidently did not have "brains enough to get some one to write for the proof of his freedom." Horton was "ten-fold happier in his cell," the paper insisted, "than the man, his near neighbor, whom the vengeance of a creditor has doomed to a dungeon."[47]

The *Intelligencer*'s description of Gilbert Horton as passive and unworldly was certainly rooted in racist stereotypes, but the editor had a point in arguing that white men, too, regularly faced imprisonment without having been convicted of a crime. Local governments acting within the poor-law tradition could remove or incarcerate people deemed vagrants or paupers, and they could do so without a legal hearing. During the second Missouri crisis, northerners who opposed Missouri's Black exclusion provision had acknowledged that paupers and vagrants did not have the same rights to untrammeled locomotion as citizens did. Congressman Joseph Hemphill of Pennsylvania, for example, had explained, "Paupers are clearly distinguishable from other citizens, and perhaps may form an exception" to the rule that all free people were either aliens or citizens. Paupers "fall helpless on the benevolence of the society to which they belong," he said, and

"I should suppose that every community would contain a power to protect itself against such palpable impositions."[48] These free staters vehemently defended free African Americans' capacity to be citizens of the states and of the nation, but they accepted the basic terms of the poor law and the long-standing idea that the dependent and migrant poor were not exactly free.

Local governments had traditionally focused much less on securing individual rights, particularly of members of marginal groups, than on guarding communities against would-be threats to harmony and good health, so it was novel to insist that everyone was entitled to untrammeled mobility. Amid the uproar over Gilbert Horton's incarceration, the *Intelligencer* editor continued to point this out, running a notice from Newburyport, Massachusetts, that a suspicious white man, presumably a sailor, had been jailed upon arriving in town. The editor snidely "hoped" that the governor of Maine—the prisoner's native state—would "lose no time in demanding the release of this individual."[49] His point was that the impulse to treat Black strangers as suspects was not dissimilar from preemptively throwing a white stranger in jail or depriving a white pauper of his liberty. In his view, all were necessary to sustain good order and public peace. He rightly perceived that the people who demanded free mobility for Black citizens such as Gilbert Horton were essentially proposing to disaggregate race from class; they wanted to make it impermissible to discriminate based on skin color without demolishing the entire poor-law edifice.

CONGRESSMAN AARON WARD of Westchester County ensured that Gilbert Horton's incarceration, and by extension the rights of free African Americans traveling in slaveholding jurisdictions, came to the attention of Congress. In December 1826, Ward introduced a resolution asking the House Committee on the District of Columbia to investigate whether the local laws permitted the imprisonment of "any free man of color, being a citizen of any of the United States" and whether it was legal to sell a free person for jail fees. Calling Horton "a free man of color, and a citizen" of Westchester County, Ward argued that it was "the duty of every Representative . . . to guard and protect the rights of the citizens of this Union." Ward claimed that several parts of the Constitution, when viewed together, defined "the absolute rights of persons" and "secure[d] to every free citizen, whatever may be his complexion, the right of personal security, personal liberty, and private property." A person could not be deprived of liberty without due process of law, Ward said, a basic principle of individual rights passed down from English tradition. Indeed, Ward called the US Constitution "the Magna Charta of the Nation."[50]

Ward's argument that the District's antiblack laws were unconstitutional was unlikely to persuade many people, not least because the US Circuit Court for the District of Columbia had upheld an antiblack measure passed by the city council of Washington in April 1821, at the end of the second Missouri debate. The 1821 ordinance had made it more difficult than ever for free African Americans to establish legal residency in the capital. Those seeking a "license" to remain in the city had to get three "respectable white inhabitants" to attest to their financial independence and good behavior and find a "respectable white person" to put up a twenty-dollar bond.[51] A locally prominent Black man named William Costin had refused to register under the harsh new law, and he appealed to the District's high court when authorities demanded that he pay the requisite fine.

Costin's suit pitted individual rights against the power of local government to regulate populations they deemed undesirable or threatening. Costin's lawyer insisted that the registration law violated the US Constitution because "the constitution knows no distinction of color," and because "all who are not slaves are equally free. . . . they are equally citizens of the United States." The court, however, was not prepared to agree. It handed Costin a partial victory, deciding that free African Americans who already lived in Washington did not need to register. But it upheld the city's racist registration laws in general, turning to poor-law principles for support.

According to Chief Judge William Cranch, a Federalist from Massachusetts, local governments had "the right to pass laws to preserve the peace and the morals of society." Whereas Costin's lawyer had argued that only criminals could be forced to post bonds for good behavior, Cranch affirmed that local governments were entitled to determine what was necessary to protect public peace and good order. "If there be a class of people more likely than others to disturb the public peace, or corrupt the public morals, and if that class can be clearly designated," Cranch wrote, governments could impose on the members of that group "reasonable terms and conditions of residence" designed to "guard the State from the evils which it has reason to apprehend."[52] With these words, the court upheld the registration law and, with it, the broader principle that the city government was entitled to regulate any class of people it deemed threatening.

In the House of Representatives, Ward's rather militant indictment of slavery and racial discrimination in Washington made the air crackle. The antiquated law that permitted free persons to be sold into slavery was likely more vulnerable than the rest. Ward insisted that the simple fact of Horton's "not being claimed as a slave" must not strip him of his "privileges as a citizen of the free and independent State of New York" and must not "create a debt to which no free act of his had contributed." Even if it could somehow be argued that Horton owed the jail fees associated with his incarceration, Ward said, it was unconscionable that he or any other free person could be sold into slavery just because they could not pay the cost of their own imprisonment. No "civilized" country permitted the "sale of the person of the debtor" to satisfy his creditor. How could Congress permit such practices in the capital? Surely Congress did not intend that "the little space of ten miles square should be the grave of rights."[53]

The "House was in the highest possible state of excitement," Charles Miner wrote to his wife. Representatives from Georgia, Louisiana, and Virginia charged Ward with raising a sensitive issue in an "inflammatory" way. There was nothing to talk about and nothing to investigate, claimed John Forsyth of Georgia. If the law was unconstitutional, as Ward had alleged, then it was void and could not be enforced. Robert Letcher of Kentucky echoed him: Let the victim seek justice in the courts, he said, while calling on the House to stop talking about this "delicate subject." Representatives from Ohio and New York insisted that the issue be discussed freely and that Ward was simply making an inquiry on behalf of a constituent. Several slave-state congressmen agreed that there was no harm in investigating the laws of the District with an eye toward reform. If a free person's rights were violated in the nation's capital, said George McDuffie of South Carolina, that was worthy of investigation.[54]

Yet Ward's characterization of free African Americans like Horton as *citizens* rankled southern congressmen. Ward had proposed to investigate whether DC authorities were permitted to imprison "any free man of color, being a citizen of any of the United States," on suspicion of being a runaway slave. In the course of debate, William Brent of Louisiana asked that the word *citizen* be removed, saying he wanted to keep the committee's charge narrow. It was appropriate for the committee to examine the laws of the District, he said, but its charge should not include the explosive question of "whether a free man of color was 'a citizen of the United States.'" Ward readily agreed to the change, perhaps thinking the phrase merely added specificity to the more important words that preceded it: "any free man of color." That view would have been consistent with the point, often expressed by northerners, that the rights of "citizens" were essentially the same as the rights of free persons. Representative Forsyth of Georgia returned to the question of Horton's citizenship later in the debate, however, as he explained why some of his southern colleagues were so distressed at the prospect that Congress would recognize a Black man as a citizen. Forsyth wanted to make the sectional differences clear: "The gentleman from New York, and others, claim, as a matter of right, that black persons, held to be citizens of the United States, in the State of New York, should enjoy in every other State the same privilege. The whole of the Southern delegation deny this claim. We hold . . . that we have the right to exclude free People of Color, to eject them, and to limit their privileges, when we admit them to reside among us." Reiterating the southern side of the second Missouri debate, Forsyth asserted states' authority to limit and exclude free African Americans, and he denied that Black people who were recognized as citizens at home enjoyed expansive rights in other states under the Constitution's privileges and immunities clause. If discriminatory state laws were unconstitutional, he insisted, then let the courts say so.[55]

After the House removed the word *citizen*, Ward's resolution passed by a large margin. The matter then moved to the House Committee on the District of Columbia for investigation. William Jay, following the debate from home, was disappointed to see *citizen* removed from Ward's proposal, telling the congressman, "Had your resolution passed in its original form, it would have been a declaration on the part of the House, that free blacks are capable of being citizens & of course of enjoying constitutional rights." Still, Jay recognized that Ward might have had to assent to the change or risk losing the measure altogether, and he declared the adoption of Ward's resolution over objections from the "hot bloods of the South . . . a victory [which] does him great credit." Southern congressmen had appeared brittle and defensive, their excoriations of Ward far louder than their occasional calls for conciliation. Jay had written to Miner that fall: "We have nothing to fear, but much to hope, from the violence and threats of our opponents. Apathy is the only obstacle we have reason to dread, and to remove this obstacle it is necessary that the attention of the public should be constantly directed to the subject."[56] The debate about African Americans' rights in the District of Columbia had accomplished just what Jay had envisioned, generating attention and raising public awareness. That was about the best New Yorkers could have hoped for.

The debate itself may have seemed a triumph for Ward and his allies, but the report of the House Committee on the District of Columbia emphatically endorsed most of the District's antiblack measures, and it never once used the word *citizen* to describe Gilbert Horton or any other free person of African descent. The committee chair was Alfred Powell, a Virginian who had supported Ward's resolution and promised a good-faith investigation. Committee members had checked with law enforcement officials on both sides of the Potomac and reported that in all areas of the District, free Black people were required to register with local officials and carry passes. Such laws "may occasionally operate a temporary hardship upon free persons of color migrating to slave-holding States," the committee wrote. Yet those hardships were a small price to pay for measures that secured the public peace and slaveholders' property. The laws were not intended "to abridge the rights or restrain the privileges of free persons of color." They were, however, necessary "to prevent slaves from escaping from their owners, and to secure their apprehension when they do abscond." The committee claimed that on both sides of the river, local officials were adequately balancing slaveholders' interests with procedural protections for alleged runaways. The lone problem was the antiquated Maryland law under whose provisions Gilbert Horton had been threatened with sale. When it came to that law, the committee acknowledged, "justice demand[ed] an alteration."[57]

The report concluded with an update on Gilbert Horton designed to demonstrate that law enforcement in the District of Columbia was working as it should. Horton had evidently decided to remain in the District after his release. It is difficult to know why he did that, although the city's large free Black community, or particular individuals within it, may have been a draw. Yet Horton, like so many other Black residents of the capital, particularly those who had not lived there long, remained vulnerable to the whims of white residents and civil authorities. Horton had been arrested again on suspicion of being a fugitive slave, but this time he was able to demonstrate to the magistrate's satisfaction his "right to freedom." He was "now enjoying an uninterrupted residence within the District of Columbia," the committee declared. And so the law worked. Periodic arrests and hearings were merely among the "temporary hardships" free Black people had to endure.[58]

The committee had proposed a bill to make the city governments of Georgetown and Washington responsible for costs associated with incarceration of suspected runaways who turned out to be free. But full-throated objections by local authorities helped the House justify its decision to do absolutely nothing, not even reform the law that permitted free people to be sold into slavery. In a letter to Congress, the mayor and city council of Georgetown, its own municipality within the District of Columbia, insisted that the existing system worked well and that if the rules proved costly to Black strangers in the city, that was their problem. "Every man," they wrote, must "conform to the laws of the community where he is, which he must be presumed to be acquainted with; and the negro can claim no exemption from this rule more than another. In coming to the South, he is, no doubt, in fact, apprized that his unfortunate caste are subjected, by the necessary policy of the slave holding districts, to many restrictions, and if he fail to ascertain and provide against them, any inconvenience that he may thereby be subjected to, is properly chargeable alone on his wilful neglect." The committee chair read the Georgetown protest on the House floor, and the House voted down the committee's proposal to revise even one law. The Washington City Council soon intensified its regime of passes, registration, and incarceration for free people of African descent, passing a new ordinance that required all "free black and mulatto persons" residing in the city to bring proof of their freedom to the city register or face a fine. Now, anyone who could not prove freedom would be committed to jail "as an absconding slave."[59]

IN NEW YORK CITY, Samuel Cornish and John Russwurm, editors of the nation's first independent Black newspaper, *Freedom's Journal*, watched and responded to events in Washington. With financial assistance from many free Black communities, Black New Yorkers inaugurated *Freedom's Journal* in the spring of 1827. They were spurred to action in part by the renewed threat they faced from the American Colonization Society (ACS). The organization had been revitalized in 1825 when Ralph Gurley, a Connecticut clergyman, became secretary and worked energetically to create local auxiliaries, secure support from ministers, and earn the loyalty of antislavery reformers. William Leete Stone, who had done so much to promote Gilbert Horton's release, became an outspoken colonizationist around this time. With good reason, then, African American activists in New York City feared that former allies in the New-York Manumission Society (NYMS) would turn to colonization. Yet they felt powerless to convey their opposition to the ACS—and to press their demands for racial equality in New York and across the nation—because white editors, both secular and religious, largely refused to cover their meetings or publish their writings. They needed their own paper to get their message out.[60]

Freedom's Journal also began as part of a movement among free African Americans who wanted to develop connections among disparate Black communities and advance their collective interests. In the 1820s, the free Black population of the Northeast continued to grow, and significant settlements began to extend westward into places such as western Pennsylvania and Ohio. Cornish's own itinerary before settling in New York reflected the mobility that free African Americans could experience in this era. Born free in Delaware in 1795, he migrated in the 1810s to Philadelphia, where he received training in Presbyterian ministry. After a stint on Maryland's Eastern Shore, he moved to New York City as a missionary to the poor in 1820; two years later, he founded the First Colored Presbyterian Church of New York. As newspaper editors, Cornish and Russwurm drew on and expanded Black networks by employing agents in cities and towns all along the Eastern Seaboard. Among their collaborators was James Forten of Philadelphia, and in 1828 they reprinted Forten's *Letters from a Man of Colour*, written fourteen years earlier.[61]

Befitting a paper founded in part to oppose the ACS, *Freedom's Journal* demanded equality for African Americans within the United States. Cornish and Russwurm published news and opinion pieces that disparaged the ACS and demanded an end to racist public policy and private prejudice. They called on African Americans to better their condition, build up their own institutions, defend against white racism, and demand full citizenship. They published an 1828 speech by David Walker urging free African Americans to "form ourselves into a general body, to protect, aid, and assist each other to the utmost of our power." Walker, best known for publishing the *Appeal to the Colored Citizens of the World* the next year, was the principal agent for *Freedom's Journal* in Boston. ACS leaders were well aware that Cornish and his allies had an entirely different vision of free Black people's future from their own. As one ACS activist wrote to another in the winter of 1827, "the ideas of Cornish & Forten are that the people of colour in this Country are by birth entitled to all the rights of freemen and ought to be admitted here to a participation of the enjoyment of citizenship." One of Cornish's Black colleagues in New York later recalled that when *Freedom's Journal* began, it "came like a clap of thunder."[62]

Freedom's Journal published David Walker's call to action around the same time that it drew attention to the restrictive new measures passed by the Washington City Council in the wake of Gilbert Horton's incarceration. The nation's capital was "the spot which alone of all others should be sacred to the right of man without distinction of colours or country." And yet public officials did precisely the opposite, targeting free people of color and forcing them to prove their freedom. Without the "prompt measures of our governor," the paper noted, Horton would have been sold into permanent bondage. *Freedom's Journal* used the Horton affair to exhort Black readers to stand up for their status as citizens: "In common with other citizens, we have rights which are dear to us; and we shall never sit patiently, and see them trampled upon, without raising our feeble voice, and entering our protest against the unconstitutionality of all laws which tend towards curtailing them in the least degree."[63] There was in fact no consensus that laws like those in Washington violated the US Constitution, but *Freedom's Journal* and its allies in New York and elsewhere repeatedly made the case that they did.

THE CONGRESSIONAL DEBATE over the Missouri Constitution had ushered citizenship into the American lexicon in an entirely new way. In the wake of the Missouri crisis, advocates for racial equality continued to turn to the US Constitution's privileges and immunities clause to elevate questions of racial equality from the state level, where they usually resided, to the federal level. The clause applied most clearly to situations in which people crossed state boundaries, so it was mainly useful when free African Americans from one state faced race-based discrimination when attempting to travel or work in another jurisdiction. In a highly mobile nation, this was far from a trivial concern. Many African Americans wanted to migrate to new places for economic opportunity, or to secure freedom itself, and free Black northerners regularly worked as sailors, their ships taking them into southern ports. Yet the official policy of many states was to prohibit free African Americans from entering or to subject them to harsh laws when they arrived. There were plenty of occasions, then, to call upon the privileges and immunities clause in an effort to confront these challenges.

The second Missouri debate also amplified the importance of state citizenship. During the debate itself, free-state politicians had begun to articulate a capacious definition of citizenship, one that included all native-born free persons, regardless of age, race, or sex (with the exception, perhaps, of paupers or criminals). They also divorced citizenship status from voting, arguing that only certain citizens—white men—were entitled to that privilege. Still, their inclusive definition of citizenship was important because it affirmed the claims of free African Americans that they were entitled to fundamental rights and that they ought not be disregarded or treated as transient outsiders, either in their communities or in the nation as a whole.

The multifaceted outcry against Gilbert Horton's incarceration also marked the critical convergence of an increasingly aggressive antislavery movement with the question of the rights of free African Americans. As Horton's case suggested, those issues came together in the District of Columbia, a space under Congress's direct jurisdiction where human beings were bought and sold, and where free Black citizens of northern states were subject to a regime of passes, imprisonment, and even sale into slavery. "The outrages . . . offered to the citizens of this state," one 1828 petition from New York argued, "afford sure and strong evidence" that slavery in the District of Columbia should be abolished. In the House of Representatives in January 1829, Congressman Charles Miner—who had not sought reelection in 1828—spoke at length about incarcerated African Americans he had met on visits to the Washington jail or read about in local papers: a woman whose children had been sold away from her one by one; a man who had suffered in jail for more than a year, emerging permanently disabled; a woman who claimed to be free but was summarily sold into slavery; and others about whom less was known. Miner's speech was published as a pamphlet, and Benjamin Lundy disseminated the information to readers of the *Genius of Universal Emancipation*. Congress took no action to curb the abuse, but antislavery activists, poised on the cusp of a new phase in the movement, responded en masse, flooding Congress with petitions calling for the abolition of slavery and the slave trade in the nation's capital.[64]

CHAPTER 3

"THE SACRED DOCTRINE OF EQUAL RIGHTS"

Ohio Abolitionists in the 1830s

IN THE FAST-GROWING river city of Cincinnati, local officials initially did not enforce state laws requiring free Black residents to register. Steamboats had begun to ply the Ohio River in the early 1810s, strengthening commercial ties with St. Louis and New Orleans. People migrated into the city from all corners, drawn there by the promise of inexpensive land and steady work in the expanding economy. With labor perpetually in short supply, arriving African Americans could be reasonably sure to find employment on the river or in clearing land and building canals. Many also worked in the homes of white people. The city's Black population grew quickly after about 1820, increasing from 433 to 2,258 in just ten years. At the end of the 1820s, African Americans were just shy of one-tenth of the city's total population of about twenty-five thousand. Most of the city's new African American residents had been born in slavery and had either escaped or purchased their freedom and migrated north across the Ohio River. They still had family and friends in bondage, and many saved their earnings in hopes of buying the freedom of others. Black Cincinnatians gradually began to build their own institutions. They founded an AME church in 1824, and by the end of the decade, Black teachers presided over independent schools.[1]

Yet Ohio's black laws still loomed as a tool for regulation and exclusion. The increase in the Black population made many white people anxious. The city's white residents had long held disparate views on the question of free African Americans' presence, and the pendulum now swung toward those who were most intolerant. In 1828, a group of white residents petitioned the city council to take action to "prevent the increase of the negro population."[2] In the summer of 1829, after the Ohio Supreme Court affirmed the constitutionality of the black laws, Cincinnati authorities declared their intention to begin enforcement. Suddenly, the city's African American residents faced grave threats to life and livelihood. They convened a meeting and decided to send a delegation to Canada to look for a place to resettle. Even as the scouts departed, however, authorities appeared determined to go forward with the plan to "rigidly enforce" the law. A Black community leader asked for forbearance while Black Cincinnatians prepared to leave. But his request was unavailing, and in mid-August, white residents erupted, accomplishing through violence what city officials had envisioned doing through laws and their orderly enforcement. White Cincinnatians pelted buildings in a Black neighborhood with rocks, demolished houses, and committed other acts of "riotous violence." Black residents, after days holed up indoors, fired into the mob, killing one man. By summer's end, about half of the city's Black population, roughly eleven hundred people, had moved away, some fleeing elsewhere in Ohio and others moving north to various destinations in Canada.[3]

Events in Cincinnati spurred free African Americans to come together in new ways and amplify their claims that they belonged in the United States and were entitled to the same civil rights as white people. Samuel Cornish, based in New York and now publishing a short-lived newspaper called *Rights of All,* condemned the onslaught in Cincinnati and called on African Americans to form a national movement that would link together, "by one solid chain, the whole free population." Turning to the US Constitution as the source of rights, he exhorted: "Let there be no compromise, but as though, 'born free and equal,' let us contend for all the rights guaranteed to us by the constitution of our native country."[4]

One year later, in September 1830, Black activists from throughout the Eastern Seaboard convened in Philadelphia for the first-ever national convention of African Americans. Presided over by Richard Allen, founder of the AME Church, the convention made racial equality before the law a central theme. It denounced laws of the free states, particularly those of Ohio, that "abridge the liberties and privileges of the Free People of Colour, and subject them to a series of privations and sufferings, by denying them a right of residence" unless they met demands "not exacted of the Whites." In an address to the "Free People of Colour of these United States," the convention promised support for the burgeoning settlement of free people in Upper Canada, where hundreds of Cincinnati residents had fled after the violence, and it pledged that in the new settlement, "no invidious distinction of colour is recognized, but there we shall be entitled to all the rights, privileges, and immunities of other citizens." The convention called for a world in which all people, regardless of color, enjoyed the same "rights, privileges, and immunities," setting the tone for a new phase in the struggle against racist laws in the free states.[5]

During the 1830s, Ohio's newly invigorated abolitionist movement made repeal of the black laws the central focus of its work. Influenced by African American activists and by the development of radical abolitionism in the East, white residents of the Old Northwest formed abolitionist societies and attacked not only slavery itself but also personal prejudice and racist laws in their home states. Some had previously supported the American Colonization Society and its vision of removing free African Americans from the United States. But traveling abolitionist agents, and William Lloyd Garrison's newspaper, the *Liberator,* encouraged them to begin to envision a society in which all people were entitled to the same basic rights and the same protection of law, regardless of race. In these years, despite sporadic and sometimes devastating violence perpetrated by white neighbors, African Americans built communities in Ohio and elsewhere in the Old Northwest, putting down roots from which a protest movement could grow. Black as well as white activists undertook a concerted movement against racist laws, consistently refuting longstanding claims that states were entitled to regulate people by race and insisting instead that all people should enjoy the fundamental rights promised in the 1803 Ohio Constitution, which declared "that all men are born equally free and independent, and have certain natural, inherent and unalienable rights."

Petitioning was the best way for this movement to make itself heard in Columbus, the state capital. People who were not permitted to vote, or whose concerns were different from those of elected officials, could elicit attention much more effectively through petitioning than through voting. This was true at the state level and with respect to the US Congress. In the late 1820s, the onslaught of petitions to Congress for the abolition of slavery in the District of Columbia marked the start of a much larger campaign, promoted by radical abolitionists in the 1830s, to draw attention to the cause and demand answers from Congress. A critical turning point in that campaign came in 1836, when slave-state legislators led the drive to pass a "gag rule" designed to neutralize abolitionist petitioning. For eight years, despite widespread objections from the free states, Congress largely refused to receive abolitionist petitions and thus avoided the responsibility of having to discuss them or send them to subcommittees for reports.[6]

Activists used petitions at the state level, too. Knowledgeable about how power worked in the federalist system, they petitioned state governments when they were looking for action on issues over which states had jurisdiction. In Ohio and across the Old Northwest, that included the black laws. Moral outrage at racist laws did not come naturally for most white Americans. In a world where discriminations of many kinds were commonplace, and where whites were predisposed to see people of African descent as a degraded class, the sense that such policies were unacceptable had to be taught and cultivated. This was no short-term project. In petitioning against the Ohio black laws, activists sought not only to achieve the straightforward goal of repeal but also to publicize their cause and to change public consciousness.

———————

IN THE WAKE of Cincinnati's antiblack riot of 1829, the state legislature adopted new measures designed to further marginalize African Americans who lived within its jurisdiction. In the spring of 1831, Ohio legislators passed a new poor law that banned African Americans from ever gaining a legal settlement in the state—that is, it made them ineligible for poor relief should they become needy, and, in a more abstract sense, declared that they were perpetual outsiders to the state's community. The legislature also passed a comprehensive law that established public education in the state but provided that public schools were "for the instruction of the *white* youth of every class and grade, without distinction." The school law exempted African Americans from paying property taxes to support the public schools, but it, together with the new settlement law, sent a clear message that African Americans were not welcome in Ohio.[7]

That summer in southeastern Virginia, Nat Turner and his allies rose up against their enslavers, killing scores of white people. In the wake of the rebellion, white Virginians rampaged against their Black neighbors, particularly targeting free African Americans whom they saw as potential subversives. Slave-state legislatures passed new laws designed to reassert order and strengthen slaveholders' power. Among them were laws that explicitly targeted free Black people by attempting to regulate their movement and in some cases by requiring them to leave the state altogether. Turner's revolt and its aftermath made some white Ohioans more fearful than ever of Black migrants. As the Ohio legislature convened in December, Governor Duncan McArthur warned that recent events in Virginia and other slave states "will have a tendency to drive many free people of color from them, and they very naturally seek an asylum in the free States." The state needed barriers to such migration, yet the "laws relative to those people, have not been strictly enforced." McArthur instructed the Ohio General Assembly to investigate the matter and pass measures necessary to "guard against the evils which must inevitably result, unless something be done to secure us against imposition."[8]

The Ohio House of Representatives appointed a subcommittee composed of James T. Worthington of Chillicothe and John Burgoyne of Cincinnati to address the governor's request, and the pair reported back with a proposal to outlaw the "further migration" of African Americans to the state. Worthington and Burgoyne drew on typical police-power rationales, arguing that African Americans posed a grave threat to public peace. "The existence in any community of a people forming a distinct and degraded caste, who are forever excluded by the fiat of society and the laws of the land, from all hopes of equality in social intercourse and political privileges, must . . . be fraught with unmixed evil," the committee warned.[9] Across the state, they claimed, Black men competed with white men for work and drove down white men's wages. When whites associated with free Blacks, whites became demoralized, "los[ing] that status and consideration in society, which is one of the strongest safeguards against vicious conduct." Black people were also inclined to lawbreaking, the committee said. Many were not working; they filled the jails with "criminals of the most hopeless description" and set a bad example for white youth. The threat of emigration from such places as Virginia, Maryland, and Kentucky only worsened the existing problem. The legislators insisted that Ohio was in danger.[10]

Worthington and Burgoyne also affirmed the governor's view that authorities were not doing enough to enforce the state's existing antiblack laws. If the laws were applied, the committee claimed, ninety percent of African American applicants for residency would be denied. More than seventy-five percent of current Black residents were in the state illegally, the committee alleged. "Should they now be considered as having a right of settlement, it must be a right acquired by a violation of her [the state's] laws. They can have no such right." Public officials could, if they wanted, "remove them" at will, "taking care not to violate the rights of other States." Evidently hoping to preempt a counterargument, Worthington and Burgoyne insisted that white Ohioans would never be persuaded to elevate African Americans' "social and moral condition . . . that they would be received into society on terms of equality." "The blacks in Ohio" would always be unequal, they said, and repealing the black laws would lead to "ruinous" results by "inviting within our borders a depraved and dangerous population." The best course forward, the pair recommended, was to amend the "laws regulating black and mulatto persons, so as to prevent their further migration into this State."[11]

The stance that free African Americans were disruptive and could not possibly blend into civic life in Ohio was consistent with the colonizationist idea that free Black people should leave the United States. Indeed, Worthington himself was active in the Chillicothe branch of the American Colonization Society, and in the same 1831–32 legislative session, a special committee of the Ohio Senate issued a report warning that a war "of extermination of one or the other race" could extend from the slaveholding states to "our own firesides." That report, authored by Thomas Morris, an antislavery Democrat who later became a United States senator, claimed that colonization would help relieve the nation of a potentially dangerous population and was "an act of naked justice" to free Black people themselves, who would meet only oppression and degradation if they remained in the United States.[12]

———

THIS WAS THE DIFFICULT CONTEXT in which a newly confident contingent of abolitionists demanded repeal of Ohio's racist laws, a reform that pointed not toward eventual removal of free African Americans but toward their recognition as part of the fabric of the state and the nation. It was not new, in the 1830s, to argue that racially discriminatory laws were unjust and that free Black people were entitled to all the basic rights that white people expected. What was new was the groundswell of support for this idea among white people who had both evangelical passion and growing organizational power. The abolitionist movement had reached an important turning point by 1831, when the Boston-based white abolitionist William Lloyd Garrison began publishing the *Liberator*. Garrison, who had previously worked for editor Benjamin Lundy, had supported the ACS in the 1820s but turned against it as he came to understand that colonization was "directly and irreconcilably opposed to the wishes of our colored population as a body." In a widely reprinted 1832 tract, he wrote: "Their desires ought to be tenderly regarded." Around the same time, the Jackson administration's campaign against Cherokee people living in the Southeast also pushed reformers to rethink their support for the ACS and its similar vision of removal for people of African descent.[13]

Drawing on lessons they had learned from listening to organized African Americans and from witnessing the cruelties of Indian removal, as well as on theories of equality drawn from the Bible and the Declaration of Independence, white radical abolitionists of the 1830s condemned the ACS and its two central claims: first, that racial prejudice was inherent and unchanging, and second, that free people of African descent would never belong in the American republic. Instead, abolitionists proclaimed that, in the words of the 1832 constitution of the New England Anti-Slavery Society, "mere difference in complexion is no reason why any man should be deprived of any of his natural rights, or subjected to any political disability." Garrisonian abolitionism traveled quickly to Ohio's Western Reserve, the northeastern part of the state, which had been settled primarily by migrants from Connecticut and Massachusetts. There, white men and women met in small abolitionist societies and, with others who despised slavery, debated the merits of rejecting colonization and adopting the abolitionist position.[14]

In southern Ohio, abolitionist students at Lane Seminary in Cincinnati rejected the colonizationist stance of the school's founder, Lyman Beecher. The most populous city west of the Appalachian Mountains, Cincinnati was a hub for transportation on the Ohio River and an inspiration to restless easterners. Beecher moved his family there in 1832 to launch his reformist evangelical seminary. The conflict began almost immediately because radical students could not abide Beecher's support for colonization. The young radicals—white evangelicals intent on doing good—believed that free African Americans belonged in the United States and that the struggle against slavery also required advocating civil rights for all persons regardless of race. The Lane radicals demanded that the conflict be aired publicly. During the winter and spring of 1834, the students hosted open debates about abolition, colonization, and the rights of free African Americans.

The Lane radicals tried to attack racism and prejudice everywhere they encountered it. "We believe that faith without *works* is dead," wrote Theodore Dwight Weld, a student leader who had already made his name as an evangelical orator in New York. The students quickly discovered that access to education was one of African Americans' central concerns. Black residents of Cincinnati had sponsored schools for Black children in the 1810s and 1820s, but educational activities had suffered in the wake of the 1829 riots. That same year, the state legislature had stipulated that "black or mulatto persons" were not permitted to attend Cincinnati's public schools. Looking to help, the Lane activists opened schools where they taught literacy and religion, organized a lyceum that sponsored lectures, and created a library. By March 1834, two students had left the seminary and were working exclusively in the Black community. Separately, white abolitionist women opened a school for African American girls and women and raised money to outfit it with supplies. Finding it impossible to heal the fissures at Lane Seminary, in 1835, most of the Lane rebels departed for Oberlin College in the Western Reserve, where administrators promised to begin admitting Black students on the same terms as whites.[15]

In the course of their work, Lane students grappled with questions of race and inequality in personal, day-to-day relationships. One white woman teacher reported in a personal letter that her white colleagues did not use the term *blacks*. Rather, she said, "with us, we call them gentlemen and ladies, as much as if white, and when necessary to distinguish, we say 'colored people.'" For his own part, Theodore Weld lived, ate, socialized, and worshipped amid Cincinnati's Black community. When a white New York abolitionist suggested that Weld was not truly living his principles, Weld shot back, "If any one wishes to know what my *principles* and *practice* have been and are as to Intercourse with the Colored people, I say let him ask the three thousand colored people in Cincinnati." Yet the Lane students' proximity to Cincinnati's Black community also drew smears from critics, who insinuated that their activities would inevitably lead to interracial sexual relationships, which they viewed as inappropriate and immoral.[16]

That controversy may have contributed to the decision by Ohio's white abolitionists to emphasize policy change over personal connection. In the summer of 1834, James Birney suggested that Ohio abolitionists focus on "the elevation of the Col'd people to *civil* privileges" rather than pressing for African Americans' "social" equality at the same time. Birney, a former slaveholder from Kentucky, had begun his antislavery work as a colonizationist but had declared himself an abolitionist amid the ferment of the Lane debates. Birney was concerned that the Lane students' commitment to racial equality in their private lives made them vulnerable to attack and could prevent them from reaching their larger goals. He suggested that if "civil privileges" could be gained, "it would be a long stride" toward equality in social life. Weld readily agreed. Echoing Birney but using the term *rights* instead of *privileges*, Weld recommended that "we should make it our *great* object to put our colored brethren in possession of their *civil* rights— social rights will follow naturally in their wake."[17]

Weld and Birney's emphasis on pushing for civil equality significantly shaped antislavery organizing in Ohio and the Old Northwest, where both men were influential. From the beginning, their brand of abolitionism emphasized energetic action directed at government, particularly repeal of racially discriminatory laws. Commissioned as an agent of the New York–based American Anti-Slavery Society, Weld traveled throughout the

state, lecturing on what it meant to be an abolitionist, not a colonizationist, and urging people in villages and towns to form their own local antislavery societies. His electrifying, revival-like addresses appealed to both
men and women, whom he invited to profess their new commitment at the
end of his sermons. He soon moved to the East Coast, but not before he
convened abolitionist activists in the summer of 1835 in Cleveland, where
they received training and then dispersed to continue evangelizing. Birney,
for his part, moved to Cincinnati that year and soon began publishing
the *Philanthropist,* an antislavery newspaper that managed to persevere
through two mob attacks and served as a vital antislavery voice in the West
and nationwide.[18]

When the white-led Ohio abolitionist movement convened for its first
statewide meeting in April 1835, the status of free African Americans was
central to its agenda. The Ohio Anti-Slavery Society (OASS) drew its leadership from the new generation of white radicals as well as from older
ministers, many based in southern Ohio, who had been leading antislavery churches and assisting fugitive slaves for decades. Acknowledging that
supporters of the black laws feared vagrancy and vagabondage among free
Blacks, the OASS affirmed in its opening declaration that "by immediate
emancipation we do *not* mean that the slaves shall be deprived of employment and turned loose to roam as vagabonds."[19] In a lengthy study focused
on the Cincinnati community, however, the society countered widespread
claims that Black migrants were a pauper class, dependent on public
resources, by describing Black Ohioans as hard workers who had overcome
serious disadvantages. Many had labored to purchase their own freedom
or had experienced illegal kidnapping or incarceration. They sought education and wanted to improve their station in life.[20] Above all, the society
insisted that African Americans were capable of supporting themselves.

> The question is often asked, Can slaves, if liberated, take care of themselves?
> We cannot answer this question better than by pointing to the colored
> population of Cincinnati. It is amusing to see the curious look which an

emancipated slave assumes, when he is asked this question. He seems at a
loss to know whether he shall consider it a joke or an honest inquiry. "We
did," they say, "take care of ourselves and our masters too, while in fetters.
We dug our way out of slavery—and now that we are free, all we ask is a fair
chance." We know of no class of men who are better qualified to take care
of themselves if placed under proper influences.[21]

Black Ohioans were impoverished and hard-pressed to accumulate wealth,
the abolitionists insisted, not because they avoided work but because whites
so severely constrained their employment opportunities.

The society not only sought to rebut those who characterized free Black
people as a disruptive class in need of regulation but also advanced rights-
based, universalistic claims. Like its abolitionist counterparts elsewhere,
the OASS often couched arguments for racial equality in Christian terms,
urging ministers to speak out against not just the great national sin of slavery but also its associated evils, including racial prejudice. In a message to
clergy, the society asked ministers to help "reform public sentiment" in the
same way they had done in their temperance work. "Prejudice against the
colored race," the society argued, was "always sinful" and "not invincible."
Prejudice implied ill will toward one's neighbor and was "incompatible"
with the Bible's "law of love." "The removal of this prejudice implies neither
an admiration of color, nor complacency in character," the society insisted.
"It only implies that love which we ought to bear to *every human being*, a
disposition to do justice, and to do him good."[22]

The OASS also invoked more secular visions of human equality, alluding to the natural-rights ideals of the Declaration of Independence and
the Ohio Constitution. A special committee assigned to explore the state's
black laws and their impact began its report by stating that the central aim
of government was to "promote the happiness, and to secure the rights and
liberties of man." The black laws abridged African Americans' fundamental rights, the committee argued; the "enjoyment of liberty and freedom"
included "the privilege of going into any community we please—of staying

as long as we please, and of 'pursuing after and acquiring happiness' by the same means, and on the same terms, as other people." These were rights to which all "men" were ostensibly entitled, to be limited only if the person was convicted of wrongdoing in a fair legal process. Arguing against popular associations of Blackness with criminality and degradation, the committee insisted that free African Americans were, as "a class, convicted of no crime—no natural inferiority—no conspiracy."[23]

The committee insisted that Ohio's black laws, even if not consistently enforced, had terrible consequences. The laws compelled Black Ohioans to live illegally and on the run, the committee said. They were cast "friendless and houseless into the open arms of poverty, and virtually *compell[ed]* . . . to roam like vagabonds over the land,— for they cannot obtain a residence until they have given their bond with competent sureties, which it is very seldom they will be able to do." Most white people would be incapable of meeting such qualifications, the committee argued, "much less the blacks, who are strangers and pennyless, and against whose race there exists a general prejudice." The law that penalized employers who hired African Americans unable to prove residency denied to the fugitive from bondage "the poor privilege of working for his daily bread" and discouraged whites from extending hospitality or support.[24] It was understandable, the committee said, that people who were prohibited from working might turn to "dishonest means" to support themselves. To make matters still worse, the racist testimony law allowed unprincipled whites to defraud and abuse Blacks with impunity.

OASS leaders realized that repealing Ohio's black laws would take time. Neither major political party, the Whigs or the Democrats, supported repeal. Politics in the 1830s generally revolved around economic questions. At the national level, the partisan turmoil that had characterized the 1820s gradually resolved into a clear two-party rivalry in what scholars have called the Second Party System. The Democrats, strongly aligned with two-term President Andrew Jackson of Tennessee, generally stood against "centralization." They claimed they were the party of everyday Americans

and, with Jackson, squarely opposed the National Bank and the elite interests it ostensibly represented. The Democrats tolerated religious heterogene-
ity and tended to attract the European immigrants who were increasingly
arriving on American shores. But slaveholders also were a critical part of
the Democratic coalition, and in the free states, Democrats often adopted
profoundly racist rhetoric to cement support from working-class whites,
who were most likely to see African Americans as competitors for jobs.

The Whigs were a weaker party that began as an anti-Jackson coalition and only gradually developed an independent party identity. Like the
Federalists before them, Whigs tended to favor federal spending on infrastructure and other forms of government planning and promotion of economic development. In the free states, Whigs attracted members of the
aspiring middle class, including Protestant reformers interested in causes
such as temperance and antislavery. Yet the Whig Party also depended on
slaveholder support. The party's standard bearer and perennial presidential hopeful was prosperous slaveowner Henry Clay of Kentucky, who was
among the founders of the American Colonization Society. Both parties,
then, relied on slaveholder support in national politics, and leaders of both
parties sought to sideline the explosive issue of slavery.[25]

In Ohio in the 1830s, legislators from both parties were apt to defend
the black laws as necessary for public peace and good order. Yet there were
opportunities to change minds. Whigs were more likely to favor repeal.
Although some were avid colonizationists, they could also be open to
the idea that as long as African Americans were in Ohio, they ought to
enjoy the same civil rights as white people expected. Democrats, who in
the 1830s were generally the majority in the statehouse, were less likely
allies, yet some were persuadable. Democratic US Senator Thomas Morris, for instance, saw the black laws as part of the matrix of oppressive
policies favored by slaveholders and other members of the wealthy elite.
Likeminded Democrats might be willing to support repeal of the black
laws and other measures supporting the civil rights of African Americans.

Seeking to make inroads into state politics, the OASS chose state

Senator Leicester King as its president. A successful businessman, King was born in Connecticut and had moved to Ohio as a young man. He had once visited Natchez, Mississippi, with an eye toward going into business there, but he was repulsed by slavery and returned to settle in northeast Ohio. There he became a promoter of the Pennsylvania and Ohio Canal, an inland shipping route that connected the Western Reserve with points east. His large home in Warren was known as a way station on the Underground Railroad, and King devoted a portion of his ample resources to helping fugitive slaves reach freedom. The OASS's selection of King, a Whig, to lead the organization suggested that abolitionists wanted to make themselves heard in the capital, which in 1816 had moved from Chillicothe to Columbus.[26]

With neither party on their side, however, Ohio antislavery activists needed to publicize their cause and build support in any way they could. The OASS turned to petitioning as a means of drawing attention to the black laws and nudging public opinion toward repeal. Petitioning was a critical and distinctive form of political action. It was different from voting in that, consistent with traditions deeply rooted in English practice, petitioning was understood as an act of supplication available to even the most marginalized individuals. From the earliest days of the republic, all manner of people—women, African Americans, Native Americans, and immigrants—had been able to petition state legislatures and Congress for redress. Also, unlike electoral politics, which channeled voters toward parties and candidates, petitioning allowed people to emphasize the specific issues with which they were most concerned.

Beginning in the late 1820s with the petition campaign against slavery in the District of Columbia, abolitionists increasingly adopted petitioning, encouraged by editors such as Lundy and Garrison. The process of circulating petitions itself led organizers into conversation with friends and neighbors. Abolitionist newspapers published petition forms for organizers to cut out, and activists often traveled door-to-door seeking signatures. By the second half of the 1830s, women signatories outnumbered men in many abolitionist petition drives. But this was not just about building community. According to longstanding tradition, legislatures were obliged to take petitions seriously. Legislators had to introduce the petitions submitted to them, read them aloud, and formally receive them. From there, the legislative body could decide to table a petition (ostensibly for future consideration) or refer it to a committee for investigation and recommendation. Subcommittees usually reported back to the larger body, offering information on the petition question and sometimes recommending legislative action. In this way, petitioners pushed legislatures into a dialogue. Regardless of the legislature's decision on the petitioners' demands, the reports that petitioning generated could be published, debated, and discussed in the press, public lectures, sermons, and meetings.[27]

Already in the legislative session that began in December 1833, the Ohio House of Representatives received multiple petitions calling for the repeal of "every statute denying or withholding any right or privilege from black persons which are enjoyed by whites." Petitioning increased as the antislavery movement gathered momentum. In 1835, an OASS report called on activists to continue petitioning the state legislature "until they wipe away this foul stain from the statutes of Ohio." That year, a House committee acknowledged abolitionists' growing influence and warned that their "efforts contemplate revolution, and necessarily strike at the existence of the Republic." Two years later, another House committee reported a record number of signatures on petitions calling for repeal of the black laws. Responding to such petitions, virtually every session of the Ohio House produced a report explaining why the black laws were necessary and needed to be sustained. In those reports, legislators insisted again and again that the black laws were a legitimate exercise of the police powers of the state. Free Black people posed a threat to public safety and well-being, they argued, so it was important to impose special restrictions on them. In one such report, legislators claimed that African Americans were fated always to be impoverished and criminally inclined. There was, the report claimed, "an insurmountable barrier to their becoming useful or orderly citizens" of Ohio.[28]

Reports produced by Ohio's House and Senate offered powerful spring-boards for further activism in the state and elsewhere. The Ohio House's 1835 report attracted the attention of William Lloyd Garrison, who published it in the *Liberator* with extensive commentary. The Boston-based paper lambasted the Ohio legislature for caring more about public opinion in neighboring slave states than about "the rights of the victims" of racial oppression. Typical of the abolitionists in their struggle to undermine the colonizationist agenda, the editorial reminded readers that there was "no natural antipathy between the white and colored races." If African Americans were overrepresented in jails, Garrison said, it was "not their fault." It was white people's contempt, and racially repressive laws themselves, that created the poverty and ignorance from which crime stemmed.[29] The *Liberator*'s attention to Ohio in 1835 foreshadowed the state's rising profile in the antislavery movement as well as growing national attention to the evils of racially discriminatory laws.

ABOLITIONISTS COURTED VIOLENCE simply by speaking out. Albert G. Riddle, a lawyer and Whig politician from the Western Reserve, wrote in the 1880s that future generations would be hard-pressed to imagine the "real conditions of the great first stages of the slavery struggle. . . . This was the era of civil strife, of mobs, violence, murder." David Smith, an itinerant AME minister, recalled of the early 1830s that Black "churches and houses were stoned and many were compelled to sell out and go to Canada. . . . The mean and fiendish treatment the colored people received from the low class of whites, encouraged and urged on by the intelligent and wealthy, can not be described."[30] Town leaders denied to traveling white abolitionists the use of venues where they could lecture. Hostile crowds harassed and assaulted white speakers, often throwing rocks and running them out of town. The threat to Black activists was even more acute. Black Ohioans, activist or not, were vulnerable to claims that they were illegally residing in the state, that they had not registered and posted bonds according to the law. They were subject to eviction and abuse, and the racist testimony law severely limited their access to the courts. White Ohioans, seeing Black people as consummate outsiders, readily turned to mob action. Although lawless by definition, violent mobs complemented the black laws. The mobs' purpose, like that of the laws themselves, was to maintain or restore what their participants believed was the proper social order.

Theodore Weld's experiences as a white abolitionist organizer in Zanesville and Putnam in the spring of 1835 suggested the disparate risks faced by white and Black activists. Weld arrived in the area—about seventy miles northeast of Chillicothe on the Muskingum River—to lecture in advance of the first statewide meeting of the OASS. At first, he could find no location from which to speak. When he finally found a place, a mob attacked, breaking windows and menacing him with clubs and stones. The impact of his presence on the local Black population was far more dire. The Black community of Zanesville, a contemporary wrote, comprised four or five hundred people. It operated a school for children and a Sunday school attended mainly by adults. The town also had its own antislavery society. Yet when Weld arrived in town, he wrote, "Large numbers of poor Colored people were turned out of employ." "Men were prosecuted under the vandal laws of Ohio for employing them," he told a colleague in New York, and the Black residents of the two towns "were greatly oppressed in continued apprehension and panic." Black residents called their own meeting and, after extensive discussion, resolved to stay away from the abolitionist lectures. They sent a delegation to inform Weld of their decision, urging him on but saying they could not be involved in any public way.[31]

In Weld's view, their decision was "common sense." If African Americans attended the meetings, he argued, the "*prejudiced*" white people who needed to hear the message would be less likely to go. Besides, Black people were likely to face "insult and outrage while there," and their presence would "be seized as ground for the pretence of mobbing them, tearing down their houses, etc." One Black man showed up at a preparatory gathering held two hours before the big meeting, but, Weld related, the group—including the man himself—decided that "for him to sit in the Convention would peril his limbs at least if not his life, and would without doubt bring down on our poor panic struck brethren, the Colored people in Z. and P., the vengeance of the mob." It was not worth the risk, and the Black man departed.[32]

These sorts of experiences taught Weld that activists had to be flexible, adjusting strategies and expectations based on context and respecting the judgment of African Americans about which battles to fight and which to leave aside. He told a white abolitionist colleague in New York that their movement must, when "*carrying out principles* . . . take into consideration the *modifications* produced in those principles by the *bearings* of *other* principles." Weld explained, for example, that he never felt compelled to demonstrate his antiracism by walking "arm in arm with a Colored lady at mid-day down main street in Cincinnati." This was not because he was prejudiced or because he feared going against "public sentiment," he said. Rather, it was because doing so would "bring down a storm of venge[a]nce upon the defenceless people of Color, throw them out of employ, drive them out homeless, and surrender them up victims to popular fury." It would, he argued, seem an "ostentatious display of superiority to prejudice" that would turn attention away from "the main point." Weld counseled deference to Black colleagues, concluding, "I say give me the colored people for counsellors. They have vastly more common sense in such matters than any of the rest of us. I have talked these matters all over a hundred times with Colored men and women, and never found one who did not agree with me in toto on this point."[33]

UNDER THE VOLATILE CONDITIONS that prevailed in many parts of Ohio, significant African American organizing occurred in churches and other private forums, efforts that are difficult for historians to see except in fleeting glimpses. The state's first independent Black church was founded in

Cincinnati in 1815, and by 1833, the state was home to more than twenty AME churches with a total membership of around seven hundred people. In 1834, African Americans in Chillicothe formed the Chillicothe Colored Anti-Slavery Society and announced it in a local newspaper. Black Ohioans were active in Freemasonry and organized myriad self-help societies. Wherever they could, Black men and women helped fugitives from slavery make their way to safety, sometimes risking their own lives in the process. Sporadic threats of violence and expulsion continued. In the summer of 1836, Cincinnati whites rioted again, this time against the city's newly established abolitionist newspaper, the *Philanthropist*. A mob destroyed editor James Birney's printing press and threw the pieces into the Ohio River, but Black residents faced the more severe terror when whites rampaged through Black neighborhoods, attacking businesses and looting private homes.[34]

Those circumstances make it all the more remarkable that in 1837, African Americans mobilized statewide to petition the Ohio General Assembly to repeal the black laws and support schools for their children. The movement began in Cleveland. Located in northeast Ohio on the banks of Lake Erie, the city had begun to grow in earnest when the Ohio and Erie Canal, completed in 1832, made it a crossroads for commerce moving from the Great Lakes into the interior. Cleveland was newer and smaller than Cincinnati, but it was also a safer place for African Americans to begin organizing a statewide movement. One of the leading figures in Cleveland's tiny Black community was John Malvin, a Virginia native who had migrated to Ohio in 1827. Starting around 1832, he began to work on establishing private schools for Cleveland's Black children. Malvin was an ordained Baptist minister who sometimes preached in the city's First Baptist Church, a white-led church where, in 1836, he waged a struggle for racially equal seating.[35]

In January 1837, Malvin and other Cleveland Black activists met to consider "the expediency of petitioning" the general assembly for repeal of the black laws and to begin organizing African Americans in a statewide movement to secure schools for their children. Malvin had previous experience, having petitioned for repeal of the black laws after the Cincinnati riot of 1829. Northern Black activists were increasingly turning to petitioning to demand changes that white majorities in their states, if left to their own devices, would likely never deliver. In 1835, a national Black convention in Philadelphia had recommended that free people of color petition Congress and their state legislatures "to be admitted to the rights and privileges of American citizens."[36] At the January 1837 meeting in Cleveland, one delegate seemed to anticipate the argument that African Americans, as marginal members of the state's body politic, were not entitled to petition. He insisted that Ohio's "colored citizens" were "subjects of this government, as the child is the subject of parental government," and therefore they had a "right to petition" for redress of grievances. Another argued that the black laws would be repealed only "when they, the colored people themselves, rightly and prudently petition, for their removal." Malvin urged the group to organize, "irrespective of any of the great movements of the day," suggesting that he and his colleagues saw their efforts as separate from those of white abolitionists. Having decided to move ahead with the petition, the group arrived at a longer-term strategy. They issued a call for a statewide meeting in Columbus that summer, and they decided to hire an agent to travel the state, soliciting signatures for the petition and gathering facts about African American life in Ohio. They appointed as their agent one of their number, Molliston Madison Clark, who had attended college in Pennsylvania and was teaching in Cleveland and studying theology at Oberlin.[37]

Clark's tour through Ohio evidently helped generate petitions to the legislative session already underway in Columbus, and the results were modestly encouraging. The Senate formally received a petition from Black residents of Hamilton County (home of Cincinnati) but tabled it, taking no further action. In the House, legislators received a repeal petition from Black residents of Columbus and referred it to the Judiciary Committee, alongside numerous similar petitions from whites. The committee, led by

John M. McNutt of Preble County, returned a report defending the black laws in the usual terms: that the existence of a free Black population was a problem, that the black laws were not particularly harsh, and that abolitionists were a threat to public order. The committee report excluded Black signatories from its tally of Ohioans who had signed petitions for repeal, suggesting its reluctance to recognize African Americans as petitioners. Still, some observers viewed the relatively subdued response to African Americans' petitions that winter as a victory. The *Cleveland Journal*, a Presbyterian paper, commented that the petitions had been "received more favorably than was anticipated," and the editors of the *Colored American* in New York reprinted the *Journal*'s story and praised Black Ohioans for their "moral and intellectual strength."[38]

The state's first general convention of African Americans met in Columbus in July 1837, the product of the January organizational meeting in Cleveland and Molliston Clark's work as traveling agent. Published proceedings of the meeting have not been found, but we know from newspaper reports that the convention delegates wrote a constitution for a "school fund institution of the colored people" designed to receive funds from private donors and, they hoped, from the state government.[39] The convention also resolved to continue pushing for repeal of the state's racist laws. The group hoped to advance both goals through petitioning. In fact, there was little else they could do in formal politics, since only white men were allowed to vote and since, in any event, African Americans comprised only about one percent of the state's population. To facilitate petitioning, the convention published two petition forms that could be cut out of the newspaper and pasted onto larger pages that people could sign.

The petition forms notably did not identify the signers as citizens. Instead, both forms began by identifying the petitioners as "the undersigned, colored people, residing in the State of Ohio." Many African Americans in Ohio certainly believed themselves entitled to the same rights and privileges as whites, and Black activists regularly referred to themselves as citizens of Ohio and of the United States. Yet the rights that Black

Ohioans demanded were widely considered to be fundamental rights that did not depend on a person's citizenship status. They were linked to God and nature, not to status or belonging in a particular state or nation. The Ohio Constitution's declaration of rights reinforced this idea, promising fundamental rights to "all men," while mentioning "citizens" only in connection with the rights to vote and hold office. A person did not have to be a *citizen* to claim the right to be free of racial discrimination, so the organizers of the petition claimed rights based not on citizenship but on personhood and their residency in Ohio.

The first petition form declared that signatories had empowered the executive committee of the newly constituted "school fund institution" to ask the legislature for an appropriation "for the support of our schools throughout this State." In the second petition form, signatories "respectfully ask[ed]" the assembly to "repeal all laws and parts of laws that do restrict them in this State." The discriminatory testimony law, the petition stated, "prevent[s] us from claiming our lawful rights when any wrong is practiced upon us," and the racist residency law drew "a distinction" between Black and white persons that was "not found in justice and equality." To reinforce their claims to financial solvency and independence—to insist that as a group they did not threaten the welfare of the state and its white population—the petition informed the legislature that Black Ohioans owned property worth $500,000 and paid state and local taxes amounting to $2,500. The petition concluded with the hope that the legislature would see fit to recognize the taxpayer status of Black Ohioans by appropriating public funds for their use. As "men[,] christians and republicans," the petitioners promised to continue exercising their "inalienable right to freely expressing our opinions . . . till justice be done."[40]

Black Ohioans likely knew, when they pledged to continue raising their voices, that they could not take for granted that their petitions would even be received, much less acted upon. In the US Congress, slaveholders and their allies were challenging the longstanding idea that petitioning was open to all people, regardless of their stature in society. Faced with an onslaught of abolitionist petitions, southerners in Congress demanded that slavery-related petitions be rejected without printing them or referring them to committee. Antiabolitionist legislators greeted petitions from enslaved people and from women with the argument that petitioning was only for voters or those who were said to have a direct political stake in the community. Likewise, legislators in the Pennsylvania statehouse in the summer of 1837 debated whether African Americans residing in the state were entitled to have their petitions received. The claim that race or sex could preclude a person from petitioning contradicted decades of practice. It was another way of trying to silence African Americans and women of all kinds who wanted a voice in public life and turned to petitioning to express their views and demand change.[41]

<hr>

As a new Ohio legislative session began in December 1837, white abolitionists and Black activists felt hopeful. A correspondent in Columbus informed the *Philanthropist* that the movement to repeal the black laws appealed not just to abolitionists but to "all lovers of justice" in the Ohio General Assembly. The campaign for what Theodore Weld had called equal "civil rights" seemed to be gaining ground. The assembly was inundated with abolitionist petitions that touched on all manner of concerns. In addition to calling on the legislature to repeal the black laws, petitioners asked for protection against violent mobs, the end of race-based disenfranchisement, and new protections for alleged fugitive slaves. In the Senate, Leicester King, who remained president of the Ohio Anti-Slavery Society, introduced many such petitions, including one "from sundry colored inhabitants," calling for repeal of "all laws which impose disabilities upon them on account of their color."[42]

The Senate quickly became embroiled in a debate over who was entitled to petition the legislature and for what purposes. In late January 1838, Benjamin Wade, a first-term state senator from Ashtabula County in the Western Reserve, presented a petition calling on the Ohio General Assembly to condemn the US Congress's latest gag rule. In a local echo of the gag-rule politics in the US Congress, one of Wade's colleagues recommended that the petition be laid on the table rather than sent to committee. Wade, in turn, demanded that the petition be treated with respect. "I care not whether it goes to the Judiciary, or to a select, or to some other committee," he said. "But to a committee it must go." The right of petition was a natural right, he insisted, one that "stands above and out of the reach of all constitutions, all laws, all legislation," and it must be honored scrupulously.[43]

The debate over the Ashtabula petition proved merely a warm-up for a fight over African Americans' right to petition. That conflict began when Senator Leicester King introduced a petition from Cincinnati African Americans seeking repeal of the black laws and "for other purposes." Several of King's Democratic colleagues objected strenuously. The state's African American residents had "no constitutional right to petition," argued John H. James, who represented three counties in west-central Ohio. Black people had "no right to ask" for repeal of the black laws. "They have come in contravention of our laws," and their residence was "only tolerated." If their petition were received, he said, it would be "only as a favor not as a right." Fellow Democrat Elijah Vance of far western Ohio insisted that Black Ohioans were "not citizens, and none but citizens of Ohio have a right to petition for the alteration of laws." Only people who were "parties to the constitution and laws" had a right to petition for their repeal. African American men were not entitled to vote, he said, and therefore they had no right to petition for changes to the statutes.[44]

For the moment, however, momentum and political power lay with the Whig majority, which honored African Americans' right to petition for redress and, more broadly, accepted the idea that there were certain rights that adhered to all persons, not just that special class called citizens. Wade, who became a US senator in 1851 and was a prominent Republican during the Civil War and Reconstruction, insisted that the right to petition "is inherent in man—... it is natural to him." Indeed, he added, "it is natural to animals." Just as supplicants were always permitted to pray to God, so too could the oppressed always petition those who held worldly power. Isaiah Morris, who came from a southern county east of Cincinnati, added that Black Ohioans had a right to petition because they paid taxes and were subject to state laws. The speaker of the Senate, George J. Smith of Warren County, northeast of Cincinnati, added that citizenship status had no bearing on a person's right to petition. "Aliens had no more a constitutional right than blacks and mulattoes; yet who would reject a petition from them, if couched in proper and decorous language?" The right to petition, he insisted, "was a *natural* right—above constitution, and above laws." King, who had introduced the petition, spoke last and with great force, arguing that the founders who wrote the Ohio Constitution never intended to deny fundamental rights to persons of color. Finally, the Senate voted to receive the petition. The day's debate had been "warm, animated and instructive," wrote a correspondent for the *Philanthropist.* The members had shown "their knowledge and their feelings on the subject of Human Rights."[45]

About a month later, Leicester King had the opportunity to publicize his views at length. Having served as chair of the special committee assigned to investigate and report on petitions for repeal of the black laws, he delivered the committee's findings in a report to the Senate on March 3, 1838. The report lambasted those who claimed that because Ohio had never legalized slavery, its white residents were exempt "from all moral obligation to the colored race." Against those who insisted that the state's founders had envisioned Ohio as a white republic, King argued that racially discriminatory laws violated both the spirit and the letter of the state constitution. He pointed out that Ohio lagged behind the many other states where African Americans already enjoyed all the "rights and privileges of citizens."[46]

But it was personhood, rather than citizenship, that King emphasized when he called for repeal of the black laws. He described the injustice of the existing legal order, pointing out that Ohio African Americans were "deprived of the protection of law, and denied the means of obtaining justice in our courts, or a redress for 'injuries done in their lands, goods, and persons,' contrary to the provisions of the constitution, declaring they should be secured to 'every person.'" He insisted that laws barring Black children from public schools violated the state constitution, and he argued that the state must pass a law guaranteeing jury trials for persons arrested as fugitive slaves. The report offered several concrete proposals, including repeal of the racist testimony law, affirmation of the Ohio Constitution's promises of universal individual rights, and a pledge that, "in the administration of justice, and in the protection of these natural and constitutional rights, the same rules and principles of law should be extended to all persons, irrespective of color, rank or condition."[47]

Leicester King's report was unlike any other that the Ohio General Assembly had produced, a grand departure from the usual warnings about disruptive Black migrants. Yet the session was ending, and there was no time—and probably little inclination, even among Whigs—to press the Senate to act. In the House, a committee again responded to repeal petitions with a report insisting that the black laws must remain, but a fulsome minority report condemned the laws and called for their repeal. The general assembly then ordered publication of a thousand copies of King's report, making it widely available to the public.[48]

Ohio abolitionists were thrilled with the results of the 1837–38 legislative session. Gathering in Granville in May, the OASS singled out Senators King and Wade, as well as US Senator Thomas Morris, who had denounced the gag rule in Washington, for "the fearless manner in which they have vindicated the rights of *all* men, and for the eloquence and fixed determination with which they have asserted and maintained the rights of petition." Special praise was reserved for King's report, which had "excited profound interest in the Assembly." "The tide of injustice, we rejoice to believe, is at length arrested," the society crowed. "The legislature begins to feel the pressure of a public opinion, to which it has not been accustomed;

hereafter, whatsoever changes may be made in our policy towards the colored people will, no doubt, be dictated and regulated by a regard to the
sacred doctrine of equal rights, and the fundamental principles of civil
liberty."[49]

———•◦•———

THE SOCIETY'S OPTIMISM, at least for the near term, was unwarranted. The
Democrats swept into power in the fall 1838 elections, winning the governorship and a majority of both houses in the Ohio General Assembly.
Among those who went down to defeat was Leicester King, who lost to
David Tod, a Democrat who was later elected governor. Some of this was
the abolitionists' own doing. That spring, the OASS had resolved that abolitionists who "believe in the lawfulness of our representative governments"
were "sacredly bound" to vote for political candidates who supported their
agenda. This was the first time the organization had taken a stand on the
question of whether and how abolitionist men should vote. In the East,
the question contributed to a major schism in the movement. In the Old
Northwest, however, most white abolitionists readily agreed that voting
was one of many weapons in the arsenal of antislavery.[50]

Things became complicated in the fall of 1838, when Gamaliel Bailey,
the new editor of the *Philanthropist,* urged abolitionist voters to support
the Democrats in the upcoming elections. The strategy was born of several priorities. Bailey wanted to punish Ohio Whigs for their lukewarm
stance on slavery and the black laws. Most immediately, he was frustrated
that the Whig governor had betrayed the cause by agreeing to extradite
to Kentucky an antislavery minister accused of helping someone escape
from slavery. Bailey also hoped abolitionist voters would ensure that the
antislavery Democrat Thomas Morris was returned to the US Senate. In
1838, it was possible—albeit difficult—to be a northern Democrat who
spoke out against slavery, but Morris was steadfast, and Bailey and his
allies in Cincinnati wanted to cultivate that beleaguered tendency in the
Democratic Party.[51]

Bailey touted antislavery voters' success when the Democrats prevailed, only to be blindsided by the agenda the Democrats pursued once in office, in the winter of 1838–39. The legislature replaced Senator Morris with a more conventional Democrat and embarked on a set of racially reactionary policies for Ohio. The debate about African Americans' right to petition reignited immediately. In the newly convened House of Representatives, George Flood, a Democrat, demanded that the House reject a petition from Black Ohioans and then introduced a raft of resolutions affirming the black laws and repudiating all forms of antislavery action. The House voted on each resolution separately and passed every one. When that exercise was over, Flood's colleague, John Brough, offered an additional resolution stating that "blacks and mulattos" who lived in Ohio "have no constitutional right to present their petitions to the General Assembly for any purpose whatsoever; and that any reception of such petitions on the part of the General Assembly is a mere act of privilege or policy, and not imposed by any expressed or implied power of the constitution." The House easily passed it. The Senate took up the question days later, when Wade introduced a petition from African Americans asking again that the legislature incorporate their proposed school-fund organization. A senator moved to reject the petition, whereupon the Senate reprised many of the arguments from the previous session and narrowly defeated the House motion.[52]

The Ohio General Assembly also distinguished itself that session by adopting a stringent new fugitive slave law at the behest of a two-man delegation sent to Columbus by the Kentucky legislature. Powerful Kentuckians feared the growth of abolitionism in Ohio, and with it, the development of networks of people willing to shelter and protect escapees from slavery. The Kentucky legislature saw the Democratic ascendancy in Ohio as an opening, and, as the legislative session began, sent the two commissioners to urge legislative action. This was not the first such delegation. The Kentuckians of 1839 recalled that in 1826, the Maryland legislature had sent emissaries to Pennsylvania, New Jersey, and Delaware to press for laws favorable to slavecatchers, and the Marylanders had won significant concessions.[53] The Kentucky delegates arrived in Columbus in mid-January of 1839 amid great popular interest. The newly elected Ohio governor, Democrat Wilson Shannon, conveyed their desires—and specific suggestions for legislation—to the general assembly. Despite strong Whig opposition, the assembly passed a law that gave the Kentuckians almost everything they wanted, including harsh penalties on Ohioans who refused to cooperate with fugitive slave renditions and a mandate that local authorities imprison alleged runaways who were awaiting a hearing.[54]

Leaders of the American Colonization Society were always ready to intensify their recruitment efforts at moments when free African Americans seemed most vulnerable. In the summer of 1829, as it became clear that Cincinnati authorities expected free Blacks to leave the city, a Philadelphia colonizationist had urged ACS secretary Ralph Gurley to send agents to Ohio. As free Black people learned "that this is not the place of their rest," he predicted, they would be increasingly open to emigrating "to Africa." But the colonization movement in Ohio had been sputtering in the 1830s, in no small measure due to abolitionist gains. When the Democrats took charge in 1838, the ACS seized the moment and sent Gurley to the state. He held five meetings in Columbus in late January 1839, including one in the hall of the House of Representatives, where it was none other than George Flood, progenitor of the House's dramatic antiblack resolutions, who introduced a resolution to revive and reorganize the state colonization society. Soon thereafter, a new state society took shape. Gurley solicited support in a variety of smaller towns and then made his way to Cincinnati, where he debated abolitionist Jonathan Blanchard on four consecutive afternoons. Gurley claimed satisfaction with his Ohio sojourn, having recruited new members and raised funds across the state. The *Philanthropist,* for its part, declared that although Gurley had won some converts, the colonization movement had "no intrinsic vitality" and would soon fade from view.[55]

If the 1838 elections had one small silver lining for antislavery people, it was the election of Joshua Giddings to the US House of Representatives.

A Whig from Ashtabula in the Western Reserve, Giddings had studied law under the tutelage of a prominent colonizationist, who was also state Senator Benjamin Wade's law teacher. Wade and Giddings shared a successful legal practice in the early 1830s, but the two were estranged by 1836. Giddings had been a member of the local colonization society in the mid-1830s. It is not clear exactly when he became an abolitionist, but in 1835 he spent time in Ashtabula with Theodore Weld, and by 1838, when he ran for Congress, he was fully committed. Voters in Whig-leaning Ashtabula sent Giddings to Washington that year, despite the generally miserable outcome for antislavery politics statewide. On arriving in the capital, Giddings found "our Northern friends" cowering before "Southern bullies." No northern man, he wrote in his journal, "dares boldly and fearlessly declare his abhorrence of slavery and the slave-trade. This kind of fear I have never experienced," he continued, "nor shall I submit to it now."[56] Few could have known it at the time, but Giddings's election was a harbinger of antislavery politicians' rising significance, both in Ohio and in the US Capitol.

Another person who refused to cower was Thomas Morris, the Democratic US senator whom the new legislature had replaced with a more pro-southern man. As he finished out his term in the winter of 1839, Morris rebuffed pressure from southern members of his party to denounce abolitionists and all aspects of their agenda. On January 10, he introduced an antislavery petition in the US Senate, blasted the gag rule, and expressed his "deep mortification and regret" that the Ohio legislature had stooped so low as to question African Americans' right to petition. A month later, as the Ohio legislature debated receiving the Kentucky delegation, Morris challenged Kentucky's most powerful politician, Henry Clay. After Clay gave a long speech on the Senate floor denouncing abolitionist activism, Morris countered that, like the "bank power" before it, a dangerous "slave power" now threatened to undermine American ideals of equality and independence. Morris complained bitterly of violations of Ohio's "sovereignty and independence" by the "slave interest" of Kentucky, and he excoriated the "slave power" for sending "its agents into the free States for the purpose of influencing their Legislatures to pass laws for the security of its power within such States."⁵⁷ Morris's address, calling out and defining the Slave Power, became renowned as a rebuttal of Clay and an inspiration for antislavery Democrats. Yet the much-lauded speech also had more specific purposes, for it drew attention to the reactionary politics of the Ohio legislature and cautioned residents of the free states not to wilt when faced with pro-slavery demands.

Oᴴɪᴏ's ᴍᴏᴠᴇᴍᴇɴᴛ ᴡᴀs the largest and most influential in the Old Northwest, but abolitionists launched similar attacks on racist laws in other states as well. Indiana, Illinois, and Michigan all had racist residency laws that dated to their periods as US territories. Illinois and Indiana forbade Black testimony in cases involving whites, and in those states, pressure for repeal yielded no concrete results. In Michigan, too, activists protested the racist laws of the territorial period, and there they were successful. Statehood arrived in 1837, and when the legislature published its first code of laws the next year, it silently omitted the offensive statutes. One of the members of the Judiciary Committee that proposed the new code was Jacob Howard, who, three decades later, became a framer of the Fourteenth Amendment. In 1838, Howard was thirty-three years old and a member of the Michigan House of Representatives, where he introduced a petition from African Americans asking for the right to vote and supported legislation to secure a jury trial for alleged fugitive slaves. As a US senator from Michigan noted in 1841, "Our constitution makes no distinction as to civil rights."⁵⁸

During the 1830s, African American abolitionists consistently pushed their white would-be allies to think more expansively about racism and inequality. The dynamic was particularly clear in New York City, where Black activists had a strong foothold and some of the most prominent white leaders of the movement were based. Theodore Wright, the Black Presbyterian minister who succeeded Samuel Cornish as pastor at First

Colored Presbyterian Church, consistently challenged his white colleagues, pointing out that elementary schools and colleges often denied access to African Americans and that white abolitionists themselves, while professing antislavery beliefs, did not always accept "man as man, all of one blood and one family." The white lawyer and judge William Jay was in direct contact with Cornish and subscribed to the newspaper Cornish now edited, the *Colored American,* which regularly published articles about white northerners' refusal to treat Black neighbors as equals or even with a modicum of respect.[59] Jay was becoming an important theorist of the antislavery movement. Erudite but physically infirm, he had little taste for formal politics or speechmaking, but he readily applied his subtle legal mind to the moral and constitutional problems created by slavery and racism.

William Jay had shown concern for free Black New Yorkers ever since pushing for the release of Gilbert Horton from jail in Washington in 1826. He had discussed the rights of free Black people in an 1834 pamphlet in which he denounced the American Colonization Society for promoting racial prejudice and inhumane policies. The Horton controversy remained on Jay's mind when he wrote *A View of the Action of the Federal Government, in Behalf of Slavery* (1839), in which he devoted almost fifteen pages to racist practices in the District of Columbia. Jay explained in a footnote that he felt especially strongly about the topic because some years earlier he had been involved in freeing a Black man from unjust incarceration there. In 1839, Jay also took special interest in the travails of Alexander Crummell, a talented young Black man who attempted to enroll at the Episcopal seminary in New York. The *Colored American* published a long article on the seminary's decision to deny Crummell admission, and Samuel Cornish personally approached Jay, himself a devout Episcopalian, about the New York bishop's stance. Jay met with Crummell and found him entirely sympathetic. He wrote Gerrit Smith, another white New York abolitionist with deep pockets, that Crummell was "suffering persecution on account of the complexion which God thought proper to give him," and he asked Smith to contribute to a fund, begun by Crummell's friends, that would pay for his religious education abroad. Smith contributed to the cause, telling Jay that he knew Crummell well and had been following the reports of the injustice against him in the *Colored American*. Indeed, he wrote, the Black minister had "been at my table regularly."[60]

New York activists were closely following developments in Ohio. Jay subscribed to the *Philanthropist* and occasionally corresponded with its editor, Gamaliel Bailey. After Ohio's reactionary legislative session in 1838–39, James Birney, who had moved to New York to become corresponding secretary of the American Anti-Slavery Society, suggested to his colleague Lewis Tappan that the society commit new resources to Ohio, writing that the new fugitive slave law was "unpopular—decidedly so. It will be totally disregarded—and never enforced." That summer, the publisher of the *Colored American*, Charles Ray, traveled to Ohio to solicit subscriptions to the newspaper and report to readers on the fortunes of African American communities there.[61]

Likely prompted by interest from men like Birney and Tappan—and by his contact with Black men like Cornish, Crummell, and Wright—in 1839 William Jay wrote a pamphlet titled *On the Condition of the Free People of Color in the United States*, which focused extensively on Ohio. The pamphlet opened with an attack on colonizationists and their view that racial prejudice was an intractable feature of human life. Whereas colonizationists believed human beings were naturally prejudiced, he wrote, abolitionists viewed prejudice as cultural, and they were determined to fight against it. He laid out examples of white northerners' racial prejudice—how it was manifested in both law and custom, and how it hurt free African Americans. He argued that Ohio's black laws violated the state's own constitution—the product of a more enlightened time—and were the harshest of any free state. He lambasted the Ohio House resolution against receiving petitions from African Americans, the assembly's affirmation of the black codes, and its cooperation with the Kentucky delegation in narrowing the rights of alleged fugitives from slavery. The state had taken a malevolent turn, he argued, and these were egregious violations of fundamental rights.[62]

Jay also took up the much-contested question of free African Americans' relationship to the US Constitution's privileges and immunities clause. Again he singled out Ohio for special criticism. Free Black people who lived in New York were understood to be citizens of the state, he wrote. Suppose "a New York freeholder and voter of this class, confiding in the guaranty given by the Federal constitution, removes into Ohio. No matter how much property he takes with him; no matter what attestations he produces to the purity of his character," the man still had to abide by Ohio's racist registration law. This, Jay argued, was a violation of the US Constitution's promise that citizens of the states were entitled to "all Privileges and Immunities of Citizens in the several States."[63]

Jay's pamphlet received notice in the antislavery press. He entertained an inquiry from someone hoping to donate three thousand dollars to aid free people of color, and he mailed the pamphlet to an acquaintance in England, describing it as "a melancholy exhibition of human depravity called into action by the . . . foul influence" of slavery. In Cincinnati, Gamaliel Bailey's *Philanthropist* printed the text, urging members of the state legislature to learn from this "eminent jurist" the harms they inflicted on "these innocent, deeply-wronged people." "By common consent," Bailey lamented, "it would seem, that to Ohio is awarded pre-eminence in that atrocious policy which crushes the colored man."[64] Bailey's reprint inspired abolitionists in northern Illinois to insist that Illinois laws were even more restrictive, and they were right. In Illinois, the group pointed out, it remained legal to buy and sell people of African descent as servants. The northern Illinois group believed their neighbors were insufficiently aware of their state's repressive antiblack laws, so they published a pamphlet that included extracts of the laws and commentary about their injustice. Jay may have declared Ohio the worst free state for African Americans, the group wrote, but Illinois could "appeal" that judgment "with good hope of success."[65]

THE CHALLENGE OF repealing racist laws seemed monumental. Still, during the 1830s, Ohio's Black and white antislavery activists had advanced profound and lasting arguments against those laws. They had promoted principles of fundamental human rights grounded in the Bible and Enlightenment universalism. Through petitioning, they had pushed those arguments into the state legislature, generating reports and further discussion. White activists had publicized evidence of Black industriousness and prosperity to challenge the widespread claims that the state needed to guard against African American migrants because they were paupers and vagrants. African American activists had entered the conversation by taking what everyone understood as the bold step of petitioning the legislature. In advocating for policy changes—for a share of the school fund and repeal of the black laws—these activists not only pursued better conditions for their communities but also challenged the idea, implicit in the black laws, that they did not really belong. While gathering petitions, they had made connections with one another, laying the groundwork for future actions.

Yet the possibility that the Ohio legislature would repeal the black laws seemed as remote as ever in 1839. How could a radical movement whose most committed participants were denied the right to vote make meaningful headway in the halls of power? The 1838 Democratic victory in Ohio suggested a rocky road ahead. Similar conclusions could be drawn from Pennsylvania, which in 1838 adopted a new constitution that restricted the vote to white men only, thereby ending the state's history of rejecting racial qualifications for the franchise. Protests and petitions from Pennsylvania African Americans and white allies had been useless in the face of a Democratic-led effort to deprive Black men of the vote.[66] The movement for racial equality in the states would need to increase its numbers dramatically or, at the very least, find a better way to navigate the two-party system.

CHAPTER 4

"THE RIGHTS OF THE CITIZENS OF MASSACHUSETTS"

African American Sailors in Southern Ports in the 1830s

IN LATE NOVEMBER 1833, a veteran ship steward named Joseph Thompson gave a sworn affidavit about his harrowing experiences as a free Black sailor in New Orleans. A voyage four years earlier had taken Thompson first to Bordeaux, France, and then to the Crescent City. When he arrived, the thirty-year-old Thompson asked to be paid a portion of his salary. The ship's mate reacted angrily, charged Thompson with stealing, had him arrested, and then—while he was in jail—attempted to sell him as a slave. "I refused to go," Thompson recounted. Proficient in French, he persuaded a jail guard to send word to two white acquaintances living in New Orleans, a landlord and a merchant whom he had known for years. The two men arrived at the jail and secured Thompson's freedom. Painfully aware that things could have turned out quite differently, Thompson concluded: "If I had not had friends in New Orleans, or if I had had them, but could not have sent a message in French by the guard, I should not have been able to recover my liberty, and should, in all probability, have been in slavery at this time."[1]

Thompson knew whereof he spoke. In the jail he had encountered other free Black northerners—three fellow ship stewards whom he knew from past voyages, as well as two men from Boston, three from New York, and one from Portland, Maine. There was also William Johnson, a free man Thompson had first encountered in Baltimore, now shackled and forced to work on the levee. All were slated to be sold as slaves after twenty days in jail. Thompson asked one of his white friends to help the other prisoners, but nothing came of it. Thompson himself went to the levee and found the ship where one of the stewards worked. He implored the ship's mate to send the man's free papers, or at least visit him in jail, but the mate refused, chasing Thompson away under a barrage of racial epithets. "A continual stream of free colored men from Boston, New York, Philadelphia, and other seaports of the United States," Thompson reported, is "passing through this calaboose into slavery in the country."[2]

The man to whom Thompson provided his testimony was David Lee Child, a Boston abolitionist lawyer and justice of the peace who, in January 1833, had delivered a speech outlining the horrors of American slavery, with particular attention to the oppressive laws of the slaveholding states. These laws not only sanctioned inhumane punishments for the enslaved. They also dramatically restricted the liberty of free people of African descent and established special regulations aimed at free Blacks who came from beyond state lines. In the published version of his speech, Child included as appendices the sworn testimony of Thompson and two other Black men, demonstrating to his New England audience that this was no abstract or distant matter. The discriminatory laws of the southern states had a very long reach—effectively stretching into Massachusetts. Right in their midst, the affidavits demonstrated, people of African descent lived in fear of kidnapping and sale into slavery. Sailors simply trying to make a living feared incarceration and sale if caught up by police in southern ports.

Unlike Ohio and other states in the Old Northwest, Massachusetts did not impose special legal burdens on Black migration and settlement. It did not exclude Black children from public education, and it did not restrict the testimony of African Americans in court. Not only did African Americans enjoy the same civil rights as whites, but Black men could also vote on the same terms as white men. Two racially discriminatory laws did remain on the books: one banning interracial marriage, and the other barring Black men from enrolling in the state militia. Abolitionists pressed for repeal of those laws, and they also worked for a bar on racial discrimination by railroad companies. The most significant of their political efforts at the national level, however, was their struggle in the 1830s and 1840s to persuade the state government to stand up for the rights of Black citizens of Massachusetts who were arrested while traveling or working in slaveholding jurisdictions. Unlike the movement to repeal the Ohio black laws, here the goal was not to repeal racist state laws at home but rather to seek ways of protecting the freedom of Black residents when they worked in other states.

Operating initially at the local and state levels, abolitionists and their allies gathered troves of evidence showing how frequently southern authorities arrested and incarcerated Black men who were simply pursuing their livelihoods in the shipping industry. People who passed through Charleston reported dozens of Black sailors incarcerated at any given time; in New Orleans in the 1840s, there were perhaps three dozen per month. Like their Ohio counterparts, Massachusetts activists petitioned the legislature and tried to influence public opinion. Efforts on behalf of Black sailors eventually involved a panoply of lawyers, sailors, ship captains, and state legislators. Individuals and organizations, working within their own networks and sometimes cooperating with newspaper editors, went to great lengths to get northern Black prisoners released from southern jails. Petitioners pressed the Massachusetts General Assembly to denounce slave-state authorities for such practices and to allow the Massachusetts governor to allocate funds when necessary to secure prisoners' releases.[3]

The possibility that they could somehow force unwilling southern officials to change their practices remained remote indeed. In the 1830s, most legal and political authorities believed state legislatures were within their rights to impose special regulations on groups they considered dangerous, including, if they chose, Black sailors. Activists offered up a range of alternative arguments. They insisted that antiblack laws violated fundamental rights to which all persons were entitled, whether by natural law, the US Constitution, or even the Declaration of Independence. They also claimed that southern practices violated Massachusetts sailors' rights as citizens under the Constitution's privileges and immunities clause (Article IV, Section 2). Finally, they sometimes argued that free Black citizens of Massachusetts were, by definition, citizens of the United States and therefore entitled to protection by the US government, just as an American citizen would be entitled to government protection if unjustly imprisoned by a foreign nation. Not all of these arguments could prevail in a court of law, but all of them reflected the determination of activists in the civil rights movement to meet the limitations of the constitutional order, and the racism of their compatriots, with serious constitutional arguments of their own.

———◦•◦———

In December 1822, the South Carolina legislature passed a law that drastically constrained the liberty of free Black sailors who entered the state's ports, touching off a struggle that established many of the terms of later debates. Adopted in the aftermath of a threatened slave rebellion led by a free Black man named Denmark Vesey, the law that targeted Black sailors was one section of a larger measure that placed stringent new regulations on free African Americans. Vesey, a former sailor and a member of Charleston's AME Church, plotted a slave uprising in the summer of 1822 and was found out. The extent of Vesey's plot and the threat it posed has been the subject of considerable debate, but at the very least it is clear that Vesey—who regularly quoted the Declaration of Independence and was believed to be seeking connections with Haiti—had terrified many in South Carolina's slaveholding elite. Vesey and dozens of his supposed conspirators were executed, after which the state legislature proceeded to tighten its laws. Lawmakers were worried particularly about Black sailors from outside the state, who in their travels propagated the revolutionary ideas about rights and equality that had shaken the Atlantic in the late eighteenth century and might inspire slave revolts close to home.[4]

The part of the new South Carolina law that applied to sailors demanded that all "free negroes, or persons of color" arriving in the state by water "shall be liable to be seized and confined in gaol [jail]" until their vessel was ready to leave. The law obliged the Charleston harbormaster to report to the sheriff the arrival of "all free negroes or free persons of color." The sheriff, in turn, was empowered to enforce the law by seizing and incarcerating Black sailors. Captains were responsible for picking up their sailors before they departed the port; those who did not do so were subject to fines, and their Black employees could be sold into slavery.[5] The law exacerbated the vulnerability that free African Americans already experienced when arriving or traveling in slaveholding jurisdictions. Prior to the new law, they were required to carry passes and faced arrest as fugitive slaves; now they would be forced to forfeit their liberty, spend time behind bars, and risk sale into lifelong slavery.

In January 1823, in keeping with the law's provisions, the Charleston sheriff and his deputies boarded ships docked in the harbor and demanded custody of Black workers—cooks, stewards, and mariners. A group of northern shipmasters immediately resisted this violation of their customary powers over their shipboard domains. Jared Bunce of Philadelphia began legal proceedings, filing a writ of habeas corpus to have his cook and steward brought before the local court. The Charleston sheriff argued that their imprisonment was justified under the new law, while Bunce's lawyers insisted that the law violated the US Constitution and could not be enforced. When the local court rejected the protest, Bunce appealed to the state's high court, whose judges split. The sailors remained in jail as Bunce and forty other "masters of American vessels, lying in the port of Charleston" petitioned the US House of Representatives. The captains argued that the South Carolina law violated the Constitution because it "destroy[ed] the liberty of freemen" and impinged on "the freedom of navigation, and the employment of seamen," something only Congress was permitted to do. They emphasized that the Black sailors on their ships were "native citizens of the United States" and had been seized "without a writ or any crime alleged."[6]

Congress had in fact obliquely recognized that African American sailors were "native citizens of the United States." Since the 1790s, federal laws had permitted US Customs officials to provide certificates that sailors used as proof of their citizenship while working on the high seas and in foreign ports. Customs collectors regularly issued such certificates to Black sailors, thus affirming their status as US citizens.[7] Yet that status seemed to mean little while Black sailors were inside the United States, where a person's status under state law mattered more than his status under federal law. As the 1820–21 debate about Missouri statehood had revealed, many states did not acknowledge their free Black residents as citizens. Racially discriminatory immigration and settlement laws were commonplace, and authorities in slaveholding states were permitted to arrest free Black people simply on suspicion of being fugitive slaves. It is little surprise, then, that after the captains' petition was sent to the House Judiciary Committee, it was never mentioned again.

It may have been relatively easy for the US government to ignore unhappy northern shipmasters, but legal action by British officials prompted a federal judge, South Carolinian William Johnson, to condemn the South Carolina law in 1823. The British case involved a Black sailor named Henry Elkison, whose lawyer sought a writ of habeas corpus in Charleston's federal court to bring his client out of state custody and test the law's constitutionality. Elkison's lawyers insisted that the law violated commercial treaties between the United States and Great Britain and interfered with Congress's power to regulate international commerce.[8]

The commerce clause, located in Article I, Section 8 of the US

Constitution, was in some ways similar to the privileges and immunities clause, in that it offered an avenue for limiting the power of the states, particularly when people (or, in the case of commerce, goods) moved across state lines. The commerce clause gave Congress authority over interstate and international commerce, as well as over commerce with "Indian tribes." Yet it was often difficult to answer the question of where Congress's authority ended and the states' power began. States regularly made regulations associated with the operation of ports—they licensed pilots, secured the health of people and goods entering the port, regulated the arrival of passengers, and oversaw harbors. All those functions of state governments were widely considered part of the police powers of the states, areas they oversaw to secure the broader public peace and good health. But such activities could also be perceived to affect relations beyond the bounds of the state, such as when states imposed taxes or regulations on shipmasters arriving from elsewhere. Several early Supreme Court cases attempted to discern the line between state and federal authority over commerce. Under the leadership of Chief Justice John C. Marshall (1801–35), the court favored congressional authority as it took steps to knit the nation together. Even Marshall, however, took pains to identify places where states' police powers prevailed, particularly in matters related to public safety and health.[9]

Defenders of what became known as the South Carolina Negro Seamen Act claimed that it did not infringe on congressional authority and was necessary to the state's "self-preservation." Attorney Benjamin Faneuil Hunt, a transplant from Massachusetts, acknowledged Congress's "exclusive" power over interstate and foreign commerce but said the Negro Seamen Act was a "*mere* police regulation," designed to safeguard the state. The law, he said, was little different from New York laws requiring ships to be quarantined in harbor or ill passengers confined in hospitals. In the case of South Carolina, the goal was to protect the state "against the moral contagion which the intercourse with foreign negroes produces." Invoking Emer de Vattel, a widely respected eighteenth-century Swiss theorist of international law, Hunt insisted that laws of this nature were critical to a

state's most basic function. Were there limits to a state's authority to issue
"arbitrary and severe enactments" in an effort to "guard against impending
danger"? Hunt believed that the state itself was "the sole judge of the means
necessary for its self-preservation."[10]

Justice William Johnson sided unequivocally with Elkison and his
lawyers. He was an associate justice of the US Supreme Court, but, in
keeping with practices of the era, in this case he was sitting as a federal circuit court judge. In a straightforward and damning opinion, Johnson held
that the Negro Seamen Act violated the US Constitution for precisely the
reasons Elkison's lawyers had suggested: It abrogated treaties with Great
Britain and interfered with Congress's power over commerce. Johnson
was unsympathetic to South Carolinians' arguments about dire necessity,
telling Secretary of State John Quincy Adams in a private letter that he
believed the "whole of the alarm of 1822 was founded in causes that were
infinitely exaggerated." Chief Justice John Marshall privately expressed
surprise at Johnson's decision, particularly his apparent disregard for local
public opinion. "The decision has been considered as another act of judicial usurpation," he wrote a colleague, and the "sentiment . . . avowed that,
if this be the Constitution, it is better to break that instrument than submit to the principle."[11]

As Marshall anticipated, Johnson's opinion in the Elkison case incited
outrage in South Carolina, where officials defiantly continued to enforce
the Negro Seamen Act. In short order, the Georgia legislature passed a
resolution asking Congress to adopt a constitutional amendment clarifying that the "import or ingress of any person of color" into a state was a
matter of state discretion. In subsequent years, Missouri, Mississippi, and
Louisiana expressed support for the proposed amendment, even as nine
other states rejected it. President James Monroe's administration, however,
aligned squarely with Judge Johnson on the unconstitutionality of South
Carolina's Negro Seamen Act. In the spring of 1824, US Attorney General
William Wirt stated publicly that the law interfered with congressional
power under the commerce clause, though he avoided questions of race,

citizenship, and personal liberty. That July, John Quincy Adams formally conveyed British complaints to the South Carolina governor, together with President Monroe's "hope" that the "inconvenience complained of will be remedied by the Legislature of the State of South Carolina itself." Federal officials appealed to the good sense of South Carolina authorities, but they did not threaten intervention by Congress or any other federal force.[12]

The election of Andrew Jackson to the presidency in 1828 marked a dramatic change in American party politics. Jackson, a slaveholding Democrat, distinguished himself for asserting federal authority over a rebellious South Carolina legislature that refused to enforce the federal tariff. Jackson had no patience for such extreme assertions of state sovereignty. In 1831, however, Jackson's attorney general, John M. Berrien of Georgia, basically reversed Wirt on the question of South Carolina's still-controversial Negro Seamen Act. Responding to continuing pressure from Great Britain, Berrien insisted, as Benjamin Hunt had earlier, that there was "perfect harmony" between the South Carolina law and the US Constitution. The Negro Seamen Law was a matter of "internal police" only and did not interfere with Congress's power over international or interstate commerce. Drawing on language in the US Constitution, Berrien claimed that federal laws, including those regulating commerce, could override state laws only if the federal laws were "both *necessary and proper* to the preservation of the commerce of the Union." Free movement of Black sailors in southern ports was by no means *necessary* to the nation's commerce, he argued, and therefore laws that excluded or regulated them were "a justifiable exercise of the reserved powers" of the states. Berrien added that the practice was analogous to a quarantine, which Chief Justice Marshall, in *Gibbons v. Ogden* (1824), had explicitly recognized as an area where states wielded expansive police powers.[13]

From the late 1820s through the 1840s, other slaveholding states followed South Carolina's lead in passing laws explicitly aimed at free Black sailors and defending those laws by invoking the states' powers to protect their own public peace and good health. They insisted that such laws concerned the states' internal affairs and therefore did not impinge on areas where Congress had authority. Nor was this type of argument for states' rights exclusively southern. Many free-state residents also held fast to a vision of the states' expansive authority to secure collective good health and safety. That, after all, was how Ohioans had defended their racist black laws—as measures required to preserve the safety and harmony of the Ohio population. Any argument that antiblack laws were morally wrong or violated people's individual rights had to compete against the deeply entrenched and, at the time, deeply legitimate belief that state legislatures had virtually unrestricted power to do what they believed necessary to secure the community's well-being.[14]

<hr />

ONE OF THE BOSTONIANS who knew the challenges African American sailors faced in southern ports was Samuel Snowden, a Black Methodist minister. Born in Maryland, Snowden had migrated northward around 1810. In Boston eight years later, he founded the May Street Church, a Methodist congregation. Among Snowden's parishioners was David Walker, author of the radical 1829 antislavery tract, *Appeal to the Colored Citizens of the World,* and both men were active in the Massachusetts General Colored Association (MGCA), an organization founded by Black activists in the late 1820s that hoped to "unite the colored population . . . through the United States," insofar as it was "practical and expedient." The MGCA was active for about five years, working to bring African Americans together to strategize about improving their condition. After Walker died of tuberculosis in 1830, Snowden carried on the endeavor. He was particularly known to welcome African American sailors to his church. Black sailors, like all sailors, were often young men and itinerant. They came home for short stints on shore, where they were subjected to criticism for drinking and carousing. Ministers and reformers worried about sailors' morality, but white-led organizations that attempted to furnish wholesome accommodations for sailors often excluded Black sailors. Snowden and his church offered a refuge. A white abolitionist recalled that Snowden's sermons were "nautical" and "full of salt." Snowden was also very political: In one sermon, he prayed that the American Colonization Society would be "smitten through and through with the fiery darts of truth, and tormented as the whale is between the sword-fish and the thresher."[15]

Snowden was among the Black leaders who helped William Lloyd Garrison and his white allies connect with Boston's African American community. Garrison had given an abolition-tinged July Fourth address in Boston in 1829 before going to work on Benjamin Lundy's newspaper in Baltimore, where the two white men were in close contact with Black Baltimoreans such as William Watkins, who were outspoken opponents of colonization. Snowden and other Black activists attended abolitionist lectures that Garrison gave in Boston before he launched his paper, the *Liberator*, in 1831. Snowden approved. The *Liberator* covered the activities of the MGCA, and in early 1833—around the time that David Lee Child gave his address on "The Despotism of Freedom"—the MGCA applied to become an auxiliary of the New England Anti-Slavery Society (NEASS), and Snowden was immediately elected a "counsellor" of the society. Snowden also began occasional work rescuing Black men incarcerated in southern jails.[16]

David Lee Child and his wife, Lydia Maria Child, were close white allies of Garrison. David had lived abroad in the early 1820s, trained as a lawyer when he returned, worked as an editor, and served briefly in the Massachusetts legislature. He was among the drafters of the constitution of the New England Anti-Slavery Society and had presided over the meeting in early January 1832 at which it was adopted.[17] The central point of his oration, given on the society's first anniversary, was that the United States was a place of historically unprecedented cruelty to people of African descent, both enslaved and free. Drawing comparisons with ancient Greece and Rome and with modern-day Europe and Latin America, he argued that nowhere else did slaveowners wield as much power to whip, torture, and kill their slaves, and nowhere did formerly enslaved people and their descendants face such extraordinary oppression. Child described the many southern state laws that criminalized the lives and behaviors of free African Americans and subjected them to harsher punishments than whites faced, drawing attention to the prima facie principle that all Black people traveling on their own were assumed to be runaway slaves unless they could prove otherwise. As other governments took steps to abolish slavery and end racial distinctions in law, the United States lagged far behind.

Child insisted that the impact of such laws on Black northerners should be a matter of common concern. Invoking the Constitution's privileges and immunities clause, he argued that because Black sailors were state citizens, they were also American citizens whose treatment by state officials in the South should draw the attention of the federal government, just as the US government would seek to protect its citizens from abuse when they traveled outside the country. The mistreatment of American citizens by foreigners could be seen as a cause for war. The plight of northern Black sailors sold into bondage in southern states was similar, Child argued. They "were torn from the protection of *that flag* of which we boast." In Child's view, then, the fate of Black sailors was not merely a private matter—a difficulty for the men's families or the ship captains who employed them. Rather, it was an issue of public policy affecting not just Massachusetts but also Maine, New Hampshire, Vermont, Rhode Island, Connecticut, New York, and Pennsylvania. At the very least, he concluded, Black sailors were "citizens" of their home states, entitled to protection from the governments of those states.[18]

As Child prepared his speech for publication in the fall of 1833, he interviewed not only the ship steward Joseph Thompson but also two prominent members of Boston's African American activist community, James G. Barbadoes and Robert Roberts. Both men knew what it was like to have family members kidnapped or unjustly arrested. Eighteen years earlier, Barbadoes's brother had spent more than five months in a New Orleans jail and was only rescued when another prisoner was released and sent word to his parents to get free papers and mail them south. Roberts told the story of his former father-in-law, a Black veteran of the American Revolution from New Hampshire, who had no fewer than three sons kidnapped into slavery from New England. The old man, Roberts said, "was kept running from one lawyer and judge to another, until he died without being able to help" his imprisoned children.[19] These two affidavits, together with Joseph Thompson's, were published as appendices to Child's speech. The men's narratives powerfully demonstrated that hostile southern laws put the freedom of Black New Englanders at risk. The testimonials suggested to white readers in particular that, out of concern for their Black neighbors and fellow state citizens, they should take an interest in the oppressive laws of distant states.

Child's published address—released as the first in a series of pamphlets planned by the NEASS—articulated a concern for free Black sailors working in the southern states that only increased as new evidence emerged. Antislavery organizations had long made it their business to prevent the kidnapping and sale of free Black northerners. In the 1830s, however, they insisted that they could not rely exclusively on private resources and required help from state governments. State governments had little power to affect the policies of their "sister states," particularly in matters concerning individual rights. Still, legislatures could issue formal condemnations, and they could devote money and personnel to defending the rights of their vulnerable citizens. They could also appeal to the US government, either by protesting racist state laws in federal court or by asking Congress to pass laws bringing other states to heel. The Massachusetts legislature would ultimately try all these options.

———◦•◦———

AS THE CAMPAIGN for Black sailors' safety got underway in the mid-1830s, the abolitionist movement faced a ferocious reaction. In New York, Philadelphia, and other northern cities, white mobs attacked abolitionists, directing particular fury at evidence of the movement's commitment to racial equality. The summer of 1835 marked the apex of antiabolitionist mobbing. By that fall, five southern state legislatures had passed resolutions condemning abolitionism and urging northern legislatures to clamp down on the movement. Across the free states, political and civic leaders denounced abolitionists as traitors whose movement threatened to destroy the Union. Whig-dominated Massachusetts was no exception. Boston was a hotbed of abolitionist organizing, home to antislavery radicals like David Walker, William Lloyd Garrison, and the African American woman orator Maria W. Stewart. Yet the city and the state's political establishment steadfastly opposed the abolitionist movement, which it considered overzealous and a threat to hard-won national unity.[20]

Bay State antiabolitionism boiled over in the fall of 1835. In late August, leading figures representing both major political parties gathered in Boston's Faneuil Hall to denounce the movement. Fearing for his safety, Garrison went into temporary exile in New York but was back in Boston by mid-October. On the twenty-first of that month, a mob of more than a thousand—including people considered by many to be "gentlemen of property and standing"—gathered at the office of the *Liberator*, where an interracial women's abolitionist organization, the Boston Female Anti-Slavery Society, was meeting. The mob demanded that the meeting disperse, grabbed Garrison as he tried to flee, and dragged him down State Street with a rope around his neck. The Boston mayor insisted that the abolitionists, not the mob, were the agents of chaos, and the state legislature soon appointed a joint committee to consider the southern states' resolutions. Garrison and other abolitionists testified before the committee, but its members disapproved of their "vehemence" and worried that the crowd that gathered to watch the second hearing was "evidently in a state of much excitement." The hearing ended abruptly, and the subcommittee denied the abolitionists' request to return and make their case under calmer conditions.[21]

In this overwrought climate, when it came to demanding attention to abuses of Black sailors in southern ports, activists sought to present the issue as one of universal concern, separating it from the perceived excesses of the abolitionist movement. That strategy is evident in the first major petition to the legislature on behalf of free Black sailors, submitted in late March 1836, a few weeks after the abolitionists' disastrous subcommittee appearance. The petition's lead signer was George Odiorne, a prosperous businessman, co-owner of a water-powered nail factory near Boston, and a former state legislator. His son, James, was among the founders of the NEASS, and father and son were evidently close, working as business partners in the 1820s and 1830s. Upon his death in 1846, an obituary lauded George Odiorne as "an ardent friend of liberty, humanity, and equal rights" who "held slavery in abhorrence." Still, the senior Odiorne publicly stood apart from organized abolitionism—a small distance to be sure, but perhaps far enough to give him and his cosignatories credibility when they averred, in a petition asking the state legislature to denounce southern state laws that oppressed free African Americans, that none of them were "connected with any anti-slavery society."[22]

Their petition was wide-ranging. Centrally concerned with violations of the liberty of free Black northerners sojourning in the southern states, it mentioned other unsavory southern laws as well. Some stipulated harsh punishments for ship captains whose vessels transported stowaway slaves, even if the captain was unaware that a fugitive was on board. In Georgia, the legislature had recently appropriated a $5,000 reward for the arrest and conviction of Garrison himself. Yet the majority of the group's complaint was devoted to condemning the laws of the slave states that had a direct negative impact on Black citizens of Massachusetts. The petitioners indicted not only those targeting Black sailors directly but all laws that treated people of African descent as a suspicious class and denied them rights to due process of law.

Beyond insisting that Black sailors from Massachusetts were citizens of the state and therefore entitled to the state's protection, the petitioners argued that southern state policies violated the US Constitution in two specific ways: First, the policies contradicted the preamble, which held that the government of the United States was designed to "establish justice, insure domestic tranquility, provide for the common defence, promote the general welfare, and secure the blessings of liberty to ourselves and our posterity." It was difficult, however, to demonstrate that the preamble was on their side. It did mention "liberty" and "justice," but it also bolstered more security-based visions of government with its allusions to "defence" and "the general welfare." Their other constitutional argument was stronger and more common among people of their political bent. Racially discriminatory laws, they insisted, subjected "a portion of our fellow citizens of this Commonwealth . . . to heavy losses, cruel treatments, and even to the deprivation of their liberty for life." Such laws violated the privileges and immunities clause, "which explicitly provides, that 'the citizens of each state shall be entitled to all the privileges and immunities of citizens in the several States.' "[23]

The petitioners' demand for action was straightforward. The Massachusetts legislature should ask states committing such violations to "repeal all their laws which violate the rights of the citizens of Massachusetts and contravene the provisions of the Federal Constitution."[24] State governments often passed resolutions making requests or recommendations to other states, which governors formally conveyed. This was what the slaveholding states had done in 1835, when they asked free states to adopt resolutions against abolitionists. Massachusetts could not force South Carolina or any other state to change its laws, but the legislature could use this common mode of state-to-state politicking to make known its views and the views of its constituents.

The legislative committee assigned to deal with the Odiorne petition gave the matter an extensive hearing. It listened to lawyers who corroborated the petitioners' claims, one of whom said he had witnessed the operations of the South Carolina Negro Seamen Act. A Black sailor named George Tolliver told the committee that "he had been imprisoned seven times on arriving as a seaman in Southern ports" and that he always encountered in southern jails "more or less of his Northern colored fellow citizens." The petitioners also provided transcriptions of the relevant southern state laws, intended to help show that their allegations were correct.[25]

The committee was not persuaded. While the subcommittee's majority declared it "inexpedient" to recommend action, however, two members stood firmly in support of the petitioners. State Senator Seth Whitmarsh and Representative Josiah Caldwell wrote a minority report that rang with righteous outrage. In a document that included not only their own views but also summaries of much of the evidence presented to the subcommittee, the dissenting legislators insisted that the well-being of Black sailors pertained to "the rights, liberties and lives of our citizens, as also the sovereignty of the State." At issue was "whether this Commonwealth shall protect its citizens against violence which by the operation of the laws complained of they are now subjected to."[26] Just as antislavery people had wanted Ohio to assert its sovereignty against the demands of Kentucky slaveholders in 1839, so too did the Massachusetts legislators argue for recognition of the state's sovereign power to protect its citizens in the face of South Carolina's abuses.

But these were not claims for state sovereignty as an abstract principle; they were arguments for recognition of a particular vision of race and citizenship. Above all, Whitmarsh and Caldwell condemned laws that discriminated on the basis of skin color or complexion as arbitrary and unjust. The idea was certainly not new or unique to them or their state, yet they discussed it as a matter of state pride. From its earliest days as an "independent community," they argued, the state had construed Black and white people as equals when it came to citizenship, and Black citizens were no less entitled to the state's protection than whites. "Are they not Citizens, and in this state having the right to vote when qualified as such? Have they not the same right which is enjoyed by all others, that of being protected by the Government under which they live?"[27]

Examining norms and directives concerning interstate tensions, Whitmarsh and Caldwell suggested that the conflict could be managed by recourse to the legal principle of "comity." *Comity*, a term from international law, provided that a host country would extend to visitors the courtesy of allowing them to maintain practices that were legal in their home places but not in the place they were visiting. Americans were already engaged in a debate about interstate comity as it applied to slaveowners. As northern states increasingly abolished slavery, the question of whether slaveowners traveling in the free states retained rights to their slaves, as property, had become increasingly fraught. Early on, free states extended comity to slaveowners, allowing them to claim ownership of their slaves while visiting free states for fairly lengthy periods of time. Yet as antislavery feeling and resentment of what activists dubbed the Slave Power spread in the free states, those states gradually limited the practice.[28] Already in 1833, David Lee Child had pinpointed the hypocrisy of traveling slaveowners who expected northerners to honor their property rights in slaves but refused to take seriously the freedom and self-ownership of northern Black people sojourning in southern states.

In a move that became increasingly widespread and important in coming years, Whitmarsh and Caldwell turned to the Constitution's Article IV to connect the rights of free Black sailors in the slave states with the rights of slaveowners in the free ones. The Constitution's first three articles defined the responsibilities of the different branches of government: legislative, executive, and judicial. Article IV concerned relations among the states and their inhabitants, and it contained both the fugitive slave clause and the privileges and immunities clause. The fugitive slave clause held that "person[s] held to service" who escaped to the free states must be "delivered up" when claimed by their owners. The privileges and immunities clause declared "the Citizens of each State . . . entitled to all Privileges and Immunities of Citizens in the several States." Whitmarsh and Caldwell saw the two provisions through a single lens. If white southerners expected the people of Massachusetts to permit enforcement of the Constitution's fugitive slave clause, southerners themselves "should as rigidly observe the other portion of that compact which secures to the Citizens of Massachusetts, in every other state, the immunities and privileges enjoyed by their own Citizens."[29]

Whitmarsh and Caldwell's powerful minority report did not generate a change in state policy, but it did draw attention to the cause. The Massachusetts Senate ordered the report printed, and readers of the April 23, 1836, edition of the *Liberator* found it at their fingertips. Later that year, the report was a resource for the antislavery lawyer Ellis Gray Loring as he defended the freedom of a girl named Med in the acclaimed case of *Commonwealth v. Aves*. Med's owner had brought her from New Orleans to Boston, where abolitionists took the owner to court for holding a person in bondage in a state in which slavery was illegal. Lawyers for the owner insisted that principles of comity required Massachusetts officials to recognize the owner's right to retain her slave. Loring, however, argued that the usual rules of interstate comity did not apply when people claimed other people as chattel; he also pointed out that southerners had already substantially eroded principles of interstate comity. As Whitmarsh and Caldwell's report had shown, citizens of Massachusetts were exposed to "outrage and injustice . . . *by law,* in those parts of the country from whence the call for comity proceeds."[30] The Odiorne petition had increased the visibility of the plight of free Black sailors in the southern states and established a template, in both form and content, for future struggles. Three years later, advocates for Black sailors were even more successful.

———————

ANTISLAVERY ACTIVISTS AND EDITORS repeatedly drew attention to southern authorities' disregard for the rights of free people of African descent, especially sailors. Their newspapers carried stories of free people incarcerated in southern states, often giving detailed accounts of attempts at rescue. Many people linked the travails of Black sailors with the problem of kidnapping of free Black northerners and the voracious and inhumane interstate slave trade in the Upper South. A person spirited away from the relative safety of a northern community could be imprisoned on a boat, conveyed into a slaveholding jurisdiction, and sold for profit with few questions asked. An 1837 editorial in Cornish's *Colored American* connected the issues, emphasizing the scourge of kidnapping and cautioning Black sailors "against going among those soul-searchers and man-stealers." As Lydia Maria Child pointed out, "In many instances written documents of freedom have been wrested from free colored people and destroyed by kidnappers," and the "lucrative internal slave trade furnishe[d] constant temptation to the commission of such crimes."[31]

Once a free person of African descent was imprisoned in a southern jail, his or her fate often hinged on chance alone. As in the case of Gilbert Horton, a northern editor might see a southern paper publicizing the arrest of someone whose attributes sounded familiar. A Memphis slaveholder named Jonathan Simpson advertised in a Mississippi newspaper for a runaway named Isaac, who "speaks quick, and very correctly for a negro." "He was originally from New York and no doubt will attempt to pass himself as free," the advertisement read. A New York editor saw the announcement and knew it described Isaac Wright, a free man, "sold as a slave at New Orleans from on board a steamboat, on which he had shipped as a fireman." A friend of Wright's traveled to Mississippi and managed to rescue him.[32]

Then there was Prince Matice, a free Black sailor from Athens, New York, arrested as a runaway slave in Virginia. Matice, who was described as a veteran seaman, managed to contact his home community via the jailer and promised to pay the expenses of his own rescue. Back in New York, his associates assembled documentation showing that he was free, but they also publicly rejected the idea that he—or they—should pay any fees assessed by Virginia authorities. They told the New York governor, Democrat William L. Marcy, that "justice" required compensation to Matice himself, not to his imprisoners. Calculating the expense and the risk of sending an emissary to Virginia, they asked Marcy to intervene on behalf of Matice, a "citizen of the State, not charged with any crime." Finding the governor unresponsive, the community raised eighty dollars and sent an agent to Virginia to secure Matice's release. The mission was successful, but an editor noted that the larger problem remained unresolved. Matice's release rested on "favorable circumstances only," not on any sort of consistent public policy. If New York's Black citizens continued to be subject to arrest and sale into slavery, then New Yorkers would have to continue providing "funds for their redemption, or abandon them to hopeless and perpetual servitude."[33]

As in New York, New Englanders created networks dedicated to helping imprisoned Black sailors and others regain their liberty. In 1833, David Child reported that Black Bostonians had pooled their resources to get imprisoned friends and family members out of southern jails. Already some of the kidnapped "have been redeemed with the hard earnings of their wives, children or parents, at home; aye, in Massachusetts,—in this very city." Three years later, Methodist minister Samuel Snowden testified that, "by the aid of various benevolent individuals," he had secured the release of six Massachusetts citizens who, without such efforts, would otherwise "have been sold into perpetual bondage."[34]

In southern cities, the written or oral testimony of a respectable white person was usually required to vouch for an imprisoned Black person's freedom. One person who attempted to fill that role was the Boston abolitionist and lawyer Ellis Gray Loring. In 1840, Loring worked on behalf of Luke Thompson, a sailor from Maine imprisoned in New Orleans. Thompson had been picked up in a gambling house. He carried a "protection" provided by a deputy customs collector, but New Orleans officials distrusted it because, they said, it described his eyes as "black," whereas authorities thought they were "light coloured." Such a discrepancy, real or imagined, could have meant a lifetime in slavery for Thompson. Loring assembled evidence of Thompson's freedom and mailed the New Orleans mayor a copy of the "protection certificate," together with an affidavit from a ship captain and a description of a scar on Thompson's head that would demonstrate to New Orleans officials that this was the right man. "The mother of the boy is in great distress about her son," Loring told the New Orleans mayor, "and I doubt not that your private feelings, as well as your sense of public duty will induce you to give your immediate attention to the case: & to order his liberation."[35]

New Orleans was by then notorious as a place where northern Black sailors faced great danger. Even before Louisiana passed a law that directly restricted Black maritime workers, officials arrested Black sailors at will under laws designed to constrain the migration of free Black people to the state. The city had a special curfew for free Blacks, and any sailor not back on board his ship by that time was subject to arrest. Sailors seem to have been most vulnerable when eating and drinking in the city. They were regularly apprehended in bars, gambling houses, and other public places, and they usually were given no opportunity to prove their freedom before a judge. Those who were swept up by police were often forced to work on the city's chain gang. This was how visiting northerners sometimes encountered people they knew; they saw them working in chains, threatened with sale into permanent slavery. Prisoners who spoke to passersby were whipped by the driver.[36]

As Joseph Thompson learned in 1829, there were wealthy and esteemed white men who might be appealed to for help. By the late 1830s, one such person was Jacob Barker, a prominent merchant and attorney. Born in 1779, Barker grew up on Nantucket, raised by his widowed mother, a member of the island's longstanding Quaker community. The island was home to a close-knit and prosperous whaling industry that drew on the labor of men of African and Native American descent, whose communities also had a long history on the island. As a young man, Barker moved to New York and went into business as a merchant and shipowner. All the while, he remained strongly connected with Nantucket, choosing to employ men from the island as captains on his many ships. Barker settled in New Orleans in 1834, ostensibly to deal with business-related lawsuits. Critical of slavery, he imported a ship full of Germans and attempted to run a sugar plantation based on free labor. The experiment failed within a year.[37]

In 1837, Barker warned a friend on Nantucket of the dangers facing Black sailors in New Orleans. He had learned the depth of the problem when he visited the jail of the Third Municipality, one of the city's three districts, to secure the release of a free Black man from Baltimore named Ephraim Larkin. There he found three other free men of color incarcerated alongside Larkin, one of whom happened to be the grandson of a Native American man whom Barker remembered from childhood. The prisoners were completely at the mercy of the recorder of the jail, Barker reported. Those who could not prove their freedom to the recorder's satisfaction could be sold into lifelong bondage. Moreover, the recorder had no consistent standard for what constituted adequate proof of freedom. Officials also disregarded state laws providing that only persons of "full" African descent were presumed slaves, holding captive the Native American man from Massachusetts and a "yellow" man from New York, both of whom should have enjoyed the presumption of free status.[38]

The threat of incarceration and abuse in New Orleans was so great, Barker told his friend on the seafaring island, that if Black sailors were not so indispensable to northern shipping interests, he would recommend they stop coming altogether. Customhouse-issued certificates were no longer sufficient to prove their freedom. If they must sail into New Orleans, they should obtain free papers directly from the governor of their home state. He also recommended that captains take action by avoiding the Third Municipality, where the laws were enforced most stringently. If they sailed past that district and docked farther upstream, in one of the city's other two jurisdictions, Barker felt, they would deprive the offending district of revenues and perhaps encourage officials there to adopt new policies. For his part, Barker had recently secured the release of six free men from jail, bitterly paying the fees demanded by their captors. "How free men can obtain satisfaction for having been thus wrongfully imprisoned and made to work in chains on the high way, is not for me to decide," he concluded. Little would change "without more active friends, willing to espouse their cause."[39]

Barker was no abolitionist. In fact, he said he detested abolitionists, believing they had no understanding of true conditions in the South. Louisiana slaves were in better health than free blacks in the North, he maintained, and the abolitionist movement was doing harm by contribut-ing to slaveowners' paranoia and thus worsening conditions for African Americans in Louisiana. Besides, he argued, the "abstract question of slav-ery" was not debatable, as it had been "settled by the Constitution." But Barker, who sometimes worked directly for other northerners seeking to liberate free African Americans from New Orleans jails, also insisted that, as a lawyer, he was entitled to advocate for his clients. Part of the problem, he insisted, was that corrupt officials were violating local and state laws. Defending his actions to critics in New Orleans, he questioned: "Why pass laws protecting free men of color if it is to be considered wrong for counsel to appear in their behalf?"[40]

Barker also collaborated with Rowland G. Hazard, a Rhode Island textile merchant who supplied "Negro cloth" to southern planters and spent winters in southern Louisiana. Barker's wife, Elizabeth, was Haz-ard's cousin. In the early 1840s, the two men made a practice of investi-gating the imprisonment of Black northerners in New Orleans, and when jail officials tried to bar them, they obtained court orders. The men scored an important victory in 1842, when they persuaded a New Orleans grand jury to take notice of the abuse. In an omnibus report on conditions in several New Orleans jails and the parish prison, the grand jury singled out the Second Municipality for imprisoning men without cause, refusing to allow hearings before a judge, and holding them in unconscionable squa-lor. The report provided details on the cases of ten men held indefinitely without a chance to prove their freedom. "Most of these persons and many others now confined," the grand jury acknowledged, "came to this port from different ports of the United States; and all are made to work in the chain-gang, as slaves."[41]

Both Barker and Hazard would come in for criticism of their work. Barker continued to disavow abolitionism and remained in New Orleans (eventually running for office during Reconstruction), while Hazard, the more morally committed of the two, faced censure from southern buyers and ultimately ended his "Southern business." In 1842, however, at least one person saw the men's success in New Orleans as evidence of what civic-minded businessmen could accomplish. The prominent Unitarian minister William Ellery Channing praised them for demonstrating that commerce established "connection . . . with our fellow-creatures" that "may be turned to good in a thousand ways."[42]

--- ⋅ ◦ ⋅ ---

By 1839, THE MASSACHUSETTS LEGISLATURE had become a more hospitable place for measures both against slavery and in defense of Black sailors' rights. One reason was abolitionists' growing interest in shaping party politics. Their influence was evident as early as the spring of 1837, when New York Democrat Martin Van Buren became president. Many viewed Van Buren—who had been instrumental in building the party in the late 1820s—as Andrew Jackson's logical successor. But southern Democrats worried that the New Yorker might not be sufficiently pro-slavery. In the run-up to the 1836 presidential election, then, Van Buren and his allies went to great lengths to show that he would stand up for slaveholders' interests. He publicly condemned abolitionists for pushing the nation into conflict and promised never to sign legislation abolishing slavery in the District of Columbia, themes he reiterated in his March 1837 inaugural address. Some northern Democrats were aghast at such genuflections to slavery. That spring, the abolitionist poet John Greenleaf Whittier joined others in Boston to lobby Democrats in the state assembly to declare their independence from Van Buren. They were gratified when the legislature passed resolutions defending the right of petition and calling for the abolition of slavery in the District of Columbia, as well as a new law providing jury trials for alleged fugitive slaves. Whittier declared happily to a friend, "The legislature is abolitionized, the whole State is coming."[43]

Encouraged by the prospect of a receptive Massachusetts legislature, African American activists and their white allies continued to draw attention to public and private discrimination against people of African descent. In 1838, white women abolitionists mounted a campaign for repeal of the state's longstanding ban on interracial marriage, one of two state laws that made distinctions based on race. Activists also attacked the law that limited militia service to white men.[44]

On the issue of free Black sailors, the turning point in public opinion and public policy came in 1839, when George Bradburn of Nantucket took up the work that George Odiorne's petition had launched three years earlier—this time with far greater success. Nominally a Whig, Bradburn later wrote that he "cared almost nothing at all for Whiggism, in comparison of liberty, of anti-slavery, of measures and principles technically neither Whig nor Democratic." Bradburn had studied theology at Harvard and then moved to Nantucket, where he served as a Unitarian minister. Black islanders—including prosperous ship captain Edward Pompey—had formed an abolitionist organization by the end of the 1820s, and Black abolitionists in the 1830s distributed the *Liberator* and the *Colored American*. Finally, in 1839, a group of white residents, mostly Quakers, formed an abolitionist organization of their own. Bradburn later recalled that he had at first seen Garrison and his allies as "hair-brained fanatics" whose course might foment slave uprisings and destroy the nation. But he changed his mind on hearing a July Fourth oration by the British abolitionist George Thompson, which persuaded him that the movement would seek abolition by peaceful means alone. In the Massachusetts legislature, Bradburn earned a reputation as a political independent whose positions on issues were unpredictable. An unabashed abolitionist, he was a confident and engaging speaker and often used humor and teasing to advance his arguments.[45]

Upon joining the state legislature in January 1839, Bradburn called for the appointment of a joint special committee to consider what one newspaper glossed as "the protection of citizens of Massachusetts from imprisonment and sale into slavery in other states of the Union." The legislature duly formed a subcommittee. Weeks later, it looked as though Bradburn's effort had stalled. The Senate portion of the committee recommended against action, and the House members soon followed suit. Bradburn kept up the fight, constituting himself as a minority committee of one and launching a campaign to change his colleagues' minds. He believed they needed more information, so he compiled what he called a "somewhat elaborate" report that drew heavily on Whitmarsh and Caldwell's 1836 minority report and introduced new evidence about Massachusetts citizens imprisoned and forsaken in southern jails. The Black minister Samuel Snowden could provide sworn testimony, he wrote, as could George Tolliver, who in 1836 had described having been imprisoned in southern ports seven times. Bradburn even alluded to a fellow member of the state assembly who, while visiting New Orleans, encountered "an old and valued acquaintance" laboring on a chain gang and managed to secure his release. Bradburn's evidence went beyond Massachusetts, illustrating the plight of free Black sailors from elsewhere, particularly New York. The examples he gave, he said, were but "specimens" of the larger problem.[46]

Bradburn, like Whitmarsh and Caldwell, distanced himself from the "peculiar doctrines of the abolitionists" but insisted that the incarceration of Black sailors in southern ports violated the Constitution's privileges and immunities clause. The safety and freedom of Black sailors, he said, "seriously concerns all—whether abolitionists or anti-abolitionists—who have the slightest regard, either for the personal safety of our seven thousand colored citizens, or for the interests and undoubted rights of our merchants and masters of vessels." Moreover, he argued, the state owed it to "her citizens, and to her own dignity and honor" to protest the southern laws that "rob so many of her citizens of the 'privileges and immunities' guaranteed them by the Constitution." Racially discriminatory laws, he insisted in an impassioned peroration, were "palpably contrary to both the letter and the spirit of the Constitution" and "in utter derogation of that great principle of the common law, which presumes every man to be innocent, and treats him as such, until he be proved guilty." Black citizens were just as entitled to protection as white ones, and the state must not be cowed into silence just because the perpetrators of abuse were their "sister states," not foreign nations.[47]

Bradburn's report offered a compelling moral call to action. On the constitutional issues, however, his argument was much less persuasive. He invoked two legal authorities: Justice Bushrod Washington's opinion on the privileges and immunities clause in the circuit court case of *Corfield v. Coryell* (1825), and Justice Joseph Story of Massachusetts in his acclaimed *Commentaries on the Constitution* (1833). In *Corfield v. Coryell*, often considered the most important ruling on citizenship offered by a federal judge before the Civil War, Washington acknowledged that the "privileges and immunities of citizens in the several states" encompassed "fundamental" rights, among which was the "right of a citizen of one state to pass through or reside in any other state, for the purposes of trade, agriculture, professional pursuits, or otherwise." Eight years after the *Corfield* decision, Story explained in his treatise that the privileges and immunities clause was intended to "confer on" state citizens "a general citizenship; and to communicate all the privileges and immunities which the citizens of the same state would be entitled to under the like circumstances."[48] Bradburn claimed that the writings of Washington and Story supported his argument that southern states were violating the constitutional rights of Black sailors.

Yet these authorities were not unambiguously on Bradburn's side, and many more authorities directly contradicted him. Black sailors traveled to other states for precisely the sorts of economic reasons Bushrod Washington mentioned in *Corfield*. The problem was that many American states explicitly denied that free African Americans were entitled to that kind of personal mobility, whether through stringent laws like those of South Carolina or looser ones like those of Ohio. Such laws had never been held unconstitutional in federal court. And Justice Washington's decision itself contained an exception that acknowledged the abiding power of the states to protect the public peace. An individual's citizenship rights, he wrote, were subject to "such restraints as the government may justly prescribe for the general good of the whole." Justice Story's statement was also ambiguous. In mentioning "general citizenship," it did suggest a kind of national citizenship that might be carried across state lines. But its phrase "under the like circumstances" could easily be construed as implying that outsiders could be subjected to local definitions of who was a citizen.[49]

Moreover, Bradburn ignored an obvious source that even more directly contradicted his interpretation of the privileges and immunities clause. In the original (1826–27) edition of his *Commentaries on American Law,* James Kent, then the nation's most prominent legal intellectual, provided the following interpretation of the privileges and immunities clause: that if "natural born or duly naturalized citizens . . . remove from one state to another, they are entitled to the privileges that persons of the same description are entitled to in the state to which the removal is made and to none other." Kent used "free persons of colour" to illustrate the principle. If free persons of color were not entitled to vote "in Carolina," he wrote, then such persons "emigrating there from a northern state, would not be entitled to vote." Kent was unequivocal: "The laws of each state ought, and must, govern within its jurisdiction; and the laws and usages of one state cannot be permitted to prescribe qualifications for citizens, to be claimed and exercised in other states, in contravention to their local policy." Kent's *Commentaries* were reissued many times over the next several decades, but this language remained largely unchanged. For instance, in *Inquiry into the Character and Tendency of the American Colonization and American Anti-Slavery Societies* (1834), William Jay argued that free African Americans were, by virtue of birth in the United States, citizens of the United States and therefore entitled to travel freely among the states. Jay's pamphlet made an impression on Kent, who in the 1836 edition of his *Commentaries* affirmed that free Black people, whether formerly enslaved or not, if born in the United States, were citizens of the United States. Yet Kent maintained his position that states could single out free African Americans for special regulations, adding that they were US citizens "under such disabilities as the law of the states respectively may deem it expedient to prescribe to free persons of colour."[50] Reflecting the complexities of American federalism, Kent implied that states were not obligated to treat Black citizens from other states with even a modicum of respect.

Challenging the views of the legal establishment, then, Bradburn and his allies insisted that the Constitution *ought to* render null and void racially discriminatory state laws; the Constitution *should* empower Congress to take action against officials who continued to enforce such laws. Those laws were wrong, they believed, because they drew immoral distinctions based on race, and because they violated the fundamental rights associated with being a free person: rights to life, liberty, and property. They associated those rights with the common law and construed them part of a sort of "higher law" that transcended the nation's founding charter. In courts and in Congress, however, such expressions of principle were pitted against the widespread commitment not to rights but to the public good, to the idea that states enjoyed plenary power to define and protect their people's welfare.

Whatever the limits of constitutional interpretation, nothing prevented the state of Massachusetts from taking independent action. After the designated subcommittee reported adversely, Bradburn introduced his own resolutions, together with his report, and pushed the general assembly to act. He wanted his colleagues to formally denounce the oppressive southern laws and to authorize the governor to use public funds to secure the release of Black Massachusetts citizens imprisoned in other states. Having emphasized the limited effectiveness of private networks, which depended on the idiosyncrasies of personal connections and private wealth, Bradburn argued that it was time to use the power of the state to protect the rights and honor the citizenship of free Black people from Massachusetts.[51]

Bradburn later recalled that he had entered that debate "with more feeling than I remember to have done into any other." He was furious with the subcommittee's "truckling subserviency to a corrupt and blind popular opinion, and the legal cobwebs with which those quibbling lawyers had attempted to fetter me." When a colleague warned him to back off lest he damage his political prospects, he paid no attention. Soon his peers began coming over to his side. The "quibbling" arguments of the committee members, he recalled, "found no favor in the masses of the House when once I had succeeded in getting before them the facts." The House voted to form a new subcommittee and instructed it to report out Bradburn's resolutions or "others containing the principles of the same." The House having changed its mind, the Senate soon followed, and Bradburn's bill passed on April 8, 1839.[52]

Abolitionists hailed the Massachusetts resolutions as a great victory. The state could now dispatch emissaries southward to liberate free Blacks languishing in jails, whether kidnapped from the North or arrested in southern ports. Before the resolutions, people had regularly sought governors' intervention in kidnapping cases. Governors could write diplomatic-style letters to their southern counterparts, but they could do little else to secure the liberation of incarcerated people. The Bradburn resolutions gave the Massachusetts governor new power by authorizing him to spend public funds. The antislavery press was elated. The *Liberator* printed Bradburn's entire report, and it was soon picked up by the *Emancipator* of New York. In Ohio, Gamaliel Bailey's *Philanthropist* called the legislature's action "one of the most important movements ever made in behalf of the colored citizens" and predicted that Massachusetts now had the power to keep its citizens safe from "the unconstitutional and atrocious laws" of the slave states.[53]

Bradburn took credit for changing his colleagues' minds, and many contemporaries concurred. According to one newspaper, the resolutions represented a "triumph of humanity over prejudice and tyranny, which will long and honorably identify the name of Mr. Bradburn with the legislation of Massachusetts." In a private letter, the Boston abolitionist Samuel May told a colleague that Bradburn had "made a movement, which has long appeared to me an important one, and which ought to be pressed with vigor." There were some seven thousand "colored people" in the state, he said, "but nothing has been done by our Legislature to extend to them the protection of the commonwealth, whenever they go beyond its borders." May now urged further African American activism, saying, "The colored people ought to importune the government of the state until they receive what every citizen has a right to claim—protection."[54]

Bradburn himself soon had the opportunity to invoke the state's new power in a case that, in turn, helped spur New Yorkers to action. In the fall of 1839, he learned that two Black men who had been kidnapped from Massachusetts had been rescued by a sympathetic "vigilance committee" in Richmond, Virginia. Bradburn visited the home of one of the missing men, Nahum Hazard, whose mother recounted her son's story. Three white men—two strangers, along with a collaborating neighbor—had come to her house and offered her son an apprenticeship at a tavern some sixty miles away in Washington, Massachusetts. Caira Hazard thought the opportunity seemed promising, and her son left voluntarily. She had begun to worry, however, when she heard of the kidnapping of a young man from Worcester. Bradburn's investigation helped expose a Virginia-based kidnapping ring whose tentacles reached far into New England. Massachusetts Governor Edward Everett—drawing on the legislature's recent resolution—sent an agent to Richmond to bring Nahum Hazard home.[55]

A New York antislavery newspaper picked up the story of Nahum Hazard and praised the Massachusetts law for allowing the state to fulfill "one of the first duties of a government, the protection of the liberty of the subject." William Seward had become New York governor in January 1839 and was more sympathetic than Governor William Marcy, his predecessor, to the plight of kidnapped Black citizens of New York. Immediately on taking office, Seward told a Quaker abolitionist that "the state ought to assume the burden" when a kidnapped African American could not afford the "legal proceedings to recover his liberty." Later that year, New York abolitionists called on the state assembly to pass a law like the one in Massachusetts, "that our governors may be saved the pain of saying to a distressed father, as Gov Seward had to tell a worthy citizen the other day, when he applied for help to recover a kidnapped son, 'I will cheerfully do all that is in my power, I will write to the Governor of the State, but I have no authority to expend a dollar of money to rescue a citizen from slavery.'" The New York–based *Emancipator* noticed changing public opinion, publishing excerpts from papers in Massachusetts, New York, and Pennsylvania that expressed outrage at kidnapping and at southern-state laws that assumed that people of African descent were slaves. In May 1840, the New York legislature followed the lead of Massachusetts, passing a resolution providing public funds for agents designated by the governor to free Black citizens from southern jails.[56]

Across the free states, Black and white residents insisted that racially discriminatory laws were wrong and that no one—regardless of citizenship status—should be subjected to them. When interstate mobility was at issue, they argued that African American citizens of their home states were entitled to move freely within the United States and to enjoy protection of their rights wherever they traveled. In Massachusetts and Ohio, the issues presented themselves in distinct ways, and the struggles looked different. In Ohio, African Americans faced racially discriminatory laws that impinged on every facet of their existence. Black activists and their allies attacked those laws first. In Massachusetts, state laws were less offensive, but the state's many Black sailors faced injustice when merely pursuing their livelihoods. In both instances, however, activists targeted legislatures, seeking reforms at the state level and—in the case of Black sailors' citizenship—looking for ways to bring the issue to the attention of federal authorities. The new governor of New York hoped that would happen. Seward told a New York abolitionist that when it came to protecting the rights of free Black sailors in southern ports, the best course was either "to test the constitutionality of the laws of sister-states" in court or to seek "an act of Congress."[57] These were precisely the two options Massachusetts activists tried next.

CHAPTER 5

"SELF-PRESERVATION IS THE FIRST LAW OF NATURE"

*State-to-State Conflict and the Limits
of Congress in the 1840s*

IN JANUARY 1839, Gamaliel Bailey informed Joshua Giddings, the newly installed Whig congressman from Ashtabula County, Ohio, of the task ahead of him. Slaveholders in Congress were so "tremblingly alive to the slightest demonstration of hostility to their beloved institution," the *Philanthropist* editor wrote, that just about any antislavery proposal would trigger their outrage. "Only make a beginning," Bailey counseled. "It is only by aggression, that we can put a stop to the further encroachment of slavery."[1] For the next several years, Giddings, John Quincy Adams, and a few other antislavery Whigs in Congress did precisely as Bailey suggested.

Antislavery people well understood that introducing petitions was one way to keep slaveholders on edge. Petitioning was open to everyone and allowed perspectives that were marginalized from formal politics to make their way into the halls of power. The right to petition was ancient and revered, and the Constitution's framers had believed it important enough to mention in the First Amendment. According to convention, legislatures were obliged to respond to petitions. At slaveholders' behest, however, in 1836 the House had begun to refuse abolitionist petitions. The policy, which was renewed each year until 1844, was intended to suppress discussion of slavery. It accomplished just the opposite. Abolitionists inundated Congress with petitions, and the gag rule galvanized nonabolitionist northerners who saw it as an affront to basic principles of democracy and self-government. During the years 1833 to 1845, Americans submitted more than 8,600 slavery-related petitions to the US House of Representatives. Antislavery petitioners pushed Congress to abolish slavery in the District of Columbia and to outlaw the interstate slave trade. They broadened their horizons, submitting petitions that raised slavery-related issues without calling directly for abolition in hopes that their petitions would be less easily suppressed.[2]

The people of Massachusetts and Congressman John Quincy Adams found particularly ingenious ways of pressuring the system. Adams, the former president who first became a congressman at age sixty-four, was the most prominent and relentless congressional critic of the gag rule. He was a close ally of Giddings, who wrote to his wife in 1841 that Adams had "made the entire South tremble before him" and "opened a new era in our political history." In 1842, Adams took to the House floor to raise the problem of Black sailors' rights, and scores of eminent Massachusetts merchants soon joined a petition asking Congress to protect the rights of free Black sailors in southern ports. The next year, Adams introduced a resolution passed by the Massachusetts legislature that called on Congress to repeal the "three-fifths" clause of the Constitution.[3]

Antislavery allies did not have nearly the power they needed in the House, much less in the Senate, either to repeal the three-fifths clause or to pass legislation protecting northern Black sailors working in southern states. For the moment, then, the movement's strategy was to pursue what Gamaliel Bailey and others had suggested: to agitate, publicize, and incite slaveholders' outrage. In this respect, the Massachusetts proposals worked precisely as intended. They generated debate and yielded reports that congressmen could disseminate to constituents—all of which drew attention not just to slaveholders' power in the US government but also to violations of the civil rights of free African Americans. The Massachusetts legislature continued to provoke in other ways. It sent antislavery resolutions to southern state legislatures and, ultimately, dispatched agents to New Orleans and Charleston to search out imprisoned Black citizens and file suit in federal court to challenge state laws that deprived them of their liberty.

ANTISLAVERY PEOPLE TOOK THEIR FIGHT to Washington, DC, in new ways in the early 1840s, and with these efforts came new demands to protect free African Americans' civil rights. In the late 1830s and 1840s, questions associated with slavery and territorial conquest arrived regularly on Congress's agenda. Beginning in the mid-1830s, the United States fought a costly war against the Seminole people and other tribes in Florida, under the presumption that, when the war ended, Florida would join the Union as a slave state. In the Southwest, a mostly Anglo group of settlers fought to secure Texas's independence from Mexico and then pushed the US government to annex the slaveholding republic as a state. In both cases, congressional votes would determine whether slaveholding territories became states with full representation in Congress. Those conflicts and others allowed antislavery activists to continue developing their argument that an anxious and aristocratic Slave Power controlled the US government.[4]

The New York–based antislavery editor Joshua Leavitt became especially interested in helping sympathetic members of Congress fight the Slave Power. Leavitt spent time in Washington during the winter of 1841, meeting with such allies as Giddings and Adams and covering the session for his paper, the *Emancipator*. The next winter, Theodore Dwight Weld, who had done so much to organize abolitionists in Ohio in 1835, joined the antislavery lobby as a researcher with a desk in the Library of Congress.

There were by now several antislavery Whigs in the House. Adams and Giddings, the best-known and most politically skilled, were joined by William Slade of Vermont, Seth Gates of New Hampshire, and a few others. Most of the members of what Giddings called their "select committee" on antislavery lived together at a boardinghouse run by Ann Sprigg, frequently known as "Abolition House." Later in the 1840s, Abraham Lincoln, a one-term congressman from Illinois, lived there too, coming to know Giddings and several others in that circle and regularly—though not always—voting as they did.[5]

By the end of January 1842, the "select committee" had launched an antislavery onslaught that brought the question of Black sailors' rights into the House. Massachusetts congressmen took turns introducing petitions concerning slavery and related matters. The petitions demanded, among other things, that Congress protect fugitive slaves in the free states, abolish slavery in the District of Columbia or move the US capital, ensure "a republican form of Government" for every state, refuse to admit Florida as a slave state, and, of course, rescind the gag rule. Amid the maelstrom, Adams introduced a petition from "sundry colored seamen and citizens of the United States" seeking relief from "certain vexations" they experienced in ports in the southern United States and in Cuba, where Black sailors also faced arrest and incarceration upon arrival in Havana.[6]

A few days later, Adams faced censure by the House after introducing the most inflammatory petition yet: a request from forty-six citizens of Haverhill, Massachusetts, that Congress peaceably dissolve the Union rather than continue the untenable alliance between slave and free states. Adams recommended sending the Haverhill petition to a select committee with instructions to report "the reasons why" the request "should not be granted." That gesture did not spare Adams the wrath of Representative Thomas Gilmer of Virginia, who demanded that the House censure him for even introducing the idea of disunion. The southerners' strategy backfired as Adams held the floor for days, defending himself against censure. Giddings reported Adams's speeches as a triumph. The Massachusetts

congressman had shown how "the slave interest has insidiously crept into
our whole policy, subsidized our papers, poisoned our literature . . . fright-
ened our statesmen, and controlled the nation." Adams had humiliated his
southern adversaries while winning support from the "entire Whig party of
the North" and even the admiration of some Democrats. "He is, I believe,
the most extraordinary man living," Giddings effused.[7]

While refuting the censure, Adams demanded an investigation into
southern states' violations of Black sailors' rights. By this time, Alabama,
Georgia, Florida, and North Carolina had all passed laws that directly
targeted Black sailors. Those laws merely gave additional specificity to the
legal regimes that characterized all the slaveholding states, where authorities could incarcerate Black people virtually whenever they wanted by
exploiting laws that required free African Americans to carry passes and by
drawing on the prima facie principle, which permitted authorities to treat
all Black people as escaping slaves. Adams, intent on exposing abuses of
Black sailors, offered a slate of resolutions that included a request for State
Department records of earlier protests against South Carolina's Negro Seamen Act and, especially, Justice William Johnson's 1823 opinion declaring
the law unconstitutional. Adams knew such documents existed because he
had been secretary of state when South Carolina first passed its controversial law, and he had corresponded with Johnson about the conflict. He told
a correspondent that his goal was to meet southern congressmen's outrage
at the Haverhill petition with evidence that their own states routinely violated the Constitution by depriving free Black sailors of their rights under
the privileges and immunities clause.[8]

Members of the northern public were prepared to work in concert
with Adams and his allies. A wave of petitions flowed into the House,
reflecting widespread concern about southern states' infringements on
Black sailors' rights and on ship captains' ability to do business. In New
York City, William P. Powell, a Black abolitionist who had previously
lived in New Bedford, Massachusetts, and was strongly connected with
William Lloyd Garrison, had started a boardinghouse for Black sailors in

1839. Powell's home became a refuge and a place of political education. In the winter of 1842, some 220 self-identified "free Coloured citizens of the United States and State of New York"—likely organized with help from Powell—claimed that the Constitution guaranteed them "rights of life, liberty and the pursuits of happiness." In the course of working as sailors in South Carolina, Georgia, and Cuba, they said, many had been "arrested and thrust into lonesome prisons and dungeons," and all were "liable to be thus incarcerated . . . without any crime being brought or alleged against us except that of our complexion." The petitioners wanted Congress to protect them in their "lawfull business and constitutional rights and privileges as Citizens of the United States." Black sailors and their supporters in Boston sent a petition bearing sixty names, asking Congress to protect them from the "unjust and unconstitutional statutes" of the southern states. Among that petition's signers were Black abolitionists William Cooper Nell, Charles Lenox Remond, and Frederick Douglass, all of whom would become increasingly prominent figures in the movement.[9]

Ship captains also mobilized. From New York came a petition complaining that in Cuba and in the coastal US cities of Charleston, Savannah, Mobile, and New Orleans, their Black crew members could be "taken out of their vessels and incarcerated in prisons greatly to their prejudice and detriment of their interest." A group of "ship-owners, masters and seamen of Nantucket," Black as well as white, complained of the "perplexities and burdensome expenses" that not only required masters to pay for sailors' release from jail but also forced them to hire substitutes while in port to do the work normally required of seamen. The laws were still harder on Black sailors themselves, who were subjected to "loathsome jails" or forced to stay home "at the cost of abandoning their best means of an honest subsistence."[10]

Petitions were not confined to the Eastern Seaboard. Free African Americans regularly staffed Ohio River steamers that stopped in slaveholding states and sometimes traveled all the way down the Mississippi River to New Orleans. In 1835, the Ohio Anti-Slavery Society had noticed that Black sailors "suffer severe persecutions by coming in constant contact with slave laws." Trade on the Ohio River offered "employment to thousands of free colored men and women," recalled Black memoirist William H. Gibson of Louisville. To avoid arrest in New Orleans, free Black sailors sometimes pretended to be slaves belonging to some white person on their ship. Other times, Black sailors paid "a white woman or creole" to swear in court that they were local residents, not from out of state. When such schemes failed, he noted, free Black sailors faced sale and hard labor on the chain gang. Yet, Gibson remembered, "These cruel, unjust laws and punishments did not deter these free men and women from contesting and contending for the right to make a living on these great highways."[11]

Steamboat owners and merchants on the "Western Waters" were also inconvenienced by slave-state laws targeting Black sailors, and in 1843 they submitted a petition of their own. A Cincinnati-based group complained of the "great inconvenience & injury in the prosecution of their business" resulting from laws in Louisiana and Mississippi that prohibited the entry of free persons of color and subjected them "to impressment & other penalties, by which laws your memorialists are prevented from employing such persons as cooks, stewards, firemen or otherwise." The signers, asking for redress of "wrongs," said they believed the laws were "unjust to the colored persons themselves" and were "incompatible with the constitution of the united states." From Cincinnati, Salmon Chase informed Lewis Tappan of their actions and crowed: "Congress does not seem likely to have much rest from the exciting theme."[12] The petitions arrived at the US Capitol to support John Quincy Adams's effort to draw attention to southern state laws that impinged on the rights of free Black northerners. For the moment, however, they were tabled.

———————

BACK IN MASSACHUSETTS, where activists and legislators had been working for years on the problem of Black sailors' rights in southern ports, Adams's resolution spurred an initiative among elite men associated with maritime trade. In the spring of 1842, Jonathan Ingersoll Bowditch, a merchant and captain from a prominent family (and author of a renowned book on maritime navigation), organized a petition to Congress that garnered signatures from one hundred fifty-five of "the most respectable and distinguished citizens of Boston," some of whom were "owners and masters of vessels." Among the signers was Benjamin Robbins Curtis, who in 1857 would write a powerful dissent in the *Dred Scott* case.[13]

Like George Odiorne before him, Bowditch was not directly associated with the abolitionist movement, though his brother Henry, a physician, was an active participant and part of Boston's Liberty Party organization. Jonathan Bowditch's highly respectable petition was brief and to the point, and it adopted the language of constitutional citizenship that Massachusetts activists and politicians had honed over several years. In Charleston, Savannah, Mobile, and New Orleans, the petitioners asserted, "free persons of color" who labored on their ships were frequently "taken from the vessels, thrown into prison, and there detained at their own expense." The practice hurt the sailors themselves as well as commerce among the states, they said, and they asked Congress to grant sailors "relief, and render effectual in their behalf the privileges of citizenship secured by the Constitution of the United States." A draft cover letter in Bowditch's papers, unaddressed and undated, argued that the petition's august signers were most concerned "with the commerce of the country" and hoped that "no fancied connection of this subject with any others" would prevent Congress from paying attention.[14]

The Bowditch petition did not find its way to Congress until the next session, which began in December 1842. By then, Robert C. Winthrop, a Whig, had agreed to introduce it. Although generally known as a conservative, Winthrop had won George Bradburn's admiration when, as speaker of the Massachusetts House of Representatives in 1839, he had supported Bradburn's push for action on behalf of Black sailors.[15] Winthrop now took up the challenge of bringing Bowditch's petition before the House and consulted with Adams about how to avoid having it tabled under the gag rule. He decided to give the petition to the clerk of the House, a move that guaranteed that it would be sent directly to a committee. Regardless of which committee received it, Winthrop told Bowditch in a private letter, the ensuing report

> can, of course, propose no very definite action. Congress cannot reach the State Laws. The Courts are alone competent to act on the subject, & even they would find it hard to get at them. The most that can be done by a Committee, is to recognize the seizure of free colored sailors as a violation of their privileges as Citizens, & the Laws under which the seizure takes place, as a violation of the Constitution of the United States.

After some deliberation, Winthrop decided to send the petition to the House Committee on Commerce, of which he was a member, rather than to the Judiciary Committee.[16] The tabled petitions submitted the previous winter—from sailors and captains in Massachusetts, New York, and Ohio—were filed with the papers of the Committee on Commerce.

Against prevailing convictions that states had virtually unlimited power over their own "domestic police," Winthrop and his allies looked for a way to justify congressional intervention, and they advanced the idea that southern laws that targeted Black sailors infringed on Congress's power over the "commerce of the country." The Marshall court in the 1810s and 1820s had begun to delineate the meanings of the Constitution's commerce clause, amplifying congressional power over interstate commerce in an effort to knit the disparate nation together. But the court had avoided taking up the relationship of human movement to commerce, or what Marshall called the question of "men" rather than "merchandise."[17] Was the movement of people across state lines—whether in the course of work or immigration or internal migration—part of commerce and therefore in Congress's domain? For many years, the Supreme Court gave no answer.

Yet ship captains regularly claimed—as northern captains had done in 1821 when they protested the South Carolina Negro Seamen Act—that state laws regulating people's mobility across state lines conflicted with Congress's power to regulate commerce.

The ship captains who litigated this question most successfully were not those who were inconvenienced by policies that constrained Black sailors but, rather, those in the business of bringing foreign immigrants to the United States. The first major Supreme Court decision on foreign immigration and the commerce clause was *New York v. Miln* (1837). The case involved state statutes generally known as passenger laws, which required captains to report the name and status of persons arriving on their ships and often to post bonds on behalf of passengers deemed paupers or likely to become public charges. States expected captains to transfer the expense of such bonds to their passengers, thus raising the cost of migration and potentially reducing shippers' business. In *Miln,* captains seeking to free themselves from such regulation argued in federal court that New York's passenger laws were void because they conflicted with Congress's power to regulate commerce that moved across state lines.[18]

The court—whose tenor had changed dramatically with Chief Justice John Marshall's death in 1835 and the addition of seven justices appointed during or immediately after Jackson's presidency—upheld the passenger laws on grounds that they were a legitimate exercise of the state's police powers. Justice Philip P. Barbour of Virginia penned the *Miln* decision. As a congressman in 1821, Barbour had vociferously defended the Black exclusion clause of the Missouri Constitution. Barbour now determined that "persons" were not "the subject of commerce" and therefore Congress did not have exclusive jurisdiction over the movement of people across state lines. New York's immigration laws, he said, were entirely appropriate uses of the state's power to "regulate internal police." New York, more than perhaps any other state in the country, he said, was "exposed to the evil of thousands of foreign emigrants arriving there, and the consequent danger of her citizens being subjected to a heavy charge in the maintenance of those who are poor. It is the duty of the state to protect its citizens from this evil."[19] The *Miln* decision was a boon for New York and other states seeking to strengthen their regulations on immigration.

Many people recognized the implications of *Miln* for questions of interstate migration and, in particular, for the movement of free African Americans. During arguments, one of the lawyers for New York, defending the passenger laws, cautioned that if the court decided that the commerce clause gave Congress exclusive jurisdiction over "the admission of passengers from Europe," then the power to regulate "the arrival of passengers by land" would also fall under Congress's authority. "If the one be exclusive [to Congress], the other is exclusive; and all vagrant laws, all poor laws, and police regulations, become, at once, solely of federal jurisdiction," he warned. Among the state laws that would likely be invalidated were those that regulated the migration of free African Americans, as well as those that limited the entry of enslaved people transported in the interstate slave trade. These issues, too, would "become the subjects of federal jurisdiction, and the state laws are abrogated." Barbour avoided this scenario with his holding that passenger laws—and by extension other state laws, many of them drawn from the poor-law tradition, that regulated people as they arrived—concerned matters of "internal police." Such measures were required to "advance the safety, happiness and prosperity of its people, and to provide for the general welfare."[20]

Congressman Winthrop had suggested that the federal courts would find it "hard to get at" southern laws, and that was true in many respects. First, the *Miln* decision suggested that the Supreme Court would be unsympathetic to the argument that state laws targeting free Black sailors violated the commerce clause. But that did not mean there were no other possibilities for challenging such laws. *Miln* was just one case, dealing with one kind of state law and making one kind of constitutional argument—an argument about the commerce clause. What of the privileges and immunities clause (Article IV, Section 2) and its applicability to free African

Americans? The Supreme Court had never heard a case on the question. To make the situation more complicated, back in 1823, Justice William Johnson had identified an impediment to getting such a case into federal court. Lawyers for the Black British sailor Henry Elkison had asked Johnson to issue a writ of habeas corpus that would remove him from the custody of the Charleston sheriff and bring him before the federal circuit court. Many saw the writ of habeas corpus, a staple of English common law, as the foundation of individual liberty because it enabled people held in custody to be brought before a judge who could assess the validity of their incarceration. Yet Johnson said he was powerless to do as the lawyers had requested. The laws governing the federal judiciary did not permit a federal judge to issue a writ of habeas corpus for a prisoner held by local or state authorities.[21] Thus, the Elkison case had highlighted a critical problem: How could the federal courts assess the constitutionality of a state law if the potential plaintiff had already been taken into state custody? If people arrested under such laws were, by definition, held by local or state officials, how could the federal courts establish jurisdiction? Without enhancement of the powers of the federal judiciary, the answer was far from clear.

Advocates for the rights of free Black people were looking for ways around this problem. Since at least the incarceration of Gilbert Horton in 1826, antislavery people had talked of a federal court challenge to laws that restricted the mobility of free African Americans. In the Horton case, the idea was to test the law in the US Circuit Court for the District of Columbia, from which appeal could be made to the US Supreme Court. In the spring of 1842, the Massachusetts legislature renewed its crusade on behalf of Black sailors by passing resolutions that called for a test of the southern laws in federal court.[22] In the meantime, prominent Massachusetts residents had forwarded their concerns to Congress, publicizing abuses of Black sailors in southern ports and insisting that Congress had the power—whether under the commerce clause or the privileges and immunities clause—to nullify state laws that unconstitutionally infringed on the liberty of free African Americans.

RESPONDING TO THE Boston merchants' petition, the House Committee on Commerce produced a report that argued, strongly and unequivocally, that free African Americans were entitled to move at will across American jurisdictions and that the southern-state laws that constrained them were unconstitutional. The report, authored by Robert Winthrop and supported by seven of the nine committee members, drew heavily on Justice William Johnson's 1823 decision in the Elkison case. It argued that southerners' treatment of free Black sailors violated the Constitution in three separate ways. Where American-born sailors were concerned, the practice violated the Constitution's privileges and immunities clause, which held that the "citizens of each state shall be entitled to all privileges and immunities of citizens in the several states." Where it involved sailors from nations with which the United States had treaty agreements, it infringed on Congress's treaty-making power. And finally, it violated Congress's power over interstate and international commerce. It was "monstrous," the committee argued, that people charged with no crime could be seized, incarcerated, and denied legal processes to determine their guilt or innocence—and that they could be whipped or even sold into slavery. States possessed significant powers to make their own "police regulations," but those powers could "never be permitted" to violate citizens' "constitutional privileges" or to render entire classes of people suspect based on "distinctions which originate in their birth, and which are as permanent as their being."[23] This was a powerful indictment of the laws on both moral and constitutional grounds.

Yet the committee remained doubtful about Congress's power to act. The nation's legislature "seem[ed] to have no means of affording such relief, or of effecting such a repeal," it observed. As Winthrop had written in his private letter to Bowditch, the conventional view was that under the Constitution, Congress could not "reach state laws" such as these. Bowditch had suggested to Winthrop that even if the Constitution did not permit Congress to repeal or directly nullify the laws, Congress might be able to intervene in enforcement, perhaps by making it a federal offense to imprison sailors "without proper legal authority" or by prohibiting anyone who had enforced such a law from holding federal office in the future.[24] Yet those ideas did not make it into Winthrop's committee's report, which only went so far as to offer a set of resolutions denouncing the noxious state laws.

The committee's majority report professed high ideals but proved a dead end in terms of lawmaking, while the minority report—authored by Kenneth Rayner, a North Carolina Whig—was less idealistic but more consistent with contemporary understandings of federalism and power. Rayner's report, echoing the 1831 opinion written by Attorney General John Berrien, argued that the original South Carolina Negro Seamen Act, passed in the aftermath of a threatened slave conspiracy, was a "means of safety, of protection, of self-defence, forced on [the state] by stern necessity." Other southern states had followed South Carolina's model, he claimed, out of concern for "self-preservation" brought on by what they saw as the destabilizing impact of the abolitionist movement. Rayner rejected the argument that the laws violated the Constitution's privileges and immunities clause, quoting Joseph Story's *Commentaries on the Constitution* and its argument that the clause was intended "to communicate all the privileges and immunities which the citizens of the same State would be entitled to under the like circumstances." As Rayner put it, "The 'privileges and immunities' of citizenship mentioned in the Constitution must refer to those of the State *in* which, and not to the State *from* which, the citizen happens to be."[25] A free Black man might be a citizen of Massachusetts, but when he was in South Carolina, he had the status of other free Black men in that state: that is, he was not a citizen there and need not be treated as such.

It likely pleased Rayner to quote a prominent Massachusetts jurist in support of his argument, and Rayner drove home his point by suggesting that northerners be careful what they wished for. One of the privileges and immunities of a South Carolina "citizen," he said, was to "seize his runaway slave wherever he finds him." In *Commonwealth v.*

Aves, however, the Massachusetts Supreme Court had decided that if a slaveowner carried a slave into the state, the slave was, in Rayner's words, "*ipso facto,* a free man, and the master cannot reclaim him."[26] The Massachusetts court had refused to recognize slaveholders' rights as citizens, Rayner suggested, yet Massachusetts petitioners now wanted Congress to reach into southern states' affairs to protect the privileges and immunities of Black citizens. If Congress could do that, Rayner implied, then it could surely also demand that *Commonwealth v. Aves* be ignored and that northern states respect the property claims of white citizens who brought their slaves into free states.

The problem that Black sailors and their allies faced in Congress was both constitutional and political. The constitutional problem was federalism itself and the Tenth Amendment principle that the states (or "the people") retained all powers not delegated to the federal government or prohibited to the states. This system offered few opportunities for federal oversight over how state governments managed their own populations. There was no constitutional guarantee that all people living in the United States would be free, or that all free people would enjoy even the most basic rights to personal liberty or due process of law. The Constitution did not prohibit racial discrimination in state laws or define who was a citizen and what the rights and obligations of citizenship were. State and local governments set the rules that governed people's lives. When state and local officials enforced racially discriminatory laws against free people of African descent, there were few constitutional channels through which to appeal to the federal government for help.

With enough political will, however, many things were possible under the US Constitution. If antislavery people had been in charge, Congress might well have found a way to try to protect Black sailors. It might have adopted measures tailored to enforcement, such as those suggested by Bowditch, or passed legislation designed to enforce the privileges and immunities clause, just as it had passed legislation in 1793 to enforce the Constitution's fugitive slave clause. But in the Congress of

1842–43—and in every other Congress until the Civil War—there was no such will. Southern legislators deeply feared the migration of free Black people into their jurisdictions. They recoiled at the ideas that Black sailors might disseminate and the influence they might gain. Many northern state governments likewise feared the northward migration of free African Americans, and any federal law that clarified that Black citizens were entitled to the same privileges and immunities as white citizens would likewise impinge on northern states' authority. Perhaps it is not surprising, then, that although a decisive majority on the House Committee on Commerce viewed state laws targeting Black sailors as unconstitutional, that same majority believed that all Congress could do was pass disapproving resolutions. And when Robert Winthrop introduced those resolutions, the House promptly tabled them.[27]

Yet the investigation sparked by the Bowditch petition had not been in vain. It advanced the question of Black sailors' rights into Congress, providing the opportunity to revisit and amplify twenty years of resistance to southern laws under whose authority free Black sailors were subjected to abuse, incarceration, and enslavement. The majority report itself, with its seven signatories, suggested that the will to challenge racist laws was growing. Still more significant was the vote of the House, over the objection of several southerners, to publish five thousand copies of the majority and minority reports, together with documents illustrating the history of the debate since 1823. Opposition to printing the report was an attempt by the "Jackson jackals" to "suppress circulation among the people," John Quincy Adams wrote in his journal. His side had prevailed, and the report was available to be mailed to constituents.[28]

———————

THE ABOLITIONIST MOVEMENT's political arm had gained considerable strength in Massachusetts by the early 1840s, leading the state legislature to take ever-more-audacious positions on slavery and the rights of free African Americans. In the late 1830s, some of the free states' most committed abolitionists had turned their attention to party politics. Believing that both major parties were in the thrall of the Slave Power, many moved toward forming a third party capable of upsetting traditional rivalries and perhaps drawing in disillusioned Whigs and Democrats. The result was the Liberty Party, which coalesced first in New York in 1839 and then, after the 1840 presidential election, in Ohio. From its inception, Liberty Party organizing efforts in Massachusetts divided abolitionist societies, as William Lloyd Garrison insisted with growing vehemence that abolitionists must avoid formal politics. The nation's founders had made a "guilty and fatal compromise" with slavery, Garrison wrote in the spring of 1842, and abolitionists ought to "withdraw from the embraces of the monster"— meaning from any activities sanctioned by the US Constitution, including local politics. Others, including many of Garrison's erstwhile allies, came to a different conclusion. When George Bradburn of Nantucket joined the Liberty Party, Garrison was unsparing in his criticism: "Poor man!" the abolitionist leader wrote to a friend. "There is more of the politician than of the Christian in his composition, and therefore he clings to political action, even if it must be at the expense of principle."[29]

The Massachusetts Liberty Party made significant advances in the fall of 1842, amid a hard-fought struggle to secure the freedom of a fugitive slave named George Latimer, who, along with his wife Rebecca, had escaped slavery in Norfolk, Virginia. The couple traveled by ship to Boston, but they were soon discovered by a former employee of Latimer's owner. Slavecatchers seized George, while Rebecca found refuge in the home of abolitionists. Judge Joseph Story, in keeping with his understanding of the requirements of the 1793 federal Fugitive Slave Act, ordered Boston authorities to detain Latimer while his status was adjudicated. Black and white abolitionists resisted fiercely, demonstrating in the streets and pressuring public officials for his release. The jailer eventually declared that he could no longer keep Latimer behind bars, whereupon the owner's agent reluctantly agreed to accept the offer made by attorney Samuel Sewell, a Liberty Party leader, to purchase Latimer's freedom. The Liberty Party had mobilized quickly and effectively in the maelstrom, and it saw results in that season's elections. The Liberty Party's influence, along with growing antislavery sentiment among regular Whigs and Democrats, dramatically shaped the winter 1843 legislative session in Massachusetts. Not only did the general assembly continue advocating for the rights of Black sailors in southern ports. It also repealed the state's ban on interracial marriage and, responding to the Latimer crisis, passed a personal liberty law forbidding public officials from participating in fugitive slave renditions.[30]

Amid all the ferment, the Massachusetts assembly adopted an audacious resolution calling on Congress to repeal the US Constitution's three-fifths clause. The clause represented a compromise struck at the 1787 constitutional convention. The question was how to count the population of the United States for the purpose of apportioning representatives to the US House of Representatives (and for imposing direct taxes). The decision also shaped the electoral college, where representation was linked to apportionment in the House. Delegates from states with large enslaved populations had wanted slaves counted as persons to give their states maximal weight. By contrast, some delegates from the northern states had argued that slaves should not be counted at all, because slaveholders claimed them as property and largely did not recognize their legal personhood. In the end, the convention arrived at the compromise position that for purposes of enumeration, each slave would count as three-fifths of a person. As elsewhere in the Constitution, the framers alluded to slaves as "persons" in this clause, writing that the number of representatives to which a state was entitled depended on the "the whole Number of free Persons . . . excluding Indians not taxed" plus three-fifths of "all other Persons." But that was small consolation for enslaved people themselves and for others who loathed slavery. The three-fifths clause acknowledged that human bondage would continue in the new nation, and it enhanced the slaveholding regions' power in the federal government.[31]

Some antislavery Americans never reconciled themselves to the three-fifths clause, but, given the explosiveness of the slavery question in

American politics, there was considerable pressure to accept it as a prereq-uisite of Union. The issue had become heated when New England Federal-ists protested the War of 1812 on grounds that southerners had provoked it to protect slavery and blamed the three-fifths clause for helping slavehold-ers secure their hold on federal power. The Republicans, then the domi-nant party, blasted the Federalists as unpatriotic, and for years afterward, slaveholders and their allies linked demands for repeal of the three-fifths clause with Federalist elitism and disloyalty to the nation. After amending its charter twelve times in the first two decades of nationhood, the country entered a period of constitutional stasis, and the Constitution became a sacred symbol of national cohesion. As party configurations shifted, politi-cal leaders of all stripes increasingly insisted that constitutional compro-mises over slavery had made the nation itself possible, and that to criticize pro-slavery provisions such as the fugitive slave clause and the three-fifths clause was, essentially, to advocate disunion. The nation's survival, they said, depended on leaving the Constitution undisturbed.[32]

Most Liberty Party leaders and antislavery Whigs of the 1840s avoided criticizing the Constitution directly and argued instead that slavery could be abolished without altering it. Some Libertyites insisted that slavery was unconstitutional everywhere, and that Congress already had the power to abolish it in the states. But most took pains to acknowledge that Congress lacked authority to regulate or abolish slavery in the states where it already existed. In its founding charter, the Ohio Anti-Slavery Society affirmed "that the several States and Congress have, by our Federal constitution, the exclusive right to legislate for the abolition of slavery in their respective lim-its." In 1839, William Jay cautioned that Congress must never "be guilty of the consummate folly and wickedness of passing a law emancipating the slaves held under State authority" or "the Union would most unquestion-ably be rent in twain." Three years later, the Ohio abolitionist Leicester King cast the state's Liberty Party as a constitutionally conservative orga-nization, writing: "We ask no amendment of the Constitution, we seek no evasion of its obligations, we justify no infringement of its provisions, we desire no violation of the national compact, the principles of the Constitution, or of laws made in conformity to them." Garrison and his allies considered such concessions immoral. Liberty Party leaders and antislavery Whigs viewed them as realistic and politically useful. By arguing for a gradual end to slavery under the existing Constitution and representing the Constitution's relationship to slavery in a way that meshed with actual practice, political antislavery activists hoped to broaden their appeal well beyond the tiny group drawn to Garrison and his absolutist approach.[33]

In 1839, Congressman John Quincy Adams took the unusual step of introducing a constitutional amendment that would end slavery gradually, but his intent was to make a political statement, not to push for the measure's adoption. Adams abhorred slavery, but he was tired of abolitionists who imagined slaveholders would end it voluntarily or who called on Congress to abolish it in the states. He believed Congress did not have the power to interfere with slavery in the states where it existed, and he felt that slavery would only end by war or constitutional amendment. His proposal was modeled on gradual emancipation statutes from Pennsylvania and New York and provided that all persons born in the United States after July 4, 1842, would be free. It made no mention of colonization, nor of compensation for slaveholders. Adams later wrote that he had "no expectation" that the House would receive or discuss the proposal. Rather, he presented it "to the *petitioners,* as comprising the only mode by which I believe the abolition of slavery could possibly be effected without violence and without injustice."[34] Adams's amendment was a reminder of how difficult it would be to abolish slavery. Perhaps at some future time, both houses of Congress would pass an abolition amendment by the necessary two-thirds majority, and three-quarters of the states would ratify it. In 1839, however, that possibility was virtually unimaginable.

The Massachusetts legislature's 1843 call for an amendment repealing the Constitution's three-fifths clause did a different kind of work. The proposal that representatives would be apportioned based solely on a state's population of "free persons, excluding Indians not taxed," was at odds with

the constitutional conservatism that often characterized antislavery politics. Yet it was consistent with another aspect of the political antislavery
movement: the focus on the Slave Power. Liberty Party activists and their
allies regularly drew attention to the remarkable power that slaveholding
interests enjoyed in the US government. They provided pointed account-
ings of the large numbers of presidents, speakers of the House, presidents
pro tem of the Senate, Supreme Court justices, and cabinet officials who
had come from slaveholding states. They argued, rightly, that the three-
fifths clause was an important foundation of this injustice. As activists
often noted, the three-fifths clause meant that in the US House of Representatives, four free northerners had the same representation as one slaveholder plus five enslaved people whom he could buy and sell as chattel.
With an unfair advantage in apportionment in the House, and therefore
in the electoral college, the slave states in fact garnered far more power
in Congress and the presidency—and therefore also in the executive and
judicial branches of government—than their free population warranted.
The clause also provided an incentive for southerners to increase slavehold-
ings: The more enslaved people who lived in a district or state, the greater
the state's power in Washington. Moreover, Libertyite activists argued, the
clause essentially used a "property" basis for representation. That is, it gave
people who owned a particular kind of property greater political power
than those who did not—a situation that, they argued, smacked of aristocratic privilege rather than republicanism.

On December 21, 1843, John Quincy Adams introduced in the US
Congress the proposed constitutional amendment that his state legislature
had so audaciously requested and suggested that it be referred to a select
committee of nine congressmen that he would chair. Americans across the
free states soon added their own calls for repeal of the three-fifths clause.
Writing from LaPorte County, Indiana, petitioners suggested that if the
ostensible human chattel belonging to white southerners continued to be
enumerated, then "the animals belonging to the free states" should likewise be counted. Residents of Ashtabula County, Ohio, objected that "one

portion of the United States should have a property representation while the other has not." "We enthusiastically prize the Union of the States," the Ohioans wrote, "yet if the Constitution cannot be so amended, we should prefer to have the Union amicably dissolved." The "additional representatives" gained by the slaveholding states as a result of the three-fifths clause, wrote a group from Brooklyn, New York, "are not elected by the persons to whom they are apportioned, but by others who claim these persons as their chattels." That winter, the Massachusetts legislature—which had shifted from a Democratic to a Whig majority—again passed the repeal resolution to show that it had strong bipartisan support.[35]

Adams's nine-member committee returned with a recommendation that the motion be tabled—a result that was not surprising, given the composition of the committee. But the report offered Adams and Joshua Giddings another chance to publicize their goals and principles. It helped inform the northern public of the way the Constitution not only protected slavery in the states but also bolstered Slave Power dominance of the US government. During the House debate on the Massachusetts proposal, when southerners charged Massachusetts with fomenting disunion by proposing the amendment, Giddings had presented a resolution affirming "that the right of amendment extends as clearly to that portion of said Constitution which fixes the ratio of Federal representation as to any other part of the instrument." His resolution had been swiftly tabled. Now the two men had coauthored a report that declared "slave representation . . . repugnant to the first and vital principle of republican popular representation."[36]

Antislavery congressmen were growing adept at using the tools available to them, as a political minority, to amplify their voices. They continued to fight the gag rule itself, but they also found ways around it. They introduced petitions like those for the protection of Black sailors and for the repeal of the three-fifths clause, ensuring that they were sent to committees. They knew they could count on antislavery activists across the free states to support their efforts with petitions of their own. Their work generated reports that they could send back out to constituents. Their abrasive tactics and grandstanding elicited coverage in the press, as did the outsize reactions they provoked from slave-state representatives. The House was not going to pass favorable legislation on these issues, to say nothing of the Senate. But through these other means, men such as Adams and Giddings delivered the struggle against slavery, and for racial equality in civil rights, into the heart of the federal government.

In some ways, however, the work of antislavery petitioners and congressmen in the early 1840s also illuminated an impasse. Slavery itself was protected in the states. The three-fifths clause, however unrepublican, was politically unassailable, and there was no chance Congress would take seriously a gradual emancipation amendment like the one Adams proposed in 1839. Meanwhile, the Constitution could not be wielded to protect the rights of Black sailors, at least not in the prevailing political climate. And even if a federal court did take up the constitutionality of laws that targeted Black sailors, it might well find, in keeping with the *Miln* decision, that the laws did not violate either the privileges and immunities clause or the commerce clause. It seemed abundantly clear that movements for racial equality had to remain within the states themselves, or else that something very dramatic needed to change at the federal level.

Some imagined the impasse would not last forever. For Garrisonians in the 1840s, the answer was to seek dissolution of the Union. William Seward, the Whig ex-governor of New York, imagined something different: a future moment when antislavery people might be in a position to change the Constitution. Noting Americans' veneration for the Constitution and perpetual fears of civil war, in 1845 Seward told Liberty Party leaders in Ohio that when an "independent Congress" was finally elected, "Amendments to the constitution may be initiated, and the obstacles in the way of emancipation will no longer appear insurmountable."[37] Elsewhere, Seward observed that "the apparent hopelessness" of efforts to reform the Constitution drove many "to the conclusion that Slavery can never be abolished." Yet he continued to believe there was reason for optimism. He told Salmon Chase that the challenge was less in the amendment process stipulated by the Constitution than in the lack of "popular conviction." New Yorkers, he said, had grown frustrated with their 1821 constitution and had decided to draft an entirely new one. With popular approval, the old constitution had been "subverted and a new one established. . . . It was a Revolution, but a peaceful one, by general consent." The New York story offered a lesson about what could happen at the federal level. "If Slavery will not suffer amendment of the Constitution in a constitutional way, the Constitution will nevertheless be amended, when the People need and will it."[38] Speaking in Cleveland during the 1848 political season, Seward exhorted, "Whenever the public mind shall will the abolition of slavery, the way will open for it."[39] He could not have known, of course, that for the United States, the revolution that would bring about the constitutional abolition of slavery would be violent indeed.

———

For decades before the Civil War, there were no constitutional amendments and there was no congressional intervention on behalf of free African Americans. And so the conflict over the three-fifths clause and the rights of Black sailors in southern ports reverted to the states. Within the federalist system, states sometimes functioned like small nations, with diplomatic rules and customs invoked during conflicts conducted in more-or-less-polite terms. State legislatures instructed their governors to send to their counterparts in other states copies of newly passed laws or resolutions. That was what slave states had done in 1835, when they had asked free-state legislatures to take steps to silence abolitionists. Virginia and Kentucky officials regularly expressed displeasure at Ohioans' lack of interest in returning alleged fugitives from slavery. The Virginia legislature was outraged with New York, starting in 1839, because the state refused to extradite three Black sailors accused of helping a slave escape; Virginia retaliated by subjecting all New York ships to rigorous inspection as they departed its ports. A succession of Maine governors likewise refused to extradite to Georgia two white men indicted for aiding a fugitive slave.[40]

In the spring of 1843, the Massachusetts legislature raised the ante by voting to send official agents to major southern port cities, the latest in the legislature's series of efforts to protect the rights of Black citizens. During that legislative session, several well-known "Colored Citizens, and Seamen" of Boston, including William Cooper Nell, Frederick Douglass, and Charles Lenox Remond, had urged state officials to bring the question of Black sailors' rights before the US Supreme Court. Jonathan Bowditch and his allies also had asked the state to send agents to Charleston and New Orleans in an effort to find all Massachusetts "citizens" imprisoned "on account of their color," secure their release, and bring suit in federal court. The legislature complied, instructing the governor to appoint agents in New Orleans and Charleston, for one year, to determine how many Massachusetts citizens were imprisoned there and to find a way to initiate a lawsuit.[41]

The state's first effort to appoint such agents came to absolutely nothing. Governor Marcus Morton tried to select men who already resided in each southern city. In Charleston, he chose Benjamin F. Hunt, a Massachusetts native who had lived in South Carolina for decades. Word of Hunt's commission evidently leaked out before he even received direct notice from the governor, and Hunt took to the *Charleston Courier* to announce that he was refusing the assignment. In fact, he reminded readers, two decades earlier as a state legislator he had voted for the original Negro Seamen Act, and he had served as the state's lawyer in the 1823 Elkison case. He had no intention, he stated, of doing anything on behalf of the Massachusetts governor or his constituents. The prospective agent in New Orleans, John A. Maybin, according to one report, "declined the office on the ground that it was incompatible with the duties he owed to the State of which he was a citizen."[42]

Meanwhile, southern legislatures responded with hostile resolutions that they sent zinging from state to state, the tone growing ever more rancorous. Responding to the Massachusetts demands that southern states respect the liberty of free Black sailors, the Georgia legislature deplored such "sickly effusions of a wild and restless fanaticism" and declared that "Negroes, or persons of color, are not citizens under the Constitution of the United States, and that Georgia will never recognize such citizenship." Florida's territorial legislature was quick to side with its neighbor to the north. With a vast coastline and innumerable harbors and ports, Florida also needed "wise laws, prudently but certainly enforced, against the introduction of a population calculated to corrupt and render discontented our slaves." To northerners who might object, the Florida legislature issued a warning grounded in police powers: "Let them remember that self-preservation is the first law of nature; and that, whilst they continue to brandish the incendiary torch, we shall endeavor to throw around our homes and firesides all those safeguards which the constitution permits, and public and private security demands."[43]

Several southern legislatures also disparaged the Massachusetts proposal to repeal the three-fifths clause. In resolutions passed in mid-February 1844, the Virginia legislature condemned the abolitionist movement and charged that Massachusetts's real purpose was to "dissolve the Union." In keeping with protocols for communication among the states, the Virginians instructed their governor to transmit its resolutions to other states. Breaking with tradition, however, they also instructed the governor to "return the original resolutions" to the Massachusetts governor. The new Massachusetts governor, George Nixon Briggs, received the Virginians' provocative gesture and urged the legislature to respond firmly. The lawmakers in turn issued a joint report affirming, on behalf of "the people of Massachusetts," that they had proposed repeal of the three-fifths clause "in truth and in good faith," seeking not to destroy the Union but rather to advance "a principle which is essential to its stability and permanence."[44]

In the spring of 1844, after another request by the legislature, Governor Briggs appointed men who would need to travel, in the manner of diplomats, to what appeared increasingly foreign domains, where they would attempt to deal with governments that did not share their values. Briggs chose as his envoy to Charleston Samuel Hoar, a former congressman and esteemed lawyer. Hoar, who was in his sixties and had retired from the bar, was not associated with the abolitionist movement, though during his one term in Washington he had argued for outlawing slavery in the District of Columbia. Hoar ventured to Charleston with his adult daughter, Elizabeth, and carried with him the names of several African American sailors who were believed to be imprisoned in Charleston, including two in whose names he felt authorized to begin a lawsuit in federal circuit court that could be appealed to the US Supreme Court.[45]

The Hoars arrived in Charleston early in the morning of November 28, 1844, and Samuel Hoar informed the governor of his portfolio. The governor, in turn, urged the South Carolina General Assembly to "maintain the police regulations" of the state. Meanwhile, Charleston officials greeted Hoar with obfuscation and threats of violence. The sheriff demanded his credentials and insinuated that he could not protect Hoar if a mob formed. Hoar insisted that he had come on official business and would not be dissuaded. As rumblings of riot continued, members of the Charleston elite entreated Hoar to leave. The owner of the hotel where the Hoars were staying wanted them out. Finally, after a weeklong standoff and continuing threats, locals made clear that Hoar and his daughter could either walk or be dragged to a carriage that would convey them to a ship and points north. At that point, Hoar realized he had no other good option. He paid his bill at the hotel, Elizabeth joined him, and together they stepped into the carriage.[46]

The South Carolina General Assembly responded to Hoar's mission with a righteous defense of the state's police powers. South Carolina was entitled to exclude "conspirators against the public peace, and disaffected persons whose presence may be dangerous to their safety," the assembly declared. That right was "everywhere exercised by independent States," and South Carolina had never ceded to the federal government "her right of internal government and police." Echoing views that were commonplace even among northern legal theorists like James Kent and Joseph Story, a subcommittee of the assembly asserted that laws aimed at restricting Black sailors did not violate the Constitution's privileges and immunities clause.

Black citizens of Massachusetts were entitled to no "greater rights, immunities and privileges, within our territories, than are enjoyed by persons of the same class in South Carolina." Going still further and repeating Georgia's declaration of a couple of years earlier, the assembly added provocatively: "But your Committee deny that they are citizens, within the meaning of the Constitution." With just one dissenting member in each house, the legislature voted to instruct the governor to expel Hoar from the state.[47] By that time, Hoar was already on his way.

The South Carolina General Assembly next passed a law designed to make it even harder for unjustly imprisoned Black sailors to get a hearing in court by denying them access to the writ of habeas corpus. Across the slave states, free Black people hoping to demonstrate that they were being illegally imprisoned frequently used habeas corpus to force an investigation into the reasons for their incarceration. Access to this process was widely considered a common-law privilege to which all people were entitled. South Carolina now rejected common-law tradition by denying even this basic right to African Americans. The US Constitution prohibited suspension of the writ of habeas corpus, but that provision was part of Article I, meaning it was most readily understood as a bar on Congress. As in so many other areas, the states were technically left to do largely as they pleased when it came to individual rights.[48]

In New Orleans, the Massachusetts emissary, Henry Hubbard, faced less overt hostility but was no more successful than Hoar. The Louisiana governor tried to handle the matter quietly. He first ignored Hubbard's missives and then sent the New England–born Jacob Barker to visit Hubbard at his hotel. Barker, who had done a great deal to rescue free Black northerners from New Orleans jails, embraced the governor's purpose and took along four locals to ensure that no one could later accuse him of colluding with the visiting Yankee. Barker duly warned Hubbard that he would make no progress in securing the freedom of Massachusetts citizens incarcerated in New Orleans jails and that, in fact, his own life would be in danger if he remained in the city. Hubbard was quickly persuaded. In a long letter to Governor Briggs, he explained that he had abandoned the mission not merely out of fear for his own life but also from the conviction that the task was completely futile. Jacob Barker was above all an opportunist who picked his battles. He continued his banking business in New Orleans, and when Benjamin Butler and the US Army arrived in 1862 to crush the rebellion, he was quick to offer the general personal loans and otherwise serve the Union cause.[49]

Responding to the spate of interstate conflicts prompted by the Massachusetts resolutions and to Hoar's trip to South Carolina, the Alabama legislature heralded the powerful principle of domestic police cherished by Americans of all regions. Massachusetts was now working against the "*domestic police* of the South, founded in the highest State necessity," the Alabamians complained. Quoting directly from *New York v. Miln,* the 1837 decision that upheld state-level immigration regulations, the Alabama legislature insisted that South Carolina had "the same authority for the enactment of these laws, as she would have—'to provide precautionary measures against the moral pestilence of paupers, vagabonds or convicts.'" As if to add an exclamation point, the Alabama declaration finished with a lengthy quotation from Justice John McLean, the Ohioan who in the 1817 *Carneal* case had ruled that Ohio was free territory. In a concurring opinion in the 1841 case of *Groves v. Slaughter,* McLean had supported the power of states to bar the sale of slaves from out of state. "Each state has a right to guard its citizens against the inconveniences and dangers of a slave population. The right to exercise this power, by a State, is higher and deeper than the Constitution. . . . Its power to guard against, or to remedy the evil, rests upon the law of self-preservation; a law vital to every community and especially to a sovereign state."[50] McLean, the most openly antislavery justice on the US Supreme Court, used the logic of self-preservation—the same logic southerners used to defend antiblack laws—to justify a state's authority to keep slavery out. Indeed, northerners and southerners shared a commitment to state control over matters traditionally considered part of their domestic police.

In Massachusetts and across the free states, however, people increasingly rejected the argument that state police powers should be permitted to outweigh the fundamental rights of free African Americans. Some people framed Hoar's expulsion from South Carolina primarily as an example of the Slave Power's disregard for the rights of a respectable white man—or for the sovereignty of the State of Massachusetts itself. Two decades later, for instance, Republicans in Congress regularly referred to South Carolina's expulsion of Hoar as an example of how, under the antebellum constitutional regime, a citizen of Massachusetts could not even exercise his constitutional right to file suit in federal court in a southern state. Yet the conflict was about more than that, as years of broad-based and persistent mobilization in Massachusetts and New York would suggest. Hoar was not in Charleston to test whether he personally could get a case into court. He was there to challenge South Carolina's laws on behalf of free Black citizens of Massachusetts and to demand that the federal judiciary address the question of free African Americans' rights under the privileges and immunities clause.

In the short term, authorities in the slave states continued to do as they pleased with respect to free Black sailors from the North, while northeasterners kept the sailors' plight before the public. Black activists and editors were particularly devoted. In the summer and fall of 1846, William P. Powell, the Black abolitionist who ran a sailors' home in New York City, wrote a series of articles on Black sailors for the New York–based *National Anti-Slavery Standard*. Powell, born free in New York in 1807, had spent five years at sea and then settled in New Bedford, Massachusetts, where he had opened his first sailors' boardinghouse. Powell had been among the founding members of the American Anti-Slavery Society and continued his activist work in New York, including holding abolitionist meetings at his sailors' home. In his columns, Powell sought to acquaint readers with the "character and condition" of African American sailors. He offered statistics emphasizing the number of Black seamen in the United States and their service in the War of 1812. He detailed the various kinds of maritime work in which Black sailors engaged, ranging from the merchant marine to the long-distance whaling industry to navigation of internal waterways to the US Navy.[51]

Shot through Powell's series was the argument that African American sailors were citizens of the states and of the United States. In the War of 1812, he said, they had "sacrificed their lives on the altar of their country," eventually securing "to every white American citizen, and NATURAL-IZED FOREIGNERS . . . rights, privileges, and immunities, which alas the coloured sailors do not now enjoy!" In another article, he included the Constitution's privileges and immunities clause followed by South Carolina's Negro Seamen Act, drawing attention to the contradictions. As the series concluded, he portrayed the mistreatment of Black sailors in southern ports as one among many offenses perpetrated by the Slave Power. White southerners were disingenuous when they claimed such laws were necessary "to prevent insurrection among their slaves." At least in Mobile, he noted, the real aim was to immobilize northern crews on board their ships so that slaveowners could hire out their slaves to load and unload the vessels. The "great question" of Black sailors' rights, he insisted, "must be met by the people of the North."[52]

Others in the free states pointed to white southerners' hypocrisy about interstate relations and to Article IV, Section 2, which included both the privileges and immunities clause and the fugitive slave clause. Slaveholders wanted northerners to help recapture alleged runaway slaves who made it to free soil, yet they would not reciprocate by recognizing the basic liberties of free Black northerners working in southern ports. A correspondent of New Hampshire Senator John P. Hale was incredulous that South Carolinians could drive Hoar from the state even as John C. Calhoun, from his seat in the Senate, "whines and growls because we are not willing to compete with their bloodhounds in catching fugitive slaves!" In a series of influential essays on the Slave Power, John Palfrey, a Massachusetts Whig, lambasted southerners' police-power argument, calling white South Carolinians cowards as he demanded that Massachusetts protect its citizens when they traveled to other states just as it would if they were abroad. The Constitution, Palfrey pointed out, provided recourse to federal courts when states could not resolve their internal disputes. In violently expelling Hoar, he argued, South Carolina had rejected the Constitution itself. What now? "Disunion? Retaliation? Prisons, stocks and lashes for South Carolinian travellers whom we may lay hands on?" These were not good answers, but the Slave Power had "outrageously maltreated our citizens" and "refused us a peaceable arbitration of differences." It had "broken [the] Constitution down."[53]

Palfrey could not have predicted that fifteen years later, the nation would arrive at the point of rupture, the Constitution so broken down that it could no longer serve as a stabilizing force. For now, the frustration was palpable. New Englanders had insisted that the US government should accept some level of responsibility for securing the rights of free Black sailors in the slave states, sometimes tying that argument with slaveholders' demand for protection of their right to claim slaves who had escaped to free states. But legislatures of the slave states had rejected such arguments, returning instead to the idea that police powers trumped any fundamental rights that Black sailors might claim. Congress would not pass legislation to enforce the privileges and immunities clause, nor would it seek to amend the Constitution in a way that weakened the power of enslavers in American politics or guaranteed African Americans' personal liberty. Efforts to get a case into federal court had failed as well. It appeared that the only possibility for tilting the country toward freedom and racial equality was political change at the state level.

Decades later, Henry Wilson, a political veteran from Massachusetts, wrote a multivolume history of the Civil War era in which he devoted an entire chapter to the struggle to defend the rights of free Black sailors in southern ports. Wilson was in the Massachusetts statehouse during the tumultuous 1840s, having first been elected to office as a Whig in 1840. A staunch opponent of slavery and racial discrimination, he worked for repeal of the state's law banning interracial marriage and battled racial discrimination aboard railroads and in public schools. Looking back decades later, he recalled the sense of frustration in Massachusetts after Hoar's and Hubbard's missions had failed. The state's "colored citizens, guilty of no crime, were still doomed, though in the pursuit of their lawful avocations, to arrests, imprisonments, fines, and, for a second offence, to be sold at public sale as slaves," he wrote. Southern policies, Wilson added, were plainly "in violation" of the Constitution's privileges and immunities clause, and the "injustice" meted out to Black sailors continued until the Civil War. All the while, the people of Massachusetts felt humiliated, "powerless either to maintain the rights guaranteed by the Constitution, which she felt herself bound to support, or to vindicate her co-equality among her sister States." Wilson was unsure where his state's stand against the invidious southern laws ranked among the "combination of causes" that brought the country to war. He was certain, however, that the conflict had contributed "to the building up of that power which, sixteen years later, grappled with slavery in arms and closed its career of crime."[54]

CHAPTER 6

"THAT ALL MEN ARE CREATED FREE AND EQUAL"

The Liberty Party and Repeal of the Ohio Black Laws in the 1840s

IN HIS YOUTH, Norton Townshend thought he would never take part in politics. An abolitionist from Ohio's Western Reserve, he believed both parties and the entire system were irredeemably tainted by slavery. But, after spending the winter of 1837 in Cincinnati as a medical student, Townshend reconsidered that position. During his stay, he heard a charismatic lawyer named Salmon Chase argue a case on behalf of Matilda, an alleged fugitive from slavery. He met Gamaliel Bailey, the editor of the city's controversial antislavery newspaper, the *Philanthropist*. He visited way stations of the Underground Railroad and saw schools for Black children run by white abolitionists. Townshend soon traveled to England to pursue his medical education and visit extended family, but he never forgot that winter in Cincinnati, where the antislavery community had deeply impressed him. He even imagined, he later recalled, that Chase was the sort of man he could someday vote for.[1]

Within a few years, Townshend was stumping for the Ohio Liberty Party. In 1848, he successfully ran for office on the Free Soil ticket and was elected to the state House of Representatives. Townshend was part of a rising tide of antislavery politics that reshaped Ohio and the nation. The Liberty Party, which formed at the end of the 1830s, attracted a relatively small number of voters, most of them committed abolitionists, but it drove questions of slavery and racial equality into the center of northern party politics. The third-party movement grew between 1845 and 1848, as Congress, after years of deliberation, decided to annex the slaveholding Republic of Texas and then went to war with Mexico to protect its claim. Many northern Whigs and Democrats bridled at these costly and consequential acts, which both major parties officially supported. Many sought new political coalitions that might be capable of stopping slavery's further extension. In the 1848 election season, the Free Soil Party united Libertyites with disillusioned Whigs and Democrats in a broad coalition determined to fight the Slave Power. Voters in the Western Reserve sent Norton Townshend to the statehouse, and in the winter of 1849, he played an essential role in persuading the legislature to repeal most of Ohio's black laws.

The state legislature's repeal of the notorious black laws, particularly the testimony law, was a monument to the transformative politics of the 1840s. African American activism in the free states flourished amid a vibrant convention movement, the establishment of newspapers, and a growing sense of confidence in claims to equality and citizenship. In Ohio, the Virginia-born David Jenkins and his allies in Columbus founded a newspaper, the *Palladium of Liberty,* and advocated racial equality alongside uplift and organization within the Black community. William Howard Day, a student at Oberlin College, began a career in public life that lasted decades. White leaders such as Norton Townshend welcomed the collaboration with African Americans and campaigned relentlessly for repeal of the black laws. Similar patterns were evident across the Old Northwest states, but only in Ohio was the movement strong enough—and the Whigs and Democrats closely enough matched—to make repeal possible. Many of the architects of Reconstruction got their start in the antislavery politics of this era. Men such as John Hale, Henry Wilson, Charles Sumner, Joshua Giddings, and William Seward—whether they joined an antislavery third party or not— were in close discussion in these years. Theirs was a struggle over ideas, but it was also a political struggle waged through coalition-building and vigorous debate. The fight had the potential to change the nation's orientation not only toward slavery but also toward the racist state laws and policies that white Americans had for so long accepted.[2]

DESPITE ALL THE NEGATIVE ATTENTION Ohio had received for its racist laws, African Americans continued to move there, purchase land, and prosper in many places. Lewis Woodson, a Pittsburgh-based AME minister and educator, advocated westward migration by African Americans in an 1839 series in the *Colored American,* the weekly paper edited by Samuel Cornish. Born in Virginia, Woodson had grown up near Chillicothe, Ohio, and began his teaching career there. His series of articles touted landownership and farming in Ohio and western Pennsylvania as an alternative to wage labor in the crowded cities of the Northeast, where expanding immigrant populations threatened to put African Americans out of work. Black farmers and mechanics were prospering in independent communities beyond the Alleghenies, Woodson told readers. Ohio's infamous black laws were "bad laws," he wrote, but law-abiding, respectable African Americans had little to fear from them. He acknowledged that Black Ohioans were shut out of public schools but said they regularly pooled resources to create their own. People who "have no strong disposition to mingle in politics . . . will never be made very unhappy," he claimed. "Their neighbors will generally be content to leave them alone, and leave them [to] grow as rich, and as happy, and as good, as they may choose to make themselves."[3]

Most African American migrants who reached Ohio arrived from the slave states, moving with more or less desperation toward a place where they could be free. Overall population growth in Ohio was tremendous; by 1840, the state was the third most populous in the Union, trailing only New York and Pennsylvania. The 1840 US Census indicated that Ohio's Black population had almost doubled in ten years, growing from 9,568 in 1830 to 17,342 in 1840. Because the white population was increasing rapidly too, African Americans remained around one percent of the state's total population. For Gamaliel Bailey, editor of the *Philanthropist*, the 1840 census numbers demonstrated the utter ineffectiveness of the black laws at discouraging Black migration. Even though the state had "done all she could to exclude" Black people "by grinding legislation," the African American population had increased at a far greater rate than that of New York, where no similar laws existed. A committee composed mainly of Black Ohioans recommended further migration to the Old Northwest at a convention that met in Buffalo, New York, in 1843, pointing out optimistically that the discriminatory laws of the states and territories were "subject to change, and time and the growing intelligence of the people . . . are destined to make those laws obnoxious to the people themselves."[4]

Cincinnati remained the West's largest city, and it was a metropolis of formidable contrasts. Despite the city's 1829 riots, the Black community became more deeply rooted and economically diverse in the 1830s. Industries related to shipping and the river trade continued to provide jobs for working-class Black men. Despite entrenched discrimination by employers and white laborers, African Americans found niches in some trades, in business, and in the service sector. One correspondent reported in 1839 that the city's African Americans had created multiple "companies for trading, or speculating purposes," including the Iron Chest Company, which had constructed three "commodious brick buildings." The diverse Black community sustained its own Methodist and Baptist churches as well as numerous schools for their children. Black men and women were active in the Freemasonry movement, and by 1843 there were five female benevolent societies counting some 340 members. The city's Black community also remained closely connected with family and friends across the Ohio River in Kentucky. Many Black residents were working to purchase freedom for relatives still in bondage, and many also provided refuge for those escaping slavery. At the same time, explained the Ohio Anti-Slavery Society, "those who have friends in slavery, live in continual dread and anxiety, lest they should be sold and taken down the river." "Boats loaded with slaves" regularly stopped in Cincinnati, and Black residents were often stricken when they encountered "friends and relations . . . in chains."[5]

Cincinnati's white community was also exceedingly diverse. Business leaders remained largely proslavery or at least sympathetic to slaveholders' interests. Yet a small white abolitionist community was also active, including teachers in Black schools, the antislavery readers of Bailey's *Philanthropist,* and people willing to help runaway slaves make their way to freedom. The mix of white residents also included a growing population of European immigrants, particularly from Germany. The always-combustible city was made more so by a protracted economic slump that began in 1837. White artisans experienced downward mobility, and working-class white men competed with African Americans for jobs, sometimes forcing them out of lines of work to which they had long had access.[6]

In the spring of 1841, two court decisions that reinforced African Americans' rights in Ohio exacerbated existing tensions in the city. The case of *State v. Farr* involved seventeen Ohioans whom a lower court had found guilty of riot for encouraging the escape of a group of enslaved people in transit from Virginia to Missouri. The Ohio Supreme Court overturned their convictions on a technicality, but the chief judge, in announcing the decision, declared that a slave "became free when brought to this State by his master." Around the same time, the Court of Common Pleas of Hamilton County (which encompassed Cincinnati) insisted that in Ohio, "liberty is the rule, involuntary servitude the exception." Both decisions affirmed the "free soil" principle—that is, the idea that no one could be claimed as a slave in a place where slavery did not exist in law.[7]

These decisions had significant implications in a border city like Cincinnati. They clarified that Kentucky slaveholders would get no help from authorities if they brought an enslaved person to the city and that person decided to make an escape. The decisions also jeopardized the investments of slave traders, who regularly stopped in the city as they traveled down the Ohio River on their way to markets in Missouri and the Southwest. That summer, the city's main Democratic newspaper, the *Cincinnati Enquirer*, whipped up resentment toward free Black people and white abolitionists. The editor, John Brough, was a former state legislator who in 1838 had introduced the measure to bar reception of petitions from African Americans. Now, his newspaper ran articles claiming that the city's commercial fortunes were being damaged by its growing reputation as a haven for enslaved people seeking freedom. The *Enquirer* worried that Kentucky slaveholders would no longer want to do business there. In mid-August, the newspaper called on the township government to "enforce the law of 1807," complaining that the city was "overrun with free blacks" who took jobs from "white citizens" and lived by "plunder" when they were not working.[8]

On Tuesday, August 31, 1841, a fight between Irish and Black workers touched off days of sporadic violence, and on Friday of that week, white residents carried out an organized onslaught against the Black community. One white observer estimated that some two thousand white residents took to the streets as the mob set upon an African American neighborhood. Black residents fired guns in self-defense and the crowd retreated, but then it returned with increased fury. White rioters planted a cannon in a major thoroughfare and fired it three times "among the negroes," causing chaos and terror. To quell the uprising, a Saturday meeting of white "citizens" and city officials resolved to disarm the Black population and enforce the 1807 black law as well as the 1793 federal Fugitive Slave Act. The meeting, led by the mayor, empowered the militia and the city police to arrest African Americans at will. Authorities grabbed more than three hundred people, and crowds continued to threaten the prisoners' safety even after they arrived at the city jail. The mob remained on the offensive that night, charging into the office of the *Philanthropist* and throwing the printing press into the river before continuing on to destroy Black-owned properties and assault Black residents. The next day, a Sunday, Governor Thomas Corwin arrived in the city. The mob's energies waned as duly constituted authorities took charge. The Black prisoners were required either to prove their "nativity" in Ohio, show "non-residence" and promise to leave, or secure bonds to remain. All children were let go, but the adults who had no documentation were "held for further disposition under the laws." The *Enquirer* kept up its campaign of defamation, calling the city's free Black residents "characterless vagabonds" who had been led astray by "white fanatics."[9]

John Mercer Langston, who later became the state's first African American lawyer and officeholder, was just eleven years old when he experienced the uprising. A recent migrant from Virginia, Langston was living with members of Cincinnati's Black elite while attending school. As an adult, he recalled that he had felt safe in the city until the day when someone warned him about the mob, and he ran for his life. When he finally reached the drugstore where his brother and friends were hiding, he was so exhausted and scared that he "fell to the floor . . . as if dead." The riot was horrifying. It underscored how tenuous African Americans' lives and institutions remained in southern Ohio. White residents' tendencies toward violence were abetted by the black laws, which, even if dormant for long stretches, could be mobilized in attempts to give legal sanction for acts of terror.

At the same time, however, Langston was among those who believed that the conflagration had stiffened people's resolve. White antislavery activists became "bolder, braver, more outspoken and eloquent" in its wake, he wrote. Adverse experiences taught African Americans "what their rights were, and how to advocate and defend them." After the riot, Black orators and writers found their footing as "fearless and able defenders of the rights of their people."[10] Over the next several years, in fact, African American activists in Ohio became increasingly militant, demanding the overthrow of slavery in the South and calling for racial equality at home.

The 1841 riot coincided with the origins of the Liberty Party in Ohio.

Generous donations from antislavery societies allowed the *Philanthropist* to rebuild quickly, and editor Gamaliel Bailey urged supporters to double down on efforts to repeal the black laws and demonstrate to "our enemies . . . that every act of violence only inflames our zeal."[11] But Bailey and his allies were envisioning something quite different from the petition campaigns that had characterized the 1830s. Frustrated that neither the Whigs nor the Democrats were receptive to their agenda, Bailey—together with former US Senator Thomas Morris, Cincinnati lawyer Salmon Chase, and others—began organizing the Ohio Liberty Party after the 1840 presidential election. In the fall of 1841, just after the riot, they called their first statewide Liberty Party convention.[12]

The Ohio Liberty Party quickly became a significant force in state politics, and Chase emerged as one of the era's most prominent politicians, later serving as Lincoln's treasury secretary and Chief Justice of the US Supreme Court. Originally from New Hampshire, Chase had studied law in Washington, DC, under the direction of former US Attorney General William Wirt. He moved to Cincinnati in 1830 and was there during the Lane Seminary debates of 1834, when he sympathized with the colonizationists, not the abolitionists. He changed his mind two years later, when slaveholders and their agents rioted against the *Philanthropist*. Chase served as an attorney for the newspaper's owners, and in short order he began to take cases defending fugitive slaves and their allies. He associated politically with the Whigs in the late 1830s, but conversations with Gamaliel Bailey persuaded him to reject colonization, advocate repeal of the black laws, and work to form an antislavery political party. He became one of the Liberty Party's most important advocates and organizers, drafting party platforms and addresses and working behind the scenes to build the coalition.[13]

The Ohio Liberty Party developed a precise vision for abolishing slavery within the existing constitutional order. Drawing on arguments made by activists like Benjamin Lundy in the early 1820s and advanced by William Jay, Theodore Dwight Weld, and others in the 1830s, the Ohioans conceded that under the Constitution, the US government had no power to regulate or abolish slavery in the states where it already existed. They insisted, however, that the federal government could not sanction or support slavery in places under its direct jurisdiction, such as the District of Columbia and the federal territories. The Fifth Amendment, they often emphasized, prohibited the government from depriving "any person" of life, liberty, or property without due process of law. Violations by the states were another matter. Like most of their contemporaries, Chase and his allies believed that the individual rights promised in the Constitution's first eight amendments were guaranteed against infringement by the federal government but not by the states.

Ohio Liberty Party leaders often positioned themselves as conservatives who sought to restore the founders' vision for the nation. The Constitution's framers had rejected the terms *slave* and *slavery*, they pointed out, because they did not want the institution to be a defining feature of American life. Governed under the current party system, they argued, the country had strayed from the founders' ideals of liberty and equality. The Liberty Party wanted to bring back those ideals, and the first step would be to divorce the federal government from slavery. As Chase explained to a friend in the fall of 1841, the aim of "antislavery political action" was "complete deliverance of the Government of the Nation from all connection with & all responsibility for slavery." When the US government stopped abetting slaveholders, he argued, slavery would be driven "back within her legal limits," the institution's true evil would become visible, and slaveholders would finally see fit to end slavery in their own states.[14]

Attacking slavery was not all that Liberty Party leaders cared about, however. They also fought to strike down racially discriminatory laws. At the end of 1840, Gamaliel Bailey had argued that the black laws were not only ineffective in stopping Black migration but also "wicked," "gratuitous," "absurd," and "ridiculous." In speeches and exhortations in Ohio and elsewhere in the Old Northwest, Liberty Party activists invoked the Declaration of Independence and its promises of liberty and equality for all men. Sometimes they recited the biblical injunction that God had made "of one blood all nations of men." The Ohio Liberty Party's initial declaration to the public called for repeal of "the oppressive laws which degrade the Black man without benefitting the white; whose legitimate tendency is to drive from among us the respectable, the intelligent and the pious men of color." These were goals long supported by the Ohio Anti-Slavery Society, and most of its members became Liberty partisans, including its longtime president, Leicester King. As Chase wrote of the party: "The great principle of action is the same throughout the country—that all men are created equal—and this principle ought to govern in state Legislation as well as in National Legislation.[15]

The Ohio Liberty Party's choice of Leicester King as its candidate for governor in 1842 underscored the significance of black-law repeal in the party's vision. A former Whig, King was the author of the unequivocally pro-repeal report published by the state Senate in 1838. In answer to a set of questions posed during the 1842 election, King declared himself "in favor of securing to all persons in this state without distinction of color the 'political civil & social rights' guaranteed to them by the constitution." Although he might prefer a mostly white state, he said, there was no excuse for treating Ohio African Americans as anything less than fully vested members of the community, including by providing schools for Black children. King concluded with an exhortation to voters that was typical of the Liberty Party. "Equal & exact justice to all men irrespective of color or condition is regarded by me as a sound maxim of free democracy," he wrote. And yet, "the great question between liberty & slavery" did not concern only the rights of "colored persons." The malign influence of the Slave Power impoverished and dishonored everyone.[16]

Liberty Party organizers like King and Chase well understood the challenge of competing for votes among a population with deeply held partisan loyalties. While the Whig–Democrat rivalry often focused on issues of trade and transportation, the parties had latent differences over slavery-related issues, and those differences made Whigs better candidates for defecting to the Liberty Party. Many Whigs were political descendants of Federalists who had opposed racially discriminatory laws and had stood up for abolition in the early republic. Many Whigs also loathed the brazenly proslavery tendencies of the southern-dominated Democratic Party. In the Western Reserve, antislavery people, insofar as they became involved in politics, tended to be staunch Whigs, which is why they repeatedly elected Joshua Giddings to Congress. Yet Liberty leaders also stood a chance of attracting Democrats—though in some places more than others. Around Cincinnati in particular, some Democrats were open to arguments such as those made by former Democratic Senator Thomas Morris: that the "Slave Power" was just another incarnation of elite rule, similar to the Bank Power the Democrats had earlier opposed.[17]

The impetus to form a third party came in part from past frustrations. In 1838, Ohio abolitionists had thrown their political weight behind the Democrats, only to be frustrated when the men they helped elect pursued a strenuously proslavery, antiblack agenda. The idea of a third party was different. In a closely divided legislature, a small number of Liberty Party members could shape policy by throwing their votes to one side or the other. As Chase explained to Giddings, whom he regularly tried to recruit into the Liberty Party camp, Liberty men would "secure the balance of power in the Legislatures of the Free States and in Congress" and extract antislavery concessions in exchange for siding with one of the two major parties. The goal was to get Liberty candidates elected, but if Liberty campaigning impelled a faction of Whigs or Democrats to push their party toward antislavery, pro–racial equality positions within their party, that might be all to the good. After all, the larger aim was to change people's priorities, and from there to change policy. Giddings stood firm with the Whigs for the time being, but he refrained from publicly criticizing the Libertyites for running a candidate for governor in 1842. He told Chase he would not condemn his antislavery friends when he disagreed with their strategy but would, instead, try to "persuade them to what I believe the correct policy."[18]

OHIO'S AFRICAN AMERICAN ACTIVISTS were invigorated by the emergence of an antislavery political party that embraced the principle of racial equality. The state capital, Columbus, was becoming the center for Black political organizing. Although the city's Black population (and overall population) remained much smaller than Cincinnati's, Columbus was far removed from Ohio's volatile southern border, and whites who lived there were less prone to antiblack violence. Besides, it was the seat of state government, and Ohio African Americans were increasingly interested in making their voices heard in the halls of power. The city's most prominent Black activist was David Jenkins. A Virginia native, he had moved to Columbus in 1837 and immediately advanced to the forefront of statewide Black organizing. By the 1840s, he was a man of many trades whose work included contracts with the state government. After what appears to have been a lull in political activity, he and other Black residents of Columbus convened in early March 1843 to discuss the "disabilities" under which Black people of Ohio were "suffering" and to begin planning for a statewide meeting that August. Embracing the idea of Black independence and self-help—and perhaps reflecting post-1841 assertiveness—the meeting resolved, "We owe it to ourselves, to our friends and to our posterity to make at least some effort to silence the charge which has long been preferred against us, of indifference to our rights."[19]

That summer, Ohio's leading African American activists were busy. By May, several were in New York City, where they convened with peers from other states and announced a plan for a national Black convention in Buffalo in mid-August. It had been eight years since the last national convention, and organizers felt that free African Americans' efforts had faltered amid generational change, internal divisions, and the overarching "tyranny" of slavery. By midsummer, an African American correspondent to the *Philanthropist* linked the upcoming statewide convention of African Americans with Liberty Party organizing, urging

Black Ohioans to action while noting that their "anti-slavery friends" were already hard at work. He exhorted, "We must come out as men, and engage in the work; stand up and claim our rights as citizens of a free and independent state." At the August meeting of African Americans in Columbus, a rump group of white Garrisonians presented their brief against the Liberty Party and the OASS's merger with it. The convention opted not to endorse the party, but it did pass resolutions praising Bailey and his Libertyite newspaper, the *Philanthropist*. The convention also sought to advance the cause of racial equality in Ohio by urging Black residents to continue petitioning the legislature and by appointing a committee to draft an address to the state's white citizens.[20]

From the meeting in Columbus, several men traveled onward to the national Black convention in Buffalo. That meeting of some forty people was held in a public hall, and Henry Highland Garnet opened the proceedings. Garnet's family had escaped bondage in Maryland in the 1820s, and he had attended school in New York City, worked as a sailor, and pursued advanced education before becoming a Presbyterian minister in New York. Garnet made the most controversial proposal of the meeting: that Black northerners publish an "address to the slaves," calling on them to rise up against their masters. Many delegates objected that such an address would endanger not only enslaved people who might try it but free Black northerners as well. Attendees also disagreed over whether to endorse the Liberty Party. They recognized the party's growth but questioned how far its leaders would advance the cause of racial equality and Black men's enfranchisement. Some delegates, particularly New Yorkers, were already active in the party and wanted to formally support it. New York Black activists had continued to emphasize voting even after the 1821 state constitution had disenfranchised all but the wealthiest Black men in the state. On the other side of the debate were those, including Frederick Douglass, who had strong ties to the Garrisonians and avoided association with political parties. In the end—against the wishes of Douglass and several others—the convention passed resolutions supporting the Liberty Party and urging Black men who lived in the six states where they were enfranchised to vote for Liberty candidates.[21]

The Ohio delegates brought two distinctive perspectives to the Buffalo meeting. First, most Ohioans objected to Garnet's controversial address. A. M. Sumner said Black residents of Cincinnati "were prepared to meet any thing that may come upon us unprovoked, but we were not ready injudiciously to provoke difficulty." Speaking as someone who lived adjacent to slavery in a city that had endured a white rampage two years earlier, he cautioned that endorsement of Garnet's address "would be fatal to the safety of the free people of color of the slave States, but especially so to those who lived on the borders of the free States." The Ohioans also distinguished themselves for their advocacy of westward migration and agricultural settlement. Three of the five members of the convention's committee on agriculture were Ohio men, and the committee's report focused mainly on the successes of Black farming communities in Ohio. Energized, perhaps, by the emergence of the Liberty Party, the committee claimed that whites were becoming increasingly enlightened and that the infamous black laws were destined to be "rescinded" or at least to become "a dead letter." The committee also urged Black settlers toward the federal territories of Wisconsin and Iowa, affirming that the government's land preemption policy was "open to all." African Americans should "strike for that region, that we may be found there forming acquaintances with the people, and making the people acquainted with us . . . that we may be on the spot, with our influence, to aid in giving character to their constitution and laws, when the time shall have come for those Territories to become States."[22] It was clear that these men, at least, were optimistic about prospects for expanding African American settlement in the Old Northwest.

Soon after the African American convention concluded in Buffalo, the Liberty Party opened its national convention in the same city. Henry Highland Garnet and other Black New Yorkers played important roles, speaking publicly and sitting on various committees. The Liberty Party convention's practical purpose was to nominate a ticket for the presidential election of

1844, and the party selected—by earlier agreement—the Kentucky-born abolitionist James G. Birney for president and Thomas Morris of Ohio for vice president. Yet it was the party's platform and proceedings that best suggested the party's commitment to racial equality. The platform, drafted in part by Salmon Chase, began not only with a demand for the "absolute and unqualified divorce of the General Government from Slavery" but also with an argument for "the restoration of *equality of rights*, among men, in every State where the party exists, or may exist." Touting full adherence to the principle of racial equality, the delegates resolved to "cordially welcome our colored fellow citizens to fraternity with us in the Liberty Party, in its great contest to secure the rights of mankind and the religion of our common country." And the party declared that, "in all those free States where any inequality of rights and privileges exists on account of color," the "friends of Liberty" must "employ their utmost energies to remove all such remnants and effects of the slave system."[23] It would be an understatement to say this was unlike anything the Whigs or Democrats would have said. Such statements on the part of either major party were inconceivable.

African American activists in Ohio were inspired by the summer's developments. At the national Black convention in Buffalo, there had been much talk of Black newspapers and their importance for building a sense of shared identity and encouraging collective action. That fall, several of the Ohio men who had attended the Buffalo meeting founded the weekly *Palladium of Liberty* in Columbus. The paper, which published its first issue on December 27, 1843, sported a masthead that read, "We hold these truths to be self evident, that all men are created free and equal." It launched with the "address to the citizens of Ohio" that had been commissioned at that summer's statewide Black convention. The address focused exclusively on the black laws. Invoking the Declaration of Independence, Black Ohioans demanded nothing more than "those rights to which we, as Americans and Ohioans, are entitled." These were rights that "God has given, and which man should enjoy." The Declaration also articulated a right to revolution, they added. They were not asking white Ohioans to abolish their form of government, they said, but simply to "repeal all laws and parts of laws that make a distinction on account of color, and which degrade us on that account."[24]

The *Palladium of Liberty* existed for just over a year, but during that short lifetime it gave remarkable expression to leading Black Ohioans' values and aspirations for political and social life. The newspaper's name and epigraph suggested that its editors were aligned with the Liberty Party and its ideals, yet the substance of the paper was wide-ranging. Articles highlighted Black achievements and advertised Black businesses. Reports discussed religious life and temperance activities, child-rearing and personal comportment. It ran fiction and news stories from other newspapers in the Old Northwest, particularly Liberty Party papers such as the *Signal of Liberty* in Michigan and the *Western Citizen* of Illinois, as well as Martin Delany's the *Mystery,* published in Pittsburgh. The *Palladium of Liberty* repeatedly highlighted the injustices of the black laws, drawing attention to cases in which African Americans were unable to secure justice in court because they were not permitted to testify. David Jenkins and other *Palladium* editors used the paper to organize support for another statewide Black convention in 1844. This time, they not only demanded repeal of the black laws but also called for the right to vote in no uncertain terms. Their disenfranchisement by the 1803 Ohio Constitution, they claimed, was an "aberration" that white Ohioans had the power to remedy.[25]

The 1844 election season offered an opportunity to assess the effectiveness of third-party antislavery organizing across the free states. In the presidential contest, Henry Clay, Whig of Kentucky, faced off against Democrat James K. Polk of Tennessee, a proslavery expansionist who strongly favored Texas annexation. Many northern Democrats were demoralized at the party's choice of Polk over Martin Van Buren of New York, the former president and party standard bearer. In Ohio, the Whigs triumphed, winning the governorship and both houses of the legislature and delivering the state for Clay. Liberty Party presidential candidate James Birney received just three percent of the vote, but Ohio Democrats nevertheless claimed that defections to Birney had cost them the election. It is not clear that Liberty voters made the crucial difference in Ohio, but in New York they may well have determined the outcome of the presidential contest. There, it seemed that defections from the Whigs to the Liberty Party hurt Clay's vote totals and thus helped secure the state for Polk, who could not have won the presidency without New York. Overall, the 1844 election revealed weaknesses in both major parties and suggested that even with relatively low voter totals, an antislavery third party could significantly shape election outcomes.[26]

With the Whigs in charge of Ohio state government during the 1844–45 legislative session and Liberty Party pressure continuing, many hoped the legislature would finally repeal the black laws. Major Whig newspapers advocated repeal, and Whig representatives appeared increasingly supportive. Petitioning continued. At the beginning of the session, a select committee of the Senate issued a report strongly condemning the black laws and proposing a bill for their repeal. The House was deeply divided, however, and its investigating committee delivered widely divergent reports: The three-man majority favored repeal, but the two-man minority adamantly insisted that the state needed the laws as a matter of self-defense. The bill ultimately failed in the House. Still, Joshua Giddings hailed the session as a breakthrough, assuring David Lee Child in Boston that Ohioans were making good progress. Whigs from southern Ohio tended to oppose repeal while northerners supported it, he explained, yet the pro-repeal faction had needed just eleven more Whig votes to pass the measure. Those eleven dissenters had "admitted the correctness of our position but said it would require another year to bring their people to that point." Giddings was pleased that "the subject was fully and ably discussed."[27]

Liberty Party leaders were not so sanguine about the Whigs. In June 1845, Salmon Chase and his allies hosted the Southern and Western Liberty Convention in Cincinnati, an effort to bolster the Liberty Party by recruiting people who previously had maintained traditional party allegiances. An exchange with Horace Greeley, the Whig editor of the *New-York Tribune*, revealed Ohio Liberty leaders' deep commitment to repeal of the black laws, as well as their frustration with the Whigs. Greeley declined an invitation to attend the convention but sent a letter in which he presumed to advise the Westerners to spend more time focusing on the condition of free blacks "in their own States and neighborhoods." He wanted them to "devote their political energies in the first place to a removal of the shameful, atrocious civil disabilities and degradations under which the African race now generally labor." Not surprisingly, the New Yorker's advice did not sit well with the convention, which included delegates who had been demanding repeal of the black laws for years. The *Cincinnati Weekly Herald and Philanthropist*, Gamaliel Bailey's current paper, voiced incredulity at Greeley's message, whereupon Greeley claimed he honestly had known of no efforts to repeal the infamous Ohio black laws. Bailey in turn described a decade's worth of abolitionist petitioning and voting for repeal. "The legislative table has groaned under their petitions from year to year; their papers have been filled with expositions of the unconstitutionality and inhumanity of the Black Laws." Yet, the Cincinnati paper lamented, they had been repeatedly betrayed by Whig politicians who failed to support repeal. "One of the chief objects" of a third party, the paper explained, was "the practical establishment of the doctrine of equal rights, by the removal of all the disabilities referred to."[28]

One person who took an interest in Liberty organizing in the summer of 1845 was the twenty-nine-year-old John A. Bingham, later the author of Section 1 of the Fourteenth Amendment. Bingham's father and uncle were locally prominent Whigs, and in the mid-1830s, Bingham attended the abolitionist-leaning Franklin College in New Athens, Ohio. Young Bingham was clearly interested in the Liberty Party, for he implored Salmon Chase and other Liberty leaders to send a lecturer to his region—five southern Ohio counties that bordered both Virginia and Kentucky. "Liberty men generally in this vicinity" were trying to mobilize, he wrote. The area was "perhaps as inveterately proslavery" as any group of counties in the state, he said, but that was precisely why "an onset should be made."

His neighbors were primed for change because they were set back from the Ohio River, "just far enough from that miserable proslavery atmosphere to be able to take breath without the danger of suffocation." Local abolitionists had already created "an under-current in our favor," he noted. This was the moment to broaden their appeal.[29]

THE 1846 OHIO gubernatorial campaign revealed how Liberty Party pressure to repeal the black laws had helped deepen fissures within the state's two major parties. The Liberty candidate was Samuel Lewis, the state's first superintendent of public schools and an important member of Chase's Cincinnati circle. Lewis, a Methodist minister, was an excellent speaker and campaigned hard, lecturing throughout the state from February through September with only a short break in the summer. Lewis and the Libertyites called consistently for repeal of the black laws, and this forced the other two candidates to delineate their positions. William Bebb, the Whig candidate, at first surprised many Ohioans by unequivocally demanding repeal of the law prohibiting African Americans from testifying in court cases involving whites. Yet Bebb changed his tone dramatically while speaking in southern Ohio at the end of the campaign. Instead of arguing for repeal of the law on grounds of justice and humanity, he claimed that repeal would enable African Americans to testify in support of slavecatchers, and he proposed a special land tax on African Americans to discourage further migration.[30]

Meanwhile, the Democratic candidate, David Tod, at first declined to take a position on the black laws. He found himself suddenly vulnerable, however, when it emerged that he had supported repeal while running for office in the late 1830s. In response to pressure, Tod came out squarely in support of the black laws. Among those following the election was Edwin Stanton, later Lincoln's secretary of war. Stanton, a Democrat who privately opposed slavery but to that point had not spoken publicly against it, complained to Chase that Tod had abandoned economic questions in favor of a last-minute attempt to unify the party "in a common shout for 'Tod & the Black laws.'" Frustrated, Stanton disparaged "the mean passions, selfish interest and petty feelings" that "somehow, guide and control a great party."[31]

Bebb managed to win the election, retaining the support of the Whigs in the Western Reserve despite his last-minute pandering in the southern part of the state. Samuel Lewis finished a distant third but garnered more votes than any previous Liberty candidate. More important than the vote totals themselves was the way the Liberty Party's campaign against the black laws had exacerbated divisions within the two major parties. The drive to repeal the black laws split the Whigs along regional lines, with residents of the Western Reserve favoring repeal and southern Ohioans opposed. Bebb could not please both sides, and if he went too far in either direction, frustrated voters might bolt the party—in one case for the Liberty Party, and in the other for the Democrats. Bebb's inconsistency on the black laws also seemed to affirm the Liberty Party's perennial message that the Whigs could not be trusted and that the best course for people who were serious about opposing slavery and the black laws was to join the third-party movement. Finally, the Democrats, by staunchly defending the black laws and the racism on which they were founded, managed to alienate partisans such as Stanton who were reluctant to embrace such positions.[32]

During the campaign, Democratic defenders of the black laws mingled traditional arguments for state police powers with rigid theories of biological race. The *Cincinnati Enquirer* insisted that the black laws were not designed to degrade or oppress African Americans, but simply to prevent Black "settlement within our borders." Governments had always adopted measures "for the protection of peace of the actual settlers of a State." To that end, the paper said, Ohio could "discourage the ingress of any class or complexion of persons." The newspaper's assessment of which traits marked people as part of a separate "class or complexion" was not surprising. European immigrants were pouring into Ohio by the mid-1840s, but the

Enquirer saw them quite differently from new arrivals of African descent. The state should welcome people who could "safely and freely *assimilate,* after the accidental barriers of language and habits are removed," the paper intoned. By contrast, "Providential law" had created separate "*races*" that must not, and could not, commingle as equals.[33] Nature had ordained that people of European descent could become Ohioans, the paper concluded, while people of African descent must remain as outsiders.

The *Enquirer* also charged the Whigs of northeastern Ohio with hypocrisy, playing up differences between Democrats, who welcomed Catholic immigrants as constituents, and Whigs, many of whom had a nativist streak. The previous few years had witnessed a spike in anti-immigrant sentiment, including mob violence and the brief rise of an anti-immigrant political party that called itself the Native American Party. The movement had ebbed somewhat after anti-immigrant rioters in Philadelphia burned down two Catholic churches in multiple days of violent conflict during which more than a dozen people were killed and scores more were injured. But anti-immigrant sentiment lingered. The *Enquirer* pointed out that in the recent legislative session, Ohio Whigs had pushed for a law to discourage foreign immigration even as they demanded repeal of the black laws. Ohio's new immigration law was similar to ones adopted by those in the East. It penalized people—usually ship captains—who imported into the state persons who were "poor or indigent, or lunatic," who would likely be dependent on public resources for support. Northern Ohioans ought to recognize, the *Enquirer* insisted, that southerners' desire to limit Black migration was no different from northern Whigs' own interest in limiting the entry of foreign immigrants through Cleveland and the Great Lakes.[34] Why should one kind of restriction be acceptable and the other not?

Leading Liberty Party people rejected both the nativist tendencies in the Whig Party and the antiblack racism of the Democrats. African Americans were Americans, the *Philanthropist* declared. They have "as good a title by birth, by residence, by labor, to this country, as the various classes, who trace their origin to Sweden, France, Spain, Germany, Holland, England or

Ireland." The paper also condemned "Native Americanism" and its efforts
to "create unjust distinctions between classes of our population." The rights
of "our naturalized citizens" were newly in jeopardy, the paper pointed out,
a result of the "project to exclude the naturalized citizen from office, and
prolong the period of naturalization to twenty-one years." Such measures
were the "legitimate offspring of that same Principle which has given birth
to the Black Laws against colored Americans—a Principle which claims for
the dominant class the right to legislate, not in accordance with the rules of
Justice, but the dictates of *Prejudice.*" The Ohio Liberty Party stood against
prejudice in all its forms, adamant that all men should be treated as individuals, permitted to rise or fall on their own merits.[35]

NOT ONLY IN OHIO but across the free states, many people who had joined
antislavery societies in the 1830s reconstituted themselves as Liberty Party
organizations, and the movement developed an ethos that was remarkably
inclusive for its time. Women played significant roles, much as they had
in abolitionist petition campaigns of the 1830s, although the question of
how they should participate was not without controversy. In the late 1830s,
William Lloyd Garrison and his allies had extended their radical vision of
individual freedom and human equality into a critique of women's oppression under patriarchy. Driven by the claims of women activists, Garrisonians put their principles into action by inviting women to speak at political
meetings, a significant departure from convention. The Garrisonians' position on women's equality generated tremendous conflict among eastern
abolitionists. Many movement leaders, particularly those based in New
York, argued for focusing exclusively on the evils of slavery and racism,
concerned that advocating a radical position on sex equality would drive
away potential supporters.[36]

Liberty Party leaders in the Old Northwest were generally in the anti-
Garrison camp, but they promoted women's participation in different ways.
White women activists taught in schools for Black children, raised funds to

support those schools and help impoverished Black women, and developed and signed petitions against the black laws. They continued to petition for repeal of state-level black laws and an end to the federal government's support for slavery. Several became prominent correspondents to Liberty Party newspapers. Often claiming special moral authority derived from their role as mothers and guardians of the home, organized white women sought to influence the political choices of male relatives. In Henry County, Indiana, for instance, members of the women's antislavery association urged their husbands, brothers, and fathers to purify "our statute books from the odious and oppressive laws now grinding our sisters in the dust and depriving them of the protection of common law and subjecting them to the brutal insults of the most accomplished villany."[37]

True to the party's platform, Liberty Party leaders also welcomed African American men as partisans and lecturers, even in states such as Ohio and Illinois, where they were not permitted to vote. And African American activists, in turn, supported the Liberty Party movement and took to the road, often speaking to mixed-race audiences. In northern Illinois in 1844, for example, a free Black man named William Jones, the victim of an attempted kidnapping in Chicago, stumped with white Liberty activist Ichabod Codding. The same year, Henry Bibb, who had escaped slavery in Kentucky, was a regular Liberty Party speaker in Michigan and southern Ohio. Lewis Hayden, another escapee from Kentucky, had encountered James Birney in Michigan and went on to lecture for the party in the East. In relating their experiences and their political views before largely white audiences, African American lecturers—many of whom knew firsthand the cruelties of slavery—offered an embodied and visceral demonstration of the "manhood" of Black men and their entitlement to the same benefits that white men enjoyed.[38]

In state after state, Liberty Party organizations insisted that racial discrimination in basic rights was unjust and demanded repeal of antiblack laws, sometimes following in the footsteps of antislavery Whigs. In 1839, when Iowa's territorial government adopted racist settlement and testimony laws modeled on those of Ohio, the territory's abolitionists mounted a campaign for repeal, and Whig representatives brought the issue to the floor in the 1840–41 session of the territorial legislature. In the fall of 1843, at its first major meeting, the territory's Liberty Party passed stringent resolutions against the black codes. The Iowa Liberty Party condemned laws that made a distinction on account of color as "wrong, and a stigma upon our statute books," and urged residents to petition for repeal.[39]

Likewise, in Democrat-dominated Illinois, the Liberty Party prioritized repeal of the black laws from its inception in 1841. The Illinois party was anchored by Zebina Eastman and his newspaper, the *Western Citizen*. Eastman, a Massachusetts native, had migrated to Illinois in 1839 and began helping Benjamin Lundy publish the *Genius of Universal Emancipation*. The veteran antislavery editor had arrived in the state a year earlier, hoping to fill the void left after a mob murdered Elijah Lovejoy, an antislavery minister who had published a newspaper in Alton. Lundy died soon after Eastman began working with him, but Eastman carried on. The *Western Citizen* and the nascent Illinois Liberty Party became tireless advocates of repeal of the state's antiblack laws. In 1841, the party published five hundred petition forms to aid Illinoisans in pressuring their legislature. The *Western Citizen* touted the petitions and called for action.[40]

Black men's right to vote was also on the Liberty Party's agenda across the free states. Most contemporaries uncoupled the vote—which they viewed as a "political" right—from such basic "civil" rights as the right to move freely from place to place, enter into contracts, and enjoy equal protection of the laws. Some called access to the vote and office-holding a "privilege," to emphasize that these prerogatives were available only to a certain elevated subset of people. The relatively expansive definition of citizenship that northerners had developed since the 1820s was compatible with this rather restrictive vision of the vote. White northerners regularly argued that all free, native-born people were citizens (except perhaps paupers, vagrants, and criminals), but most also insisted that only certain citizens—namely, white men—were entitled to vote.

Neither Black activists nor, increasingly, women activists were willing to settle for this understanding of the franchise. Black and white women had become increasingly involved in public life in the 1820s and 1830s, working on a variety of causes including abolitionism, poor relief, prison reform, temperance, and protection for Native Americans. By the mid-1840s, women activists increasingly attacked sex-based inequality in public policy. They made some progress in persuading state legislatures to repeal married women's property laws—laws that required women to forfeit control over their property to their husbands when they married. Some went so far as to insist that women should be permitted to vote on the same terms as men, a radical idea that challenged conventional ideas about gender and dependency. In the early republic, New Jersey had been the only state to allow women to vote. Still, a group of New York women petitioned the 1846 state constitutional convention for the right to vote, and activist women went on to intensify their demands for the vote through conventions and petition drives in the East and the Old Northwest. Women's enfranchisement was not broadly popular, however, and activists had little success persuading state legislatures or constitutional conventions to take them seriously. They could not overcome contemporaries' commitment to patriarchy and the view that men and women were naturally suited to distinct roles.[41]

By contrast, advocates of Black men's right to vote were working against a strong tide of disenfranchisement. At the nation's founding, Black men had been able to vote in most states. Over time, however, states moved to make voting a prerogative of white men only. Among those that entered the Union after 1800, only Maine permitted African American men to vote. Meanwhile, older states increasingly restricted Black men's right to vote or disenfranchised them entirely, even as they extended the vote to poor and propertyless white men who had previously been excluded. In its 1821 constitution, New York imposed a special property requirement on Black men, and Pennsylvania disenfranchised Black men in its new constitution in 1838. During these decades, it became clear that previous justifications for excluding large swaths of citizens from the vote—that only those who were economically independent or truly vested in the community were entitled to the privilege—were no longer valid. The vote had become associated with the static, inborn traits of whiteness and maleness. Black activists fought race-based disenfranchisement and pointed out its injustice. In 1841, responding to years of organized pressure by Black New Yorkers, Governor William Seward, a Whig, denounced the property requirement for Black men as "arbitrary" and "incongruous with all our institutions." He continued to advocate Black men's full enfranchisement, arguing after he left office that Black votes would help the antislavery movement. "Give them this right," he wrote to Salmon Chase in 1845, "and their influence will be immediately felt in the national councils, and it is needless to say will be cast in favor of those who uphold the cause of human liberty."[42]

The states of the Old Northwest were among those that had come into the Union after 1800 and had never permitted Black men to vote. Their state constitutions contained declarations of universal basic rights but limited the vote to white male "inhabitants" or "citizens." It was not always clear who belonged in these categories. In some Ohio locales, authorities permitted voting by white noncitizens who were long-term residents of the community. Moreover, two Ohio Supreme Court decisions in 1842 recognized the right to vote of a limited number of men of color. The court had previously held that, in the matter of giving testimony in court, persons who were more than one-half white should be accorded the privileges of white people. Ohioans of racially mixed background pressed the court to apply the same principle to voting, and the court obliged in two decisions—one concerning a person of mixed Black and white background, and the other a person whose mixture included Native American ancestry. In both cases, the court found that because mixed-race people who were deemed more than one-half white were viewed as white for legal purposes, they should also be treated as white for purposes of voting. As a result of the decisions, some mixed-race people could and did vote in Ohio elections.[43]

Still, the constitutional barriers to voting for most African Americans remained in place in Ohio and elsewhere. An Ohio Black convention in 1844 called the state constitution's restriction of the vote to white men "the only dark spot upon that otherwise truly republican document." The convention claimed that the white population had grown more enlightened over time and insisted that white Ohioans now remove the offending clause. The next year, speaking to a gathering at Cincinnati's African Union Baptist Church, Salmon Chase agreed that when the state next revised its constitution, the "anti-suffrage restriction" should be erased. "True Democracy," he argued, "makes no enquiry about the color of the skin, or the place of nativity, or any other similar circumstance of condition."[44]

Liberty Party activists and antislavery Whigs brought demands for Black men's enfranchisement into the many state constitutional conventions that met in the 1840s. In the aftermath of a devastating nationwide economic crisis that began in 1837, many states moved to write new charters, primarily to address issues of banking and public debt. These were opportune moments to alter a state's qualifications for voting. Liberty Party activists ensured that Iowa's initial constitutional convention, meeting in 1844, entertained numerous petitions for Black men's voting rights. The New York convention of 1846 discussed at length whether to drop the property requirement for Black men. The question was put to a referendum, which failed decisively. In Michigan and Wisconsin, too, activists persuaded constitutional conventions to provide referenda on Black men's enfranchisement. More voters supported than opposed Wisconsin's 1849 referendum, which would have instructed the legislature to pass a law eliminating the racial qualification for voting. The state's Board of Canvassers, however, ruled that an insufficient number of voters had cast ballots on the referendum (in comparison to the total number of voters in the canvass) and declared that the referendum was defeated.[45]

These state-level campaigns for Black men's enfranchisement failed everywhere except Rhode Island. There, in 1842, Whig Party leaders allied with African Americans to oppose an insurgent movement seeking to drop property requirements but reserve the vote to white men only. The conflict ended with a new state constitution that permitted Black men to vote on equal terms as white men, while all voters had to meet residency and taxpayer requirements, and naturalized citizens faced more restrictions than the native born. Everywhere else, however, constitutional conventions or the voters themselves rejected proposals to end race-based restrictions on the vote. Yet pressure and publicity did make a difference. Studies have shown that the percentages of northern white voters willing to vote in favor of Black men's enfranchisement grew steadily during the antebellum years, despite never reaching a majority.[46] Among prominent politicians who openly favored Black men's equal right to vote in the 1840s were men like Salmon Chase of Ohio and William Seward of New York, who became Republicans in the 1850s and were prominent figures in the federal government during the Civil War and Reconstruction.

Black activists extended their arguments for racial equality into public schools and public accommodations in these years. Owners of steamboats and railroads routinely required African American passengers to sit in "Jim Crow" sections or denied them access to first-class facilities. Massachusetts activists were particularly effective in protesting such practices. They petitioned the state government, refused to comply with conductors, and filed lawsuits against railroad companies when they were ejected. The state government did not take action, but railroad managers in Massachusetts stopped their iniquitous practices. On a steamboat on the Ohio River, a dignified Black traveler named Dr. Brown explained to Samuel Gridley Howe, a white reformer from Massachusetts, that simply refusing to be "sent into the kitchen to eat his meals" and other humiliations had "cost him many a severe & painful dispute, & brought on him harsh treatment." In 1849, a statewide Black convention in Ohio condemned "Stage Houses and other hotels" that "will not accommodate respectable colored persons," and urged their white friends to withhold their business from such places. The few times lawsuits made it to court, results were mixed, with some courts finding that race was not a reasonable ground for separating passengers and others declaring that it was.[47]

In the Northeast, where state and local governments provided public schools for Black children, many activists in towns and cities fought for racial integration. This was sometimes controversial within African American communities, as some parents and leaders believed that separate schools, staffed by African American teachers, were indispensable community institutions that helped shield their children from the racism of white teachers. Some, however, fought segregated schools on the principle that any form of racial distinction was abhorrent and that separate schools reinforced racism and denied their children opportunities for upward mobility. The most significant school desegregation lawsuit of the period was *Roberts v. City of Boston,* argued in the Massachusetts Supreme Court in 1849. In that case, Benjamin Roberts, a Black printer whose parents had been part of an earlier generation of New England Black activists, sued the city of Boston for establishing segregated schools that barred his daughter from attending the school in her neighborhood. Roberts's lawyers were Robert Morris, the state's second African American attorney and the first to argue a case before a jury, and Charles Sumner, a white man and a rising figure in Massachusetts Whig politics.

Sumner's brief against Boston's segregated schools encapsulated and advanced many of the arguments that civil rights activists had been making for decades. The central theme was "equality before the law." Sumner argued that the impulse to draw racial distinctions was a residue of slavery and that it reflected a spirit of "caste" associated with monarchies and feudalism, not republics like the United States. The state constitution's declaration that "all men are born free and equal" made racial discrimination illegal, he argued. Addressing legal questions about the appropriate scope of regulation, he argued that it might be "reasonable" for the school board to classify students by age, sex, or ability, but that it was entirely inappropriate to "brand a whole race with the stigma of inferiority and degradation, constituting them into a *caste*." The Massachusetts Supreme

Court disagreed with this argument, upholding the school board's policy on grounds that segregation by race could indeed be construed as "reasonable," although it did not explain why. The state legislature sent Sumner to the US Senate in 1851, where he became, during the Civil War and Reconstruction, a stalwart advocate of the principles he and Morris had articulated in the *Roberts* lawsuit. In the meantime, in 1855, the Massachusetts legislature outlawed racial discrimination in public education, thus accomplishing through political processes what Roberts, Morris, and Sumner had been unable to do through litigation.[48]

***

THE LIBERTY PARTY reached its apex in the presidential election of 1844, but the reformist energies that sustained it—including the drive for racial equality in civil and political rights—continued long afterward. In the lead-up to the 1848 election, the Free Soil Party emerged as the next iteration of third-party antislavery organizing. The Free Soilers brought under one umbrella longstanding Liberty Party activists, antislavery Whigs, and new recruits from the Democratic Party. The alliance, although distinct from the Liberty Party, was the fruit of years of third-party organizing. In the mid-1840s, Chase and other Liberty organizers had continued to seek out disillusioned adherents from both major parties. They found increasing purchase among Democrats amid the national crisis over the annexation of Texas in 1845. The question of Texas annexation had roiled politics since 1836, when a largely Anglo group of settlers in the northernmost province of Mexico, Coahuila y Tejas, had led a rebellion against the Mexican government, declared Texas an independent republic, and applied for US statehood. Leaders of both parties at first refused to annex Texas, concerned that incorporating a new slave state under such conditions would be politically destabilizing to the nation. Yet demands for Texas had continued to grow, particularly among southern Democrats, and after the 1844 election of James K. Polk, a pro-annexation Democrat, Texas statehood appeared inevitable.

Northern Democrats' refusal to simply fall into line behind annexation became clear in January 1845, when John P. Hale of New Hampshire, a popular Democratic congressman, announced his opposition to annexation. New Hampshire's Democratic establishment ostracized him, but many voters embraced his strong stand against the Slave Power. In the ensuing months, Hale and his allies, calling themselves Independent Democrats, forged a coalition with New Hampshire Whigs and Libertyites, eventually securing Hale's election to the US Senate and the election of an antislavery Whig to the state's governorship. Hale's triumph suggested that many northern Democrats were willing to break with their party.[49]

Cleavages among Democrats deepened as the conflict over slavery's extension continued. Just before Polk took office, in March 1845, President John Tyler signed a law accepting Texas into the Union. War with Mexico followed soon thereafter. On August 8, 1846, David Wilmot, a Democratic congressman from Pennsylvania, introduced a proposal to forbid slavery in any territory the United States might acquire during the Mexican War. Mexico itself had abolished slavery, and supporters of the Wilmot Proviso argued that the US government had no right to reinstate it. Large numbers of northern Democrats and Whigs proved willing to vote for Wilmot's proposal, defending the principle of nonextension of slavery and denouncing the Slave Power with growing determination. The Wilmot Proviso became a symbol of the extent to which northern Democrats, in particular, were willing to choose section over party. In 1847, Martin Van Buren's allies—known as the Barnburners—walked out of the New York State Democratic Convention when it failed to endorse the principle of nonextension of slavery. Members of the renegade group met a week later to register their grievances and declare "their uncompromising hostility to the extension of slavery into territory now free."[50]

The Free Soil movement of 1848 emerged from this stew of dissent and nascent realignment. The alliance was cemented at a convention in Buffalo, where—in a nod to the importance of the New York Democrats—the party chose Martin Van Buren as its candidate for president. In Ohio as in New York, ferment within the Democratic Party created new possibilities for third-party organizing. As Salmon Chase explained, Ohio Whigs' increasing antislavery sensibility, and "especially" their "opposition to our Black laws," had driven Ohio Democrats toward "pro-slavery positions and into professed support of the Black laws." That dynamic, in turn, repelled many Ohio Democrats, making them susceptible to alliances with the Libertyites or the Whigs.[51] By the mid-1840s, a number of Democrats in the Ohio General Assembly considered themselves "Free Democrats" who were not obliged to conform to the racist and pro-slavery positions of the larger Democratic Party.

The 1848 election season also proved the final straw for the many antislavery Whigs who loathed their party's nominee for president: slaveholder and Army General Zachary Taylor of Kentucky. Intended as a safe choice in a polarized time, Taylor was anathema to many antislavery or "conscience" Whigs who were tired of yielding to the southern wing of their party. Joshua Giddings, who had heretofore insisted that the goals of the antislavery movement were best advanced within the Whig Party, now joined the third-party movement and campaigned for Free Soil candidates in the Western Reserve and across Ohio. Likewise in Massachusetts, antislavery Whig politicians who were committed to dismantling racist policies at home—including Henry Wilson and Charles Sumner—joined the Free Soil movement in 1848.[52]

The Free Soil Party was larger and more diverse than the Liberty Party, and its stance on racial equality before the law was more opaque. Some of its adherents, particularly northern Democrats such as David Wilmot himself, were uninterested in questions of racial equality in the free states—or were outright opposed. Wilmot had told the House his goal was to preserve the territory acquired from Mexico for "the sons of toil, of my own race and own color." To knit the movement together at the national level, leaders emphasized opposition to the Slave Power and slavery's extension; the party's catchy slogan was, "Free Soil, Free Speech, Free Labor, Free Men." Unlike the Liberty Party platform of 1844, the Free Soil platform of 1848 made no mention of the rights of free African Americans, the repeal of antiblack laws, or Black men's right to vote.[53]

At the state level, however, many Free Soilers continued to work for repeal of the black laws, and this was nowhere truer than in Ohio. In 1848, Norton Townshend was a candidate for the Ohio House of Representatives, running on the Free Soil platform. As a medical student in 1837, Townshend had met Salmon Chase and his abolitionist allies in Cincinnati. Townshend had helped organize the Liberty Party in the Western Reserve, and in 1844 he stumped for the party's agenda of repealing the Ohio black laws and ending federal support for slavery. In 1848, Ohio Free Soilers campaigned on both national and local issues. Defining his position on state policy, Townshend emphasized: "First of all, I desire the repeal of the disgraceful Black Laws, no vestige of them ought to remain, and for the honor of our noble State, I wish all record of them could be blotted from the otherwise fair pages of her history."[54]

Whig leaders recognized the significance of the black laws as they deployed heavy hitters in the Western Reserve to try to shore up support. Visiting Cleveland in 1848, William Seward sought to persuade his audience that the Whigs, not a small and untested third party, remained the best conduit for bringing the antislavery movement into politics and for repealing the black laws. Sounding much like Liberty Party leaders, Seward put equality at the center of his argument. Whigs recognized that "our democratic system . . . is founded in the natural equality of *all* men— not alone all *American* men, nor alone all *white* men, but all MEN of every country, clime, and complexion, are equal—not made equal by human laws, but born equal." The black laws of Ohio, he said, like the laws requiring Black voters to meet a property requirement in his home state, reflected continuing "corruption" of the free states by slavery. He called on Ohio Whigs to stick with their party, to "inculcate . . . the love of freedom and the equal rights of man" in their homes, to see that such values were taught in schools, and to reform their "own code" of laws.[55]

Seward and the Ohio Whigs were right to worry about defections to the Free Soilers. When the election results were tallied, it became clear that Ohioans had sent eight Free Soilers to the legislature, most from the Western Reserve. The vote suggested that many antislavery Whig voters were now, like Giddings himself, tired of compromising. Most of the newly elected Free Soilers were former Whigs who retained strong Whig attachments, but two—Norton Townshend and John Morse—turned out to be genuinely independent. Morse was a former Whig and had even served in the legislature as a Whig, whereas Townshend, the longtime admirer of Chase, had been a Libertyite for as long as he had been involved in politics.[56] Their distinct backgrounds notwithstanding, both men were prepared to stake their political reputations on using the third-party "balance of power" strategy to secure repeal of Ohio's black laws.

The opening of the Ohio legislative session in early December 1848 was chaotic and at times seemed poised to devolve into violence as party leaders shouted over one another and spectators crowded in to witness the proceedings. The two major parties were almost evenly matched in both houses. The party to which the Free Soil men threw their support would have power to appoint a US senator and two Ohio Supreme Court justices, as well as to control various state-level patronage positions. In the House, the majority party would choose the speaker and engineer a favorable resolution to a controversy over who had won two House seats from Hamilton County (the Cincinnati area). With respect to the US Senate seat, a Democratic majority in the legislature might choose Chase, avatar of the Liberty Party in Ohio and nationwide. A Whig majority might send Giddings, one of the US House's preeminent opponents of slavery's extension. Both Giddings and Chase saw this as a great opportunity for the Free Soilers to "hold the balance" and exert significant influence over policy and personnel, although Chase was more aggressive in promoting his vision for what that would look like.[57]

Reflecting their determination to speak directly to the legislature, the state's African American leaders had called for a statewide convention to meet in Columbus just as the legislative session got underway. Their first priority was repeal of the black laws. Although they were disenfranchised and therefore unrepresented in the statehouse, they hoped their "moral power" could be "mighty to the pulling down of the strongholds of oppression." Convention delegates addressed a variety of matters, including the merits of emigration out of the United States and support for escaped slaves who had made it to Ohio. They demanded Black men's enfranchisement and, on learning that colonizationist David Christy was lobbying the legislature to support Black migration to Liberia, strongly condemned the American Colonization Society. The convention also reflected the uptick in women's incursions into political life. A Black woman attendee, Jane P. Merritt, offered a resolution that reprimanded convention leadership for depriving women of "a voice" and promised that women would "attend no more after to-night, unless the privilege is granted." The male-dominated convention acceded to the women's demands.[58]

The most spectacular aspect of the convention was a public meeting held on the evening of Thursday, January 11, 1849, in the chamber of the state House of Representatives. It was novel and even daring for a Black convention to ask for use of the hall, and Norton Townshend had been their conduit. The speakers that evening were William Howard Day and John L. Watson, and the audience was large and racially mixed. The two lecturers came from very different backgrounds. Day was born free in New York and benefited from formal education in New York City and Northampton, Massachusetts. Just twenty-three years old, he had recently graduated from Oberlin College and lived in the town of Oberlin, which was in Townshend's district. Watson, a prosperous Cleveland barber, was born enslaved in Virginia and thus represented the migrant class to which so many white Ohioans had long objected. The speeches of the two men came off well, with newspapers hailing the evening as a success. The *Ohio State Journal* called the event "an incident in our history well worthy of reflection and remark." It was an indicator of progress, the paper said, that Black men had been permitted to speak in a venue "hitherto deemed sacred to the white man alone." Echoing a well-known abolitionist phrase, the

paper heralded "the colored man . . . standing there to plead his right to
be deemed a man and a brother, and to claim a community of interest in
all that appertains to humanity—to say '*our* God,' and to beg permission
to say '*our* Country.' "[59]

It remained an open question whether the legislature would finally
repeal the black laws. In the frenzied first days of the session, Townshend
publicly predicted that whatever the ultimate partisan alignment in the
assembly, "there is almost a certainty that the Black Laws will all be
repealed." He and John Morse met with Salmon Chase, who happened
to be in Columbus to argue a case, and they asked him to draft a bill for
repeal. Chase complied, but no one knew precisely how Townshend and
Morse would secure enough votes to pass the bill. As days elapsed, it was
still unclear which party had the majority in the House. In the fight for
the speakership, most Free Soilers threw their weight to the Whigs. Townshend and Morse, however, withheld their support from both parties in
hopes of trading their votes for concessions. Repeal of the black laws was a
significant part of their calculation. Growing numbers of Ohio Whigs had
voiced support for repeal during the 1840s. Many Ohio Whigs believed
their party was ready to repeal the laws at last, but Townshend and Morse
refused to take anything for granted. They planned to wait for a firm promise before delivering their votes to one side or the other.[60]

The pair managed to wield the balance of power extraordinarily effectively. In retrospective accounts, Townshend explained that he and Morse
were open to collaboration with either the Whigs or the Democrats—
whichever party was willing to agree to their terms. At first, it appeared
that the Whigs would join them. In response to overtures from Morse, a
large majority of House Whigs agreed to a bargain that would repeal the
black laws, send Joshua Giddings to the US Senate, and put their party
in the majority. Four Whigs refused, however, and the negotiation failed.
Meanwhile, Townshend tried to make common cause with the Democrats.
Whig editors denounced Townshend and Morse as traitors. Chase, back
home in Cincinnati, tried to reassure them that the Whigs, "under the

influence of the great doctrine of Equal Rights," would join in "carry[ing] their fundamental principle into practical application." He believed repeal was popular and that Townsend, Morse, and others who "take similar ground" would be "triumphantly sustained by the People." Ultimately, Townshend and Morse made the deal that Chase had hoped for. The Democrats agreed to vote to repeal the black laws and send Chase to the Senate, in exchange for a Democratic majority in the House and the patronage and appointments associated with it.[61]

Finally, then, on February 10, 1849, the Ohio legislature passed a bill that announced the repeal of all state laws that "enforce any special disabilities or confer any special privileges *on account of color*." The measure was a triumph of decades of activism by Black and white Ohioans. People like David Blackmore and Benjamin Lundy had spoken out against the laws in the 1810s and early 1820s, but the rise of the Second Party System, in which both major parties relied on slaveholder support, had made what was already a difficult task—persuading a majority of state legislators to repeal racist laws—even harder. Black and white activists had petitioned for repeal in the 1830s, using every adverse report as an opportunity to further publicize the laws' injustice. In Ohio, relentless pursuit of repeal by white Libertyites and Black supporters had helped fragment both the Whigs and the Democrats. Now, the legislature had abolished the anti-black testimony law, which made African Americans vulnerable to all manner of exploitation by whites, and had ended the local registration system that Ohio had established in the first decade of the nineteenth century. The new law made African American children eligible for public school funding, providing that where separate schools were created, the property taxes paid by African Americans must be reserved for the Black schools. It also permitted African American male taxpayers to vote to choose their own local "school directors." In meetings across the state, church organizations celebrated the bill and proffered thanks to Townshend, Morse, and others who forged the coalition that accomplished these long-sought goals.[62]

Momentous as it was, however, the law provided two exceptions and a coda that rendered it less than satisfying to many who had so long sought to expunge racial distinctions from state laws. The law left intact an 1831 statute that made African Americans ineligible for jury service and another that prohibited them from benefiting from poor relief. Nineteenth-century Americans often viewed jury service as a political right or a "privilege" similar to voting, so it is not completely surprising that the jury provision was left in place. More telling was the legislature's decision to retain the law formally declaring that no "black or mulatto person" could "gain a legal settlement" in the state and to include a coda making it a criminal and civil offense to bring or "induce" into the state "any person or persons, who is or are likely to become chargeable as paupers in any township . . . or to become vagrants."[63]

These provisions reflected the longstanding link between traditional concerns about relief of the poor (handed down in the English poor-law tradition) and special worries about Black poverty and criminality. Barring African Americans from gaining a "legal settlement" was tantamount to saying they were not eligible for poor relief. Black Ohioans who had nowhere else to turn still remained vulnerable to the whims of local officials, who could, if they chose, deny them access to relief funds or even remove them from their communities. The new law's race-neutral coda, which barred from the state people who were "likely to become" economically dependent, suggested how legislators readily moved from race-specific prohibitions—which the new legislation mostly condemned—to race-neutral ones that could be used to serve the same purposes. As in Pennsylvania in 1814, the Ohio legislature showed a kind of flexibility about categories of race and class that later served southern legislatures after the Civil War. The language of class-based discrimination could help recoup what was lost when race-based provisions were repealed.

An Ohio correspondent offered a sobering synopsis that Frederick Douglass's *North Star* published alongside praise for the new legislation. Writing from Eaton, Ohio, Alfred J. Anderson, a barber and longtime activist, condemned the "pandering" and "graceless demagogues" in the legislature who had supported repeal while expressing contempt for Black people. Racist laws served to "foster and keep alive a prejudice seriously injurious to our interest," he argued, and therefore the legislature's decision to retain prohibitions on jury service and poor relief—and to provide for segregated as opposed to fully integrated schools—was barely worthy of praise. African Americans' "difficulties will always continue," he wrote, "as long as partial legislation predominates, denying the doctrine of the equality of all men, and making invidious distinctions on account either of caste or color, sect or condition." His position was one of many. The following year, the statewide Black convention focused squarely on the right to vote, while praising the legislature for repealing the black laws and nominating William Howard Day to serve as superintendent of the state's Black public schools.[64]

SOME COMMENTATORS WERE QUICK to diminish the significance of what happened in Ohio, labeling it an anomaly born of shady political dealings and, above all, Salmon Chase's ambition for the Senate seat and more. In 1851, Whig editor Horace Greeley asserted that the repeal "amount[ed] to very little," since it was "palpably the result of a political accident, such as may not again happen in a century." "There was not one-third of the Legislature which repealed those Black Laws heartily in favor of such repeal," the New York editor claimed. The 1880s and 1890s saw renewed interest in the momentous legislative session of 1849, and Morse and Townshend's unorthodox moves became the stuff of Ohio legend. By then, Ohio's black laws had become emblems of a less enlightened era, and the story of their repeal seemed heroic if somewhat quaint. People were fascinated by the tumultuous winter of 1849 legislative session and its role in advancing Chase's career, since his term as a senator proved a stepping-stone to the governorship, the Lincoln administration, and the US Supreme Court.[65]

Yet all the attention on Townshend, Morse, and Chase rendered invisible the many years of petitioning, lobbying, reporting, and political agitation that preceded the repeal. It sometimes sounded as if—as Greeley had suggested—Townshend and Morse were alone in supporting repeal, as if they had made it happen through sheer force of will and savvy politicking. The reality was much different. In Ohio and across the free states, Black activists had persistently and creatively demanded repeal, and growing numbers of white people had become persuaded that racist laws were unacceptable and un-American. By 1849, it was not just a few independent-minded Free Soilers who supported repeal, but most of the state's Whig politicians and not a few Democrats.[66] And Ohio's repeal stuck, despite challenges at the constitutional convention in 1850 and in the general assembly for years thereafter. Repeal of the black laws in Ohio, particularly the hated testimony law that so blatantly denied Black residents equal protection of the laws, served as a beacon for activists elsewhere. Ohio's evidence of what was possible was important, as other developments in the 1850s—the Fugitive Slave Act and newly repressive state policies in Illinois and Indiana—suggested that the nation might be moving in the opposite direction.

CHAPTER 7

"INJUSTICE AND OPPRESSION INCARNATE"

Illinois and a Nation Divided in the 1850s

LIKE MANY AFRICAN AMERICANS who migrated to the Old Northwest, John Jones began life in the slave states. Born free in North Carolina in 1816, he moved to Memphis as a tailor's apprentice and there met and fell in love with Mary Richardson, a free Black woman. When Jones's apprenticeship ended in 1841, he took his small savings and relocated to Alton, Illinois, where Mary and her family then lived. Alton was a dynamic riverfront town, the largest on the Illinois side of the Mississippi River. Yet the official policy of the state of Illinois, like that of most other Midwestern states in the early 1840s, was to treat Black residents with contempt. Its laws required them to register with county officials and forbade them from testifying in court cases involving whites. John and Mary married in Alton and, in 1844, registered as Black residents of Madison County, where Alton was located. Shortly thereafter, they moved 290 miles northeast to Chicago.[1]

The fast-growing city was a place where a man like John Jones could find a way into public life. Abolitionists had begun organizing in Chicago in the wake of Elijah Lovejoy's murder in Alton in 1837. Five years later, the city became the state's center of Liberty Party activity when editor Zebina Eastman moved his paper there, naming it the *Western Citizen*. The Joneses became important members of the city's small Black community. John established a tailoring business and made connections with white abolitionists who helped him improve his reading and writing skills. He affiliated with the white-led Tabernacle Baptist Church, founded in 1843 when members of the city's First Baptist Church split off to form a deliberately antislavery congregation. In 1848, Jones was one of two Black Illinoisans who traveled to a national Black convention that met in Cleveland, where he was named a vice president. He publicly fought the Illinois black laws for almost two decades. Meanwhile, he and Mary helped raise money to purchase runaways hunted by slavecatchers and opened their home to fugitives from slavery. Jones managed to prosper by investing in real estate, and by the 1860s, he had amassed a small fortune.[2]

In the summer of 1847, John Jones published three letters in the just-launched *Chicago Tribune* that made the case for repeal of the state's black laws and Black men's right to vote. His letters would have sounded familiar to anyone following Black activism in the Old Northwest and the broader movement for racial equality. The nation's founders had considered free Black people as citizens, Jones argued. The fact that the Articles of Confederation granted rights of interstate transit and settlement regardless of race was evidence, he said, that the "Revolutionary Congress" believed that "we, the free negroes, of whatever caste, are entitled to all the privileges and immunities of the citizens of the several states." Racist laws like those in Illinois, he insisted, were a malignant departure from the founders' vision and ought to be repealed.[3]

At the same time, powerful forces were pushing in the opposite direction. The Fugitive Slave Act of 1850 provided no procedural protections for alleged runaways and thereby endangered all free Black northerners, who, regardless of their actual status, could be accused of being fugitive slaves and dragged into bondage. Several free states adopted antiblack policies that were more restrictive than ever, including Illinois, where an 1853 statute banned free African Americans from migrating into the state and allowed authorities to sell violators of the law into bondage. The American Colonization Society enjoyed a revival, as some Americans insisted that free Blacks were a source of sectional tension and needed, at last, to leave the country. Many speculated that newly stringent free-state laws like those of Illinois would induce them to go. In 1857, the Supreme Court intensified the argument, declaring in *Dred Scott v. Sanford* that people of African descent were not US citizens and never had been.

The northern debate about the rights of free African Americans thus reached a new apex in the 1850s. The central political conflict of these years concerned the expansion of slavery itself, but the question of free African Americans' future in the United States was never far from view. Most northern Black activists agreed with John Jones: They should continue to demand racial equality in civil rights and citizenship, as well as the right to vote. Some, however, looked at the political situation and concluded that such goals could never be achieved and that it was better to leave the United States altogether. Yet white northerners increasingly joined the cause of racial equality, particularly in the area of civil rights. In the face of the Fugitive Slave Act, they demanded new legal protections for the African Americans who lived in their midst. In Washington, DC, a growing coalition of northern congressmen and senators stood up for racial equality in federal law, though they did not yet have the votes to prevail.

By 1858, when Abraham Lincoln and Stephen A. Douglas traversed Illinois, debating the major political issues of the day, the central fissure over race and rights that had long characterized the antebellum North had etched itself into party politics. On one side were Douglas and the Democrats, who insisted that nature had made Black people subservient to whites and that the egalitarian promises of the Declaration of Independence were intended for white people only. On the other was Lincoln and a new political party, the Republican Party, and they stood for something rather different. Building a coalition after the collapse of the Whig Party, the Republicans drew in people with a wide array of prior affiliations: radical abolitionists and advocates of racial equality who had joined the Liberty Party and other antislavery third parties; former Whigs, some of whom were colonizationists; and former Democrats, some of whom were avowed white supremacists. By the end of the 1850s, however, Republican partisans stood firmly opposed to Democrats' brand of white supremacy and their vision for the nation. Republicans largely agreed that free African Americans were entitled to the same civil rights and perquisites of citizenship as white people were. No major political party had ever before embraced those ideals.

———————

JOHN JONES's CALL for repeal of the Illinois black laws in the *Chicago Tribune* coincided with a state constitutional convention held in the summer of 1847. Economic issues were front and center, but Black migration to Illinois was a major concern. Benjamin Bond, a delegate from southwestern Illinois, introduced a measure to bar Black migration, arguing that free African Americans "had become a great annoyance, if not a nuisance, to the people of Illinois." At the time of the Missouri crisis more than twenty years earlier, plenty of slaveholding states already had banned Black migration. Missouri itself had adopted increasingly stringent measures after statehood. An 1843 law cracked down on Black sailors and almost entirely barred Black migration, but—in a concession to the terms of the Missouri Compromise—it contained an exception for Black or mulatto persons who could produce a certificate of citizenship from another state. The Missouri General Assembly erased that exception in February 1847, enacting a complete ban on Black migration.[4] No free state had enacted such a ban. Now, Illinois was considering it.

Divisions over Bond's Black exclusion measure fell out along sectional rather than partisan lines. It was "north" against "south" within the state. Southern Illinois delegates insisted that northerners had no idea what it was like to live adjacent to slavery. Some said they had moved into the state to get away from the institution. They wanted nothing to do with slaveholders, but neither did they want to live in proximity to free Black people, whose presence was a baneful reminder of the region they had left. One delegate claimed that free African Americans were "idle and lazy" and that his area "was overrun with them." Some alleged that slaveholders sent elderly slaves into Illinois to avoid the cost of caring for people who could no longer be productive laborers. One insisted that the Black population was growing because slave states were forcing out free Blacks.[5] Indeed, some Illinois delegates may have felt special urgency because of Missouri's new bar on Black migration.

In describing free African Americans with such words as *idle, lazy,* and *worthless,* delegates trafficked in racist stereotypes but also drew on the poor-law tradition that had authorized governments to monitor or exclude people whom they believed threatened public order or were likely to drain public resources. Their arguments were bolstered by their view that differences in "race" were natural and immutable. One southern Illinois delegate asserted that nature had created "a barrier between the two races," and he found it inconceivable that "negroes are entitled to all the privileges of citizenship—social and political." Another, who happened to be a South Carolina native, raised the *sine qua non* of sovereignty. "Self preservation was the first law," he said, "and for the purpose of peace and harmony, it was our duty to so fix the constitution so that this matter should be forever settled." As the debate wore on and northerners fought back, a delegate from an Ohio River county threatened genocide. If the convention did not pass a measure to protect "the south [that is, the southern part of the state] from being overrun by these swarms of free negroes . . . the people of the south would take the matter into their own hands, and commence a war of extermination."[6]

Opponents of Black exclusion challenged every argument. Many insisted that the measure was morally wrong and contrary to the principles of freedom that its proponents supposedly embraced. The measure would make the Illinois legislature "the objects of scorn to the world," one argued, and discourage industrious settlers from coming into the state. Whig delegate Jesse Olds Norton, who later served as a Republican in the US House of Representatives, refuted the racist generalization on which the law was premised. Even if some people of African descent appeared disinclined to work, he argued, that did not mean all should be banned from the state. Finally, critics insisted that the measure was unconstitutional. Invoking the Missouri debates of 1820–21, they argued that Black citizens of other states could not be denied entry to Illinois. More broadly, the US Constitution made no mention of "the word white, or black, or yellow," and neither should that of Illinois.[7]

The debate was explosive—filled with interruptions, invective, and insults. Finally, after tabling the issue for two months, the delegates forged a compromise in the final week of the convention. Bond reintroduced the measure, now worded more indirectly. The proposed constitution would not ban Black migration outright, but it would instruct the legislature to do so. Also, when voters were asked to ratify the new constitution, the Black exclusion measure would be separated from the rest of the document. That way, if voters chose to reject Black exclusion, they would not scuttle the whole constitution in the process. Neither side had secured exactly what it hoped for. Southern Illinoisans had hoped to end the debate by putting the exclusion measure directly in the constitution itself; most northerners had hoped for no exclusion clause at all. After another bitter confrontation, more name calling, and another threat of racial extermination, the convention adopted the revised proposal by a vote of 97 to 56. In March 1848, the voters of Illinois weighed in, approving the Black exclusion clause by a large margin. The voters had made their choice clear, although nothing would formally change until the legislature took action.[8]

The impulse to ban Black migration also prevailed in Oregon Territory, Kentucky, Iowa, and Indiana. Oregon Territory's provisional government had passed a Black exclusion measure in 1844, and five years later the first territorial legislature repassed the ban. In the summer of 1850, Kentucky's constitutional convention adopted a measure similar to the one in Illinois, instructing the Kentucky General Assembly to make it a felony for "any free negro or mulatto" to migrate into the state and for any newly emancipated person to remain there. In neighboring Indiana, a constitutional convention met soon after that, and, following extensive debate, passed measures that prohibited entry of free African Americans, voided contracts made by Black people who were in the state illegally, fined employers who hired illegal migrants, and channeled all fines collected in enforcement of the measure into a fund for promoting colonization. By putting its Black exclusion clause directly in the constitution rather than leaving the matter to the legislature, and by specifying a series of other violations, Indiana outdid both Illinois and Kentucky. The following summer, in 1851, "the people" of Indiana—that is, the voters, who were exclusively white men— approved the constitution. Meanwhile, in the winter of 1851, the Iowa legislature passed a law prohibiting Black settlement.[9]

Support for such bans was far from unanimous among white northerners, however, even those living in the Old Northwest states. In Indiana and Illinois, white men who went on to significant careers in state and national politics strongly rejected the new policies. Among the most vocal opponents of the new measures in Indiana was Schuyler Colfax, later Republican speaker of the House and vice president of the United States during Grant's first term. At the Ohio constitutional convention of 1850, a Black exclusion proposal was discussed but defeated. The following winter, Ohio Democrats tried to revive laws similar to those repealed in 1849 but failed again. Wisconsin and Michigan never passed Black exclusion laws, nor did any of the Mid-Atlantic or northeastern states. Opponents of racist legislation continued their advocacy even in the face of defeat. In the Illinois legislature's first session under its new constitution, Black residents and their allies again petitioned for repeal of the existing black laws. Richard Yates, a future Republican governor, was among those in the Illinois House of Representatives who supported repeal, calling the state's black laws "tyrannical, iniquitous, and oppressive" and "unbecoming the statutes of a free, magnanimous, enlightened, and christian people."[10]

STILL, THE BLACK EXCLUSION MEASURES passed by the free states of Illinois and Indiana in 1848 and 1850 made a strong impression, particularly
as this was a moment of unprecedented national upheaval over slavery. At
the end of the 1840s, the epicenter of the national conflict was Congress,
and the crisis began when California applied for admission to the Union
as a free state. Congress had never resolved the question of whether slavery
would be permitted in the territory gained in the Mexican War of 1846–
48. Free staters of all political parties had supported the Wilmot Proviso,
which would have prohibited slavery's extension into the newly acquired
territory, but the proviso did not pass Congress. Thus, while northerners opposed slavery's expansion ever more vocally, slaveholders and their
allies insisted that Congress continue to divide the land into slave and free
territories, as it had done in the past. California's 1849 bid for admission
brought the matter to a head. In wide-ranging debates, amid threats by
slave staters to dissolve the Union and President Zachary Taylor's death of a
stomach ailment in the summer of 1850, Congress confronted not just the
status of slavery in the territories acquired from Mexico but a range of longstanding federal-level issues concerning slavery and race. These included
abolitionists' demand for the abolition of slavery and the slave trade in the
District of Columbia, slaveholders' desire for a stricter fugitive slave law,
and New Englanders' concerns about the rights of free Black sailors in
southern ports.

Southerners wanted a new federal fugitive slave law to better enforce
the Constitution's provision that enslaved people—glossed as persons "held
to Service or Labour"—who escaped to free states would be "delivered
up" to slaveholders who claimed them. The 1793 Fugitive Slave Act had
provided mechanisms for enforcement of the fugitive slave clause but did
not specify which officials—federal, state, or local—were required to help
slaveholders seize runaways. Concerned about alleged fugitive slaves' rights
to due process of law, free-state legislatures in the 1820s and 1830s had

adopted measures designed to fill in the blanks, and some of those state-level "personal liberty laws" afforded considerable protections for alleged fugitive slaves, including—as in Massachusetts and New York—the possibility of a jury trial. Some antislavery lawyers and activists, including Salmon Chase of Ohio, had gone so far as to argue that the 1793 law itself was unconstitutional. In the 1842 case of *Prigg v. Pennsylvania*, the US Supreme Court had weighed in. Justice Joseph Story of Massachusetts, writing for the majority, upheld the constitutionality of the 1793 law and affirmed slaveholders' right to reclaim enslaved people who escaped to free territory. Story also sought to resolve the question of which authorities were responsible for enforcing the law. His view was that the recapture of fugitives was a matter of exclusive federal jurisdiction and that state officials—judges, justices of the peace, sheriffs, and the like—need have nothing to do with it. After *Prigg*, free states passed new laws that explicitly forbade state and local officials from cooperating with fugitive slave renditions and prohibited the use of jails for holding alleged fugitives. Slaveholding politicians saw such measures as acts of bad faith and demanded a new and stronger federal fugitive slave law. Those demands were in play during the crisis over California statehood.[11]

Southern calls for a new fugitive slave law reignited the debate about Black sailors' rights. New Englanders had long connected the two issues, which were associated with interstate relations and represented in Article IV, Section 2 of the US Constitution. If free states had to honor slaveholders' claims on free soil, they insisted, then slave states should respect the privileges and immunities of traveling Black citizens. If Congress passed legislation to satisfy one side's interests, they said, then it ought to do the same for the other. In the spring of 1850, Roger Baldwin, a Whig from Connecticut, made the case in the US Senate, insisting that any new federal fugitive slave law must include "an independent tribunal" to assess the validity of slaveowners' claims, and that such tribunals must also operate to protect the rights of free Black northerners in places "where every colored man is presumed to be a slave." That summer, Senator John Davis of

Massachusetts again linked the two issues, proposing to amend the fugitive slave bill with a measure empowering federal courts to issue a writ of habeas corpus when any "free colored person," arriving in a state by sea, was deprived of his or her liberty.[12]

Senator Robert Winthrop joined the fray with evidence of the injustices visited on Black sailors and a far-reaching argument about personhood rights. Winthrop had moved from the US House to the Senate at the end of July 1850, replacing Daniel Webster when the latter became secretary of state. Drawing on his experiences in 1842 and 1843, Winthrop offered testimonials from ship captains and others showing that—contrary to southern senators' claims—authorities in southern ports did indeed enforce laws targeting Black sailors. When southern senators split hairs over the question of the "privileges and immunities" of state citizenship under the Constitution's Article IV, Winthrop sought to rise above it all. This was no "mere question of citizenship," he said. It mattered little whether Black "stewards and mariners" were "citizens or not." Rather, the question was whether, "upon the ground of police regulations, or upon any other ground," states had the right to remove free people from their ships "and imprison them, and even sell them into slavery for life, for no other crime than their color." Paring away the constitutional language of "privileges and immunities," Winthrop insisted that all people, citizens or not, were entitled to basic rights to personal liberty and due process of law. Winthrop later wrote that this was the moment of his legislative career of which he was most proud. He had followed his "own convictions of duty, & sustained [his] honest opinion of what was right, independently & fearlessly."[13]

The New Englanders had made their point. Anyone following the Senate's tense debates would have understood that the matter of free Black sailors' rights in the southern states remained a live issue. Still, they did not have the numbers to ensure that if the nation was going to have a strict new fugitive slave law, it would at least also have a law designed to protect Black sailors in southern ports. The Fugitive Slave Act of 1850—one of a series of measures known as the Compromise of 1850—dramatically enhanced the federal government's authority and capacity to reach into the states. Consistent with the *Prigg* decision's holding that the federal government was responsible for enforcement of the Constitution's fugitive slave clause, the new Fugitive Slave Act established a corps of federal commissioners charged with adjudicating slaveholders' claims. The legal procedures it established were manifestly biased in favor of slaveholders. In the summary proceedings required by the law, alleged fugitive slaves were explicitly denied the right to testify; commissioners were paid ten dollars if they ruled in favor of the slaveholder and just five dollars if they did not. The law also commanded "all good citizens" to help with enforcement and made it a federal offense to resist the law.[14]

The Fugitive Slave Act, passed on September 18, 1850, sent shock waves through the free states. Prominent northern Whigs and Democrats held meetings urging people to accept the new law for the sake of keeping the nation together. They hoped northerners would fall into line behind yet another compromise with the Slave Power. For Black people living in the free states, the law was an existential threat. They recognized immediately that it not only jeopardized the many runaways among them—some of whom had lived in the free states for decades—but it also made free Black people more vulnerable than ever to kidnappers abetted by unscrupulous commissioners. In many places, Black northerners responded with militancy, organizing vigilance committees to resist enforcement of the law. Some decided to leave altogether, including the Syracuse-based minister and abolitionist Samuel Ringgold Ward, who felt that it was "vain to hope for the reformation of such a country," and moved with his family to Toronto. The Fugitive Slave Act radicalized some white northerners, who were shaken out of complacency by the sight of federal commissioners, often acting against the wishes of local communities, forcibly grabbing Black neighbors and dragging them southward. Many viewed the new law as further evidence that slaveholders were willing to go to un-American extremes—including in this case trampling the customary authority of the states and the basic right to due process of law—to defend human bondage.[15]

Amid this national crisis, the American Colonization Society enjoyed a renaissance. Whigs in particular argued that colonization would solve a host of problems. Most prominent was Henry Clay of Kentucky, one of the founders of the ACS, the Whig Party's standard-bearer, and the owner of dozens of enslaved people. Clay urged Congress to invest in a "line of steamers" that would ply the Atlantic, enhancing trade and transporting free African Americans to Liberia while also helping intercept illegal slave traders: "Commerce will be promoted; civilization will be promoted; religion will be promoted, by the transfer of the free people of color with their own consent from the United States to Africa." One writer for the ACS's *African Repository* suggested that colonization could resolve the entire sectional conflict. "If politicians would stop talking and act a while in concert, to provide a home for our free blacks where they would be welcome and well off, perhaps then the question of slavery might be compromised to the satisfaction of all parties."[16]

ACS leaders promoted a cheerful vision of Liberia while touting their organization's plan as a solution to the ostensibly intractable challenge that free African Americans posed to the United States. The ACS emphasized that Liberia had become an independent republic in 1847 and was now governed by formerly enslaved people from the United States. This was a place that, unlike the United States, Black Americans could truly make their own. Meanwhile, in an annual report published in early 1851, the society forecast increasing white animosity toward free African Americans and solicited donations from the states. The recently adopted constitutions of Illinois and Indiana revealed that "the people at large are arrayed in favor of some energetic State action for carrying on the work of Colonization," ACS leaders wrote. One article in the *African Repository* warned that exclusionary measures in the Old Northwest would drive African Americans into free states that had no such restrictions and that whites, in turn, would leave those states, "to avoid the inconveniences of the preponderance of that race." Gloomy scenarios such as these also preoccupied Whig editor Horace Greeley, who, reflecting on developments in Illinois and Indiana, commented that "the will of a Majority of the Enfranchised is the law of the land. That Majority may do wrong, but it is well nigh irresistible." Washington Hunt, the Whig governor of New York, jumped on the bandwagon, calling on the state legislature to make an appropriation to the ACS.[17]

Black activists fought hard against signs that the ACS was gaining momentum and that, amid the panic wrought by the Fugitive Slave Act, some free Black northerners appeared willing to consider moving to Liberia. In an "Address to the People" of New York, African Americans in Albany called the ACS "a gigantic fraud, professing to love, whilst it systematically encourages hate among mankind." The group countered Governor Hunt's claim that Black New Yorkers were "condemned to a life of servility and drudgery." Black New Yorkers were active and prosperous citizens, they insisted. Many owned real estate and sent their children to school. Black men voted regularly and had even helped put Hunt in office, supporting him in part for his strong opposition to the Fugitive Slave Act.[18]

Frederick Douglass was not interested in the pessimistic assessments of leading Whigs and the ACS. Douglass, who had escaped slavery in Maryland and became a renowned abolitionist speaker in the 1840s, published his autobiography in 1845 and started his own newspaper, the *North Star,* in 1847. By the early 1850s, he was the most renowned Black man in the United States. Douglass had also become critical of the Garrisonian position that the American political system was so irredeemably tainted by slavery that the only moral answer was to avoid politics and the state altogether. In the winter of 1852, Douglass adopted a hopeful tone as he tried to reframe the conversation. The new Indiana Constitution reflected a desire to "conciliate the South," not "a disposition to get rid of the few colored people" who lived there, he argued. How one assessed the existing situation was a matter of perspective, he continued: "Those who take counsel only of the outrages and proscriptions of which we are the victims, will lean on colonization. . . . Yet this is altogether the result of a partial view of our past history and present condition." Douglass urged readers to note Black Americans' successes and white Americans' growing acceptance of them. "The 'Jim Crow pew,' and the 'Jim Crow car,' are becoming relics of American barbarism," Douglass wrote. "Men are everywhere becoming ashamed of the littleness of despising a man for the complexion which God has given him."[19]

As Douglass suggested, the impulse to imagine and demand a better future for African Americans in the United States required a measure of optimism. Those brought low by significant new assertions of white supremacy in the late 1840s and early 1850s were more ready to imagine that the best course was to leave the country altogether. Nor was Liberia the only option for African Americans looking to escape American abuses. In the early 1850s, thousands departed for Canada, where they lived beyond the reach of federal fugitive-slave commissioners and where communities of Black refugees from the United States had been putting down roots for decades. Yet for Douglass and many others, including John Jones of Illinois, the decision was to stay and fight.[20]

THE 1850 FUGITIVE SLAVE ACT had particular ramifications in Illinois because one of the compromise's main architects, Stephen A. Douglas, was the state's senior senator and the most powerful Democrat in a Democrat-dominated state. Many believed the pugnacious Midwesterner was destined for the presidency. Yet Douglas was also one of the most prominent northern allies of pro-slavery southern Democrats, a stance that many Illinois Democrats, particularly in the northern reaches of the state, did not appreciate. Douglas was absent for the Senate vote on the Fugitive Slave Act, but constituents in Chicago demanded that he answer for it anyway. After all, he had been behind the legislative maneuvering that succeeded in getting the multifaceted Compromise of 1850 through Congress.[21]

Black and white Chicagoans rebelled openly against the Fugitive Slave Act. The city's Black population was small but mighty—about 320 people and one percent of the population in 1850. In the 1840s, Chicago's AME church, Quinn Chapel, had become a center of Black religious and civic life. Immediately on hearing of passage of the Fugitive Slave Act, Black leaders convened a meeting at the church. White supporters were also in attendance as the meeting adopted resolutions condemning the new law and created a vigilance committee to patrol the city and root out would-be slavecatchers. Several weeks later, the Chicago City Council took a stand. It declared the Fugitive Slave Act unconstitutional, condemned as traitors the members of the Illinois congressional delegation who had voted for it, and requested that "the citizens, officers and police of this city . . . abstain from any and all interference" in the capture of fugitives. The next night, a mass meeting at City Hall passed similar resolutions and declared that the portion of "our citizens" who had escaped slavery "by their own act" were already free. Stephen Douglas had sneaked into the hall, and as the crowd cheered for resistance, some called on him to defend the law, which he did the next night. In an address that ran more than three hours, Douglas characterized the city council's measure as South Carolina–style nullification, antithetical to national unity, and said it was Chicagoans' collective duty to uphold federal law. Douglas's powers of persuasion were formidable, and some called on the city council to reverse itself. The resolutions remained on the books until the end of November, when the council passed new resolutions that were softer in tone but nonetheless declared that city officers had no obligation to cooperate in the arrest of fugitives.[22]

Many Illinois Democrats remained disillusioned with Douglas and his collaboration with the Slave Power, however, and the 1852 election season revealed that traditional partisan alignments were faltering. For years, the state's nine-member delegation to the US House of Representatives had included just one non-Democrat, and that person always came from the Springfield area. That changed in 1852, when, according to editor Zebina Eastman, antislavery voters "diverted their votes to congressmen, who they knew were pledged to their principles and against Douglas' pet doctrines." That shift, particularly among Democratic voters in northern

Illinois, combined with redistricting before the election, resulted in the election of four Whigs to Congress, along with two anti-Douglas Democrats. The Democrats' "arrogant power in Illinois was broken," Eastman wrote. Among those elected to Congress for the first time that year was a future prominent Republican, Elihu Washburne of Galena. Nominally a Whig, he had campaigned as an independent to attract votes from Democrats and third-party antislavery voters.[23]

The impact on the Illinois statehouse was unclear, but the elections sparked optimism among organized African Americans. Although the Democrats remained the heavy majority in the state legislature, the party was hardly united. And Lake County, a Democratic stronghold just north of Chicago, had elected Henry W. Blodgett, a longstanding abolitionist and third-party man, as its representative. Chicago's Black activists took steps to energize their movement and make their voices heard in Springfield. At a meeting in City Hall, Byrd Parker, an AME minister, declared his hope of building "a union of sentiment and *concert of action,* on the part of the colored people, and friends, urging all to move in the matter of petitioning the Legislature." John Jones read the state's antiblack statutes aloud, describing in a "masterly and happy manner . . . the immoral, wicked, and evil tendency of such enactments." The meeting's organizers wanted to repeal all of the state's black laws but decided to focus first on the racist testimony law, believing it most damaging. A petition campaign was already well underway, as J. H. Barquet, a migrant from South Carolina, had been lecturing and collecting signatures in locales across northern Illinois.[24]

It was John A. Logan, a southern Illinois Democrat, who ensured that the hopes of Illinois African Americans would be dashed. As the legislative session began in Springfield, an ally of the Black conventioneers proposed repeal of the noxious testimony law, but that effort was overwhelmed by Logan and his campaign to ban Black migration. A veteran of the Mexican War whose father was an influential Democrat, Logan was twenty-six years old and had already been elected county clerk and district attorney. His home was in Jackson County, part of the far southern region of Illinois known as "Egypt," because its largest town was Cairo. He and his family were known locally as slavecatchers, hostile to the interests of free African Americans and to their presence in the state. In later years, Logan became a Republican and a renowned Civil War general. In 1853, however, he was serving his first term in the state legislature and was determined to bring about what many southern Illinois Democrats had long desired: fulfillment of the Black exclusion mandate in the 1848 state constitution.[25]

As it happened, a December 1852 US Supreme Court decision suggested that Logan's proposed Black exclusion measure would pass constitutional muster if challenged. The case, *Moore v. Illinois*, had begun ten years earlier, when Richard Eells, a white abolitionist from Quincy, Illinois, was convicted in a local court for violating a law that made it a misdemeanor to harbor a fugitive slave. Eells lost his appeal to the Illinois Supreme Court and then, represented by Salmon Chase, appealed to the US Supreme Court. Eells and his lawyers argued that the state law under which he was convicted was invalidated by the court's decision in *Prigg v. Pennsylvania* (1842), which held that the US government had exclusive jurisdiction over matters associated with fugitive slaves. By contrast, the Illinois attorney general argued that even if matters associated with slaveholders' rights were now exclusively under federal jurisdiction, the Illinois law was valid on the principle of state police powers—that states had a "right of self-preservation" and could "repel" dangerous populations from their borders. In *Moore v. Illinois,* the Supreme Court agreed with the state in a decision that strongly affirmed states' authority to do what they deemed necessary to regulate such unwanted groups as "paupers, criminals, or fugitive slaves."[26]

In early February 1853, then, John Logan introduced his Black exclusion law in the Illinois House, ready to fight for it and believing it was on firm constitutional ground. The bill made it a crime for anyone to bring free or enslaved African Americans into Illinois. African Americans who entered the state and remained more than ten days could be found guilty of a "high misdemeanor" and fined fifty dollars. Persons who could not immediately pay the fine were subject to imprisonment and sale "at public auction" to any purchaser willing to pay the person's fine and court costs. The purchaser, in turn, was permitted to compel "said negro, or mulatto," to labor without pay, for an amount of time agreed upon with the justice of the peace.[27] It was that provision—that a free person could be sold into slavery—that earned the measure the moniker "Slave Law."

The abolitionist Henry Blodgett of Lake County was among the legislators who decried Logan's proposal on both moral and constitutional grounds. Blodgett—who had previously edited a newspaper, the *Lake County Visitor*, whose motto was "The Primary Object of Civil Government is to Secure Justice"—called on the legislature to repeal all existing antiblack laws rather than pass Logan's measure. Then he insisted that Logan's proposal violated both the privileges and immunities clause of the US Constitution and the state's own constitution, which banned slavery and declared that "all men are born equally free and independent, and have certain inherent and indefeasible rights." Blodgett professed incredulity that the legislature would criminalize migration. "What becomes of all our notions of republican rights and liberty," he asked, if it is a crime "to pass a geographical, a mere mathematical line." If people of African descent could be oppressed this way, he continued, then so too could the "poor, debased, worn-out serfs of Europe that are thrust upon us."[28] Illinoisans were not willing to enslave or cast out impoverished European immigrants, he reasoned, and neither should they impose such penalties on African Americans.

Logan defended his bill from top to bottom, drawing on familiar arguments about the state's obligation to protect the public good. To Logan, the primary object of government was not justice but "the greatest good to the greatest number." The bill was simply good "public policy," he argued. It did no harm to the people of northern Illinois, while it offered long-sought relief to the state's southern region, where white residents needed protection against an influx of paupers and criminals of a supposedly inferior race. Blodgett seemed to want to "make the negro a citizen," Logan said,

REGISTRATION OF A FREE BLACK FAMILY, ROSS COUNTY, OHIO, 1812

This page of the registry for Ross County, Ohio, shows the kinds of steps many African Americans had to take to register in Ohio, as required by state law. The clerk in Essex County, Virginia, mailed proof that Polly and her children—Barbara, Joe, and Carter—were free. The Ross County clerk received the evidence and duly registered the family on Nov. 20, 1812. The Ohio clerk drew a picture of the Essex County seal to demonstrate the authenticity of the documentation he received. *Ross County Clerk of Courts.*

CINCINNATI, 1812

Early engraving of Cincinnati viewed from the Kentucky side of the Ohio River. The river became an important border between slavery and freedom within the new nation. Yet states on the north side, including Ohio, passed antiblack laws designed to discourage African American settlement. *Wikimedia Commons.*

"TEARING UP FREE PAPERS," 1838

This antislavery engraving illustrates how easily white people could abuse policies that required African Americans to carry papers proving their freedom. *Charles Deering McCormick Library of Special Collections and University Archives, Northwestern University Library.*

FREEDOM PAPER OF PATSEY EVANS, 1827

In this document, the clerk of Lunenburg County, Virginia, attests that Patsey Evans is "a free person, born of free parents," and that she is "entitled to all the benefits of a free person of colour, under the laws of this State." It describes Evans as "about Thirty years of age, brown complexion about Five feet three inches high, no scars." Free Black people carried such documents to prove their freedom to anyone who might question it. Freedom papers were also required when a person needed to register with county officials in Ohio and elsewhere. Patsey Evans's freedom paper shows evidence of having been folded, roughly in sixths, to fit in a pocket or purse. *Courtesy of the Ohio History Connection, VFM5314.*

BLACK LEADERS IN THE STRUGGLE FOR JUSTICE, 1820s

Samuel Cornish (left), was a Presbyterian minister in New York City and co-editor of *Freedom's Journal* and other antislavery newspapers. William Costin (right), was a widely respected messenger for the Bank of Washington who fought the Washington, DC, law requiring free African Americans to register with local officials. *Cornish image: Photographs and Prints Division, Schomburg Center for Research in Black Culture, The New York Public Library. Costin image: Library of Congress, LC-DIG-pga-06394.*

US CAPITOL AND COFFLE OF ENSLAVED PEOPLE, 1817

From an antislavery tract, this engraving of the US Capitol, with a group of enslaved people chained before it, indicates how early activists trained their attention on the District of Columbia. One of the allegorical figures at the top right is probably Columbia, a symbol of the nation. The other is Liberty, who holds a pole topped with a liberty cap—an icon of freedom associated with ancient Rome and, more recently, the American and French Revolutions. *Library Company of Philadelphia.*

IMAGES FROM THE *AMERICAN ANTI-SLAVERY ALMANAC*, 1840
(Top) *"Poor things, they can't take care of themselves."* This engraving offers a sardonic comment on the widespread argument that free Black people would become dependent on public resources. (Bottom left) "The *Negro Pew,* or *'Free' Seats for* black *Christians.*" (Bottom right) *"Mayor of New-York refusing a Carman's license to a colored Man."* This pair of images criticizes white northerners for systematic discrimination against African Americans—in churches and in public policy. *Library of Congress, Rare Book and Special Collections Division, Printed Ephemera Collection.*

"JAIL IN WASHINGTON,—SALE OF A FREE CITIZEN TO PAY HIS JAIL FEES!"
From an 1836 abolitionist broadside, this illustration insists that free African Americans are citizens and emphasizes the perils they faced in the nation's capital. If arrested on suspicion of being fugitive slaves, they could be sold into slavery to cover their jail fees. *Library of Congress, LC-DIG-ppmsca-19705.*

DAVID JENKINS

JOHN MERCER LANGSTON

JOSHUA R. GIDDINGS

WILLIAM HOWARD DAY

OHIO CIVIL RIGHTS ACTIVISTS, 1830s TO 1850s
All these men pushed for repeal of the Ohio black laws. Jenkins was an early leader in Ohio Black activism; Langston survived the 1841 Cincinnati riot as a boy and later became known as Ohio's first Black lawyer and officeholder; Day, an early Black graduate of Oberlin College, was particularly committed to opening educational opportunities for Black children; and Giddings, who was white, spent two decades in the US House of Representatives fighting against slavery and for racial equality in civil rights. *Jenkins image: Public Library of Steubenville and Jefferson County. Langston image: Library of Congress, LC-DIG-cwpbh-00681. Day image: Documenting the American South, University of North Carolina Libraries, Chapel Hill, wheel40.tif. Giddings image: Library of Congress, LC-DIG-cwpbh-02822.*

JOHN JONES AND MARY RICHARDSON JONES

Born free in North Carolina, John Jones served as a tailor's apprentice in Memphis, where he met Mary Richardson, the daughter of a blacksmith. When Mary's family moved to Alton, Illinois, John soon followed. The pair married in Alton and moved in 1845 to Chicago, where they became prominent members of the city's Black community, their home a gathering place for Black and white activists and a safe haven for fugitives from slavery. John Jones fought the Illinois black laws from the 1840s through 1865, when they were finally repealed by a Republican-majority state legislature. *John Jones image: Chicago History Museum, ICHi-022361, Mosher & Baldwin, photographer. Mary Richardson Jones image: Chicago History Museum, ICHi-022363, Baldwin & Drake, photographer.*

CONTRASTING PERSPECTIVES IN ILLINOIS

(Left) Zebina Eastman, a New England native, was an editor and third-party antislavery leader in Illinois during the 1840s and 1850s. He and his publications consistently opposed the state's black laws. (Right) Author of the notorious 1853 law barring Black migration into Illinois, John A. Logan was a Democratic state legislator from southern Illinois and an ally of Stephen A. Douglas, the state's most powerful politician in the 1850s. *Eastman image: Northwestern University Library. Logan image: Library of Congress, LC-DIG-cwpb-07018.*

"SLAVE TERRITORY. | FREE TERRITORY."

This 1846 engraving from the *North-Western Liberty Almanac,* published in Chicago by Zebina Eastman, shows how antislavery activists described the stark contrast between the sections, with the Ohio River as the dividing line. On the left, in slave territory, an overseer stands watch over enslaved laborers working in a field, with rudimentary buildings as a backdrop. On the right, a farmer is at work in a more orderly rural landscape, and a city stands behind him as a representation of economic advancement. Even the tree branches demonstrate the contrast. *Newberry Library, Chicago, Graff 1201.*

SUNDAY IN JAIL, WASHINGTON, DC, 1861
In December 1861, *Frank Leslie's Illustrated Weekly* published this spread commenting on depraved conditions on a Sunday in the Washington jail. In the center, a group of African American men and boys play cards. At top left, a lone Black woman is in anguish as, at top right, white women—portrayed in low-cut dresses as if prostitutes—groom one another. At bottom right, crowded conditions force men to congregate in a hallway. *Library of Congress, LC-USZ62-103911 & LC-USZ62-103912.*

"GLIMPSES AT THE FREEDMEN'S BUREAU, RICHMOND, VA.," 1866

In August 1866, *Frank Leslie's Illustrated Weekly* published this scene of a Freedmen's Bureau court that had opened the previous October. The image shows an African American man taking an oath before testifying in court, a visual representation of the Republican belief that African Americans were entitled to the same civil rights as whites, including the right to give testimony. The accompanying text explains, "The person sitting at the table is a colored man, who draws up petitions and transacts other business for the Freedmen, though they may employ lawyers, if they choose." *Archives and Special Collections, Dickinson College.*

"THE LOBBY OF THE HOUSE OF REPRESENTATIVES AT WASHINGTON DURING THE PASSAGE OF THE CIVIL RIGHTS BILL," 1866

During the winter of 1865-66, African American organizations across the country sent delegates to Washington to lobby for federal enforcement of racial equality in civil rights and the right to vote. The artist who created this image from *Harper's Weekly* included, at front right, a Black man as part of the crowd of lobbyists at the US Capitol. *Archives and Special Collections, Dickinson College.*

"CELEBRATION OF THE ABOLITION OF SLAVERY IN THE DISTRICT OF COLUMBIA BY THE COLORED PEOPLE," 1866

On April 19, 1866, Black residents of Washington, DC, celebrated both the fourth anniversary of the District of Columbia Emancipation Act and the recent passage of the Civil Rights Act—the nation's first federal civil rights law. After a parade that featured African American veterans and members of local political and philanthropic societies, thousands convened in Franklin Square, blocks from the White House. This illustration depicts that gathering, where the crowd was addressed by prominent Republican legislators, as well as by longtime northern Black activists Henry Highland Garnet and William Howard Day. *Library of Congress, LC-DIG-ds-07454.*

but that was "repugnant to the opinions of the civilized world." Besides, he insisted, there was little novel in a proposal that compelled idlers to work. Alluding to the state's vagrancy law, Logan pointed out that authorities were already permitted to arrest, convict, and sell "any person (no distinction as to color)" who might be found idle and without "visible means of support." It was in fact true that Illinois law permitted convicted vagrants to be sold "to the best bidder, by public outcry," for up to four months, the proceeds of their labor going to the county treasury or to their family, if they had any. This was no "question of slavery or anti slavery," Logan insisted. It was "a question merely of policy." He called on his colleagues to perform the "duty" they owed to "a rising generation." Logan's bill passed the Illinois House by a relatively close vote of 44 to 37; two weeks later, it passed the Senate by a 13-to-9 vote.[29]

The "Logan Law," like other antiblack measures, gave white people a sense of power and impelled some to vigilantism. When the law was enforced by officials, mostly in southern Illinois, people convicted under it were typically forced to labor for one month, during which time they ostensibly earned the fifty-dollar fine they owed the state. Yet the law sent a message that African Americans were not wanted in Illinois, and white residents who supported it saw it as official confirmation of their existing beliefs: that Black people had no real right to live and work in Illinois and could be subjected to expulsion at any time. Sporadic white violence against Blacks was already commonplace in some pockets of the state, but the new law surely enhanced the climate of hostility and gave ill-disposed white people a new sense of license. In Cairo, which stood at the southern tip of the state, at the confluence of the Mississippi and Ohio Rivers, a white mob lynched a Black man named Joseph Spencer in the fall of 1854. Two years later, white residents of Cairo formed a posse with the professed purpose of arresting African Americans under the Logan Law. They intensified their efforts the following summer, this time laying siege to Black homes and demanding—in many cases successfully—that African Americans clear out of the city.[30]

Yet the Logan Law also became an organizing tool for Illinoisans who wanted to see the state move in the opposite direction—to repeal all the black laws and secure to African Americans what John Jones called "fair and equal treatment." In party politics, the latest incarnation of the third-party antislavery movement was the Free Democrats. The coalition first convened in Pittsburgh in 1852, attempting to recapture some of the energy of the Free Soil movement of four years earlier. The coordinator of the Pittsburgh meeting was Samuel Lewis, the former Ohio Liberty Party gubernatorial candidate. Frederick Douglass was among the New York representatives and served as a secretary of the gathering. At the heart of the Free Democrats' endeavor stood pragmatic and committed leaders of the political antislavery movement, many of whom went on to become Republicans and play prominent roles in Congress during Reconstruction. The party's 1852 presidential ticket consisted of John Hale of New Hampshire, the US senator and former Democrat who had left the party over Texas annexation, and George Julian, a Free Soiler from Indiana who had served one term in Congress. The party also claimed as members Salmon Chase, Joshua Giddings, and Henry Wilson of Massachusetts. In Illinois, Zebina Eastman, whose *Western Citizen* had so effectively advanced the Liberty Party, energetically promoted the Free Democrats, and Owen Lovejoy, brother of the slain abolitionist Elijah Lovejoy, became one of its most prominent spokesmen.[31]

For the Illinois Free Democrats, the Logan Law was a gift. Eastman and his Free Democrat colleagues relentlessly publicized the law, calling it the "Slave Law" to emphasize its extremism and indicate that it was yet another encroachment by the Slave Power. To their surprise, editors from all parts of the state, of both major parties, denounced the new measure. Even Democratic papers in southern Illinois joined the chorus of condemnation. Eastman and his allies crowed at stories like one from a statewide convention of Universalists, where a "long, straight, six-foot-three Kentuckian" described his six-month sojourn in the southern reaches of Illinois. Rebuking a timid minister from northern Illinois who feared discussion of the law, the Kentuckian called it "so infamous that it *cannot find a single apologist in all Egypt!*" On the national scene, the passage of the Logan Law had enhanced the state's national reputation for racism and backwardness, but antislavery leaders also hailed it as a spur to action. As Gamaliel Bailey's the *National Era* put it, "If such an atrocity does not arouse the good men of that State to the necessity of making their power felt at the ballot-box, we know not what will."[32]

The Logan Law also energized Chicago's Black activists, who ramped up their work, determined to draw the nation's attention to injustices in Illinois. The members of Quinn Chapel were raising money for a new building at the corner of Jackson and Buffalo Streets, and Black women held two nights of antislavery "tea parties" in March 1853, featuring addresses and songs. Eastman urged white readers of the *Western Citizen* to contribute to the church fund, saying it was "one of the ways by which this community can bear their testimony against the negro repulsion law." The question was, "Shall these people be allowed to remain among us?" Eastman wrote. "Giving aid to this church is a very effective way of saying yes." With perhaps a similar goal in mind, of showing that they were organized and immovable, that spring Black Baptists founded their first church in Chicago, Zoar Baptist. In early May, activists assembled in Quinn Chapel and decided to form a statewide organization, and that summer, movement stalwarts John Jones, Byrd Parker, and Henry O. Wagoner traveled to Rochester, New York, for a national Black convention, the first since 1848.[33]

The Rochester convention was contentious, as activists from across the free states split over the best way forward in a nation that seemed increasingly enthralled by the Slave Power. The Fugitive Slave Act, new antiblack measures at the state level, and renewed efforts by the American Colonization Society, all suggested that the forces of Black exclusion and racial inequality were gaining ground. Pessimistic about their prospects, some Black northerners, among them prominent writers and speakers, talked of leaving the United States. In 1852, Martin Delany, a Pittsburgh-based editor and physician, had published *The Condition, Elevation, Emigration, and Destiny of the Colored People in the United States,* a book that urged African Americans to consider that their future might lie elsewhere, perhaps in Haiti or the Caribbean. For decades, Black northerners had been calling on white Americans to quell their prejudice, to treat free Black people respectfully and as equals. Finally, Delany and many others were ready to give up. They felt they had made little progress despite their efforts and needed to look abroad for freedom and self-determination.[34]

Frederick Douglass and others continued to hold out hope. The people on their side of the debate were not insensitive to the ways antiblack policies and white prejudice continued to menace free Black northerners. They experienced those oppressions themselves. Still, Douglass and his anti-emigration allies took inspiration from evidence of Black advancement in the free states. Black northerners were building and staffing schools, leading independent churches and community organizations, making money in business, and organizing to discuss shared concerns. They had grown more confident by contesting the ACS, claiming American citizenship, and demanding equal rights. And they were making their voices heard on the lecture circuit, in their own newspapers, and in writing for progressive white newspapers. Their arguments and inspiration had helped propel the movement for an antislavery third party under whose influence Ohio had repealed most of its black laws. Elsewhere, concrete gains had been limited. But in 1853, neither of the two major political parties was unified or thriving, and that instability suggested more change on the horizon.

Douglass and his allies took charge of the 1853 Rochester convention's message, purposely marginalizing the emigrationist faction. Delegates resolved to form a permanent "national council" with branches in the states, and they tackled a range of issues—including education, employment, and social uplift. In an "Address to the People of the United States," the conventioneers self-consciously demanded recognition of their national citizenship. "We are Americans," they declared at the outset. "We address you not as aliens nor as exiles, humbly asking to be permitted to dwell among you in peace; but we address you as American citizens asserting their rights on their own native soil." Their demands mirrored their mode of address. They sought equality in all spheres, and they particularly singled out laws targeting free Black people as "flagrantly unjust to the man of color, and plainly discreditable to the white man." Whether in the South or the North, they said, laws that "aim at the expatriation of the free people of color, shall be stamped with national reprobation, denounced as contrary to the humanity of the American people, and as an outrage upon the Christianity and civilization of the nineteenth century."[35]

Knowing they would be challenged in their claim to the "high appellation of '*citizen,*'" the authors of the address offered "facts and testimonials" to demonstrate that they were indeed citizens according to both the Declaration of Independence and the US Constitution. It was a historical litany that had become familiar as Black activists and their allies had repeated it again and again. The Constitution's privileges and immunities clause contained no racial exclusions. Andrew Jackson, as a general in the War of 1812, had recognized Black soldiers as citizens and promised them "the same bounty in money and land" as white soldiers would receive. New York had recognized African Americans as state citizens in its 1821 constitution, and, in the Second Missouri Compromise of that same year, Congress had acknowledged that Black citizens of the states had rights under the privileges and immunities clause. "Modern legislators" used "the word '*white*'" in laws, they argued, but the practice was "despised in revolutionary times." Addressing white Americans, they concluded: "The testimony of your own great and venerated names completely vindicated our right to be regarded and treated as American citizens."[36] Building on this historical narrative of rights acknowledged and then denied, the convention demanded unqualified citizenship and equality for African Americans, and it called on Black and white Americans to envision a future that was radically different from the present.

The three Chicagoans who had attended the Rochester meeting returned home poised to build their movement in Illinois with help from

Frederick Douglass. Delegates from all over the state attended the first statewide Black convention in Illinois, which began on October 6, 1853. Douglass headlined the event, drawing a crowd that included white as well as Black admirers. Debates about emigration absorbed considerable energy, but finally the convention denounced "all schemes" for colonizing free Black people in Africa and echoed the Rochester convention in resolving to "plant our trees in American soil, and repose in the shade thereof." The convention's address to "the people of the state of Illinois" was, like the Rochester address, unequivocal and unapologetic. Black Illinoisans wanted the state government to recognize them as citizens in every respect. The state readily acknowledged the citizenship of naturalized immigrants from all over the world, they argued, while the Logan Law doomed native-born Black men, women, and children "to life-long Slavery for the simple act of coming into the State of Illinois, peacefully to reside, and to gain an honest living by cultivating the soil."[37]

Douglass left Chicago to campaign for the Free Democrats in northern Illinois, leaving behind an invigorated African American movement. A month later, John Jones reported to Douglass that "colored men and women" were active throughout the state, "from centre to circumferences," and were forming a statewide council. R. J. Robinson, leader of the Wood River Baptists, a Black Baptist organization based near Alton, was traveling in southern Illinois, addressing "large and spirited meetings of colored men and women, urging upon them the necessity of a thorough organization." Chicago's Underground Railroad regularly moved "shipments" of fugitives to Canada. White allies "cheer us on to victory," Jones added. "They say the time has come, when 'HE WHO WOULD BE FREE, HIMSELF MUST STRIKE THE BLOW.' "[38]

Zebina Eastman criticized the antislavery press for not devoting enough attention to Douglass's visit and the associated surge in Free Democrats' activities, but he need not have worried about a return to the political status quo. In January 1854, Stephen Douglas created a political earthquake when he introduced the Kansas–Nebraska bill in the US Senate. After some modifications, the bill allowed settlers in the newly formed Kansas and Nebraska Territories to exercise "popular sovereignty" over slavery—that is, they could decide for themselves whether to legalize it. The provision nullified the Missouri Compromise of 1820, which provided that in Louisiana Purchase territories, slavery would exist only south of the 36°30′ parallel. Both Kansas and Nebraska were part of the Louisiana Purchase and lay north of that line. To make sure everyone understood the implications, the bill explicitly declared the Missouri Compromise "inoperative and void." Northerners of all political orientations found this shocking. Ever since the Mexican War, free staters of both major parties had grown increasingly adamant that no new slave states should join the Union, and many saw the Missouri Compromise line as a nonnegotiable part of the nation's architecture.[39]

Stephen Douglas and the Kansas–Nebraska Act provoked the culmination of more than a decade of third-party organizing. The Whig Party, always the weaker of the two major parties, had already crumbled. The party had run a presidential candidate in 1852, but it had ceased to be a going concern in most places after that. Passage of the Kansas–Nebraska Act shifted the political terrain, opening the possibility of creating a grand new political coalition unified in opposition to the extension of slavery. In some places, former Libertyites and Free Soilers attempted to realize that coalition by building "anti-Nebraska" parties, some calling themselves "Republicans." The anti-immigrant Know Nothing Party briefly materialized, looking to mobilize anti-immigrant sentiment among former Whigs and highlight an issue that could unite voters in slave and free states. By the time the presidential election of 1856 arrived, however, most of the uncertainty had dissipated, and a major new party had taken shape.

The Republican Party wielded formidable power from the start and was destined to become an unprecedented force in American politics. The party emerged from a core of Liberty and Free Soil partisans who drew together with former Whigs and disillusioned Democrats. To build a coalition capable of attracting mass support, leading Republicans emphasized the nonextension of slavery and the opening of the West to "free labor," themes with potential to unite great swaths of northerners. Among the Republicans of 1856 were third-party stalwarts like Salmon Chase of Ohio as well as newcomers like Abraham Lincoln of Illinois, a longstanding Whig who joined the party only that year. Republicans did not all share the same views on the rights of free African Americans. Some former Democrats, in particular, still subscribed to the antiblack views that characterized that party and its rhetoric of white nationhood. Yet those were not the most vocal or most powerful members of the new coalition. The new party was led by people like Chase and William Seward of New York, men who had a history of demanding racial equality in civil and even political rights in their home states.[40]

AMID THE POLITICAL FERMENT of the 1850s, the question of whether the US government recognized free African Americans as national citizens also came to the fore. Until then, much of the debate about African Americans' legal status as citizens had revolved around the Constitution's privileges and immunities clause, which referenced "the citizens of each state." Yet citizenship had always had different, more national meanings as well. The Constitution alluded to US citizenship in several places. It required that the US president be a "natural born" citizen of the United States. It also gave Congress power to establish a "uniform rule of naturalization," meaning that Congress could determine how noncitizens became citizens of the nation. When the United States acquired new territory from foreign powers, Congress made treaties in which it declared inhabitants of newly acquired territories "citizens of the United States." The 1848 Treaty of Guadeloupe Hidalgo, for example, gave residents of the territories acquired from Mexico one year to declare their desire to remain Mexican citizens. If they did not, the treaty stipulated, they "shall be considered to have elected to become citizens of the United States."[41]

The question of whether the United States government considered free

African Americans citizens in this more national sense had never been answered. The issue arose dramatically in 1849, when two Black men applied to the State Department for US passports, were denied, and protested vehemently. In the first several decades of American nationhood, consistent with prevailing ambiguities about citizenship and evolving international norms about documentation, the State Department had not viewed passports as certificates of citizenship and thus had issued the documents to a range of people without much consideration of their citizenship status. By the 1840s, amid growing foreign immigration and opportunities for Americans to travel abroad, the department sought to regularize its policies and tighten the link between passports and US citizenship. In that context, Secretary of State John M. Clayton, a Delaware Whig, declared in 1849 that free African Americans were ineligible to receive US passports, and he claimed, incorrectly, that the department had never issued passports to people of African descent.[42]

Five years later, as a US senator, Clayton described his surprise at the outcry evoked by his decision. He explained to the Senate that he had refused African Americans' requests for passports on the grounds that only US citizens could receive such documents, and that only white people could be US citizens. Although he thought the policy was reasonable and necessary, he was "assailed by a great portion of the northern press, and by many responsible persons at the North, who seemed to think that the point was not correctly settled at the Department." Their responses showed him that "a very respectable and considerable portion of the people of the northern States" believed that free Black people were US citizens.[43] The argument would only intensify as African Americans and their white allies continued to protest the government's refusal to acknowledge their citizenship, and as Congress continued to grapple with legislation that required decisions on the matter.

One such area was land policy. The US government claimed jurisdiction over vast territories acquired through the combined force of government agents and civilian settlers who pushed Native people off the land through violence, diplomacy, and treaty-making. As territorial conquest advanced, Congress debated how to apportion land after "Indian title" was extinguished. Early federal laws known as "preemption laws" allowed settlers to claim lands that the government had not yet put up for sale. The first preemption laws allowed "any settler or occupant" to make such claims. Faced with a rapidly growing immigrant population, Congress began to distinguish citizens from aliens, making citizenship status—or at least intention to become a citizen—a qualification for access to land. The first law to do so was an 1841 statute that permitted preemption only by US citizens or people who had formally declared their intention to become citizens.[44] The question inevitably arose: Could a free Black person preempt land under that policy?

In 1843, responding to a query from Illinois, US Attorney General Hugh Legaré, a South Carolinian, answered the question in the affirmative while also managing to avoid acknowledging that a free Black resident of Illinois was a United States citizen. Legaré pointed out that the "rights of contract and property" were fundamental to freedom. Free Black people enjoyed such rights, he noted, "even in the slaveholding States." Rights to contract and property did not depend on citizenship status, Legaré continued. They were rights that "mere birth, under the *ligeance* of a country, bestows." Throughout world history, he asserted, wherever "domestic slavery existed," people who had been freed from bondage were "considered as at once capable" of all such rights. Regardless of whether "free people of color" were US citizens, then, they were "not *aliens*." Legaré concluded that free African Americans were best described as "denizens," and that as such they were eligible to preempt land under federal law. Later that year, the agricultural committee of the Black convention in Buffalo encouraged African Americans to move to the federal territories, declaring, "The right of pre-emption is open to all."[45]

As Congress continued to make laws regulating settlement of the vast lands coming under its jurisdiction, questions of race, immigration, and citizenship remained at the fore. In the 1840s, land reform activists, many of them aligned with the Whigs or antislavery third parties, proposed "homestead" legislation designed to curtail speculation and hoarding. In early 1854, Congress took up two land-related bills: one meant to establish a land office and distribute land to settlers in New Mexico Territory, and the other a homestead proposal. In the House, some legislators sought to add the word *white* to the homestead bill to eliminate any ambiguity about who was eligible to take advantage of it. Many slaveholders could not abide the possibility that Congress would leave open the possibility that free Black people could claim land. As Congressman Laurence Keitt of South Carolina argued, a congressional affirmation that free African Americans in the territories were US citizens would "indirectly assail our institutions by affirming, through legislation, the equality of the races, which we deny in the very beginning." The states could do as they pleased, he said, "but the Federal Government can recognize none but whites as *people*." Many northern Democrats shared Keitt's view that the United States was a white man's country and that only white people should benefit from federal land policy. Since its origins in 1790, federal laws had provided procedures for the naturalization of "free white" persons only. Some invoked US naturalization policy to argue that European immigrants should have access to public land, while African Americans must not. As David T. Disney, an Ohio Democrat and the House sponsor of the New Mexico bill, put it: "This is a Government of white men—carried on by white people, and for white people."[46]

Benjamin Wade, representing Ohio's Western Reserve, rejected such logic and turned to the US Constitution instead. He replied to Disney: "Well, I did not suppose that the Government had any particular color." Disney replied: "Oh, yes, it has." Wade went on: "I had myself supposed that it was rather a human Government; and, in my judgement, if it be a human Government, it must extend to all human beings." Nothing in the Constitution indicated "that this is a *colored* government; that is, a white, or no-colored, Government, or a black colored Government. The Constitution says nothing about any tribe or race of men; it speaks of persons, and whoever bears that character is a member of the Government, if born within its territory." Black people, he said, were manifestly persons. "There is nothing in the Constitution that has aught to do with the color of a free man, or with the color of a slave."[47]

Wade was one of many northerners in Congress who were willing to speak up for racial equality before the law and to insist that free African Americans were US citizens. Their numbers were greater in the 1850s than ever before, but not large enough to outvote their adversaries. They nevertheless made their case firmly and repeatedly.[48] In 1854, the homestead bill passed the House with the word *white* intact. The Senate rejected the measure, not because of its racial language but because most Democrats saw homestead legislation as a sectional policy designed to favor the settlement of northern territories and therefore produce new free states. Congress finally adopted a homestead law—without racial exclusions—in 1862, when most slave states were not represented in Congress.

Democrats in power expressed doubts about Black citizenship or overtly opposed it. In 1856, the Pierce administration's attorney general, Massachusetts Democrat Caleb Cushing, overruled Legaré's opinion on free African Americans' eligibility to preempt federal land. In the process, Cushing crystallized the unresolved problem of African Americans' national citizenship. "The question,—what is meant by the term 'citizen of the United States' in the Constitution and laws of the United States," he wrote, "has not been fully determined, either by legislation or adjudication." He had been asked to weigh in on whether a "half-blood Indian" could claim land under the 1841 preemption law. In answering, Cushing declared himself reluctant to lay down a general principle of race and citizenship, particularly because the question at hand "involves the much more serious question of the constitutional *status*, relatively [*sic*] to the question of citizenship of the African race in the United States." Yet he criticized Legaré's view that "denizens" were entitled to preempt land, pointing out that the law itself never mentioned the word. Cushing alluded to William Wirt's 1821 opinion that a free Black man from

Virginia was not a citizen of the United States. "If a free African is enti-tled to pre-emption," Cushing said, "it can only be so considered by first overruling Mr. Wirt, and deciding that he is a citizen of the United States."[49] Cushing was not prepared to do that, so he penned a narrow decision on the case at hand and left the larger question of free African Americans' citizenship for someone else.

CHIEF JUSTICE ROGER TANEY tried to settle the question the following year. Taney's hopes for the 1857 *Dred Scott* decision were ambitious. The case began as a suit for freedom launched by Dred and Harriet Scott, a married couple who had begun their lives enslaved and had lived, sepa-rately and together, in Illinois, Wisconsin Territory, and Missouri. The cou-ple argued in a St. Louis court that they were entitled to freedom because they had spent time in free territories. After they won their case, their ostensible owner appealed to the Missouri Supreme Court. Missouri courts had regularly honored freedom claims like that of the Scotts, accepting the principle articulated in both *Somerset* and *Aves* that enslaved people became free when their owners brought them onto free soil. In 1852, however, the Missouri Supreme Court, reflecting the reactionary tenor of the moment, rejected the Scotts' claim to freedom. Dred Scott then filed an appeal on behalf of his family in federal district court, and, after losing there, took the case to the US Supreme Court.[50]

Justice Taney was eager to use Scott's case for his own purposes. He agreed with the lower courts that the Scotts remained enslaved, but set-tling their status was not his primary goal. He hoped, instead, to use the case to solve pressing political questions, and to do so in favor of slavehold-ers and their interests. The first and most urgent question was whether Congress had the power to outlaw slavery in the federal territories. The Kansas–Nebraska Act had repealed the Missouri Compromise, opening to slavery the areas north of the 36°30′ parallel. But slaveholders still were not satisfied. They sought recognition that, as citizens, they were entitled to take their human property into any federal territory they chose. Congress had barred slavery from federal territories in the past, first in the 1787 Northwest Ordinance and later in the Missouri Compromise. Slaveholders now argued that these measures had violated the Constitution, and Justice Taney took their side. In his *Dred Scott* opinion, which was designated the official opinion of the court amid several concurrences and two dissents, Taney insisted that a slaveholder's "right of property in a slave" was "distinctly and expressly affirmed in the Constitution." By that logic, he wrote, Congress was not permitted to ban slavery in any federal territory and had acted unconstitutionally in the past when it had done so.[51]

That was Taney's most critical political intervention, but the chief justice also saw fit to declare that people of African descent, whether enslaved or free, "had no rights which the white man was bound to respect."[52] In ways that sometimes go unrecognized, that resounding phrase was tied to a broader discussion of African Americans' state and federal citizenship under the US Constitution. Here too, Taney's argument was deeply embedded in contemporary politics. As Attorney General Cushing's 1856 opinion indicated, the question of free African Americans' citizenship at the federal level remained unresolved. Congress had arrived at no definition, and the executive branch—the General Land Office and the attorney general, for example—had no clear answer either. Moreover, no one had yet managed to test in federal court whether free African Americans were protected against state-level antiblack laws by the Constitution's privileges and immunities clause. In the mid-1840s, the Massachusetts legislature had hoped that Henry Hubbard would bring a case in New Orleans, or Samuel Hoar would advance one in Charleston. But legal action proved impossible when white southerners threatened the men's lives and drove them from their cities. During the tense debates that led to the Compromise of 1850, Stephen Douglas had suggested that Massachusetts politicians bring a federal case in Illinois, where "sectional prejudices" would not interfere. No such case materialized.[53]

The question of who was a citizen under the US Constitution arose in the *Dred Scott* case because of the Constitution's provision that federal courts had jurisdiction in cases "between citizens of different states," a principle known as *diversity jurisdiction*. Scott's Missouri-based lawyer argued that Scott was a citizen of Missouri and had standing to sue in federal court. Lawyers for John F. A. Sanford, the man who claimed the Scotts as slaves, insisted that Scott lacked standing because he was Black and therefore not a citizen. One of the central questions in the case, then, was who was a "citizen" of a state for such purposes. As the case moved to the US Supreme Court, Scott's St. Louis attorney sought legal help from Montgomery Blair. It was typical to enlist high-profile lawyers in momentous Supreme Court cases, and Sanford's lawyers were among the most prominent in the country. Blair, for his part, was the son of the politically prominent Francis Preston Blair, a Maryland Democrat who had recently joined the Republican Party. Montgomery had previously practiced law in St. Louis and was well-connected in Missouri.[54]

The *Dred Scott* case was argued twice before the Supreme Court, and both times Blair focused on defending Scott's status as a citizen with standing to sue in federal court. He had abundant evidence from which to choose, in part because African American activists and their white allies had been arguing for Black citizenship for years. In 1854, for example, a learned petition from John Mercer Langston on behalf of twenty-five thousand "half-freemen" of Ohio assembled a trove of evidence. Langston, who was studying to become a lawyer and was deeply involved in the Free Democratic movement in Ohio, stressed the American tradition of birthright citizenship—the idea that a free person born in a given jurisdiction was a citizen of that jurisdiction. No less an authority than the eminent New York judge and legal theorist James Kent had validated this perspective, he wrote, and during the tense debates of 1850, Senator Roger Baldwin of Connecticut had reminded Americans that Black men had voted in many states at the nation's founding. In conventions, newspapers, books, and elsewhere, Black activists also emphasized Black Americans' history of service to the nation, particularly as soldiers in the

Revolution and the War of 1812. They described their contributions as taxpayers and their work on behalf of their own communities. Some tied their arguments to constitutional definitions of citizenship, while others built on the broader cultural sense, widespread at the time as it is today, that citizenship suggested something intangible about belonging and membership. As Black organizers in Ohio had put it in 1843, "WE ARE AMERICANS, and as Americans, we desire all the rights and immunities of *American Citizens.*"[55]

As Dred Scott's attorney, Montgomery Blair emphasized legal and political precedents, insisting before the Supreme Court that many states recognized free African Americans as citizens and that the principle of birthright citizenship was widely recognized in international law. He reminded the court that the Second Continental Congress of 1775 had rejected South Carolinians' attempt to add the word *white* to the clause in the Articles of Confederation that granted "free inhabitants" of the states the "privileges and immunities of the several states." Blair alluded to James Kent and the Second Missouri Compromise of 1821, and he insisted that people who were "not voters, or eligible to office" were often considered citizens, including white women, minors, and some naturalized foreigners. Dred Scott, Blair conceded, might be a "*quasi* citizen," but he was a "citizen in the sense . . . which enables him to acquire and hold property under the States and under the United States," and it followed from there that he had standing to sue in federal court.[56]

Such claims found little sympathy in the Supreme Court, however, and the justices decided 7–2 against Scott. In a detailed and historically informed dissent, Justice Benjamin Curtis, a conservative Whig from Massachusetts, adopted many of Blair's arguments and added some of his own. Justice McLean of Ohio also dissented, though on different grounds. The justices in the majority diverged from one another on some issues, but Chief Justice Taney rendered a sweeping denial of Black citizenship, both in the national sense and under the privileges and immunities clause.

Contrary to the historical evidence assembled by Blair and so many others, Taney insisted that no one could have imagined free African Americans as citizens when the nation was founded. The egalitarian promise of the Declaration of Independence had long been a talisman for the antislavery movement. Now Taney confidently claimed that the nation's founders never meant for the Declaration to apply to people of African descent. Citing an array of discriminatory state and federal laws, he argued that "a perpetual and impassable barrier was intended to be erected between the white race and the one which they had reduced to slavery." He dwelled particularly on late-eighteenth-century New England laws. "It is hardly consistent with the respect due to these States," he smirked, "to suppose that they regarded at that time, as fellow-citizens and members of the sovereignty, a class of beings whom they had thus stigmatized." Echoing the resolutions adopted by the legislatures of Georgia and South Carolina in the 1840s, Taney insisted that free Black people had formed no part of the "political body" in the founding era. They "were not intended to be included, under the word 'citizens' in the Constitution, and can therefore claim none of the rights and privileges which that instrument provides for and secures to citizens of the United States."[57]

Taney not only denied that free Black people were American citizens. He also claimed that Black citizens of the states were not entitled to benefit from the Constitution's privileges and immunities clause. Americans had debated the question for decades, and Taney now bestowed his authority on one side of the argument. A state could confer "the rights of citizens" to whomever it chose "within its own limits," the chief justice said. But a person who had "all the rights and privileges of a citizen of a State" was not necessarily "a citizen of the United States." To admit that free Black "citizens" of the states were US citizens under the privileges and immunities clause, he wrote, would be to recognize that African Americans from Massachusetts, New York, and other northern states would have "the right to enter every other State whenever they pleased, singly or in companies, without pass or passport, and without obstruction, to sojourn there as long as they pleased, to go where they pleased at every hour of the day or night without molestation, unless they committed some violation of law for which a white man would be punished." This, of course, was precisely the kind of free movement that free Black northerners and their allies had long demanded—the same liberty to which white citizens were entitled. In equal measure, that liberty was precisely what pro-slavery southerners could not abide. Such freedom for free Black Americans would "inevitably" produce "discontent and insubordination" among free and enslaved southern Blacks, Taney said, "endangering the peace and safety of the State."[58]

Justice Taney's *Dred Scott* opinion landed in a nation deeply divided along sectional and partisan lines. Frederick Douglass called it an "insult to the people of the North" and vowed to continue the struggle to "place the Federal Government . . . in the hands of men who will not prostrate and prostitute themselves at the feet of slavery." It received decidedly mixed reviews from legal authorities, and many state courts and lower federal courts found ways to circumvent it, or, in some cases, openly rejected its conclusions. In New England, state legislatures affirmatively declared that African Americans were citizens. Republicans scorned the decision, while most Democrats embraced it. The decision also shaped a political contest that focused the nation's attention on Illinois: Stephen Douglas and Abraham Lincoln's 1858 battle for a seat in the US Senate.[59]

BY THE TIME the two Illinois men faced off, the Republican Party had become a juggernaut capable of permanently reshaping American politics. From the 1830s through the early 1850s, the two-party system had helped suppress sectional tensions. Built on support from free states and slave states alike, both major parties had emphasized issues such as infrastructure and the tariff, which could unite people across regions while tamping down disagreements over slavery. But the system had been unstable. Southern slaveholders habitually pressured northerners to accept policies that secured slavery's future and slaveholders' power, including the 1850 Fugitive Slave Act and the admission of new slave states, insisting that the nation would come apart if northerners did not accede. Free-state residents grew increasingly unwilling to swallow such measures, particularly as it became clear that their populations were growing much more quickly than in the slave states and that a sectional party—one that drew its strength only from the free states—might be capable of winning the presidency and majorities in Congress. The Republican Party was that party. Slavery was the preeminent source of party conflict, but the question of free African Americans' present and future standing in the nation was also pressing and would become only more important in years to come.

The men who became Republican leaders in the late 1850s emerged from many different political backgrounds and espoused a variety of ideas about race and equality. At one extreme was Henry Wilson, a Massachusetts senator who, as a state legislator in the 1840s, had worked to end the state ban on interracial marriage and fought racial discrimination on railroads and in public schools. Wilson saw racist laws as nefarious remnants of slavery that had lingered on in a few state laws and "in the customs of society, and in prejudices which in many minds . . . set at naught the principles of justice and humanity." He abandoned the Whig Party in 1848 and from then on worked consistently to form antislavery political coalitions that culminated in the Republican Party.[60] On the party's other extreme, a few Republicans, including James Doolittle of Wisconsin, were rank racists who continued to espouse an unalloyed vision of white supremacy. Closer to the middle were men like Abraham Lincoln and Lyman Trumbull, both prominent Republicans in Illinois. Trumbull was a former Democrat, while Lincoln had been a Whig. Both men spoke approvingly of colonization in the 1850s, and neither publicly condemned the Illinois black laws. Yet men like Trumbull and Lincoln adopted a position on racial equality that was distinct from that of most northern Democrats. Unlike their Democratic counterparts, Trumbull, Lincoln, and other Republicans believed that the United States must not be so unjust as to deny African Americans the fundamental rights invoked by the Declaration of Independence—to life, liberty, and the pursuit of happiness, or, translated into legal terms, the civil rights to personal liberty, to enter contracts, to sue and be sued, to access the courts, and to be protected by the law.[61]

In the late 1850s, most Republicans condemned the *Dred Scott* decision and defended the citizenship and civil rights of free African Americans. Northern Democrats took the opposite position, and those differences were on full display as Lincoln and Douglas sparred in 1857 and 1858. The *Springfield State Register,* a Democratic paper, threw down the gauntlet soon after release of the *Dred Scott* decision. "The issue of negro equality is now before the American people," the paper announced. As Illinois Republicans explained their objections to Taney's opinion, the editor predicted, they would likely expose themselves as radical supporters of racial equality, out of step with Illinois voters. "Negro citizenship has always been repudiated by all parties in Illinois," the paper chided. In Springfield, Douglas gave a speech supporting the *Dred Scott* decision and reiterating Taney's position that the Declaration of Independence "referred to the white race alone, and not to the African." Douglas had defended the Illinois Constitution's Black exclusion clause on the floor of the US Senate in 1850, arguing that it was among the "police regulations" necessary to "the quiet and peace of our community." Now Douglas condemned the "Republican or Abolition" party for seeking racial equality before the law, saying the policy would "open the door for the three millions of emancipated slaves to enter and become citizens on an equality with ourselves." Republicans would permit Black men to vote and hold office on the same terms as whites, Douglas predicted. They would even allow Black men "to marry white women on an equality with white men."[62]

Speaking in Springfield two weeks after Douglas's speech, Lincoln countered that the founders intended the Declaration to apply to all people. It was meant as a "standard maxim for free society which should be familiar to all . . . constantly spreading and deepening its influence and augmenting the happiness and value of life to all people, of all colors, everywhere." Somewhat later in Chicago, Lincoln urged an audience to "discard all this quibbling about this man and the other man—this race and that race and the other race being inferior." Instead, they must "unite as one people throughout this land" and "once more stand up declaring that all men are created equal."[63] Longtime abolitionists would have welcomed a call to repeal the black laws themselves, but Lincoln did not do that, likely more because he wanted to expand the Republicans' appeal in Illinois than because he did not believe it would be right.

Douglas repeatedly forced Lincoln to explain his position on racial equality during the famed Lincoln–Douglas debates in 1858. He painted Lincoln and the Republicans as radical racial egalitarians, drawing special attention to Republicans who had been part of the third-party antislavery movement—people such as Owen Lovejoy and John F. Farnsworth of Illinois, and Joshua Giddings and Salmon Chase of Ohio. In warning that Republicans favored racial "amalgamation," Douglas adopted a common tactic among northern Democrats, who regularly insisted that people of European descent were superior to all others and that any move toward racial equality would lead inevitably to sex between Black men and white women, and therefore to pollution of the white race. Democratic politicians may have genuinely worried that this would come to pass, but such rhetoric was also a political tactic designed to scare voters into casting their lot with the Democrats. Douglas never altered his position, stated early on, that the nation was "made by the white man, for the benefit of the white man, to be administered by white men, in such manner as they should determine." "I am opposed to negro citizenship in any and every form," he often said.[64]

Lincoln needed to tread carefully. The Democrats were poised to construe anything he said as advocacy of interracial sex. Meanwhile, he and his party wanted to avoid alienating potential voters and hoped to keep the focus on the parties' distinct views on slavery itself. Unlike the Douglas Democrats, Republicans condemned slavery as immoral and promised to stop its expansion. Responding to Douglas's goading, Lincoln clarified that he did not support "political" or "social" equality of the races. But he continued to insist that the Declaration of Independence was meant for all, and that people of African descent were "equal in their right to 'life, liberty, and the pursuit of happiness.'" He did not go so far as to advocate repeal of the Illinois black laws—a logical extension of his argument that "all men" were equal and entitled to the basic rights promised by the Declaration of Independence. Yet he unequivocally rejected Douglas and the Democrats' view that the founders had designed the nation for white people only.[65]

Lincoln's cautious approach frustrated the many contemporaries, white and especially Black, who wanted him to take a bolder stand. Among them was H. Ford Douglas, who as a young man had escaped slavery in Virginia and migrated to Cleveland, where he became a member of that city's Black activist community. Ford Douglas advocated Black emigration to Canada in the 1850s, and at an 1856 Black convention in Alton, Illinois, he denounced the Republicans for accepting the constitutionality of slavery in the states where it already existed. During the summer and fall of 1860, Ford Douglas excoriated Lincoln—now the Republican nominee for president—for having refused, two years earlier, to sign a petition demanding repeal of the racist testimony law of Illinois. He condemned the Republicans for claiming that all they intended to do was return the federal government "to the policy of the fathers." Americans needed "a position far higher" than the nation's founders had occupied, he insisted. Only "uncompromising opposition to oppression," he argued, "will ever make us worthy of the name of freemen."[66] Republicans would eventually come around to the position that the founders' Constitution would not serve. For Lincoln in the late 1850s and 1860, however, the preeminent goal was to propel the Republicans into power.

———————

IN THE US CONGRESS as in Illinois, Republicans ushered into the political mainstream the argument that free Black people were entitled to citizenship and the same basic civil rights as white people. The question of African American citizenship arose pointedly in 1858 and early 1859, when Congress considered Oregon's application for statehood with a constitution that not only barred Black migration but prohibited African Americans from holding real estate, making contracts, and suing in court. Reflecting white residents' concerns about Chinese migration, the Oregon Constitution also barred Chinese immigrants who arrived after the constitution's adoption from owning real estate or mining claims, and from working in mines.[67]

Oregon's bid for statehood set the stage for a reprise of the Missouri crisis of 1820–21. Did Black exclusion measures such as these violate the US Constitution? Was Congress obliged to reject a state constitution that included such provisions? The congressional debate was shaped by practical partisanship as well. Republicans advocated admission of new free states to increase free-state power in Congress, but some Republicans wanted to stall admission of Oregon because its politics were dominated by Democrats. Meanwhile, northern Democrats like Douglas were happy to support admission of a free, Democrat-dominated Oregon, but many southern Democrats opposed Oregon statehood in order to slow the proliferation of free states.

Amid the welter of concerns, many Republicans denounced the proposed Oregon Constitution's antiblack provisions, and some also condemned its anti-Chinese ones. Several insisted that the antiblack measures violated the US Constitution's privileges and immunities clause by abrogating Black citizens' basic rights to locomotion and to own property, enter contracts, and defend their rights in court. New Englanders revived the matter of Black sailors. Henry Wilson pointed out that Black whalers from Massachusetts might be forced by bad weather to disembark in Oregon, where they could be "abused" or "murdered" but could not "maintain a suit in the courts of that State to protect them in their personal rights." The Oregon Constitution, he said, was "inhuman, unchristian, devilish" and "unworthy of a free State."[68]

As in the Missouri debate, their opponents frequently insisted that it was pointless to block Oregon on such grounds, since its legislature could simply add a Black exclusion measure after statehood. The Old Northwest furnished examples. In the House, Eli Thayer, a Massachusetts Republican, prioritized adding another free state over worrying about Oregon's Black exclusion measure. The Oregon Constitution, he said, was "no more hostile to the United States Constitution than are the laws of Indiana and Illinois which exclude free negroes and mulattoes from their boundaries." And Stephen Douglas in the Senate proclaimed, "I insist upon the right of Illinois, as a sovereign State of this Union, to keep negroes out of the State, whether free or slave."[69]

Congressman John Bingham of Ohio, later the author of the first section of the Fourteenth Amendment, was among those who stringently opposed Oregon's constitution. Bingham had come of age amid Ohio's political antislavery movement and became a close associate of Joshua Giddings after being elected to the House in 1854. Now Bingham called the Oregon Constitution "in its spirit and letter . . . injustice and oppression incarnate," and he even rejected the proposition that Black exclusion laws in the existing states were constitutional. To the contrary, he said, those laws violated the rights of American citizens under the US Constitution.[70] What to do with that argument was entirely unclear in 1859. As Stephen Douglas suggested during the Oregon debate, state legislatures had long taken for granted their "right" to pass such laws. Just two years earlier, the Supreme Court had pronounced the privileges and immunities clause virtually meaningless for Black state citizens. And congressional Republicans could not stop Oregon from gaining statehood with its racist constitution, much less orchestrate federal measures to enforce the rights of free Black citizens. These challenges suggested that the cause of racial equality was faring poorly. Yet Republican power was still ascending, and the party's sweeping victory in 1860, including the election of Lincoln to the presidency, created an entirely new set of possibilities.

CHAPTER 8

"ESTABLISHING ONE LAW FOR THE WHITE AND COLORED PEOPLE ALIKE"

Republicans in Power during the Civil War, 1861–1865

A REPUBLICAN-DOMINATED CONGRESS abolished slavery in the District of Columbia in the spring of 1862, less than one year after the Civil War began. For decades, antislavery activists had pushed for abolition in places like the national capital, where Congress had exclusive jurisdiction. They also realized that Congress's role in the capital had ramifications for the rights of free African Americans. Since at least the 1820s, activists had been aware of how the capital's laws—under full control of Congress—had subjected all Black people to the suspicion of being fugitive slaves and had denied them basic liberties. In 1862, one person who was well aware of that long history was John Jay II, son of William Jay, the New York lawyer who, decades earlier, had done so much to ensure that Gilbert Horton was freed from the Washington jail and had worked to raise white northerners' awareness of the injustice of racial discrimination against Black northerners. The younger Jay thanked Senator Henry Wilson for leading the effort to reach this long-sought goal. He recalled that his father's interest in attacking slavery in Washington dated to 1826, the year of Horton's arrest, and he remembered his own "boyish efforts to arouse attention to the atrocity of slavery in Washington, commenced nearly thirty years ago." Now Jay rejoiced that "our National Government sits, at last, in a free capital."[1]

The Republicans had swept into power in the fall 1860 elections, validating slaveholders' longstanding fears that an exclusively northern antislavery party could take control of national affairs. Abraham Lincoln of Illinois ran against three other candidates, winning with a convincing plurality of the popular vote and more electoral college votes than the three others combined. As a result of the election alone, Republicans increased their majority in the House and reached parity in the Senate. Republican power in Congress only increased as slaveholding states declared themselves out of the Union, beginning with South Carolina in December 1860. The secessionist movement gathered momentum, and by April 1861, a total of eleven states had left the Union, their representatives in the US House and Senate packing their bags and returning home, many with the intention of serving in the Confederacy.

Republicans immediately began to implement a program of abolition and racial equality in civil rights, taking action everywhere they believed the Constitution gave them power to do so. Most had significant constitutional scruples. Consistent with the political antislavery tradition established by people such as Benjamin Lundy and William Jay, they believed that Congress could attack slavery in places under exclusive federal jurisdiction but not in the states—at least not during peacetime. They would pursue their agenda in places like the District of Columbia and the federal territories. They also realized, as the antebellum debates about African American citizenship had demonstrated, that cabinet officials such as the attorney general and the secretary of state could exercise authority over such matters in their own somewhat limited domains. Beginning in 1861, the State Department, under the direction of William Seward, began issuing US passports to African Americans, and congressional Republicans pushed to abolish slavery in the District of Columbia and eradicate the capital's racially discriminatory laws. The next year, Attorney General Edward Bates of Missouri wrote an opinion on citizenship that explicitly contradicted the *Dred Scott* decision by concluding that free African Americans were US citizens. The Republican-dominated Congress also recognized Haiti and Liberia as independent countries, long a priority of antislavery activists. All this occurred before January 1, 1863, when President Lincoln issued the Emancipation Proclamation. In 1864, Congress barred federal courts from allowing race-based discrimination in witness testimony; in 1865, it repealed a law prohibiting Black people from carrying the US mail.[2]

Republicans were virtually unanimous in support of racial equality in civil rights—that is, in rights to personal liberty, to enter contracts, to sue and be sued, and to basic equality before the law. They diverged, however, when it came to racial equality in other areas, particularly the right to vote. Those customarily called "radical Republicans"—with strongest ties to the antislavery movement—were most inclined to envision equality expansively, while others were more doubtful. African American activists applied pressure. They used petitions and direct action to demand equal access to public accommodations such as streetcars and railroads in Washington. At the federal level, they argued for the rights to vote, hold office, and receive equal pay in the US armed forces. Congress responded by taking up all of these questions, although the results did not always satisfy African Americans' most expansive demands. On the question of voting rights in particular, Republican politicians' reluctance stemmed not only from disagreements in principle but also from concern that if they moved too quickly, they would lose the support of voters back home. Still, Republican policy during the war years revealed a party committed to nationalizing the principles long espoused by the first civil rights movement: that there must be no racial discrimination in citizenship and civil rights.

THE STATE OF SOUTH CAROLINA, long the locus of southern separatism, declared itself out of the Union on December 20, 1860, and by the time Lincoln delivered his inaugural address on March 4, 1861, six additional states had joined the movement to create a separate nation committed to the perpetuation of slavery. In mid-April, a crisis at Fort Sumter in Charleston, South Carolina, marked the formal beginning of military hostilities. The Lincoln administration had refused to surrender the US forts in Charleston Harbor but now faced the question of how to deliver rations to the soldiers stationed there. Lincoln dispatched ships carrying provisions, but just as they arrived, Confederate forces attacked the fort. After a day and a half of bombardment, the US soldiers surrendered. Two days later, on April 15, Lincoln called up seventy-five thousand state militiamen, signaling that the government would not passively accept this outcome. In response, four more southern states joined the Confederacy. Congress was not scheduled to convene until December, but Lincoln called for an emergency session to start on July Fourth. Congress needed to begin legislating immediately to meet the challenges of war.[3]

The transformation of the District of Columbia, up to that point a citadel of slaveholders, began immediately. US soldiers started entering the capital in the late spring of 1861, the initial regiments traveling through the slaveholding state of Maryland to get there. Two bridges over the Potomac River—Long Bridge and the Aqueduct Bridge—linked the US capital with neighboring Fairfax County, Virginia. On May 23, Virginia declared itself part of the Confederacy. That night, US forces advanced across the river by moonlight, accompanied by engineers who had already scouted the terrain and knew where to establish forts to secure their positions. The soldiers occupied a strip of land along the river and soon began forays into the countryside. Confederates fired on a detachment of US soldiers assigned to explore the town of Fairfax Court House. US soldiers took five Confederate prisoners and killed or wounded twenty-five. A week later, US troops heading by train toward Vienna, Virginia, were overwhelmed by Confederates. The area had become a theater of war.[4]

Across the region, many enslaved people saw their chance and made a break for freedom. Many had been following politics closely. As a Virginia-based correspondent noted in early May, "The slaves evidently have an impression that the war may give them freedom." Near occupied Alexandria, Virginia, after ten enslaved men heard they were to be forced into labor for the Confederacy at Manassas, they instead drove— with two wagons and two mule teams—across the lines into US territory. An eleven-year-old named Alfred Montgomery left his home near Falls Church and spent six weeks with the First Ohio, accompanying the regiment to Manassas and carrying water for the soldiers during the battle at Bull Run. Montgomery remained with the soldiers until they returned to Washington, and when they parted ways at the railroad station, the soldiers paid him a dollar and a half for his services.[5]

Many freedom-seekers ended up, like Montgomery, heading into Washington. Joseph Spears, who lived near Falls Church, saw his owner leave for Confederate service and decided to join a group of Union pickets and accompany them back to the capital. Charles Jackson, also enslaved in Fairfax County, witnessed his wife and children being whisked out of the county seat by their fearful owner. A US colonel gave him a pass to "come to Washington and work for himself." Edward Parker, who according to Virginia law was the property of Confederate Colonel John A. Washington—an indirect descendant of the first president and owner of Mount Vernon—was sent to meet his master at Manassas Junction. Instead, Parker made his way into occupied Alexandria and was hired as a cook for US soldiers. He, too, soon migrated into Washington.[6] Some escapees from slavery helped build the ring of forts that eventually surrounded Washington. Others cooked, oversaw animals, or did laundry. Some worked as teamsters, for the railroad, or in the navy yard. Working for wages for the US government was an important step toward becoming free. As one supportive newspaper put it, "To engage a person as a laborer, giving him the usual wages of labor, is to acknowledge and declare his rights as a man."[7]

Yet the old order had not been decisively overturned, and the legal status of freedom-seekers in Washington remained unclear. Army commanders did not take over the traditional duties of local law enforcement, instead allowing District of Columbia authorities—mostly constables and justices of the peace—to continue enforcing the prima facie principle, that all persons of African descent on the streets were assumed to be fugitives from slavery. Local authorities arrested and incarcerated African Americans, seemingly at will. These were the same procedures that had snared Gilbert Horton in the summer of 1826, and little had changed about local law enforcement in the intervening decades.

Congressional Republicans had no patience for such practices. James Grimes of Iowa, chair of the Senate Committee on the District of Columbia, took immediate action when he learned that the Washington jail "was being used . . . as a means of oppression." Grimes had burst into prominence in Iowa politics in 1854, when he was elected governor on an anti-Nebraska platform that brought Whigs like himself together with antislavery activists and Free Soil Democrats. When he joined the Senate in the winter of 1859, he associated with William Seward, Henry Wilson, John Bingham, and other prominent radical Republicans. In the summer of 1861, Grimes was dismayed to learn that local authorities were sweeping suspected runaways from slavery into the city jail and also continuing the practice of holding enslaved people for "safe keeping" at the request of their owners. The Iowa senator approached Secretary of War Simon Cameron, who agreed to arrange "a general jail-delivery by military authority." In orders issued on July Fourth—the day Congress began its emergency lawmaking session—Cameron instructed his subordinates to let all the prisoners go free.[8]

By late summer, local law enforcement had reverted to the customary practice of arbitrarily arresting and incarcerating African Americans on suspicion that they were fugitive slaves. Cameron's order evidently was no longer in effect. Constables and other local officials collected people in their workplaces, in the market, and on the city's streets, disregarding free papers and refusing to allow suspects to contact those who might vouch for their freedom. Captives were subjected to a perfunctory hearing before a justice of the peace and then jailed. After the disastrous battle at Manassas on July 21, Lincoln had named George McClellan commander of the division of the US Army charged with defending Washington, DC, and McClellan based his operations in the US capital. But the general, a prewar Democrat entirely unsympathetic to the abolitionist cause, did nothing to intervene in the arrests. The Washington jail, a decrepit three-story stone building on Judiciary Square in the center of the city, became horribly overcrowded as alleged runaways were thrown in with a bloated population of petty offenders, debtors, prostitutes, and inebriated soldiers.[9]

A corps of northern journalists took note. For decades, the Washington jail had been a symbol of the Slave Power and its abuses, and many saw it as a perfect place to begin the assault on slaveholders' power in the federal government. A Washington correspondent for the *New York Post* wrote of his astonishment that the building held so many "unclaimed fugitives from slave-holding justice." He particularly noticed Edward Parker, whose prominent owner had been killed by US pickets in northwestern Virginia. Why should the slave of so high-ranking a Confederate be permitted to languish in jail? A correspondent for the *Independent*, a widely read New York weekly magazine, called the arrest and incarceration of people who were merely seeking freedom a "shameful injustice" in an era of Republican oversight.[10]

Just before Congress reconvened in December 1861, the army provost marshal sent detective Allan Pinkerton into the jail to investigate. Pinkerton was predisposed to find law enforcement practices in Washington repellent. An abolitionist from Kane County in northern Illinois, Pinkerton had moved to Chicago in 1849, opened his own detective agency, and become a contractor with the Illinois Central Railroad. In that last capacity, he came to know George McClellan, vice president of the railroad company. The two men's politics could not have been more different. While McClellan was a Democrat, Pinkerton remained active in radical abolitionist circles, in one instance using his railroad connections to help John Brown move a group of twelve fugitives east toward Detroit and Canada. Yet Pinkerton and McClellan were evidently friends, and in early 1861, McClellan invited the detective to direct intelligence operations for the Department of the Ohio. The men moved to Washington, where Pinkerton oversaw spy operations for the Army of the Potomac and debriefed people exiting the Confederacy. Pinkerton understood that enslaved people could be particularly good sources of information, and in the fall of 1861, he tried to persuade McClellan to take an interest in their potential as military allies and informants.[11]

Pinkerton took his assignment to the Washington jail seriously. Operating under the pseudonym "E. J. Allen," he toured the building and spoke, at greater or lesser length, with sixty African American prisoners, recording information about where they had come from, who their putative owners were, and the conditions of their escape, arrest, and incarceration. Pinkerton discovered that many of the prisoners had escaped bondage in Virginia. This was significant because the Confiscation Act passed by Congress the previous summer had instructed the military that slaveholders who required their slaves to labor for the rebellion no longer had a right to reclaim slaves who escaped. This law made it difficult to justify jailing people who had escaped from Virginia, where most enslavers were assumed to be disloyal to the United States. More generally, Pinkerton found that prisoners were forced to live in abysmal conditions in a dangerously overcrowded jail. A clear and dramatic writer, the detective penned an outrage-filled report of his findings, which made its way into the hands of Senator Henry Wilson of Massachusetts.

With Republicans in control of Congress, slavery and the black codes in the District of Columbia, long protected by the Slave Power, finally were vulnerable. Shortly after the Thirty-Seventh Congress opened its second session on December 2, Wilson introduced Pinkerton's incendiary report and called for the release of all persons arrested as fugitive slaves, regardless of their state of origin. Pinkerton had emphasized the absence of due process of law for African Americans in Washington. Local officials refused to consider African Americans' own accounts of who they were and why they were in the city and, in keeping with longstanding practice, they planned to sell inmates into slavery if no owner claimed them and they could not prove their freedom. Wilson said he had personally visited the jail the day before, and that very day he had taken several others "to witness what I had seen." Conditions, he said, were "a burning shame and a disgrace to our country." The Massachusetts senator delivered an impassioned peroration in which he argued that those who threw fugitive slaves in jail instead of treating them with respect were committing treason against the United States. Escapees from slavery were critical sources of information for the United States, he insisted, while the arresting officers were "vampires" whose actions were "calculated to weaken the Federal cause and strengthen the cause of the rebels." They, not the slaves, should be in prison.[12]

Wilson and his Republican allies were poised to destroy slavery in the nation's capital and repeal its racist laws. Among the most passionate of these allies was John Hale of New Hampshire, who in 1847 had broken with the Democrats and reached the US Senate with the support of a Free Soil coalition. In 1848, he had railed against antiabolitionist mobs in the capital city. Now, Hale indicted the District's justice system, focusing special attention on the consequences for free Black people: "No matter how long a man has lived here, no matter how correct a life he has led, no matter how exemplary he may be in all the walks of life," if his "complexion" was dark, he was "liable to be at once arrested and carried to jail, and kept in confinement." Congress had a duty, Hale declared, "to look into the administration of justice in this District, and to see to it that those who have been ground to the earth heretofore may not be ground still more under your auspices."[13]

In attacking law enforcement practices in the capital, men such as Senators Wilson and Hale were also trying to push the Lincoln administration. Some Republicans were frustrated with Lincoln that fall of 1861 for his reluctance to attack slavery head-on. They were particularly incensed by Lincoln's reversal of Major General John C. Frémont's order to free the slaves of rebels in his Missouri jurisdiction. In the capital, the head of law enforcement was Ward Lamon, the District of Columbia marshal and a personal friend of Lincoln's. A Virginia native, Lamon was known to be conservative on slavery-related issues. He was also an imperious man who had no desire to cooperate with Congress. By drawing attention to the slavery-appeasing practices of the constables and justices of the peace under Lamon's watch, Republicans were signaling another way in which the administration was dragging its feet. The same day that Wilson read Pinkerton's report in the Senate, the House instructed its Committee on the District of Columbia to investigate whether there were prisoners in the Washington jail who were "not charged with crime," and to propose legislation preventing such people from being arrested in the future.[14]

Pressure on the administration to stop the arrest of freedom-seekers may well have worked, for on that same day, Secretary of State William Seward informed George McClellan of a new order from Lincoln himself. The president's order noted that local police regularly arrested runaways in Washington "upon the presumption, arising from color, that they are fugitives from service or labor." Lincoln instructed military authorities to enforce the Confiscation Act, which required that people who were fleeing forced labor for the Confederacy must be "received into the military protection of the United States." Echoing Senator Wilson, the president told military authorities to arrest anyone who seized runaways in violation of federal law. Congress continued to pressure Lamon to divulge who was in the jail, and in January 1862, Lincoln instructed him that no one could be imprisoned for more than thirty days on suspicion of being a fugitive.[15]

In the meantime, newspapers published reporters' lurid accounts of the jail. The stench was sickening. Black prisoners were "packed into it like herrings, close, foul, without ventilation or any apparent drainage." Some reporters profiled individual prisoners by name. Charles Jackson had been

in jail five months when reporters filed in. After seeing his wife and children carried off by their owner, he had come to Washington to work. Once
there, however, he "candidly" told a policeman that he was a runaway and
was immediately arrested. Joseph Spears, who had escaped from Virginia
and found work in Washington as a baker, had been jailed since July. Most
prisoners had fled slavery in Virginia or Maryland, but several were free
men, including James Johnson, a young Pennsylvanian who had come to
Washington as a cook for his state's Fifth Regiment. Johnson was arrested
while on a marketing errand, and police had refused to allow him to contact the officer of his unit, who could attest to his freedom. An artist for
Frank Leslie's Illustrated Weekly produced a sketch of the horrid conditions
in the jail, which was published with authenticating testimony by reporters and politicians.[16]

Washington's local leaders fought back hard. The city governments of
Washington and Georgetown had always been subordinate to the will of
Congress, although members of Congress often made a show of deference
to public opinion among the white elite. As a congressman in 1849, Lincoln himself had proposed gradual abolition of slavery in the capital, but
only if local voters gave their consent. In December 1861, Richard Wallach, editor of the *Washington Evening Star,* the city's leading newspaper,
defended the local black laws, arguing that "general experience teaches that
[free negroes] require different laws for their government than those applicable to a white population." He denied that Black prisoners were ever sold
for jail fees, and, voicing the casual racism of the slaveholding city, suggested that the report of Allan Pinkerton (a.k.a. E. J. Allen) be viewed with
skepticism because "the testimony" on which it was based was "derived
wholly from negroes in jail." Locals knew that such people were not to be
trusted, wrote Wallach. "Had [E. J. Allen] lived in this community a single
decade, he would have known, as our own citizens do, how little reliance is
to be placed on such testimony." That spring, the Washington City council
passed an antiabolition resolution, insisting that "a large majority of the
people of this District" opposed abolition, and encouraging Congress to

prevent the city from becoming "an asylum for free negroes, a population undesirable in every American community."[17]

Congressional Republicans largely ignored such expressions of local opposition. After the flurry of discussion in December 1861, Congress returned to the issue of slavery in the District in February 1862. Some Republicans believed slavery had always been unconstitutional in the capital, while others worried that abolishing slavery in the capital without compensating slaveowners would violate the Fifth Amendment. To allay such concerns, a proposed District of Columbia emancipation bill included a million-dollar appropriation to be distributed as payment to District slaveholders who remained loyal to the Union. The act established a commission to hear slaveowners' claims and determine their loyalty. It also included an appropriation of $100,000 to support the voluntary emigration of any Black people who were interested in departing the country, a provision that was inserted at the behest of James Doolittle, a Wisconsin Republican whose views on race and equality were among the most conservative in the party.[18] Lincoln signed the District of Columbia Emancipation Act on April 16, 1862, setting in motion the process of compensated emancipation. In an official message, Lincoln informed Congress that he supported abolition and believed the act constitutional, adding that he particularly appreciated the compensation and colonization provisions. Doolittle was pleased, writing to his wife that he hoped those remarks would help radicals understand "what I have been endeavoring for 4 or 5 years to show them, that the *question of race* is a more troublesome one than the question of condition."[19]

Yet Henry Wilson and his allies did not forget about Washington's black codes. The prospect of ending slavery raised the question of what rights free African Americans would enjoy—a question that had long roiled the free states. The day after Lot Morrill of Maine introduced the emancipation bill in the Senate, Wilson declared his intention to offer a bill that would address certain laws "relating to persons of color" in the District of Columbia. Several days later, Wilson presented an "abstract" of the dozens

of laws he proposed to repeal—local ordinances and congressional charters dating to the earliest days of the nation that meted out special rules
for free Black and mulatto persons. When David Wilmot of Pennsylvania,
the former Democrat and author of the Wilmot Proviso in 1846, suggested
that simply abolishing slavery would take care of such matters, Wilson disagreed. His proposal did something different and necessary. It "repeal[ed]
the black code of the District—the laws applicable to persons of color."[20]

Wilson and others understood that, without further action, the capital's antiblack laws would remain on the books, subjecting free Black
people to suspicion of being fugitive slaves and exposing them to other
kinds of discrimination. It was a "monstrous doctrine," Wilson argued,
that required free people of African descent to prove their freedom or face
imprisonment. "This doctrine, that color is presumed evidence of slavery,"
had a corrupting influence on law enforcement officers and resulted in the
incarceration of scores of innocent people. Laws that required free Black
people to register with local officials invited "the most oppressive acts of
petty tyranny," he insisted. "The wrongs, the outrages, the enormities" that
such laws had visited upon "the unoffending" and "the helpless . . . will
never be known until the secrets of the last days are revealed."[21]

The process of repealing racist laws in the District began with a clause
in the Emancipation Act itself. In a section suggested by Senator Charles
Sumner of Massachusetts, the act instructed the commission charged with
assessing the value of slaves to receive testimony "without the exclusion
of any witness on account of color." Congress soon made a more direct
thrust at repealing the capital's black codes. A new law, proposed by Senator Wilson and signed by Lincoln on May 22, 1862, established a system of public schools for Black children and provided that "all persons of
color . . . shall be subject and amenable to the same laws and ordinances to
which free white persons are." Then, at Sumner's behest, a separate measure
in July 1862 declared that, "in all judicial proceedings in the District of
Columbia there shall be no exclusion of any witness on account of color."
This cluster of measures, driven by the two senators from Massachusetts

but concurred in almost unanimously by Republicans, provided for the District of Columbia the kind of regime of civil equality that antislavery activists in the free states had long demanded.[22]

But the repeal of certain laws did not instantly change local practice. In the spring of 1863, a lawyer named George H. Day explained that although the District of Columbia was now free territory, kidnappers still traversed the city, looking to grab and sell into slavery people who were not carrying free papers. In several recent cases, Day said, justices of the peace had rejected Black men's complaints of assaults by whites, arguing that police court hearings were not, in fact, judicial proceedings, and therefore that testimony from Blacks need not be admitted. Two or three of the justices of the peace allowed "colored testimony," Day said, adding that "the matter is improving."[23] Undoing decades of racist practice in law enforcement was a monumental task; changing the law itself was an important first step, but it was only the beginning.

———•———

LIKE THE REPUBLICAN-DOMINATED CONGRESS, the Lincoln administration quickly took steps to enforce racial equality in civil rights in areas where it believed it had jurisdiction. The question of whether free African Americans were citizens had never been settled, Chief Justice Roger Taney's efforts notwithstanding. Taney had insisted in 1857 that free Black people, even if citizens of their states, were not citizens "in the sense in which that word is used in the Constitution." Republicans collectively believed that Taney had based his decision on an erroneous account of the nation's history, and that the case itself was wrongly decided.

From the outset of his presidency, Lincoln hoped that Congress would take action to affirm African American citizenship. In his inaugural address of March 4, 1861, he returned to the relationship between the 1850 Fugitive Slave Act and the Constitution's privileges and immunities clause. He urged Congress to amend the Fugitive Slave Act to add "safeguards of liberty" that would ensure that "a free man be not in any case surrendered as a slave." At the same time, addressing the longstanding question of the right of free Black people to move freely from state to state, he invited Congress to "provide by law for the enforcement" of the privileges and immunities clause.[24]

Thinking along the same lines in the spring of 1862, weeks after the president signed the District of Columbia Emancipation Act, Charles Sumner was trying to envision legislation that would "carry out the clause of the Constitution ensuring to citizens their rights in other states." The Massachusetts senator wrote Horace Gray, a leading lawyer, that he wanted Congress to do something to "set aside" the *Dred Scott* case. Gray cautioned that Congress could not "overrule" a Supreme Court opinion, but Sumner continued to question whether there was "any thing in the way of legislation, or Congressional declaration" to be "done against it."[25] The question soon bubbled up in the Treasury Department, which was under the direction of Salmon Chase. Since leading the movement to create an antislavery third party in Ohio and across the free states in the early 1840s, Chase had been highly successful in politics. He had served as a US senator for six years and then, as a Republican, was elected governor of Ohio in 1855. Despite having earned his share of political enemies through his ambition and capacity for ruthlessness in politics, Chase's political career remained defined by his early leadership of the political antislavery movement and his energetic advocacy of racial equality.

In the fall of 1862, Chase saw an opportunity to help shift the government's position on African American citizenship. Late that summer, a customs official inspecting ships sailing out of Perth Amboy, New Jersey, had detained a schooner because its master, David M. Selsey, was African American. According to a 1793 federal law, masters of ships conducting trade along the coast were required to be US citizens. African Americans had long been permitted to captain such ships, but treasury officials now raised the question of whether—particularly in light of the *Dred Scott* decision—Selsey could be considered a citizen for such purposes. The query made its way up the chain of command within the Treasury Department.

The department's solicitor, Edward Jordan, believed that detaining the ship on such grounds was "illegal." "I know of no authority for denying citizenship to a *colored man*, save the 'Dred Scott' decision," Jordan wrote. He called that decision "erroneous" and said that although it had the "effect of law" where the Supreme Court had jurisdiction, it did not apply to "the Treasury Department, or the officers under its jurisdiction."[26]

In September, Chase asked US Attorney General Edward Bates for his opinion on whether free African Americans were citizens under federal law. It is intriguing that the question fell to Bates, a conservative Republican from Missouri. A longtime Whig, Bates had moved into the Republican camp only as the 1860 presidential campaign approached. He had been active in colonization society activities in Missouri and was strongly aligned with the Blair family, powerful border-state Republicans who also advocated emancipation with colonization. Yet Francis Blair's son, Montgomery, had defended Dred Scott before the Supreme Court, compiling an extensive brief for African American citizenship under the US Constitution.[27] By the 1860s, the Blairs, as well as people like Lincoln and Trumbull of Illinois, felt that support for colonization was not incompatible with a willingness to defend the citizenship and civil rights of free African Americans. These men may have expressed support for colonization for reasons of political expedience, or they may have found it genuinely difficult to imagine a United States in which all people were free and coexisted on terms of racial equality. One thing was certain: They rejected the Democrats' vision of a nation in which African Americans were excluded from the basic promises of "life, liberty, and the pursuit of happiness."

Bates's response to Lincoln's wartime colonization gambit reveals that mix of views. On August 14, 1862, Lincoln met in the White House with a delegation of prominent Black residents of the District of Columbia, hoping to encourage them to cooperate with the idea that free African Americans should start a "colony" in Central America. After the meeting—with help from appropriations by Congress—the government began taking steps to recruit volunteers. Attorney General Bates supported the plan, though he thought Black Americans who moved to Central America should be considered "emigrants" rather than progenitors of "colonies" that were extensions of the United States. At the same time, in a lengthy memorandum on colonization, Bates indicated that he viewed African Americans as citizens. He criticized those who insisted that Black Americans were not entitled to US passports for believing that they were "wiser than the constitution." He also observed that he did "not know of any *foreign* State whose laws prohibit men, only because they are negros, from coming in, acquiring a domicil among the people, owning property, & establishing a civil & social status." Perhaps this was a comment on the fact that many domestic states did precisely that.[28]

Bates was the latest in a long line of attorneys general to be asked to weigh in on the citizenship status of free African Americans. In 1821, William Wirt had ruled that a free Black Virginian was not a citizen of Virginia and therefore not entitled to a ship pilot's license. From then on, attorneys general had declined to take a decisive position. Chief Justice Taney had tried to settle the issue in his *Dred Scott* decision, but Republicans, now in power, were determined to overrule him. Bates was reluctant to enter the fray at first, but the political climate forced his hand. On September 22, 1862, Lincoln gave formal notice that on January 1, he would proclaim slaves in insurrectionary areas free. The Preliminary Emancipation Proclamation served as a warning: If the seceded states did not give up the fight, the war would take a dramatic turn in the new year. Two days later, Salmon Chase reiterated his question to Bates, this time more formally: "Are colored men Citizens of the United States, and therefore Competent to command American vessels?"[29]

Confronted with Chase's query, Bates was hesitant to respond. In correspondence with his friend Francis Lieber, a leading constitutional scholar, the attorney general lamented that American discussions of citizenship tended to be too abstract. Bates wanted to begin not with ancient Greece or Rome but with actual practices in the United States. He wrote to Lieber about the longstanding argument over the relationship between citizenship and voting. Since at least the Missouri debate, northerners had regularly separated citizenship from voting rights, claiming that all free people who were not aliens were citizens, regardless of whether they could vote. Southerners were more likely to argue that a person who could not vote was not a citizen—or that members of a group whose men could not vote were not citizens. Bates took the former position. He argued that a citizen was a person who owed allegiance to the government and was entitled to its protection, and that if the government did not recognize citizenship in this broad sense, the consequences would be "frightful" for state and society.[30]

Finally answering Chase at the end of November 1862, Bates argued that free African Americans were US citizens. From the nation's beginning, he insisted, American practice had been to assume that any person born in the United States was a citizen of the United States. Attempts to claim that free African Americans were not citizens by birthright, he said, were specious departures from that tradition. The nation was founded on "written law," and the US Constitution did not exclude people of African descent from citizenship. Indeed, "its terms are manifestly broad enough to include them." In the absence of any constitutional provision to the contrary, the only possible conclusion was that free African Americans were citizens of the United States. Bates explicitly disagreed with and disregarded the *Dred Scott* decision, accepting instead decades of arguments by free African Americans and their allies who had claimed citizenship as their birthright. Therefore, he informed Chase, "the *free man of color,* mentioned in your letter, if born in the United States, is a citizen of the United States."[31]

The Bates decision, which went public in mid-December 1862, received extensive coverage in newspapers and was often portrayed as a direct rebuttal of *Dred Scott*. One person who still had questions was Robert Winthrop, the old Massachusetts Whig who in 1843 had shepherded the Boston merchants' petition about free Black sailors' rights into the House and had authored the House committee report that declared the South Carolina Negro Seamen Law unconstitutional. By 1862, Winthrop had retired from politics, but he was still paying close attention, and he queried Bates about the lingering problems of state citizenship and the meaning of the privileges and immunities clause. Winthrop evidently wondered whether Bates had considered that his opinion on citizenship would undermine or nullify state laws like those of Illinois, which prohibited free African Americans from entering. Bates informed Winthrop that he gave less weight to such consequences than to the "fact of citizenship, because the fact is primary and independent."[32]

Bates assured Winthrop that he was well aware of the consequences of his official opinion. "The constitution was made as it is, for the very purpose of securing to every citizen, common & equal rights all over the nation; and to prevent local prejudices & captious legislation in the States," he wrote. He realized that, in recognizing Black citizenship, the US government was acknowledging that African Americans were entitled to the same rights of "locomotion" and "habitancy" as whites and thus implying that laws restricting free Black migration and settlement, in Illinois and everywhere else, would be null and void. In a second letter, Bates affirmed that he considered questions associated with slavery itself outside the purview of his analysis. He had tried to answer, as a "cold matter of law," only the question that had come before him. "Enough for me, & for the question," he said, "if I have succeeded in placing upon impregnable grounds of law & logic, the proposition that a person may be a citizen without being white. That is all I aimed at."[33]

That was a lot. No previous administration had suggested as much, and the Republican conviction that the US government ought to ensure protection of African Americans in the privileges and immunities of citizenship only grew stronger with time. In the meantime, most people understood, as Winthrop and Bates both did, the practical import of Bates's decision. The *Milwaukee Daily Sentinel*, for instance, applauded Bates's opinion as "another sign of progress" and speculated that, "under the principles and acts of an Administration like the present, there will be no more refusals of passports to 'free Americans of African descent' . . . and the bitter persecutions of colored seamen in Southern ports would be likely to cease."[34] The

Bates decision—and the direction in which the Lincoln administration and Congress were proceeding—promised the resolution of longstanding questions concerning African Americans' rights to captain ships, to travel abroad, and to move freely from state to state within the United States.

———•◦•———

LINCOLN ISSUED THE Emancipation Proclamation on January 1, 1863, about two weeks after Bates's landmark opinion was released. Constitutionally, the presidential proclamation was a war measure. Lincoln drew on his power as commander-in-chief in wartime to declare slaves free in areas that were in rebellion against the United States, excepting several places within the Confederacy that were occupied by US forces. The proclamation, like any measure, was not self-executing. But it decisively turned the US Army and the US Navy into agents of liberation. Everywhere the soldiers and sailors went, people would be free. The Emancipation Proclamation changed the direction of the war, setting in motion the enlistment of Black men into the US Army and affirming that—as abolitionists had long argued—the question of slavery's future was truly at the heart of the conflict.

While Americans were taking stock of the vast changes at hand in early 1863—the Bates decision, the Emancipation Proclamation, and the prospect of Black men in the US fighting forces—a Haitian diplomat and his secretary arrived in New York City. The beginning of US diplomacy with Haiti was prompted in large measure by the Lincoln administration's interest in relegating some forms of racist foreign policy to the past. In the late eighteenth century, Haitians had thrown off French rule, abolished slavery, and declared their nation an independent republic. The US government had, from the time of Thomas Jefferson's presidency, refused to recognize Haitian independence or engage in formal diplomatic relations with the new nation. Abolitionists had petitioned Congress to recognize Haiti in the 1830s, and John Quincy Adams carried the matter into the House of Representatives in 1839. Under Slave Power rule, however, Congress never wavered. Slaveholders and their allies could not stomach the idea of recognizing Haiti as an equal in the family of nations, nor Black diplomats as legitimate members of the Washington diplomatic corps. As Charles Sumner put it in 1852, the presence of a Black minister from Haiti, "even though silent, would be a perpetual protest against Slavery."[35]

Addressing Congress in December 1861, Lincoln suggested that legislators take steps to recognize "the independence and sovereignty of Hayti and Liberia." It was the Senate Committee on Foreign Relations, chaired by Charles Sumner, that drove the matter forward, reporting a bill in the spring of 1862 to send diplomats to both nations. Democrats immediately denounced the proposal. Garrett Davis of Kentucky complained that US government officials should not have to receive Haitian ministers "upon the same terms of equality" as other diplomats. If a "full-blooded negro were sent" as a diplomat to the United States, he warned, "by the Laws of Nations he could demand that he be received precisely on the same terms of equality with the white representatives from the powers of the earth composed of white people." Such recognition ran all the way to the "negro wives and negro daughters" of such men, he warned, who would want to attend social gatherings with the rest of official Washington. But Davis and other Democrats could not stop the Republican majority, and Lincoln signed the bill into law in June 1862. A headline in the Democratic *Cincinnati Enquirer* spoke volumes: "The Recognition of Negro Hayti and Negro Liberia,—Negro Equality Proclaimed."[36]

The arrival of the first Haitian diplomats to the United States in mid-February 1863 generated intense public commentary. The Haitian chargé d'affaires, Ernest Roumain, and his assistant landed in New York City, where they prepared to make their way to the capital. Roumain was a member of the Haitian elite and a close associate of the republic's new president, Fabre Geffrard. Educated in England, Roumain spoke French and English, and reporters described him as elegant and congenial. Arriving in Washington in early March 1863, the Haitian delegates were formally received at the State Department.[37]

The State Department, under the direction of William Seward of

New York, was happy to welcome the Haitian delegation to Washington. The department had moved early to recognize African American citizenship. In April 1861, Seward had issued a passport to Henry Highland Garnet, the prominent Black Presbyterian minister and activist. In boilerplate language, the passport declared Garnet "a citizen of the United States," and where it listed Garnet's identifying features, it described his "complexion" as "black." Seward, when governor of New York, had already advocated racial equality in voting rights, and he took his duties to the Haitian delegation seriously. In keeping with diplomatic conventions, he hosted a ceremonial dinner in which Roumain was feted alongside other Washington-based diplomats and members of Lincoln's cabinet.[38]

It was precisely the sort of event that slaveholders and Democrats had most stringently opposed, because it so dramatically marked the advance of racial equality into new spheres. The Democratic *Detroit Free Press* called Seward's party a "nigger dinner" and claimed that Republicans had prioritized recognizing Haiti just to be provocative—because they wanted to "introduce to society in the capital of the nation, as the equal, and, in some cases, the superior of the whites . . . some Haytien 'citizen of African descent.'" The paper decried Seward's dinner as a knowing affront to white supremacy, saying that, "in his high position, his every act, particularly where the negroes are affected, must bear the utmost significance." Others were determined to use the presence of the Haitian delegation to tout the progress of racial equality. George Lawrence Jr., an African American man who was in New York City promoting Black emigration to Haiti, wrote a public letter describing Roumain as "a Haytian gentlemen of education and refinement" and delighting in the fact that Roumain would meet the "other distinguished guests *as their equal.*"[39]

In July, Frederick Douglass praised Seward's dinner when he addressed a mass meeting in Philadelphia to promote Black men's enlistment. Recognizing that many hesitated to volunteer for a government that had, in so many ways, refused to recognize their manhood, he declared that he too wanted only "equal and exact justice" for African Americans. He then reviewed the recent changes that had given him hope. Congress had abolished slavery in the District of Columbia and the territories and taken action against the international slave trade. The president had issued his Emancipation Proclamation, and the attorney general had declared that "we are American citizens." The Haitian minister, Douglass noted, "sits beside" our secretary of state, "dines at his table in Washington, while colored men are excluded from the cars in Philadelphia," showing that "a black man's complexion in Washington, in the presence of the Federal government, is less offensive than in the city of brotherly love." All this was a lead-up to Douglass's exhortation that Black men enlist in the US Army. He acknowledged that African American soldiers were paid less than whites and that Black men were not permitted to be officers, but he predicted that these inequities would soon be remedied. Meanwhile, he urged, "the hour has arrived, and your place is in the Union army."[40]

———•◦•———

IN THAT SAME PHILADELPHIA SPEECH, Douglass connected Black men's military service with future citizenship claims. He forecast: "Once let the black man get upon his person the brass letters U.S.; let him get an eagle on his button, and a musket on his shoulder . . . and there is no power on the earth or under the earth which can deny that he has earned the right of citizenship in the United States." As Douglass recognized, Black men's enlistment changed the kinds of demands that African Americans could make on the nation. Citizenship was traditionally understood as an exchange of loyalty for protection, and here was a chance for African American men to demonstrate loyalty in the most vaunted way. Some African Americans thought Douglass too optimistic, but many were eager to join the fight to defeat the slaveholders' rebellion.

Joining the Army meant taking the fight for equality into a new venue. Black soldiers were dismayed to find that soldiers' pay was profoundly unequal. Congressional legislation passed in 1862 provided that

Black enlistees were to be paid $10 a month, minus $3 for clothing. By contrast, white soldiers could expect $13 per month and a clothing allowance on top of that. In Ohio, Governor David Tod found that the pay disparity made Black men reluctant to enlist. Black soldiers, civilian activists, and white supporters pushed hard for equal pay, with some soldiers facing courts-martial and even execution as punishment for protesting. In his annual report at the end of 1863, Secretary of War Edwin Stanton asked Congress to enact equalizing legislation. After a lengthy debate, in June 1864 Congress adopted a new policy: Men who were free at the time of their enlistment received equal pay backdated to the date of their enlistment. For those who were enslaved when they enlisted, the raise was dated only to January 1, 1864. In the ensuing year, Congress made additional adjustments that afforded some freedmen equal pay dating to their enlistment, though the policy never made whole many of the enslaved men who had volunteered or been drafted in 1862 and 1863.[41]

Everyday activities within the army afforded further opportunities to inch forward the project of racial equality and give substance to African Americans' claims to equal citizenship and belonging. In military tribunals, officers regularly permitted African Americans to testify in cases involving whites. Midway through 1864, John S. Rock, a Black lawyer from Massachusetts, learned that an officer of the 54th Massachusetts Regiment had refused to allow a Black sergeant, a noncommissioned officer, to serve the regiment as clerk, reputedly saying, "No negro will be allowed to hold any position . . . except that of a cook or a laborer." Rock conveyed the complaint to Massachusetts Governor John Andrew, a staunch advocate for Black soldiers, who demanded the clerk be reinstated. Many Americans cherished the ideal of the citizen-soldier who sacrificed for the nation in exchange for the privileges of full citizenship. That is why it had been important for Black activists to remind people that Black men had fought in the American Revolution and under Andrew Jackson in the War of 1812. Fighting in the Civil War made Black men's claims to the same rights white men enjoyed all the more persuasive and profound. "All we ask is equal opportunities and equal rights," Rock said in the summer of 1864. "We ask the same for the black man that is asked for the white man; nothing more, and nothing less."[42]

———————

THE OLD WASHINGTON, DC, was far from vanquished amid the rise of the Republican city. And entrenched forces found succor among some of the new white migrants to the city. As Black men began to enlist in the US Army in the spring and summer of 1863, white Washington residents—including teamsters and others working for the army—had no compunction about attacking Black neighborhoods, setting fire to buildings, and directing particular animosity toward Black men in uniform. By late June, such violence had become so frequent that white officers of Black troops met to discuss "cases of assaults, attacks, &c, on colored soldiers." Weeks later, New York City descended into chaos as working-class whites protested the military draft and then turned their rage on Black communities and institutions. When news of the upheavals in New York reached Washington, the supervisor of the city's "contraband camp"—a temporary camp for escaped slaves who could not find other housing in Washington—asked that a company from the Washington-based 1st U.S. Colored Infantry be deployed to the camp as guards and requested "a hundred and fifty muskets with ammunition to place in the hands of our laboring men . . . so that in case of riot we may be able to defend ourselves."[43]

Black Washingtonians only became more assertive, demanding public recognition of the principle of racial equality. They gathered en masse to protest when local officials tried to enforce the federal Fugitive Slave Act. They opposed efforts to galvanize support for colonization among the capital's Black community. At a military recruitment event in the spring of 1863, George Hatton, a charismatic young Black army corporal, declared "he would not ride" the city's streetcars "until he had his rights and could sit inside." Days later, a correspondent for the *Christian Recorder* reported: "The soldiers all ride in the street cars or any other cars they want to ride in; and you might just as well declare war against them as to declare that they can't ride there because they are colored." In the volatile summer of 1863, longstanding but heretofore largely clandestine Black civic organizations took to the streets in parades and public demonstrations of the kind that had been forbidden in the days of slavery. In July, for instance, the District's African American Sabbath School Union—a coalition of Sunday schools—converted its annual meeting into a citywide spectacle. Thousands of students and their teachers marched through the city's thoroughfares before gathering at Israel AME Church to hear exhortatory speeches. "The proslavery citizens could hardly believe their own eyes," reported one participant. The same month, Georgetown's Black Freemasons took to the streets displaying a "very beautiful banner" that they had "dared not" show in public "during the Dark Ages."[44]

The transformed national capital had new resonance for African American activists across the free states. As the remarkable year of 1863 came to a close, Robert Hamilton, editor of the New York–based *Anglo-African,* called for African Americans from across the nation to gather in the capital to celebrate the first anniversary of the Emancipation Proclamation and collectively nominate Abraham Lincoln for a second term as president.[45] This was an audacious proposal for a demonstration of Black political strength. Since African American men in most states (and the capital) were still denied the right to vote, meeting in Washington to renominate Lincoln was, in essence, a demand for voting rights and full citizenship. Hamilton's vision for a march on Washington did not come to fruition that year, but his proposal was just the beginning of a longer-term effort to establish a Black lobbying organization in the capital.

———

BY 1864, CONGRESS had made significant progress in codifying racial equality in civil rights in places where it had direct jurisdiction. Shortly after abolishing slavery in the District of Columbia, it ended slavery in the territories, in outright defiance of the *Dred Scott* decision. Charles Sumner in particular made it his business to push for repeal of antiblack laws and policies wherever possible. Sumner, who had called for "equality before the law" in his 1849 brief in the Boston school case, in December 1861 asked the Senate Committee on Patents to explore legislation that would secure the "right" to take out patents to "persons of African descent." In the spring of 1862, he proposed the repeal of federal laws that disqualified persons "by reason of color" from carrying the US mail. After pressing for a prohibition on racial discrimination in witness testimony in the District of Columbia, he sought similar measures for the federal courts overall. This was complicated in part because longstanding convention—affirmed in a recent statute—provided that federal courts adopt the rules of testimony of the state in which they were located. Such concessions to local practices were widely accepted. Yet Sumner pushed his point, and in the summer of 1864 he persuaded Congress to pass a law banning discrimination in witness testimony in all federal courts.[46]

Sumner was not popular among his congressional colleagues; most considered him dogmatic and impractical. Some Republicans believed the equalizing measures he advocated were premature or unnecessarily provocative. Lyman Trumbull, for instance, argued that Congress must not "assum[e] action which the exigencies of the country did not require." And James Doolittle of Wisconsin complained that such measures "seem to have no bearing whatever on the great issue," which in his view was sustaining northern unity in pursuit of winning the war. Yet Sumner and many radical Republicans were impatient. They saw opportunities to set an example, and they had no desire to wait until the war was over. Sumner often pointed out that the founding generation had eschewed the word *white* in documents like the Constitution and the Northwest Ordinance, and he demanded that Republicans in Congress take a principled stand while they had the chance.[47] Republicans extended that argument in later years, transforming the US Constitution in the process.

The war's dynamics also challenged Republicans to think beyond the somewhat limited vision of racial equality on which they had consensus—citizenship and civil rights—and to consider Black men's right to vote. African Americans and white radicals had long insisted that Black men must be permitted to vote on the same terms as white men. They had resisted the diminution of Black men's access to the vote in New York in 1821 and Pennsylvania in 1838, and in many places they had pushed the question into state constitutional conventions and referenda. Still, most white northerners—including many who supported African Americans' citizenship and civil rights—remained reluctant to permit Black Americans to become fully vested members of the body politic. They had qualms about sharing power and found it difficult to imagine Black officeholders. They also feared backlash from white voters and a Democratic Party that was wholeheartedly opposed to Black men's enfranchisement and willing to resort to racist demagoguery to ensure its defeat.

The Civil War cast the question in a new light. First, the war amplified the perspectives of principled radicals like Sumner who had long favored full racial equality and who insisted that if the United States were ever to slough off the residue of slavery, now was the time. Second, Republicans understood that the abolition of slavery—prospective in 1863 and real by the end of 1865—meant that the southern states, if readmitted to the Union without Black men's enfranchisement, could emerge more powerful than ever before in the US government. This was because the end of slavery meant the end of the Constitution's three-fifths clause. While slavery existed, enslaved people had been counted as three-fifths of a person for purposes of enumeration. With slavery abolished, freedpeople would be counted whole, thus increasing the size of the enumerated population in the southern states. If white southerners denied Black men the equal right to vote, not only would they dominate their own states' politics, but their priorities would be more heavily weighted than ever in Congress and the electoral college. As Republicans began considering this looming dilemma in the winter of 1863–64, they also began to consider new ways of exercising congressional oversight in the states.[48]

The question of who could vote in places under exclusive federal jurisdiction could be handled by Congress much more directly, and in the spring of 1864, that question arose in two such places: Montana Territory and the District of Columbia. During the war, the Republican-dominated Congress, eager to bring new states into the Union, had created the new states of West Virginia and Nevada, tried to get Nebraska and Colorado admitted, and added several new federal territories. The debate about voting rights in Montana Territory began in March, as Congress considered a bill to make Montana its own jurisdiction, separate from Idaho Territory. Minnesota Senator Morton Wilkinson introduced an amendment to strike the word *white* and add citizenship language to the part of the Montana bill related to voter qualifications.[49] Wilkinson's change would disqualify aliens from voting while opening the possibility that nonwhite citizens could vote.

The Senate adopted Wilkinson's language, whereupon a ferocious debate ensued in the House. Moderate and conservative Republicans wanted to avoid any action that implied Republican support for Black men's enfranchisement, particularly in anticipation of a difficult election season. James Doolittle of Wisconsin, for example, argued that Black men's enfranchisement was unpopular, particularly in the critical states of Pennsylvania, New York, Ohio, Indiana, and Illinois, and that George McClellan, now a presidential candidate, and his Democratic allies would eagerly use the issue against Republicans in the campaign. Benjamin Wade of Ohio, who usually aligned with the radicals, eloquently professed his opposition to all forms of racial distinction at law but supported keeping *white* in the Montana bill, particularly since there were virtually no African Americans in the territory. Wilkinson, along with Charles Sumner and John Hale of New Hampshire, bitterly rejected such arguments for expedience, comparing their opponents to those who, before the war, had urged the extension of slavery into the territories on grounds that the land would never be hospitable to slavery anyway. They wanted to stand on principle and insisted that this was a moment when they could show the nation that they rejected odious racial distinctions, even in voting. As Wilkinson put it: "I am opposed to being governed any longer by that wicked pro-slavery

prejudice that has ruled in the Congress . . . for more than thirty years."
The radicals lost this round, however, and *white* remained in the voter
qualifications for Montana Territory.[50]

The District of Columbia was worlds away from Montana Territory.
Whereas congressmen could plausibly assert that there were almost no
people of African descent in Montana, free Black people made up about
one-third of the population of the District of Columbia. In the winter of
1864, Senator James Harlan of Iowa proposed amending the election law
of Washington City by creating rules for voter registration. The existing
city charter provided that every "free white male citizen" who met certain
age and residency requirements was entitled to vote. (The policy explicitly
denied the vote to "persons non compos mentis, vagrants, paupers, or persons . . . convicted of any infamous crime," and those who had not paid
taxes owed.) In the spring of 1864, anticipating a congressional discussion of the city's election laws, Black residents petitioned for the franchise.
They insisted that African Americans' many accomplishments in the city
should discredit any arguments that Black men were less worthy of the vote
than white men. Black Washingtonians observed the same laws as others,
were subject to the same punishments, and had no more criminals or paupers among them than "any other class." They were "intelligent enough
to be industrious, to have accumulated property, and to build and sustain
Churches," and they were "educating their children without the aid of any
school fund." Moreover, their "loyalty has never been questioned," and "in
all their Country's trials they have responded voluntarily and with alacrity,
pay or no pay, bounty or no bounty, promotion or no promotion."[51]

The city government of Washington objected strenuously to Black
men's enfranchisement, resisting as it had when faced with the prospect of
abolition two years earlier. The city council passed a joint resolution opposing voting rights for Black men and sent the mayor and council chair to
the Senate to make the case. City officials could not abide the idea that the
"thousands of unfortunate contrabands that have gathered here" should
have a voice in local affairs. In the ensuing Senate debate, conservative

Republican Edgar Cowan of Pennsylvania moved to insert the word *white* into the description of voter qualifications, "so as to confine the right of voting in Washington to white male citizens." Republican moderates suggested a property requirement for all Washington voters, arguing that such a law would avoid *both* racial discrimination and the enfranchisement of thousands of propertyless freedmen. But the prospect of disenfranchising propertyless white men who already enjoyed the right to vote also elicited strong objections. Sumner proposed a policy that explicitly forbade racial discrimination in voting. Citing reports of "shocking" violence perpetrated against African Americans by white southerners, Sumner insisted that Congress's policy toward Washington ought to "set an example of justice and humanity." With Republicans unable to agree on a change, voter qualifications in Washington remained the same: white male citizens alone would be eligible to vote.[52]

Black Washingtonians' push for racial equality in public spaces, public accommodations, and voting rights in 1863 and 1864 reflected not just local conditions but a national groundswell. In the rebel states, the US government claimed extraordinary power founded in wartime exigency, and African Americans in those places regularly made their case to Lincoln and to Congress. At the end of April 1864, a delegation of five Black men from North Carolina visited Lincoln and asked him to make sure, as he encouraged the formation of loyal state governments in the Confederacy, that Black men would "exercise the right of suffrage." In Louisiana, where Lincoln's Reconstruction program was already underway, African Americans secured signatures of more than one thousand men on a petition for voting rights. Among the signers were veterans of the Battle of New Orleans, in which Andrew Jackson, then a general, had recruited Black soldiers to help defend against British assault. Two men carried the Louisiana petition to Washington, where they presented it to Lincoln and submitted it to the Senate via Charles Sumner.[53] It remained to be seen what, if anything, the US government would do to protect African Americans' rights in the rebel states—and which rights it might recognize.

In the free states, Republican dominance meant progress on repealing racist laws that abridged African Americans' civil rights. Since the formation of the Republican Party, the movement to repeal racist state laws had been decidedly partisan. In 1859, the Democratic-majority Ohio legislature had passed a law that barred election judges from permitting voting by persons with "distinct and visible admixture of African blood." The Republican-dominated Ohio Supreme Court, in turn, had declared that the new law violated the state constitution. In 1865, Ohio Republicans, now in the majority, finally repealed the state law that prohibited African Americans from receiving poor relief. Similarly, once under Republican control, the legislatures of Oregon and California repealed laws that barred Black testimony in cases involving whites. (Oregon made witness qualifications race-neutral. California, however, retained its law barring Indians from testifying in cases involving whites and explicitly banned Chinese testimony in such cases.) The Massachusetts General Assembly, under Republican leadership, passed the nation's first state law banning racial discrimination in public accommodations.[54]

In Iowa and Illinois, efforts by citizens and local authorities to enforce racist laws led to litigation and then repeal. African American migration into the Midwest increased during the war as enslaved people fled northward into free states. White residents raised familiar specters of dependent and disorderly Black populations, in some cases inciting violence. Yet Republican authorities were interested in dismantling restrictive laws, not upholding them. In Des Moines, Iowa, on January 8, 1863, the sheriff arrested a Black migrant named Archie Webb for violating the state's 1851 law barring Black migration. A Republican judge agreed to hear Webb's argument that the law was invalid. The conflict received extensive press coverage, and the judge, Maryland-born John Henry Gray, took his mandate seriously. In a lengthy and learned decision that explicitly challenged Chief Justice Taney's *Dred Scott* ruling, Gray argued that the 1851 law— which had rarely been formally enforced—violated the Iowa Constitution as well as the US Constitution's privileges and immunities clause. Webb was released, and the Republican-controlled legislature repealed the law the following year.[55]

In Illinois, the infamous 1853 Logan Law, which barred Black migration, remained in force until January 1865. The previous year, the state supreme court explicitly upheld the law in the case of *Nelson v. Illinois*. In Hancock County, which bordered both Iowa and Missouri on the Mississippi River, local officials had prosecuted six Black men under the Logan Law's antimigration provision. A local court convicted them and, in keeping with the law, sentenced them to be sold "at public auction." One of the men, identified only as "Nelson," got an attorney and challenged the law, arguing that it violated the state constitution because it permitted slavery, and that it violated the US Constitution both by contravening the privileges and immunities clause and by interfering in an area that was the exclusive domain of the US government. In a 2–1 decision, the Illinois Supreme Court held that the measure was "a reasonable police regulation, adopted for the protection of the inhabitants of the State against a class of persons which are supposed to be injurious to our community." Was Nelson entitled to the "privileges and immunities" of state citizens, promised by Article IV, Section 2 of the US Constitution? The court said flatly, "This record contains no evidence that the plaintiff in error is a citizen of any State."[56]

The best way to overturn the law was to secure its repeal by the legislature. When the fall 1864 elections brought Illinois Republicans a sweeping victory, they pressed hard for repeal of all the state's antiblack laws, with John Jones and Chicago's Black community at the forefront. Jones penned an open letter "to the people of Illinois," arguing that the discriminatory laws were far from a "dead letter." They were "a *living, active reality*" shaping the lives of African Americans in Illinois. The following month, Jones took the lead in submitting to the legislature a petition bearing the signatures of fifty thousand citizens. As the legislative session opened, the Republican governor, Richard Yates, urged repeal. A state senator from Cook County presented a petition 125 feet long bearing seven thousand names. "It will be done," the *Chicago Tribune* editorialized, "and the disability of the black race be utterly and forever removed in Illinois. The people have decreed it. It only waits for their representatives in council to execute the popular will." The legislature finally repealed the black laws that winter. By the time the war ended, Indiana was the only one of the five states in the Old Northwest that retained its racist residency and testimony laws.[57] Repeal of antiblack laws had finally come as a result of political struggle at the state level. There were still no federal limits on the states' right to discriminate.

———•—•———

GATHERING IN SYRACUSE, New York, in October 1864, a national convention of African American activists contemplated the future. That April, the Senate had passed the Thirteenth Amendment, which outlawed slavery and involuntary servitude and explicitly gave Congress the power of enforcement. The House, however, had failed to pass the amendment. During tenuous peace negotiations with Confederates that summer, Lincoln had said there would be no peace without "the abandonment of slavery" by the southern states. Yet the administration appeared to qualify that position in the fall, as William Seward and John P. Usher, the secretary of the interior, both said publicly that slavery's abolition was not, in fact, a necessary condition for peace. It was anyone's guess what would happen in the upcoming presidential election, and a victory for George McClellan, the Democratic candidate, would almost certainly mean slavery's survival.[58]

Even as the outcome of the war hung in the balance, the composition of the Syracuse convention suggested how much the war had altered possibilities for African American political organizing. No longer was a national Black convention composed of delegates from the free states and a smattering of people from places like Maryland and the District of Columbia. Now, Louisiana, Florida, Tennessee, Mississippi, North Carolina, and Virginia were all represented. Black men's enlistment in the US war effort elevated Black men's civic stature and their claims to full political "manhood," including the right to vote. New possibilities were opening for African American women as well. Before the war, Black women had increasingly moved out of traditional public roles in churches and communities and into the more overtly political world of the Black conventions. African American women, including Frances Harper and Sojourner Truth, had taken to the stump as abolitionists and women's rights advocates. During the war, correspondents for African American newspapers such as the *Anglo-African* and the *Christian Recorder* emphasized women's contributions to the war effort and to aiding needy freedpeople. At the Syracuse convention, Black women shared the dais with Black men. Both Harper and Edmonia Highgate, a teacher and writer, addressed the group.[59]

Old rivalries lingered among some leading men, but the convention ultimately published a strong address "to the people of the United States." The Democratic Party was the most pressing threat to their well-being, the convention declared, for the party, if it gained control nationally, would likely "restore slavery to all its ancient power." Yet convention leaders also worried about the fidelity of their white allies. Republican leaders were hobbled by racial prejudice, they said. Their proposals for "reconstructing" the southern states did not recognize that Black men, even soldiers, had "any political existence or rights whatsoever." What did the Black convention want? First, the total abolition of slavery. After that, racial equality before the law and the right to vote. The nation, the Syracuse convention declared, must proceed by

> erasing from its statute-books all enactments discriminating in favor or against any class of its people, and by establishing one law for the white and colored people alike. Whatever prejudice and taste may be innocently allowed to do or to dictate in social and domestic relations, it is plain, that in the matter of government, the object of which is the protection and security of human rights, prejudice should be allowed no voice whatever.

The Syracuse leaders enumerated civil rights as "personal freedom; the right to testify in courts of law; the right to own, buy, and sell real estate; the right to sue and be sued." But they were not satisfied with these rights alone. In a republican country, they insisted, such rights became "mere privileges" when people were denied the vote. The possession of that right, they said, "is the keystone to the arch of human liberty; and, without that, the whole may at any moment fall to the ground."[60]

The convention resolved to form a permanent organization based in Philadelphia. It would raise money and employ traveling agents, publish pamphlets and make annual reports. Members could create state-level leagues and auxiliaries, provided "no distinction of color or sex shall be permitted." Among the organization's goals was the uplift of Black Americans; it would encourage temperance and frugality. But it would also seek to change "the minds and conscience of the American people" and demand— by legal process if possible—the recognition of African Americans' rights as citizens.[61] Befitting the moment and the mission, the founders called their group the Equal Rights League.

CHAPTER 9

"TO RESTRAIN THE POWER OF THE STATES"

The Civil Rights Act and the Fourteenth Amendment

IN THE SECOND WEEK of May 1865, veteran abolitionists gathered in New York City's Church of the Puritans for the thirty-second annual meeting of the American Anti-Slavery Society. A choir sang Julia Ward Howe's wartime anthem, "Battle Hymn of the Republic," and the crowd joined for the chorus: "Glory, glory, hallelujah! His truth is marching on." William Lloyd Garrison, storied leader of the organization, announced that it was time to go their separate ways. "My vocation, as an Abolitionist, thank God, is ended." Armed conflict had taken the nation to a place few could have imagined four years earlier. The war had set in motion the destruction of slavery, and Congress had finished the task by passing a constitutional amendment that outlawed the institution everywhere. Their ultimate goal achieved, Garrison and many of his allies believed it was time to turn their attention elsewhere.[1]

Frederick Douglass did not share that view. Douglass had not been close to Garrison since the early 1850s, when Douglass embraced the political antislavery movement. Now, Douglass argued with Garrison again, insisting that abolitionists must work for the repeal of the racist laws that had long oppressed free African Americans, North and South. He recalled that in Rhode Island in the early 1840s, abolitionists had fought for and won a constitution "in which the word 'white' did not appear." In Massachusetts, they had "looked over their statute-book, and whenever they found the word 'white,' there they recognized slavery, and they made war upon it." "Anti-slavery ladies" had risked their reputations to circulate petitions demanding repeal of laws banning interracial marriage.[2] Now abolitionists faced a similar challenge, but on a far greater scale, Douglass argued. Even if every state ratified the Thirteenth Amendment, he said, "while the black man is confronted in the legislation of the South by the word 'white,' our work as Abolitionists, as I conceive it, is not done."

The black codes of the Midwest remained a cautionary example. No one should be surprised, Douglass pointed out, if white southerners denied Black men the right to testify against white men in the courts of law. "Why, our Northern States have done it. Illinois, Indiana and Ohio have done it." The southern states could do the same and more, and the Thirteenth Amendment would not stop them. Recalling Samuel Hoar's expulsion from Charleston, he argued that the Constitution's privileges and immunities clause had never worked as it was supposed to. There was "something down in South Carolina higher than Constitutional provisions," he said.[3] And so the abolitionists' work was not complete. They had to keep fighting for the repeal of racist laws, for the protection of the privileges and immunities of citizens, and ultimately for Black men's right to vote.

Faced with an extraordinary opportunity born of secession and civil war, most Republicans in Congress agreed with Douglass that it was time to nationalize the principle of racial equality in civil rights. Many had been fighting for that principle for decades, as part of the abolitionist movement and third-party antislavery movements. Others had come to the idea later but recognized its merits and necessity. Developments in the former Confederacy over the next several months only clarified the need. In the summer and fall of 1865, white southerners resorted to violence and intimidation to keep freedpeople under their control, and, in reconstituted state governments, they began to pass explicitly discriminatory laws, just as Douglass had predicted. When Congress reconvened in early December 1865, Republicans were ready to take action. In the first few months of 1866, they developed two measures that dramatically changed American life in that moment and for the future. The Civil Rights Act and the Fourteenth Amendment were designed to prohibit the states from discriminating on the basis of race. They were meant to ameliorate conditions in the former Confederacy, but they also served to fulfill the civil rights movement's longstanding vision—that laws drawing racial distinctions in fundamental rights had no place in American life.

When congressional Republicans turned their attention toward policymaking for the states, however, they confronted directly the nation's federal structure and Americans' longstanding deference to state power. As they sought to forge a policy that would grant Congress unprecedented power to protect individual rights in the states, they had to tread carefully, lest they lose members of their coalition and—come the fall of 1866—face defeat in midterm elections. They argued among themselves and with their Democratic colleagues over how far Congress could go in constraining the police powers of the states, whether the right to vote was a "civil right," and whether Congress had authority to enforce the Constitution's privileges and immunities clause. Even in a moment of extraordinary, almost unimaginable change, everyone carried forward political ideas and vocabularies forged in previous engagements. For Republicans, this meant invoking the promises of the Declaration of Independence and the immorality of racist laws. For Democrats, it was recourse to the argument, long used in the service of white supremacy, that states were entitled to identify, regulate, and even exclude populations they considered undesirable. The measures that emerged from that cauldron of ideology and Realpolitik marked a radical departure from the past.

THE ASCENT OF Andrew Johnson to the presidency was a defining part of the Republicans' struggle to nationalize civil rights. Congress was out of session in mid-April 1865, when President Lincoln was murdered by Confederate sympathizer John Wilkes Booth. During the previous winter, with Lincoln's support, Congress had passed the Thirteenth Amendment, which outlawed slavery and involuntary servitude and affirmatively granted Congress power to enforce the ban. When Johnson became president, the amendment was in the process of ratification by the states. The amendment itself affirmed the political antislavery movement's longstanding view that, under the original Constitution, Congress had no authority to interfere with slavery in the states. During the war, Lincoln and Congress had drawn on extraconstitutional war powers to attack slavery. The Emancipation Proclamation declared slaves free only in insurrectionary areas, and Congress had authorized emancipation through wartime confiscation acts, articles of war, and a provision to encourage enlistment of Black soldiers. None of those measures, however, purported to function in peacetime or bring a permanent end to slavery. In 1864 and 1865, Lincoln had urged white loyalists in the rebel states to form new governments and abolish slavery by state action. The consensus among Republicans remained: Only a constitutional amendment could give Congress authority to ensure that slavery in the states was permanently eradicated. The Thirteenth Amendment, ratified on December 6, 1865, did that by declaring that slavery "shall not exist" anywhere in the United States, and then, in a separate section, explicitly stipulating that Congress had the power to enforce the decree "by appropriate legislation."[4]

Abolishing slavery through constitutional amendment solved one major problem, but another loomed. On what terms would or could the rebel states rejoin the Union? The political leaders of the southern states, defeated in the war, preferred a speedy transition to new civilian governments. But federal authorities enjoyed a moment of unusual power, since the Confederate states had given up their normal relationship to the federal government in 1860 and 1861 and were now under military occupation. Would authorities use this leverage to demand that state governments protect the rights of freedpeople? Lincoln insisted that the president, not Congress, had the power to set reconstruction policy, and his plan, promulgated on December 8, 1863, granted newly constituted state governments wide latitude. He required southern political leaders to take loyalty oaths in which they affirmed their acceptance of federal emancipation policy. Consistent with the American tradition of state power in such matters, however, he did not insist that the reconstituted states eliminate racially discriminatory laws, nor that they permit Black men to vote. President Johnson's plan, announced at the end of May 1865, was similar. The new president required states to abolish slavery and insisted that new state constitutions be "republican" in form (alluding to the Constitution's Article IV, Section 4, in which the US government guaranteed to every state a "Republican Form of Government"). But Johnson did not demand the repeal of laws that discriminated against free Blacks, and he explicitly affirmed that the authority to decide who could vote and hold office was "a power the people of the several States . . . have rightfully exercised from the origin of the Government."[5]

During the summer and fall of 1865, white southerners tried to launch new civilian governments under Johnson's policy, but violence and chaos prevailed in many places. White vigilante groups, taking advantage of the absence of discernible state authority, exacted punishments and humiliations on white Unionists and African Americans. When Carl Schurz, a former major general in the US Army, traveled through the rebel states that summer, he wrote frequently of encountering freedpeople "with bullet- or buckshot-wounds in their bodies." In Atlanta, he reported, "freedmen were attacked and maltreated by whites without the least provocation, almost every day." From Montgomery, Alabama, Major General Wager Swayne estimated that "murders of blacks by whites are occurring at the rate of about one per day"—and that was only in places where federal agents were on hand to make reports.[6]

Although understaffed for the immense task, the US War Department set out to impose the principle of racial equality on the former Confederacy. In early 1865, Congress created the Bureau of Refugees, Freedmen, and Abandoned Lands (known simply as the Freedmen's Bureau), which was part of the War Department and staffed mainly by soldiers. The bureau's task was to aid in the transition to peacetime and to a system of free labor, in part by adjudicating disputes between freedpeople and whites and among freedpeople themselves. Bureau agents were a variegated bunch. Some were abolitionists with longstanding commitments to racial equality in civil rights. Others were more sympathetic to planters than to freedpeople. That spring, federal agents in several places collaborated with local authorities to create systems requiring African Americans to obtain written passes or certificates in order to travel from place to place or remain in cities and towns. The idea was to keep freedpeople on plantations, where they would work for former owners and not become public charges.[7] Black residents of Richmond quickly and vehemently protested the local pass system. After they published a letter in the *New York Times* and directly lobbied President Johnson, the army commander in charge of the area terminated the pass system, ordering that "people of color will henceforth enjoy the same personal liberty that other citizens and inhabitants enjoy."[8]

The War Department and the Freedmen's Bureau soon made that policy universal. At the urging of the Freedmen's Bureau commissioner, O. O. Howard of Maine, at the end of July 1865, the War Department issued a sweeping order designed to "secure equal justice and the same personal liberty to the freedmen as to other citizens and inhabitants." The order voided all army policies that subjected freedpeople to "restraints or punishments not imposed on other classes." Howard had earlier instructed an army captain, "Equality before the law is what we must aim at." Elsewhere, Howard advised a South Carolina planter that when making rules for the newly freed laborers on his plantation, he should "forget for the time that the laborers are black" and make the regulations "as the farmer, machinist, or manufacturer does in New York for Germans, Irish, Chinese, negroes & others, i.e. equally applicable to all."[9]

The southern white men who met in the constitutional conventions required by Johnson's policy, and who served in the new state legislatures, had scant interest in laws that were "equally applicable to all." In fact, they were moving in the opposite direction. During the summer and fall of 1865, white southerners pushed to organize their state governments and send representatives to Congress. They believed that the sooner they did so, the sooner the president would withdraw the military and they could resume the usual authority enjoyed by states in the federal system. Many high-ranking former Confederates, having received individual pardons from the president, reentered public life and were voted into office. Newly constituted legislatures abolished slavery, as Johnson had urged, but they went out of their way to deny that the Thirteenth Amendment gave Congress any power over civil rights or voting rights in the states. They also adopted racially restrictive laws that expressed their desire for white supremacy in every facet of life.[10] These were the southern "black codes" so notorious in American history.

Mississippi was the first state to launch a new legislature and begin passing laws. Starting in November 1865, the state passed more than thirty separate provisions that established an entirely different legal regime for African Americans than for whites. New statutes acknowledged that freedpeople had certain "civil rights," including the right to marry and testify in court. Yet new laws also called for apprenticing Black children and permitted judges to give preference to former owners. They established a broad, Black-only definition of vagrancy and a set of corresponding harsh punishments, made Black people who quit work subject to arrest and forced return to their employers, and permitted corporal punishment in some cases. They prohibited African Americans from owning guns, making "insulting gestures," and preaching without a license, among many other special misdemeanors. For any issues not covered by the new laws, they declared antebellum criminal statutes pertaining to slaves and free Blacks reenacted and "in full force and effect, against freedmen, free negroes, and mulattoes."[11]

It was not a foregone conclusion that Congress or President Johnson would permit such measures. Mississippi and other former Confederate states had not yet resumed normal standing in the Union. Theories varied as to the status of those states in relation to the federal government, but most northerners agreed that federal officials (perhaps the president, perhaps Congress) were entitled to dictate terms because the Confederacy had been defeated in war. Freedmen's Bureau officials pushed state governments to repeal racist laws and, in particular, to accord African Americans the equal right to testify in court. At times, Johnson himself got involved, as when he informed the Mississippi governor that he would withdraw the army only when the state adopted measures protecting "all freedmen, or freemen in persons and property, without regard to Color." Even as Johnson threatened to continue the military occupation, however, he instructed the army to demobilize rapidly. And as growing numbers of US soldiers were discharged in the second half of 1865, white southerners stepped up their violent attacks on freedpeople and white Unionists, increasingly confident that they would be permitted to define the post-slavery order for themselves.[12]

African Americans in the South knew very well what was happening and called on the federal government to expand peacetime protection of their rights. In a June 5 address "to the people of the United States," Black residents of Norfolk explained that their former oppressors had "returned to their homes, with all their old pride and contempt for the Negro transformed into bitter hate for the new-made freeman." The Thirteenth Amendment, if ratified, would not touch "the laws respecting free people of color" that predated the war and were "presumed to have lost none of their vitality." A statewide Black convention that met in August 1865 in Alexandria, Virginia, urged Congress to continue military occupation "until you have so amended the Federal Constitution that it will prohibit the States from making any distinction between citizens on account of race or color," including in the right to vote. A South Carolina group protested to Congress "against any code of black laws the Legislature of this State may enact."[13]

Northern Black activists, accustomed to lobbying state governments, also directed their attention to the federal government. George T. Downing, a veteran of the struggle for equal public education in Rhode Island, urged African Americans in the fall of 1865 to support a lobbying office in Washington. "So much is involved affecting our and our children's dearest interests, that no ordinary considerations should stand in the way of our having a special representation this winter at Washington," he wrote in the New York–based *Anglo-African* newspaper. Downing and his allies worked through channels established during decades of organizing at the state and local levels and through the National Equal Rights League, established in Syracuse in 1864. They urged local organizations to raise money to send delegates to Washington, where, in Downing's words, they would establish a central lobbying office at a "good address," receive and distribute "facts and documents" that helped their cause, and engage "every member of Congress" with "argument and appeal." In Norfolk, a mass meeting selected four delegates and instructed them "to cooperate and act in harmony and unison with similar Committees and delegations from this and other States."[14] The African American lobby that assembled in Washington that winter was a vanguard for racial equality. Its members would push not only for federal guarantees of civil rights but for Black men's political rights as well.

CONGRESSIONAL REPUBLICANS GREW increasingly frustrated as they observed events in the former Confederacy during the summer and fall of 1865. They were dismayed by President Johnson's generous pardons of former Confederates and reports of unrepentant white southerners and gruesome violence against freedpeople and white Unionists. Many also believed that Congress, not the president, was entitled to decide how and when the rebel states would return to the Union. Republican politicians of that era are often categorized as conservatives, moderates, or radicals, depending on their views on racial equality, with "radicals"—people like Thaddeus Stevens and Charles Sumner—most strongly in favor of immediate enfranchisement for Black men. Yet there are other ways to assess political radicalism. Some of the politicians commonly characterized as "moderates"—including William Pitt Fessenden and Lyman Trumbull—may have been slower to embrace racial equality but could be more assertive than so-called radicals in their use of federal power to pursue Republicans' agenda. Such differences in approach to federal power became especially clear in 1866 and later, as Republicans grappled with the question of how much to disrupt the old constitutional order— whether through their use of war powers or by transforming the Constitution itself.

As the opening of the Thirty-Ninth Congress approached, party leadership took the dramatic step of agreeing that neither house of Congress would admit representatives sent by the state governments established under Johnson's policy. The goal was to stymie the process of restoring the rebel states and, in doing so, give Congress a chance to develop a reconstruction program of its own. Republican leaders also created a Joint Committee on Reconstruction to take testimony and draft policy. The committee, dominated by ideological moderates like William Pitt Fessenden but also including radicals like Thaddeus Stevens, eventually wrote the Fourteenth Amendment.[15]

Most Republicans agreed that it was time to nationalize racial equality in civil rights. For many, this was a matter of longstanding principle. Some had pushed to repeal racist laws in their own states or had demanded attention to the way southern states' discriminatory laws impinged on the liberty of free Black northerners. Many had voiced that principle earlier, in congressional debates about federal land policy or about the admission of Oregon. Most had also supported the racial equality agenda when applying it to places such as the District of Columbia, where Congress had unquestioned jurisdiction. The black codes enacted by new southern state legislatures prodded Congress to act. By the time Congress convened on December 4, 1865, South Carolina had joined Mississippi in adopting new laws that explicitly denied African Americans basic protections. Congressional Republicans were outraged by white southerners' lawlessness and well understood that African Americans' subordinate status in state law heightened their vulnerability. President Johnson himself, addressing Congress on the first day of the session, seemed to sanction the idea that Congress should take steps to ensure freedpeople's protection. Voting was a matter for the states, he said, but it was "equally clear that good faith requires the security of the freedmen in their liberty and their property, their right to labor, and their right to claim the just return of their labor."[16]

Republicans in Congress proceeded to push for legislation that would do precisely that, protecting freedpeople's basic rights and resolving long-standing questions of citizenship. But they had to decide how to do it, and they were mindful of constitutional limitations. A conversation between Henry Wilson of Massachusetts and Lyman Trumbull of Illinois suggested two potential tracks. Wilson, an unstinting advocate of racial equality since his days in the Massachusetts legislature, proposed to draw on war powers to invalidate the rebel states' new black codes. He envisioned a statute that applied only to states that Lincoln had declared "in insurrection and rebellion" and declared "null and void" all laws that drew "distinctions or differences of color, race, or descent" among "inhabitants." Trumbull, chair of the Senate Judiciary Committee, agreed with Wilson's sentiment but argued for a statute that would apply beyond wartime and throughout the nation. Trumbull proposed to postpone further talk of a congressional civil rights measure until the Johnson administration officially certified that the Thirteenth Amendment had been ratified. At that point, he argued, under the power granted to Congress to enforce the abolition of slavery, Congress could enact a more permanent measure.[17] Wilson's views on racial equality had always been more progressive than Trumbull's, but it was Trumbull's measure that would have the larger, more enduring impact.

On December 18, 1865, five days after the Wilson–Trumbull discussion, Secretary of State William Seward issued a formal pronouncement that the Thirteenth Amendment had "become valid . . . as a part of the Constitution of the United States." True to his word, after the holidays Trumbull introduced two separate bills: the Freedmen's Bureau Bill and the Civil Rights Bill. The first would extend the life of the bureau, which had been established in April 1865 as a temporary war measure. Even with the proposed extension, the bureau was still construed as an artifact of wartime, overseen by the War Department and designed mainly to help regularize labor and property relations in the post-conflict South.[18] By contrast, the Civil Rights Bill was a permanent peacetime measure that would apply everywhere and persist beyond the official end of Congress's war powers.

With the Civil Rights Bill, Trumbull was looking to resolve questions that were pressing in the moment but that had also bedeviled civil rights activists in the free states for decades. His initial draft of the bill did not mention citizenship, but just before introducing it in the Senate, he added a provision designed to settle the longstanding question of whether free African Americans were citizens of the United States. The bill stated: "That all persons born in the United States and not subject to any foreign power, excluding Indians not taxed, are hereby declared to be citizens of the United States without distinction of color."[19] The only groups of people excluded from birthright citizenship under this measure were children of foreign diplomats and Native Americans living on tribal land. With this provision in federal law, there could no longer be any doubt about the citizenship status of native-born African Americans.

Having addressed the matter of citizenship, Trumbull's bill barred racial discrimination in a variety of areas of civil life. Here the bill aimed at inhabitants, not citizens. It stated: "There shall be no discrimination in civil rights or immunities among the inhabitants of any State or Territory of the United States on account of race, color, or previous condition of slavery." That prohibition was followed by an affirmation that inhabitants of all races and colors "shall have the same right" to make contracts, give evidence in court, hold real and personal property, benefit from legal proceedings, and be subject to legal penalties. Republicans like Trumbull were well aware that a bar on racial discrimination among "inhabitants" would apply not only to citizens but also to unnaturalized immigrants and perhaps to Native Americans as well. Ohio Congressman John Bingham, an influential member of the Joint Committee on Reconstruction, defended the use of the term *inhabitants* on precisely these terms. Bingham insisted that conscience ought not permit members of Congress to allow "discriminations . . . against the alien and stranger," and he cited a Bible verse that commanded, "Ye shall have the same law for the stranger as for one of your own country."[20]

The impulse to protect all inhabitants—not just citizens—against racial discrimination was consistent with the view long espoused by anti-slavery activists and their allies that race was not an appropriate category for discrimination, particularly not in civil rights such as the rights to enter contracts, own property, sue and be sued, enjoy access to the courts, be protected by the law, and travel freely from place to place. It also reflected the reality that people had regularly exercised such rights without being recognized as citizens. Authorities had not considered free African Americans in slave states or places like Illinois to be citizens of the state, yet they had enjoyed many of the rights at issue in the Civil Rights Bill, including rights to enter contracts, hold property, and sue and be sued. White noncitizens were also, for the most part, entitled to such rights and more. Unlike free Black people in many places, they could testify in court on the same terms as native-born whites and move freely from place to place within the country. Thus, when Republicans sought to bar racial discrimination among inhabitants, whether citizens or not, they made an open-ended and expansive claim that *all* people should be protected against racial discrimination when seeking to exercise civil rights. The "inhabitants" language in Trumbull's original bill did not survive the legislative process, but the broad-based commitment to rights for all, regardless of citizenship status, would find its way into the Fourteenth Amendment.

Trumbull's Civil Rights Bill contained nine clauses concerning enforcement, an indication of the thoroughness with which he and the Senate Judiciary Committee approached the challenges Congress faced in trying to nationalize the principle of racial equality before the law. It was no small thing to devise a system by which matters traditionally left to the states—such as who could testify in court, or which criminal penalties were associated with which crimes—were made issues of federal concern. Rather than demand directly that states repeal racially discriminatory laws—which would heighten the infringement on state sovereignty as conventionally understood—the Civil Rights Bill made it a crime to enforce such laws. State officials who enforced discriminatory laws would be subject to fines or jail time, and individuals who faced discrimination in local or state courts would be permitted to move their cases into federal court. In provisions modeled on the 1850 Fugitive Slave Act, the bill established federal marshals to oversee enforcement and, when needed, bring charges against state officials who violated the law. As one contemporary writer explained, it was "more than poetic justice" that the Civil Rights Bill used "the very means once employed to repress and crush the negro for his defense and elevation."[21]

Contemporaries well understood that the Civil Rights Bill was entirely unprecedented. Congress had never before asserted its power in states this way. How could it do so now? Trumbull offered several answers. He began by arguing that the bill would "carr[y] into effect" the "abstract truths and principles" of the Declaration of Independence and the US Constitution. Those principles were of little use if people did not have "some means of availing themselves of their benefits." Turning to a closer reading of the Constitution itself, Trumbull made two central points. First, he insisted that the Civil Rights Bill was simply a measure to enforce the Constitution's privileges and immunities clause. Referencing Samuel Hoar's

1844 expulsion from Charleston, he argued that Congress had always had authority to require states to respect the rights of citizens of other states. Prevailing legal opinion, he argued, was that "a person who is a citizen in one State and goes to another" was "entitled to the great fundamental rights of life, liberty, and the pursuit of happiness, and the right to travel, to go where he pleases." All state citizens already had such rights, he said. The problem was that many states refused to recognize them. By declaring all persons born in the United States to be citizens of the United States and barring racial discrimination against everyone, Trumbull argued, Congress was merely exercising power that it had had all along.[22]

Not all Republicans agreed with that line of argument. Before the war, many critics of the Fugitive Slave Act had believed the law was unjust but not unconstitutional. Others, including Salmon Chase, had insisted that the law was unconstitutional because Congress had no authority to pass legislation enforcing the Constitution's fugitive slave clause. The clauses in Article IV, Section 2, Chase frequently claimed, did not expressly delegate enforcement power to Congress, and therefore this was not an area where Congress could legislate. If Congress could not pass a fugitive slave law, the argument went, then it also could not pass a law enforcing the privileges and immunities clause. Some Republicans, most notably John Bingham, found that argument persuasive. Although Bingham wanted to see the federal government protect people's civil rights, he insisted that the Constitution gave Congress no authority to pass a law enforcing the privileges and immunities clause.[23]

Trumbull had an answer for people like that. The Civil Rights Bill, he also claimed, was authorized by the Thirteenth Amendment. The abolition of slavery would be meaningless if states were still permitted to "depriv[e] persons of African descent of privileges which are essential to freemen." Non-slaveholding states had adopted antiblack laws "out of deference to slavery," he said, but he had "no doubt" that, under the Thirteenth Amendment, "we may destroy all these discriminations in civil rights against the black man."[24] That position—that overturning antiblack laws in the states was part of Congress's power under the Thirteenth Amendment—echoed antislavery activists' longstanding arguments that the antiblack laws of the free states were ugly residuals of slavery. To truly eradicate slavery, it was necessary to abolish not only the chattel principle itself but all its nasty offspring.

Knowing that the measure they were proposing, however justified from a moral and constitutional standpoint, represented a radical departure from the past, supporters of the bill regularly tried to downplay its significance. In addition to insisting that such a law would have been constitutional even before the war, they reminded their colleagues that it banned *only* race-based discrimination, leaving all other aspects of state prerogative untouched. Senator Jacob Howard of Michigan, for example, told colleagues that the law did not invade the "legitimate rights of the States." Instead, "it simply gives to persons who are of different races or colors the same civil rights. That is its full extent." In the House, the bill's sponsor, James Wilson of Iowa, said that because the states refused to "shut their eyes" to differences in "race and color," it was necessary for Congress to step in "to protect our citizens, from the highest to the lowest, from the whitest to the blackest, in the enjoyment of the great fundamental rights which belong to all men."[25]

Democrats, however, were not persuaded. They homed in swiftly on the Republicans' central aspiration, which was to limit the powers of the states, and they rejected it. They denied that the Thirteenth Amendment authorized Congress to do anything other than outlaw chattel slavery itself. Congress still had no power, they said, to reach into the states and tell them to change their laws or even to stop enforcing laws associated with the rights of their residents. Senator Reverdy Johnson of Maryland, an eminent constitutional lawyer who had argued the *Dred Scott* case on behalf of Scott's owner, insisted that Congress had no right to interfere with the "police power" of the states—that is, with the states' "power of governing well and of preserving the peace and harmony of society."[26] Like so many who had advocated Black exclusion laws before the Civil War, Senator Peter Van Winkle of West Virginia maintained that "there was no right that could be exercised by any community of society more perfect than that of excluding from citizenship or membership those who were objectionable." He did not see why "we are bound to receive into our community those whose mingling with us might be detrimental to our interests."[27]

In the House of Representatives, Andrew Jackson Rogers of New Jersey, one of the few Democrats on the Joint Committee on Reconstruction, insisted that Congress had never had authority to pass such a law, nor did it now. To illustrate the radicalism of the Republicans' proposal, he asked a series of questions:

> Could Congress, before slavery was abolished in the country, have passed a law making all the free negroes of the States citizens with all the rights of white citizens, in defiance of the laws or police regulations of a State? Could Congress twenty years ago have passed an act providing that the negroes in Virginia, in South Carolina, in Delaware, in New Jersey, and in all the other States of this Union, should have all the privileges and immunities of citizens of the several States? Could they have passed a law prohibiting a State from passing laws, as many did, that the testimony of a negro should not be taken against a white man? Could they have passed a law annulling, for instance, the constitution of Indiana, which prohibits a negro from settling or owning property in that State, or the law of Illinois which prohibited a negro from coming within the limits of that State? Could Congress twenty years ago have passed a law annulling all those laws and setting at defiance the jurisdiction and powers of the States? Could it have passed a law repealing the statute of a State which made it penal for a negro to marry a white person? Could it have repealed all the laws of all the States which made a distinction between colored people and white, which existed in the laws of every State twenty years ago? Could it have legislated for free negroes in the States then? If it had no constitutional power then[,] it has none now.[28]

Everyone would have known that Rogers's catalog of state-level anti-black measures, North and South, was accurate. Whether Congress *could* constitutionally have acted in the ways he suggested was a matter of debate. It was indisputable, though, that it had never done so. Republicans now proposed to overturn practices of federalism that had held basically steady since the founding. That they did so in the name of protecting the rights of African Americans rankled Democrats all the more.

———— ⁕ ————

THE AFRICAN AMERICAN lobbyists dispatched by Black organizations across the nation arrived in Washington in mid-January 1866. With Rhode Island's George Downing taking the lead, they quickly convened and selected an executive committee to direct their efforts. Delegations of Black men then fanned out across official Washington. They met with congressmen and with Salmon Chase, whom Lincoln had appointed chief justice of the Supreme Court in December 1864. They informed the Freedmen's Bureau commissioner, O. O. Howard, of the challenges southern freedpeople faced and argued that the bureau must be renewed. And they petitioned Congress to enfranchise Black men in the District of Columbia.[29] The most visible of the lobbyists' activities was their meeting with President Johnson in the White House on February 7, 1866.

The thirteen-man delegation was there to insist on a national commitment to racial equality in civil and political rights. Black activists had always had a more robust vision of racial equality than most white people, even their political allies, and they could see that allowing white southerners to continue to determine who could vote in their states would never lead to Black men's enfranchisement or to a more genuine version of American democracy. Among the activists who met with Johnson that day was John Jones, who had done so much to demand repeal of the Illinois black laws. Downing of Rhode Island told Johnson that African Americans supported the Civil Rights Bill and believed it was constitutional under the Thirteenth Amendment. As the war itself had demonstrated, he said, "The Government may justly reach the strong arm into States and demand from them . . . their assistance and support." Now it should "reach out a like arm to secure and protect its subjects upon whom it has a claim." Frederick Douglass spoke next, advocating that the president help secure voting rights for Black men.[30]

Johnson took offense at the forthright way these Black men addressed him. He did "not like to be arraigned by some who can get up handsomely rounded periods and deal in rhetoric," he told them. The delegates had sacrificed nothing for the Union cause, he alleged, and now they brought him "theoretical" and "hollow" requests. They must think "practically." Freedpeople were too degraded by slavery to properly exercise the vote, he maintained. In light of "the hate that existed between the two races," Black men's enfranchisement would likely lead to "a war of the races." Johnson claimed that southern African Americans had always harbored special animosity toward poor whites in particular, favoring instead the paternalism of the planter class. There would be no federal push for Black men's enfranchisement, the president said, reiterating his view that this was a matter for the states. If African Americans did not want to stay in the South, he added, "I suggest emigration."[31]

The meeting wrapped up quickly from there. Downing and Douglass said they objected to much of what the president had said, but Johnson indicated that he was not interested in talking further. A reporter for the *Washington Evening Star* had taken stenographic notes, and the tense proceedings were soon reprinted widely. The delegation then denounced the president's positions in a letter published in a Republican newspaper. Likely emboldened by the knowledge that prominent Republicans supported them, and viewing this as lobbying in another form, they condemned the president's views as "entirely unsound and prejudicial." They blamed "the cunning of the slave masters" for hostility between enslaved people and poor white southerners. If Johnson truly cared about the well-being of southern African Americans, they wrote, he would support voting rights for Black men. "Peace between races is not to be secured by degrading one race and exalting another . . . but by maintaining a state of equal justice between all classes." Well practiced at refuting colonizationist arguments, they said it was "impossible to suppose" that African Americans could ever "be removed from this country without a terrible shock to its prosperity and peace."[32]

Johnson's position had shifted since December, when he had seemed to support congressional intervention on behalf of freedpeople's basic rights. On February 19, twelve days after meeting with the Black delegation, the president shocked many in Congress and in the press by vetoing the Freedmen's Bureau Bill, a move that inaugurated an epic unraveling of his relationship with congressional Republicans. Tensions increased when the Joint Committee on Reconstruction declined to recognize the congressional representatives sent by the president's home state of Tennessee. Then the House passed a resolution asserting Congress's paramount power to set the terms of Reconstruction. On George Washington's birthday, February 22, Johnson stood on a balcony of the White House and, in response to serenaders, gave a heated speech in which he denounced the joint committee as "an irresponsible central directory" and called Charles Sumner and Thaddeus Stevens traitors to the country.[33]

———————

As THE FATE of the Civil Rights Bill became caught up in the escalating rift between Congress and the president, one casualty was the promise to protect all "inhabitants" against racial discrimination. The Senate had passed Trumbull's bill on February 2, 1866, just before relations with the president spiraled out of control. When the House took up the bill a few weeks later, it seemed increasingly unlikely that Johnson would sign a federal civil rights measure. Before introducing the measure in the House, James F. Wilson, chair of the House Judiciary Committee, made several modifications that circumscribed the measure's reach. Most significantly, he narrowed its scope by replacing the term *inhabitants* with *citizens*.

Wilson's changes may have represented a response to concerns expressed in the Senate about the *inhabitants* language. Senator Reverdy Johnson had warned that the provision would invalidate state-level laws that limited immigrant aliens' ability to purchase land. Such "alien land laws" drew on longstanding English tradition that linked land with allegiance and limited aliens' right to own it. Many states, seeking to attract immigrants, had repealed their alien land laws or allowed them to go unenforced. Illinois already allowed noncitizens to own land, and Trumbull told Senator Johnson he was entirely comfortable with a federal prohibition on alien land laws. Other senators complained that banning racial discrimination among "inhabitants" would invalidate laws that targeted Chinese immigrants. Edgar Cowan, a conservative Republican from Pennsylvania, said that if he were from California, he would likely not support securing basic rights to "all men of every color." A West Virginia Republican opposed citizenship for "the negro race" and "other inferior races that are now settling on our Pacific coast."[34] Reservations such as those, among Democrats and conservative Republicans, combined with President Johnson's recent tirades, may have prompted Wilson to change *inhabitants* to *citizens*—thus ensuring that the bill excluded noncitizens from its protection.

Representative Wilson made one other significant change that narrowed the Senate version of the bill. He added the phrase *as is enjoyed by white citizens*. This mattered because the Senate version of the bill had declared simply that inhabitants of "every race and color" were entitled to "the same right" to enter a contract, go to court, own property, and so forth. The Senate's language could readily be understood to mean that all persons, of every kind, had the exact same civil rights. But that was not what most Republicans wanted to convey. They wanted to invalidate race-based laws but not, for example, laws that drew distinctions between women and men. Wilson's addition of the words *as is enjoyed by white citizens* clarified that the bill barred discrimination based on "race and color" but not other forms of discrimination. As Republican Samuel Shellabarger of Ohio explained during the debate, "Your State may deprive women of the right to sue or contract or testify, and children from doing the same. But if you do so, or do not do so as to one race, you shall treat the other likewise. . . . [I]f you do discriminate, it must not be 'on account of race, color, or former condition of slavery.' That is all."[35]

Wilson's preemptive changes silenced some potential criticisms of the
bill, but the question of congressional overreach still loomed. John Bingham believed it was time to nationalize protection of civil rights, but he
became the bill's most consequential opponent in the House when he
insisted that Congress did not have the constitutional authority to pass a
civil rights law. It was the "want of the Republic," he lamented, "that there
was not an express grant of power in the Constitution" to enable Congress
to enforce the rights of "citizens" promised in the privileges and immunities clause and the rights of "persons" promised in the Fifth Amendment,
adopted in 1791, which declared that no person could be "deprived of life,
liberty, or property, without due process of law." In a widely publicized
speech, Bingham emphasized that the framers of the Constitution had
left the states in charge of defining and enforcing individual rights. The
states were not fulfilling their obligation, he said, but the Constitution
would have to be altered before Congress could take action in the matter. In fact, the Joint Committee on Reconstruction, of which Bingham
was a member, was already considering such a constitutional amendment.
Meanwhile, in the House, Bingham joined Democrats and a handful of
Republicans in opposing the Civil Rights Bill. They were unable to outvote the Republican majority, which passed the bill on March 13, 1866.
The Senate soon adopted the House version, and the Civil Rights Bill
went to President Johnson for his signature.[36]

Republican efforts to moderate the Civil Rights Act evidently mattered little to President Johnson, who issued a stinging veto on March 27.
Sounding much like Stephen Douglas in the 1850s, and echoing Democrats and conservative Republicans in Congress, Johnson spoke for the
many Americans who believed that states were entitled to discriminate
based on race, and he rejected Republican efforts to nationalize the principle of racial equality in civil rights. The president also denounced the
act's recognition of African American citizenship, arguing that people who
had just emerged from slavery ought to go through a probationary period
before becoming citizens. He condemned Congress's incursion into what

he believed was the rightful domain of the states and their police powers. "Every subject embraced in the enumeration of rights contained in
this bill has been considered as exclusively belonging to the States," he
argued. "They all relate to the internal police and economy of the respective States" and were "matters which in each State concern the domestic
condition of its people." If Congress could "repeal all State laws discriminating between whites and blacks in the subjects covered by this bill,"
the president warned, then it could do similarly when it came to suffrage,
landholding, and other matters. The law would "sap and destroy our fed-
erative system of limited powers and break down the barriers which preserve the rights of the States," he predicted. "It is another step, or rather
stride, toward centralization."[37]

Days after his veto, Johnson intensified his break with the congressional Republicans by declaring that the rebellion was over everywhere
except Texas, a formal repudiation of Congress's continuing use of war
powers in measures such as the Freedmen's Bureau Bill. Many Republicans, including Lyman Trumbull himself, had expected the president to
approve the Civil Rights Act. Supporting the measure might have helped
Johnson isolate those, including Sumner and Stevens, who had made no
pretext of cooperating with him and demanded maximal congressional
control over the rebel states. But Johnson had other ideas. Looking ahead
to the midterm elections of 1866, the president envisioned building a new
coalition of Democrats and conservative Republicans, and he believed he
did not need the majority of the congressional Republicans to do this. Yet
Johnson's vetoes only served to drive the Republicans into even tighter
coalition. Northern Republican newspapers indicated that the public was
behind Congress and the Civil Rights Act. After a lengthy debate and a
dramatic defense of the bill by Trumbull, the Senate overrode the president's veto on April 6. The House followed suit three days later and the
bill became law on April 9, 1866, the first anniversary of Robert E. Lee's
surrender at Appomattox.[38]

President Johnson and the Democrats were correct to see the Civil

Rights Act as a radical departure. Congress had never before declared who was a citizen or pledged itself to protect the rights of all citizens regardless of race. It had never stepped in to protect the rights of free Black sailors, nor had it directly challenged or sought to nullify racially discriminatory state laws. In saying that all citizens were entitled to the same civil rights as white citizens, Congress had endorsed the hard-fought principle of racial equality before the law—a principle that the civil rights movement had long advocated but that many others, even in the free states, had long resisted. Just as the Slave Power had been willing to mobilize federal power to support the rights of slaveholding citizens in the free states, so too did the Republicans now use that power to defend the rights of African American citizens throughout the nation.

At the same time, the Civil Rights Act was not a blanket statement of universal equality. Congress had prioritized the rights of free African Americans. In altering the bill's language from *inhabitants* to *citizens*, Congress declined to outlaw discrimination against aliens—particularly the Chinese—or against Native Americans, most of whom the government did not consider citizens. Moreover, by clarifying that it was prohibiting discrimination based on "race and color" alone, Congress indicated that it was not condemning other kinds of inequality, particularly that of sex but also that of economic status. Laws that permitted authorities to force paupers and vagrants into poorhouses, or to remove them involuntarily from one jurisdiction to another, were not affected. These limitations hewed closely to Republicans' longstanding commitments. The antislavery movement had for decades prioritized racial equality in civil rights. Now that Republicans had their chance, that was the kind of equality they were willing to fight for. Most Republicans did in fact want the guarantee of racial equality in civil rights to extend to everyone, regardless of citizenship status. Responding in part to pressure from San Francisco's Chinese community, the revised civil rights statute that Congress passed in 1870 promised racial equality to all *persons* living under US jurisdiction, rather than to all *citizens*, as the 1866 compromise had required.[39]

THE CIVIL RIGHTS ACT became effective on April 9, 1866, the moment it passed Congress over President Johnson's veto. Northern cities hosted parades, speeches, and cannon salutes to honor the occasion. African Americans celebrated in churches and meeting halls. In Chicago's Mount Olivet Baptist Church, John Jones and others saluted the law as "a new *magna charta* to all persons dwelling beneath the folds of the fire-cleansed and blood baptized flag of our country." At a Cleveland event, a Black minister urged every African American to keep a copy of the Civil Rights Act at home and spread the word about its contents. Nor were festivities confined to the formerly free states. In Hampton, Virginia, Black residents celebrated with illuminations and a torchlight parade. In Washington, DC, thousands gathered to honor simultaneously the Civil Rights Act and the fourth anniversary of Congress's DC Emancipation Act. Speaking at the gathering, Senator Lyman Trumbull earned applause by addressing the crowd as his "fellow-citizens" before giving a speech defending the constitutionality of the new law.[40]

In many places, whites seethed at evidence that African Americans understood the Civil Rights Act and would seek its enforcement. In Norfolk, a mass celebration of the new law touched off a riot in which gray-clad ex-Confederates attacked US forces and several people died. A month later in Memphis, whites mobbed a Black neighborhood, burning buildings, attacking homes, and sexually assaulting women. A conservative newspaper blamed white Memphians' act of spectacular violence on African Americans' new-found assertiveness, complaining that the Civil Rights Act was an "exhaust-less theme" in pulpits and courtrooms alike. Lawsuits associated with the act, the paper warned, had "given fresh impetus to the idea that African manhood and perfect equality of races must be everywhere asserted."[41]

The newspaper was correct that African Americans were determined to pursue enforcement of the Civil Rights Act in the courts. By that time, Indiana was the only Old Northwest state where traditional antiblack laws remained on the books. The day after the Civil Rights Act passed Congress, in Lafayette, Indiana, a Black man named Isaac Barnes sued his employer, a hotel owner, for wages owed. The employer's lawyer claimed that Barnes was illegally residing in the state and therefore had no authority to make or enforce contracts there, and was not entitled to his wages. Were the racist settlement provisions in the Indiana Constitution still enforceable? A justice of the peace agreed with Barnes that they were not. The employer appealed to the county court, and there too he was defeated. State governments were entitled to "protect ourselves against vagabonds and paupers," the judge said, but Indiana's antiblack provisions were unacceptable because they "exclude[d] a whole race of men though born and reared in the United States." The judge observed that the Indiana Supreme Court had upheld explicitly racist laws in the past, as had the US Supreme Court in *Dred Scott*. But, he argued, the Thirteenth Amendment had changed everything. Citing other people's doubts about the constitutionality of the Civil Rights Act, he rested his decision on the amendment, which, he said, had swept away the "vile system" of slavery and required that "all the wrongs and oppressions built upon the wretched institution must cease." Barnes, he concluded, was "a citizen of the United States," fully entitled to the fruits of his labor. That fall, the Indiana Supreme Court took on a different case challenging the state's black laws and found them invalid, in the process affirming Congress's power to pass the Civil Rights Act: "There can be no doubt of the power of Congress to pass this act," it declared.[42]

African Americans in southern states faced more deeply entrenched opposition and fiercer conflicts between state and federal authorities. Newspapers called the Civil Rights Act an example of "Jacobin misrule," and a step "toward extinguishing the last remnant of American freedom." African Americans and sympathetic white lawyers pushed back, and in many places judges began admitting testimony from African Americans in cases involving whites. In Jefferson Parish, Louisiana, lawyers for two Black churches contended that in light of the Civil Rights Act, the state could no longer enforce a law barring African Americans from incorporating religious organizations. The parish judge agreed. In some places, however, judges and district attorneys refused to enforce the new federal law. In Alexandria, Virginia, a judge denied a request to allow an African American to testify in court, saying that his was a state court, so the federal law was inapplicable. A Louisiana judge claimed the Civil Rights Act was invalid because the Thirty-Ninth Congress itself was not a legitimate lawmaking body. In a closely watched case in Memphis that involved Robert Church, one of the city's most prominent Black citizens, the state attorney general insisted that an act of Congress could not stop the state from enforcing a law that barred African Americans from owning tippling houses and billiard saloons. The Memphis judge who heard the case disagreed, however, finding that the Civil Rights Act had "effectually repeal[ed]" the discriminatory state law.[43]

The Memphis case was a clear example of the kind of situation the Civil Rights Act was designed to tackle: state officials enforcing discriminatory state laws. It was less clear, however, that the act applied to railroads and theaters. During the congressional debates on the Civil Rights Act, little had been said about the potential impact on such places, commonly known as public accommodations. The act did explicitly bar racial discrimination in contracts, and it insisted that the principle of racial equality must override "any law, statute, ordinance, regulation, or custom."[44] A ticket was a kind of contract, and managers of public accommodations invoked regulations and customs to justify segregation and exclusion. In this sense, a strong argument could be made that the Civil Rights Act outlawed racial discrimination in public accommodations. On the other hand, the law provided punishments for public officials who enforced racist laws but not for private individuals who discriminated based on race. In theaters and on railways, employees often enforced racist regulations or customs, but they were not state officials, nor were they necessarily enforcing state law.

Was race-based segregation and exclusion in public accommodations illegal under the Civil Rights Act? African Americans aimed to find out. In Nashville, a Black man caused a controversy when he bought tickets for reserved seats at a show. In a Detroit case concerning theater tickets, a judge affirmed that a person's color "does not deprive him of the privileges he chooses and is able to pay for." In Baltimore, Black men and women refused to be segregated on trains and in train stations, and Black men tried to patronize a theater and a public house that did not customarily admit African Americans. On receiving a dispatch from Kentucky, the conservative Washington *National Intelligencer* warned of the "rapidly accumulating cases" arising from "prosecutions brought by negroes for denial to them of places with the most favored at theatres, hotels, and other public resorts."[45]

In Baltimore, it became clear that longstanding defenses of race-based regulation might still be permitted to stand. Among the many African Americans who looked to test the law was Aaron A. Bradley. Born enslaved in South Carolina, Bradley had escaped north and trained in Massachusetts as a lawyer. In the spring of 1866, he sued the Baltimore and Ohio Railroad for refusing him access to the first-class car. In a case heard before a local judge, the company insisted that it had the right to make and enforce regulations it believed necessary to govern the road. There was little novelty here. Americans were accustomed to the idea that governments—or, in this case, corporations—were entitled to prioritize good order and public peace over individual rights, and many saw race-based discrimination as an entirely acceptable form of regulation. Did the Civil Rights Act invalidate railroad companies' right to separate customers by race if they deemed it necessary to keep the line running? The Baltimore court did not think so and ruled in favor of the railroad.[46] The truth was that the 1866 Civil Rights Act did not clearly indicate whether public accommodations like railroads were included in its purview. Another federal law, passed nine years later, would attempt to remedy that problem.

———————

As the Civil Rights Act went into effect, congressional Republicans continued their work on what became the Fourteenth Amendment. Throughout the winter and spring of 1866, the Joint Committee on Reconstruction discussed what kinds of constitutional measures would be necessary to set the nation on a new footing. The committee faced a variety of thorny issues, including whether—and for how long—leading former Confederates should be disenfranchised; whether to require states to remove race-based restrictions on the right to vote; and the status of the Confederate war debt. Protections for civil rights remained a priority. Just as Republicans across the ideological spectrum had supported the Civil Rights Act, so too did they support a constitutional amendment that would make federal protection for basic civil rights more secure. Many Republicans understood the need for an amendment not only because of the southern states' black codes or because of uncertainty about the constitutionality of the Civil Rights Act, but also because for decades they had been fighting against racially discriminatory laws in the states and trying, mostly unsuccessfully, to get Congress or the federal courts to support their efforts. In the spring of 1866, Republicans had to reconcile disagreements about what precisely the Constitution needed and to write an amendment that could pass Congress and be ratified by the states, while not creating an uproar that would lead to the party's defeat in the fall elections.

One of the Fourteenth Amendment's most important and most lasting innovations was what lawyers and constitutional scholars call its "state action" language. In its final form, the amendment placed direct restrictions on the states, beginning with the instruction, "No state shall." It barred *states* from abridging the privileges or immunities of citizens and from depriving persons of equal protection and due process of law. The amendment's emphasis on limiting states emerged in the second major draft produced by the Joint Committee on Reconstruction. The committee's initial draft, which committee member John Bingham introduced in the House, endowed Congress with extraordinary new authority but said little about the states. It declared simply:

Congress shall have power to make all laws which shall be necessary and proper to secure to the citizens of each state all privileges and immunities

of citizens in the several States, and to all persons in the several States equal
protection in the rights of life, liberty, and property.[47]

Leading with "Congress shall have power," the proposal sought to remedy
what Bingham saw as the Constitution's central problem—that it did not
directly authorize Congress to enforce the privileges and immunities clause
or the rights enumerated in the Fifth Amendment. His draft declared that
Congress had power in both areas. It referred to both *citizens* and *persons*,
because the privileges and immunities clause alluded to citizens and the
Fifth Amendment promised rights to persons, as did the other amendments that we now know as the Bill of Rights. The proposal did not simply repeat the language of the Fifth Amendment, however. In addition, it
empowered Congress to secure to persons "equal protection" in the three
basic rights recognized in the amendment: life, liberty, and property.

Bingham's colleagues in the House were not enthusiastic about his
proposal. Among those who proclaimed their support for this wholesale
change in the federalist order was Republican Hiram Price of Iowa, who
asserted that Congress was "in the course of reconstruction, laying anew,
as it were, the foundations of this Government." But Democrats and a few
Republicans were wary. Robert Safford Hale, a conservative New York
Republican, predicted that the measure would allow Congress to void
almost any state law it wanted and was therefore "an utter departure from
every principle ever dreamed of by the men who framed our Constitution."
He raised the question of women's equality as an example: Wouldn't promising to all persons "equal protection in the rights of life, liberty, and property" override state laws that required married women to turn over their
property to their husbands? Bingham was vague in response, saying that
once a person owned property according to the laws of the state, then she
was "equally protected in the enjoyment of it." Bingham's colleagues could
see that the proposal was unlikely to get enough votes to pass, so Ros-
coe Conkling, who, like Bingham, was a Republican member of the Joint
Committee on Reconstruction, suggested postponing further discussion.[48]

As the debate wound down, Giles Hotchkiss, another New York Republican, offered a substantive criticism of Bingham's formulation. The language left too much to the "caprice of Congress," Hotchkiss argued. "We may pass laws here to-day, and the next Congress may wipe them out. Where is your guarantee then?" Instead, Hotchkiss suggested, "Why not provide that no State shall discriminate against any class of its citizens . . . [?]" An explicit limit on the states would ensure that, unlike in Bingham's initial proposal, the amendment would not become meaningless if "rebels" and "their northern sympathizers" took charge of Congress. Although Hotchkiss did not say it explicitly, his proposal also implied that if Congress refused to act, at least aggrieved parties might have recourse to federal court.[49]

The House ended its debate, but the Joint Committee on Reconstruction continued its deliberations and weeks later released an elaborate, five-part constitutional amendment that addressed several distinct problems associated with ending the war. To the great frustration of future judges and historians, the committee did not preserve the records of its discussions, so it is not known exactly how the committee arrived at this approach or how it chose the language of each clause. The civil rights provision was Section 1, and it was notably different from the one Bingham had introduced earlier in the House. Now, the emphasis was on restricting the states, as Hotchkiss had suggested. The clause read:

> No state shall make or enforce any law which shall abridge the privileges or immunities of citizens of the United States; nor shall any State deprive any person of life, liberty, or property, without due process of law; nor deny to any person within its jurisdiction the equal protection of the laws.

The final section of the omnibus measure, Section 5, explicitly authorized Congress to enforce every part of the amendment, stating: "The Congress shall have power to enforce by appropriate legislation the provisions of this article."[50] Echoing and expanding the Thirteenth Amendment, the

Fourteenth Amendment decisively answered those who had insisted that Congress had no constitutional authority to enforce the Constitution's privileges and immunities clause or to protect individual rights in the states. When ratified, the amendment would grant Congress precisely that power and, in doing so, transform the Constitution itself.

Section 1 of the Fourteenth Amendment took familiar constitutional concepts and put them to entirely new purposes. Bingham said of his original proposal that "every word" except the broad grant of power to Congress was "to-day in the Constitution of our country." Similarly, the second version rested heavily on existing constitutional language and addressed longstanding areas of constitutional conflict. First, invoking the privileges and immunities clause (Article IV, Section 2), it prohibited states from violating the "privileges or immunities" of citizens. Like the original clause, the Fourteenth Amendment did not say precisely *what* the privileges or immunities of US citizenship were, presumably leaving that for the courts to decide. Yet the amendment was doing something novel with this old language. Section 1, with its "no state shall" language, made it clear that states were no longer permitted to deny citizens the privileges and immunities associated with citizenship, and Section 5 provided that Congress could step in to ensure that they did not. Moreover, instead of echoing the original clause's emphasis on state citizenship, the amendment barred abridgment of the "privileges or immunities of *citizens of the United States.*" It emphasized national citizenship in keeping with the Republicans' longstanding vision of federal protection for basic civil rights. The proposal that emerged from the Joint Committee on Reconstruction did not grapple with the residual problem of *state* citizenship. That would come later.[51]

Second, the amendment declared that the states could not deprive any "person" of the three general categories of basic rights handed down from English tradition—life, liberty, and property—without due process of law, nor could they deny to persons "equal protection" of the laws. In promising rights of due process and equal protection to *persons*, the Joint Committee on Reconstruction restored something important that had been lost in the debates about the Civil Rights Act—that is, it reinserted the idea that all people, not just those considered citizens, were entitled to certain basic rights. The Fourteenth Amendment's "due process" language drew on the Fifth Amendment. Most Americans who thought about constitutional law and individual rights had long believed that the individual rights promised in the Fifth Amendment—and in the rest of the Bill of Rights—constrained the federal government but not the states. The Fourteenth Amendment's due process clause was meant to change that. It explicitly barred the states from denying certain fundamental rights, and it used the universal language of personhood that had characterized the original constitutional amendments. As Bingham had pointed out, quoting the Fifth Amendment during the House debate on the Civil Rights Act: "Your Constitution says 'no person,' not 'no citizens,' 'shall be deprived of life, liberty, or property,' without due process of law."[52] Section 5, the enforcement clause, promised that if states violated the promises now made to persons, Congress was empowered to intervene.

The amendment's "equal protection" clause was different from the rest because it added to the Constitution a new ideal, one kept alive through decades of struggle against slavery and racism. *Equality* had been a watchword of the political antislavery movement, its authority embedded in the Declaration of Independence. To promise equal protection was to guard against the injustices that had for so long characterized free and enslaved African Americans' experiences with law and policy—to prohibit racist legislation that left Black people unprotected, unable to sue in court or to move freely from place to place. Even among Republicans, however, the language of equality had its critics. In February 1864, Charles Sumner had proposed a Thirteenth Amendment that declared: "All persons are equal before the law, so that no person can hold another as a slave." Jacob Howard of Michigan had worried that such phrasing would make "a woman . . . equal to a man," "a woman . . . as free as a man." It would mean that "a wife would be equal to her husband and as free as her husband before the law." The Senate had shelved Sumner's proposal in favor of a Thirteenth

Amendment that said nothing specific about individual rights. In 1866, some had cautioned that the Civil Rights Act would incidentally outlaw sex-based discrimination. Even after the House added language clarifying that the act concerned only racial discrimination, some still worried that the act would invalidate laws barring interracial marriage.[53]

The word *equal* returned in the Fourteenth Amendment, and this time without qualification. The immediate context was Congress's desire to protect African Americans in their basic rights and to render racist laws unconstitutional. Yet the amendment's language was universal. Women activists had been demanding repeal or reform of sex-based laws at the state level since the 1840s, and contemporaries were well aware that the amendment's sweeping language of equality might open the door to new claims by women. Most congressmen certainly did not favor women's equality with men, but they adopted the language anyway. The equal protection clause was an apt tribute to the movement for racial equality and its talisman, the Declaration of Independence. After decades of elevating the Declaration—and its vaunted but vague promises of equality—participants could feel satisfied that the principle finally would enter the US Constitution.

The principle of birthright citizenship—that all persons born in the United States were citizens of the United States—arrived in the Fourteenth Amendment only at the end of deliberations. The House passed the amendment without that language, not because Republicans did not support the idea but because so many took it for granted. African Americans and their allies had long argued that in both Roman and English legal traditions, states had two basic classes of free inhabitants: citizens and aliens. If you were not one, then you were the other.[54] To be sure, many white Americans had long resisted that argument, insisting that free people of African descent were something less than US citizens, even if some states considered them citizens of the state. Even in 1866, many Democrats continued to claim that Chief Justice Taney's *Dred Scott* decision was a binding precedent. Most Republicans, however, had never wavered from the view that *Dred Scott* was wrongly decided and that the weight of historical evidence and political theory was in favor of free African Americans' status as citizens.

Some Senate Republicans urged Congress to affirm the principle of birthright citizenship in the new amendment, hoping that doing so would clarify the constitutional meaning of the word *citizen*. Senator Benjamin Wade of Ohio argued that the new amendment should put the question of who was a citizen "beyond all doubt and all cavil." A week later, Jacob Howard of Michigan proposed this phrase: "All persons born or naturalized in the United States, and subject to the jurisdiction thereof, are citizens of the United States and of the state wherein they reside." Howard's provision—adopted first by the Senate and later by the House—invalidated any claim that free African Americans were not American citizens or citizens of the state in which they happened to live.[55] They were citizens because they were born in the United States and subject to its jurisdiction. The provision also affirmed that there was no distinction between native-born and naturalized citizens; all were citizens alike. It recognized the existence of state citizenship, as the original Constitution had. But it elevated national citizenship by associating it with durable traits of birthright and naturalization, while linking state citizenship with mere residency, which could easily be changed.

The amendment's affirmation that free African Americans were citizens of the United States overruled Taney's 1857 *Dred Scott* decision, but it did much more than that. It ratified African Americans' decades of insistence that they were American citizens, fully entitled to the basic rights and responsible for the obligations associated with that status. And it served as a rebuke to decades of colonizationist agitation, which had insisted that people of African descent had no claim on citizenship and no right to assert that they were as entitled to remain in their homes and communities as any other native-born person. Yet constitutional recognition of birthright citizenship also created new categories of marginalization. By excluding from citizenship persons who were not "subject to the jurisdiction" of the United States, the framers intentionally excluded children of foreign diplomats living in the United States and Native Americans who lived in tribal nations with sovereignties of their own. At the same time, the citizenship provision intersected with federal naturalization laws that, dating back to the 1790s, permitted only "white" immigrants to naturalize. In 1870, at Charles Sumner's urging, Congress extended the right of naturalization to "aliens of African nativity and to persons of African descent." In doing so, however, Congress rejected a broader bill that would have simply opened naturalization to all people regardless of race. It provided Asians no parallel way to circumvent the white-only naturalization policy, and Chinese immigrants remained ineligible for naturalization until 1943.[56]

In this and many other ways, the Fourteenth Amendment's provisions and their impact were shaped by the historical moment in which it passed and the battles that had proceeded it. In the twentieth and twenty-first centuries, the amendment's "state action" language came in for particular criticism. Beginning in the 1870s, the US Supreme Court leaned heavily on the amendment's prohibition on the states to render the amendment largely useless for protecting African Americans. The court, for instance, claimed to have no jurisdiction in cases in which white southerners led campaigns of terror against their Black neighbors, committing violent crimes that local authorities refused to prosecute. Crimes committed by private parties, the court said, ostensibly did not involve the *state* denying people due process or equal protection. In 1883, the court also ruled that Congress had exceeded its authority in passing a law that banned racial discrimination in public accommodations such as railroads and restaurants. These were not state actors, the court said, and the amendment only provided "modes of redress against the operation of State laws, and the action of State officers executive or judicial, when these are subversive of the fundamental rights specified in the amendment."[57]

The Fourteenth Amendment's ban on racially discriminatory state action looks different, however, if we think our way forward from the antebellum period, rather than backward from later moments. For decades before the Civil War, antislavery activists fought racist laws in their home states, with varying degrees of success. They attacked racist laws in the southern states, too—attempting, for instance, to bring the Constitution to bear in defense of free Black sailors' rights but finding it impossible to do so. As Frederick Douglass pointed out in 1865, fighting the black laws of the ex-Confederacy was nothing new in principle. And yet the move to establish a federal ban on such laws, rather than continuing to fight them on a state-by-state basis, was fraught with difficulty.

In light of this, it is perhaps less surprising that Republicans were willing to accept what they arrived at in 1866. Senator Jacob Howard, introducing the final version of the amendment in the Senate, said, "The great object of this amendment is . . . to restrain the power of the States and compel them at all times to respect these great fundamental guarantees."[58] Delivering the amendment to the House, Thaddeus Stevens explained that the original Constitution limited only the action of Congress and not the states. The amendment "supplies that defect, and allows Congress to correct the unjust legislation of the States, so far that the law which operates upon one man shall operate *equally* upon all." That was no small thing.

> Whatever law punishes a white man for a crime shall punish the black man precisely in the same way and to the same degree. Whatever law protects the white man shall afford "equal" protection to the black man. Whatever means of redress is afforded to one shall be afforded to all. Whatever law allows the white man to testify in court shall allow the man of color to do the same. These are great advantages over their present codes.[59]

Stevens was right. In 1866, a constitutional ban on racially discriminatory state laws was both extraordinarily novel and critically important.

FROM THE BEGINNING, debates about the 1866 Civil Rights Act and the Fourteenth Amendment were entangled with demands for a federal provision for Black men's enfranchisement. The question of voting rights had always had a complex relationship to what contemporaries commonly called "civil rights." For decades before the war, free-state residents had found ways of divorcing citizenship and civil rights from the rights to vote and hold office. That separation—of "civil rights" from "political rights"—had allowed northerners to claim that almost all free people were citizens entitled to basic rights, but it had also helped justify the idea that the right to vote was a privilege for white men only. African American activists had railed against this logic, arguing that racial distinctions in the right to vote were just as abhorrent as racial distinctions in civil rights. But they and their allies had made limited headway in the free states before the Civil War.

As the Black delegation's meeting with President Andrew Johnson suggested, African American activists in 1865 and 1866 continued the campaign for political rights at the federal level. Many of the white Republicans most associated with the antislavery movement joined them. They insisted that Black men's enfranchisement was right in principle, but they also pointed out that if Congress did nothing to ensure that Black men could vote, the rebel states would eventually return to the Union stronger than ever. While slavery persisted, enslaved people had counted as three-fifths of a person for purposes of deciding how many congressmen and electoral votes each state was entitled to. Now that all were free, each African American would count fully in the population. If southern state governments did not permit Black men to vote, southern whites—many of them of dubious loyalty and dubious intentions—would exercise more proportional power than before. This prospect provided congressional Republicans a strong incentive for finding a way to enfranchise Black men, at least in the former Confederacy.

But those who wanted immediate and unequivocal Black men's enfranchisement in 1866 would have to wait. James Grimes, a member of the Joint Committee on Reconstruction, wrote to his wife that the Fourteenth Amendment was "not exactly what any of us wanted; but we were each compelled to surrender some of our individual preferences in order to secure anything, and by doing so became unexpectedly harmonious." The amendment's second section did, in a convoluted way, address the issue. It declared that representatives would now be apportioned based on the "whole number of persons in each State," but that if a state barred male citizens over age twenty-one from voting (for any reason other than having participated in the rebellion or having been convicted of a crime), the state's representation in Congress would be proportionately reduced. This was the best Republicans believed they could do and still pass the measure in Congress, get it ratified by the states, and survive the midterm elections.[60]

Still, many were frustrated by the amendment's failure to address voting more squarely. Charles Sumner was so disgusted that he voted against it. The measure also infuriated women suffragists, who lamented that by including the word *male*, the amendment associated the franchise with manhood and diminished women's claims to political equality. Many contemporaries believed, correctly as it turned out, that Congress was not finished with the matter of Black men's enfranchisement. Among them was William Howard Day. In 1849, Day had stood in the Ohio statehouse and demanded repeal of the state's black laws. He had continued pressing for racial equality in Ohio until fleeing the United States for Canada in 1855. He spent several years lecturing and fundraising in Great Britain before returning to the United States at the end of 1863, prepared to take up the fight in a nation wholly changed by war. Day was among the speakers who addressed a great crowd on Franklin Square in Washington just after the Civil Rights Act passed. "Justice to the colored race had not been realized all at once, but had come step by step," he told the assembly. The struggle, he said, "tends to a yet higher point, and that is, suffrage for all."[61]

EPILOGUE

MARY ANN SHADD fully understood the importance of working to repeal racist laws. In the 1850s, Shadd was editor and publisher of the *Provincial Freeman* newspaper, based in Chatham, Ontario. The descendant of free African Americans from the Chesapeake region, she lectured widely, advocating continuing Black emigration to Canada and greater equality for women.[1] Visiting Chicago in 1856, Shadd offered trenchant observations on African Americans' situation in a city where whites were generally accommodating but racist laws remained on the books. She praised white Chicagoans for refusing to cooperate with the Fugitive Slave Act and paying little mind to the state's black laws. "Fully conscious of their great power over the colored people," she wrote, white residents were "too proud spirited to strike their prostrate victim." Still, Shadd lamented the conditions produced by the Illinois black laws. In cities like New York and Cincinnati, she said, Blacks and whites were "more nearly equal by the law," and that status made possible the "proper antagonism . . . which is of vital importance to final success in any undertaking." Shadd understood that racial equality in law did not necessarily mean racial equality in practice. But she also knew that African Americans were in a far better position to fight back in places that acknowledged their basic civil rights than in those that did not.[2]

Her allies in the first civil rights movement would have agreed. The many and diverse people who lent their voices to the movement converged not around the most profound of antiracist arguments, but rather around the straightforward demand that the nation accept the principle of racial equality, first in civil rights and then in political rights. They had inherited a country in which equality was enshrined in the soaring words of the Declaration of Independence, but almost nowhere else; a country in which few believed the abolition of slavery would lead inexorably to multiracial democracy; and a country where many believed that repealing racist laws would lead directly to race war. Many white people thought the problem was so intractable that the best course for free African Americans was to leave the country altogether.

In the course of eight decades, from the nation's founding to the 1860s, a growing number of people had the courage to challenge those ideas and put forth a different vision. African Americans consistently took the lead, rejecting racist platitudes and insisting that they were just as entitled as white people to live in any American community, enjoy the same civil rights, and hold political power according to their numbers and influence. They viewed white people's racism as nonsense and believed that all manifestations of it—in both public and private life—must be eliminated. They had little patience for separating civil from political rights, or for saying that men could be citizens but not voters. They consistently pushed for more equality, and faster, than most white people—including their political allies—were willing to accept. Although they recognized that racial prejudice was deeply entrenched, like Mary Ann Shadd they readily saw the importance of trying to change laws, regardless of how fast white people managed to change what lay in their hearts.

Through petitioning and political organizing, Black and white northerners worked together to demand racial equality in civil rights. Because of the nation's federal structure and slaveholder dominance in the halls of federal power, they worked mainly at the state level. But they sometimes found purchase in national politics and turned to the few places in the

US Constitution—particularly the privileges and immunities clause—that opened the door to federal protection of free Black people's rights. The process of coalition-building required compromise, and the Republican Party, which entered national politics in 1856, encompassed people of many different political persuasions. By the time Lincoln was elected in 1860, however, the party stood unequivocally behind the principle of racial equality in civil rights and moved quickly, during the Civil War, to translate that principle into public policy. It was only the vicissitudes of war that afforded the Republicans the majority they needed and the rationale—an unprecedented constitutional crisis—to nationalize the principles of racial equality that many of them had long demanded. Despite the Fourteenth Amendment and several federal civil rights statutes, however, the world for which those Republicans and their supporters fought did not materialize. To the contrary, Americans of diverse backgrounds resisted strenuously and with great effectiveness.

FREDERICK DOUGLASS WROTE in December 1866 that "the right of each State to control its own local affairs" was an idea "more deeply rooted in the minds of men of all sections of the country than perhaps any other political idea."[3] With the Civil Rights Act and the Fourteenth Amendment, the US government had taken unprecedented steps to protect individual rights by restraining the states. It is hardly surprising, then, that so many Americans worked so hard to blunt the new measures' impact. White southerners fought back particularly vigorously, challenging the limits of the new federal policies in every conceivable way—peaceful and violent, legal and illegal. The Supreme Court, too, did its part.

Republicans of the Thirty-Ninth Congress had tried to resolve ambiguities about American citizenship by declaring that everyone born under US jurisdiction was a citizen of the United States and that states could not deny to citizens the "privileges or immunities" of US citizenship. The Constitution's original privileges and immunities clause had offered glimmers of opportunity for free African Americans. With the Fourteenth Amendment, Republicans sought to build on that promise by clarifying that African Americans were citizens, elevating federal citizenship over state citizenship, and promising that the US government would protect all citizens in the basic civil rights long associated with that status.

In its 1873 *Slaughter-House* decision, however, the Supreme Court undermined these goals by insisting that the most important privileges and immunities of citizenship remained under state, not federal, authority. The case was initiated by white butchers in New Orleans who claimed that when the state granted a monopoly to a slaughterhouse company, it violated their rights, as citizens of the United States, to pursue their trade. In a 5–4 decision written by Justice Samuel Miller, the court sided against the butchers. Miller insisted that the Thirteenth and Fourteenth Amendments had been intended not to help white men but to secure "the freedom of the slave race" and "the protection of the newly made freeman and citizen." Although the butchers had posed a question that the amendments were not exactly designed to address, Miller soldiered on. He resurrected the long history of state citizenship under the original privileges and immunities clause, insisting that states still had virtually unalloyed power to determine the rights of their own residents and that the Fourteenth Amendment had extended federal protection only to privileges or immunities that "owe their existence to the Federal government." Those were few indeed: the right to engage with the US government itself, as well as "free access" to seaports, land offices, and "courts of justice in the several States." According to Miller, to interpret the Fourteenth Amendment any other way would be to "radically" change "the whole theory of the relations of the State and Federal governments to each other and of both these governments to the people."[4] Miller and the court were unwilling to sanction a transformation of that magnitude.

Dissenting justices articulated the Republicans' earlier vision—that the Fourteenth Amendment's privileges or immunities clause was designed to protect individuals against injustices perpetrated by the states and their agents. Noah Swayne insisted that the Reconstruction amendments were indeed "novel and large," and intended as a "new Magna Charta" for the nation. The court majority, he complained, had turned "what was meant for bread into a stone." Justice Stephen Field affirmed that the new amendments did "protect the citizens of the United States against the deprivation of their common rights by State legislation." And Justice Joseph Bradley complained that the majority's claim that fundamental "rights, privileges, and immunities . . . attach only to State citizenship" was "a very narrow and insufficient estimate of constitutional history and the rights of man."[5] Yet these views lost out to the majority's conviction that most civil rights were associated with state citizenship and remained under state jurisdiction. The Fourteenth Amendment's privileges or immunities clause— drafted just seven years earlier to affirm Congress's power to protect the rights of citizens in the states—had been gutted.

The US Supreme Court also became persuaded that state-mandated racial separation did not violate the Fourteenth Amendment's promise of equal protection of the law. The most egalitarian abolitionists had always rejected the idea of "separate but equal." In Massachusetts, abolitionists had drawn on the state constitution's promise of equality to demand repeal of an anti-miscegenation statute and to challenge segregation in Boston's public schools. As Charles Sumner had argued in the 1849 school desegregation case, differences in race *can furnish no ground for any discrimination before the law.* In the early years after the Civil War, some state legislatures, adopting that principle, repealed their bans on interracial marriage, and several state courts struck down such bans as violations of state-level civil rights laws or of the 1866 Civil Rights Act or the Fourteenth Amendment.[6]

But courts soon reversed that pattern, elevating state police powers in the process. The trend began with the Indiana Supreme Court, which upheld a state statute barring interracial marriage in the 1871 case of *State v. Gibson.* The court insisted that new federal measures had no bearing on a state's power to regulate contracts such as marriage. Marriage was "essential to the peace, happiness, and well-being of society," the court said, and the state's authority to regulate it continued unimpeded. State and federal courts increasingly followed Indiana's lead, holding that the police powers of the states included the authority to regulate marriage as they saw fit. The US Supreme Court, in the 1883 case of *Pace v. Alabama*, upheld a state law that penalized sex ("fornication") between men and women of different races more heavily than sex between same-race couples. The law did not violate the Fourteenth Amendment's equal protection clause, the court said, because the "punishment of each offending person, whether white or black, is the same."[7]

That case was a precursor to *Plessy v. Ferguson* (1896), a railroad case in which the court adroitly combined traditions of state police powers with the idea that policies that required racial separation did not necessarily violate the amendment's promise of equal protection. Despite the efforts of lawyers Robert Morris and Charles Sumner, in 1849 the Massachusetts Supreme Court had made an important contribution to the doctrine of separate but equal in the case of *Roberts v. City of Boston*, when it held that the Boston school board was entitled to offer racially segregated schools if it believed the policy was reasonable and served "the good" of all. Drawing heavily on that case, in *Plessy v. Ferguson*, the US Supreme Court noted that laws requiring racial separation were "generally, if not universally" understood as appropriate exercise of states' "police power." Any exercise of the police power must be "reasonable," the court acknowledged, and "enacted in good faith for the promotion of the public good, and not for the annoyance or oppression of a particular class." Working from that standard, the court found that a Louisiana law that required racial segregation on railroads was indeed a "reasonable regulation" consistent with "established usages, customs and traditions of the people, and with a view to the promotion of their comfort, and the preservation of the public peace and good order."[8]

Deference to the police powers of the states was an American tradition, and that was precisely the problem. Republicans' Reconstruction measures were designed to protect people when they could not get justice in their home jurisdictions, but those measures and their defenders often found themselves outmatched both in the courts and on the ground. Mobilizing arguments for police powers that dated back to before the nation's founding, as well as raw white supremacy, opponents insisted that real world challenges of social order superseded any promise of meaningful racial equality. They declared that public peace and the public good required racial segregation and subordination, and that dependent poor people were not entitled to the same rights as other free people. They fought fiercely in courtrooms, in statehouses, and in party politics. All too often, they used threats and outright violence to keep advocates of equal rights from voting or speaking out.

THE LONGSTANDING CONNECTION between laws that discriminated based on race and those that targeted the mobile poor provided a powerful avenue for resisting change. The first civil rights movement had focused acutely on the problem of racial discrimination. Its spokespeople often began with the biblical concept that God had made all races of mankind "of one blood" and, therefore, that shared humanity was more important than superficial differences in physical features. They also insisted that it was unjust and immoral to make policies based on race because a person's race did not determine their behavior or their moral worth, and because doing so elided meaningful differences. As the Black activist Charles Lenox Remond complained as he testified against racial discrimination on Massachusetts railroads in 1842: "Color is made to obscure the brightest endowments, to degrade the fairest character, and to check the highest and most praiseworthy aspirations."[9] Antiblack laws construed all Black people as dangerous, threatening, or criminal. While white people benefited from the protection of the laws, Black people were presumed guilty simply by virtue of being Black.

But the movement's critique of racist laws did not automatically extend to a critique of other forms of inequality before the law, and that created some challenges for those seeking racial justice. From the nation's earliest days, many laws that singled people out by race had been connected to those that targeted people based on their economic status. Americans readily accepted policies that cast suspicion on dependent poor people, particularly those who were moving from one jurisdiction to another, and subjected them to deportation, incarceration, and even sale. In places such as Ohio and Illinois, early legislatures had constructed their black laws atop old and accepted poor-law structures, justifying this matrix of regulation as necessary for the "domestic police" of the state. State legislatures had even shown that the poor-law tradition could provide a substitute when laws that explicitly discriminated based on race seemed untenable. The Pennsylvania legislature in 1814 smoothly replaced a law barring migration of "people of color" with one that imposed new penalties for vagrancy. In Ohio in 1849, the assembly that repealed most of the black laws adopted a new statute designed to reduce migration by people who were "likely to become chargeable as paupers in any township . . . or to become vagrants."

A similar fungibility of race and class continued after the Civil War. The idea persisted in many quarters that poor people who were transient or appeared not to be working posed a threat to public peace and good order, and that such people were not entitled to the same basic rights as others. Freedmen's Bureau agents and other northerners in the post–Civil War South insisted on racial equality before the law but felt entirely free to crack down on "vagrancy" and "vagabondage." A northern clergyman in Memphis, for instance, vigorously condemned overtly racist policies but urged officials to restrict the liberty of known vagrants and, in particular, to pay attention to vagrancy and pauperism among whites. Southern state legislatures quickly adapted to Republican priorities by abandoning the flagrant black codes of 1865 in favor of race-neutral statutes that penalized vagrancy and demanded enforcement of labor contracts. "No reference to color was expressed in terms," one Freedmen's Bureau official observed of an Alabama law, "but in practice the distinction is invariable." Strict antivagrancy laws often remained on the books but went unenforced while

Republicans were in charge of southern state governments. Democrats, on regaining control, enforced them with new stringency and adopted even more draconian ones.[10]

Governments in northern states were not much more likely to feel constrained by new federal civil rights policies when making policy toward the poor. Particularly during the global economic crisis that began in 1873, states and localities intensified measures that targeted the transient poor, with little respect for ideals of due process or equal protection of the laws. Alleged vagrants, paupers, and beggars could be picked up and convicted of crimes without a formal hearing, forced to labor, or removed involuntarily from a jurisdiction. Courts occasionally struck down such laws. The Maine Supreme Court in 1876 invalidated a municipal poor law, arguing that even alleged paupers were entitled to due process of law under the Fourteenth Amendment. In the Chicago area in 1877 and 1878, the Cook County Criminal Court declared the state's anti-vagabondage law unenforceable because it denied the right of trial by jury. In the main, however, states and localities continued to deny to the itinerant and unemployed poor the same rights to liberty and settlement as other, more fully vested people enjoyed. In fact, the Supreme Court did not recognize poor people's right to move from state to state until 1941. Amid the upheavals and destitution of the Great Depression, the court finally allowed that even the migrant poor were *persons* before the law, invalidating a California law that, like the laws of many other states, punished the importation of "any indigent person who is not a resident of the State."[11]

----•-•-•----

ASSESSING COMPLICITY and assigning blame in this nation's enduring inability to confront entrenched racism is nothing new. Historians, in their efforts to take full measure of the problem, have drawn significant attention to the bigotry of white northerners. Its depth must not be underestimated.[12] In the post–Civil War years, many northern white communities continued to do everything in their power, with or without the sanction of law, to prevent African Americans from moving in. Where African Americans did reside, whites often demanded separation in housing, schools, and recreational facilities. Yet regional distinctions remained tremendously significant. For decades before the Civil War, the free states had offered a climate in which Black and white people could coalesce in a movement for racial equality that made significant inroads into state and then national politics. Many of the same people lived on after the war, and their continuing efforts—and those of like-minded younger people coming of age in a new era—made it possible for African Americans in many locales to settle peacefully and to gain access to public schools, public accommodations, and political power.

A constitutional limit on states' power to deny Black men the vote followed quickly after the Fourteenth Amendment. In January 1869, Congress passed the Fifteenth Amendment, which prohibited states from depriving citizens the "right" to vote "on account of race, color, or previous condition of servitude." In the states as in Congress, Black men's enfranchisement had become a largely partisan issue, with many state Republican parties endorsing it and Democrats standing strongly opposed. Still, northern white voters had remained reluctant to approve it at the ballot box. The Fifteenth Amendment, ratified at the end of March 1870, took the matter out of their hands. The enfranchisement of African American men allowed northern Black communities to exercise power in new ways, and many Black northerners immersed themselves in partisan politics. Among them was William Howard Day, the Oberlin College graduate who in the spring of 1866 had forecast that Congress would soon turn its attention to the vote. Settling in Harrisburg, Pennsylvania, Day regularly campaigned for Republican candidates and was elected to the city's school board in the 1870s.[13]

Across the North and in the Far West, African Americans successfully pushed state governments to make them "more nearly equal by the law," their effectiveness heightened by Black men's power as Republican voters. In many places, Black organizations rooted in churches and school communities, as well as branches of the Equal Rights League created at the Syracuse convention of 1864, made children's access to schools a priority. In Illinois, for instance, African American pressure and Republican power in the statehouse yielded an 1872 law that barred school districts from excluding Black students. Two years later, another law prohibited school officials from excluding children from any school on account of color. Everywhere, Black parents and community groups pushed state legislatures to provide their children with schools and went to court when they did not. State supreme courts differed as to whether particular schools could bar attendance by Black students, but they routinely upheld laws requiring states to make public education available to all.[14]

At the same time, African Americans continued to fight for guarantees of racial equality in public accommodations such as railroads, steamboats, streetcars, restaurants, and saloons. Beginning with Massachusetts in 1865, several states under Republican control, including some in the former Confederacy, passed measures barring racial discrimination in public accommodations. Still, African American activists and their white allies wanted to see a federal ban. Their strongest ally in Congress was Massachusetts Senator Charles Sumner, who in the early 1870s fought for a federal law that would bar discrimination by railroads, steamboats, public conveyances, hotels, restaurants, licensed theaters, public schools, juries, churches, and cemetery associations. The measure was controversial, including among Republicans. Congress finally passed Sumner's law in 1875, after the senator had died and with the sections barring discrimination in schools, churches, and cemeteries removed. But the Supreme Court struck it down eight years later in *The Civil Rights Cases* decision, ruling that Congress had exceeded its authority by prohibiting racial discrimination in public accommodations. The Thirteenth Amendment certainly did not authorize such a measure, the court claimed, while the Fourteenth permitted Congress to regulate only the behavior of official "state" actors, not ostensibly private entities like theaters and railroad companies.[15]

The court's pinched definition of state action in *The Civil Rights Cases* helped make the Fourteenth Amendment marginal in the long-term fight against racial discrimination in public accommodations. In the mid-twentieth century, activists, lawyers, and politicians found another way forward. They grounded the first major piece of civil rights legislation since Reconstruction, the 1964 Civil Rights Act, in the Constitution's commerce clause, which explicitly empowered Congress to regulate interstate and international commerce. The Fourteenth Amendment could not help them because of the amendment's state action language and the court's narrow interpretations. Yet the possibility that the commerce clause could be a mechanism for protecting individual rights—particularly the right to move freely from one place to another within the nation—would not have surprised those ship captains and Black sailors who lived before the Civil War.

In the wake of the 1883 *Civil Rights Cases* decision, an enduring regional distinction emerged regarding the question of race in public accommodations. In the 1880s and beyond, eighteen states—all of them in the North, Midwest, or Far West—passed laws barring discrimination in public accommodations. For instance, in 1885 the Republican-dominated Illinois legislature passed a measure, introduced by John W. E. Thomas, an African American legislator from Chicago, that guaranteed to all "persons" within the state's jurisdiction the "full and equal enjoyment" of various public accommodations. State supreme courts upheld the new public accommodations laws, and many states strengthened their antidiscrimination provisions in the 1890s. Meanwhile, developments in the states where slavery had been legal in 1861 were starkly different. Faced with the prospect of the federal Civil Rights Act in 1875, Delaware and Tennessee explicitly affirmed the right of public accommodations to discriminate as they saw fit. Then, from the late 1880s through the turn of the century, southern states passed stringent "Jim Crow" laws requiring racial segregation in public schools and in all manner of public accommodations.[16]

There was also a marked regional split on race and voting rights. Beginning in the late 1860s, white southerners had already distinguished themselves for violent voter suppression directed at Black voters and white men who voted Republican. In the 1890s, southern Democrats followed two decades of terror and fraud with legalized disenfranchisement, rewriting their constitutions to reduce the Black vote and cement their party's power. By contrast, Black men continued to vote across the North, and by the early twentieth century, Black women joined them as voters in many places. Party competition in the North and West remained far more robust than in the South, and Black voters influenced local elections—and shaped policy—often by asserting independence from the Republican Party. In the early decades of the twentieth century, massive Black migration from South to North enabled Black voters—bolstered by rich networks of churches, women's clubs, and mutual-aid societies—to elect Black men to office, secure patronage positions, and eventually pursue their interests at the federal level.

————

THE ASPIRATIONS OF antebellum civil rights activists notwithstanding, the federal measures adopted during Reconstruction did not secure a baseline guarantee of racial equality in civil rights. Operating on the principle of "separate but equal," state and local governments continued to insist that race was a legitimate distinction in public policy and to reinforce forms of racial subordination that, as antebellum activists well understood, had originated in race-based slavery. Governments regularly used facially neutral laws—including those associated with vagrancy and other crimes linked to poverty—to perpetuate racial inequality. Meanwhile, white supremacist violence, as well as racial discrimination by private property owners, by employers, and in the administration of justice, went largely unchecked. From the 1890s to the 1950s, Congress chose not to use its powers under the Fourteenth Amendment to mitigate the damage.

And yet the legacies of the first civil rights movement lived on. In 1939, lawyers in the newly created Civil Liberties Unit of the US Justice Department (soon renamed the Civil Rights Section and later the Civil Rights Division) began using Reconstruction-era federal statutes to pursue cases on behalf of exploited and vulnerable Black and white laborers, particularly in the South. In 1947, the President's Committee on Civil Rights, commissioned by Harry S. Truman, delivered a report outlining the many ways in which the United States was failing to live up to the Fourteenth Amendment's promises of equal protection and due process of law for all people. Recalling the first civil rights movement, the committee emphasized the still-unmet goal of securing for "each individual" the right "to physical freedom, to security against illegal violence, and to fair, orderly legal process." Meanwhile, activists, including Black lawyers, turned to the federal courts for redress, hoping the Supreme Court might breathe new life into the equal protection clause in particular. In 1954, they secured a signal victory when the court declared, in *Brown v. Board of Education*, that "separate educational facilities are inherently unequal" and therefore Black students who were subjected to segregated schools were "deprived of the equal protection of the laws guaranteed by the Fourteenth Amendment."[17]

The mid-twentieth-century civil rights movement echoed and expanded the agenda of its antebellum predecessor. The new movement demanded federal protection for African Americans' basic rights to life, liberty, and property, but it also sought to end the racialized exploitation of laborers, which it likened to slavery itself. It demanded repeal of racially discriminatory laws and a newly robust understanding of equal protection of the laws. In addition to advocating racial equality in public education and public accommodations, which the nineteenth century's most progressive activists had envisioned, the twentieth-century campaign also sought protections against discrimination in private employment and housing. Like the first civil rights movement, the mid-twentieth-century movement pursued federal legislation to advance its goals.

In the early 1960s, nearly a century after Congress passed the Civil Rights Act of 1866 and the Fourteenth Amendment, some said it was impossible to "legislate morality" and that equality could be achieved only by changing attitudes through education and religion. Martin Luther

King Jr. explained why legislation mattered. In the years before Congress adopted the 1964 Civil Rights Act, King's response became familiar:

> It may be true that morality cannot be legislated, but behavior can be regu-
> lated. It may be true that the law cannot make a man love me, but it can
> keep him from lynching me. . . . It may be true that the law cannot change
> the heart, but it can restrain the heartless, and this is what we often do and
> we have to do in society through legislation.[18]

King's brief for antiracist lawmaking sounded much like Mary Ann Shadd's quest more than a century earlier. In the United States—a country born in slavery and steeped in racism—changing the law was not everything, but it was a start.

The federal government's role in American life and its capacity for administration had grown immensely in the twentieth century, and the 1964 Civil Rights Act was accompanied by far more extensive enforcement measures than would have been imaginable a century earlier. For a while, it seemed that policy changes might finally deliver the nation from its terrible past. Additional pressure—through grassroots activism, lobbying, litigation, and electoral politics—generated further advancement in the 1960s and 1970s, as African Americans gained access to schools, jobs, neighborhoods, and other places from which whites had long excluded them. Yet that more recent struggle also revealed familiar impediments. Removing racist laws did not remove racism, and ostensibly race-neutral laws were readily put to discriminatory purposes. Hard as it was to eradicate policies that explicitly discriminated based on race, it was even more difficult to take the next step: to confront the longstanding interpenetration of racism with the criminalization of poverty, and to address meaningfully the ways seemingly race-neutral policies perpetuate racial inequality.

Much remains to be done. Yet the first civil rights movement can teach us a few important things about American history, politics, and law, dating back to the earliest years of the republic. The men and women of that movement looked at their flawed country and demanded something better. They unflinchingly attacked the enduring legacies of slavery in American life. They deplored racism in public policy. They sought due process and equal protection for everyone, everywhere. Members of the coalition did not always agree with one another, and they had their blind spots. Some were in the radical vanguard and others proceeded with great caution. Still, the agitators, petitioners, and politicians of the first civil rights movement built a coalition that pushed the principle of racial equality into the center of American life, demanding policy changes that would edge the nation closer to its most egalitarian promises. When they prevailed, it was often by slim margins. When they failed, they kept trying. When the Civil War provided an opening, they propelled their quest for justice onto the national stage and into the US Constitution. We are fortunate that they did.

ACKNOWLEDGMENTS

WITH THE WORLD engulfed in a pandemic and so many institutions in free fall, it feels especially poignant to recognize the people and organizations that made this book possible. My gratitude begins with Mary Lou Reker, who in 2010 shared with me a remarkable document that tells part of the story related in chapter 8, of the dozens of African Americans whom Washington authorities arrested and incarcerated in the fall of 1861. In entrusting me to think and write about the document, which had been passed down within her family, Mary Lou set me on the path that led to this book.

I completed much of the work during two academic years of leave from teaching and service at Northwestern, and I'm indebted to the Hutchins Center for African and African American Research at Harvard University and the National Endowment for the Humanities for funding those leaves. At the Hutchins Center in 2014–15, Henry Louis Gates, Jr., the staff, and the other fellows provided a congenial atmosphere that allowed me to begin to understand what I was up to. My NEH leave year in 2018–19 was enriched by a residency at the American Bar Foundation, where Ajay Mehrotra and many others welcomed me as a member of that vital community.

Countless librarians and archivists helped me secure access to sources I needed, and I have never appreciated their contributions more than I do now, when most institutions are physically closed, yet staff members continue working to support researchers. I am indebted to archivists and librarians at the collections that I visited: the Chicago History Museum, the libraries of Dartmouth College and Harvard University, the Illinois State Library and Archives, the Indiana State Library and Historical Bureau, the Burton Historical Collection at the Detroit Public Library, the Legislative Division of the US National Archives, the Manuscript Division of the Library of Congress, the Massachusetts Historical Society and Massachusetts State Archives, the New Hampshire Historical Society, the Newberry Library, the Ohio History Connection, the Historical Society of Pennsylvania, the Western Reserve Historical Society, and the University of Illinois Archives. For going out of their way to answer my research queries, I particularly thank Jeffrey Flannery at the Library of Congress; Robert Ellis and Rodney Ross, both now retired from the National Archives; Lily Birkhimer at the Ohio History Connection, and Christopher Schnell at the Abraham Lincoln Presidential Library and Museum. The library staff at Northwestern University, including the Interlibrary Loan office, deserve my special gratitude. Among them, Harriet Lightman, Kathleen Bethel, Victoria Zahrobsky, Anne Zald, Kurt Munson, and Basia Kapolka have all been patient and generous with their time, expertise, and resources. And I have surely taxed them.

I have benefited incalculably from Lori Matten's research assistance over the last two years. A smart, probing, and steady researcher, Lori was also truly heroic in securing illustrations and permissions amid the pandemic. A number of Northwestern undergraduates also aided with research, dating back to the days when I had no idea what this project was about. Thank you to Eric Barrone, Sofia Lopez Franco, Anthony Iglesias, Andrew Jarrell, Joshua Levin, Fiona Maxwell, and Hannah Springer, as well as to Jeane Em DuBose, an enterprising history major from the University of Michigan. Northwestern University—particularly the Leopold Fellows program of the Chabraja Center for Historical Studies, and the Wayne V. Jones II Research Professorship—provided the resources that made research assistance possible. I thank History Department chairs Ken Alder and Laura Hein, as well as Dean Adrian Randolph of Weinberg College of

Arts and Sciences, for their support of my work in all its facets. The History Department and Chabraja Center staff—led by Annerys Cano, and including Jasmine Bomer, Susan Delrahim, Elzbieta Foeller-Pituch, Tricia Liu, and Eric West—has provided crucial assistance. I'm also grateful to the Alice Kaplan Institute for the Humanities for a 2017–18 faculty fellowship, which offered me the chance to meet new colleagues and rediscover the pleasures of cross-disciplinary conversation. At Northwestern, I work with an extraordinary number of brilliant, kind, and ethical people. I'm constantly mindful of my good fortune and delighted by the many opportunities I have to learn from them.

Historical scholarship is best and most gratifying when it's a collaborative enterprise, and I could not have written this book without the colleagues and friends who patiently answered my questions and listened as I tried to sort through events and ideas that were new to me. I'm grateful to the many scholars who invited me to present portions of this work in seminars or included me in conference programs, providing venues in which I received generative feedback. I was particularly energized by workshops on the history of American democracy sponsored by the Tobin Project and coordinated by Maggie Blackhawk, Laura Edwards, and Naomi Lamoreaux. Above all, I'm indebted to the historians who took time from their own busy schedules to engage with draft chapters and in some cases read the entire manuscript. For their critiques and encouragement, I thank Richard Blackett, Roger Bridges, Corey Brooks, Laura Edwards, Eric Foner, Sarah Gronningsater, Craig Hammond, Steve Kantrowitz, Bill Novak, Jim Oakes, Dylan Penningroth, Chris Schmidt, and Kyle Volk, as well as my wonderful Northwestern colleagues Henry Binford, Kevin Boyle, Caitlin Fitz, and Susan Pearson. My special gratitude goes to Leslie Harris for her probing analysis of a late draft, and to Joanna Grisinger not only for commenting on the manuscript but also for almost twenty years of conversation about US legal history. Greg Downs offered characteristically insightful readings and, still more important, made this business a lot more fun as a stalwart friend and collaborator.

This book made its way to W. W. Norton because of Steve Forman, my editor, who took an early interest in the project, stood back while I developed it, and then supported it with expert editorial interventions and wise counsel. I'm also grateful to Geri Thoma for help navigating the publishing process, Kathleen Brandes for her sharp and generous copyediting, and the team at Norton, including Amy Medeiros and Lily Gellman, for overseeing the production process. I've tried my best to get everything right; any remaining errors are of course my responsibility.

For their friendship and solidarity inside and outside History World, I also thank Amy Boyle, Gerry Cadava, Margot Canaday, Kate Diana, Andrea Durbin and John Audley, Brodie Fischer, Libby Garland, Martha Jones, Lisa Levenstein, Daryl Maeda, Tracy Van Moorlehem, Deborah Tuerkheimer, and Gillian Weiss. The graduate students with whom I've worked over the years, particularly those who have been my primary advisees, have challenged and inspired me, making me a better historian and a better person. Thank you to Gideon Cohn-Postar, Carl Creason, Amanda Kleintop, Hope McCaffrey, Heather Menefee, Mary Kate Robbett, Ana Rosado, and Leigh Soares.

History is all about understanding the convergence of time with human activity, yet I remain confounded by the mysteries of time in my own life. While I worked on this book, my sons, Isaac and Milo, grew into almost-adulthood. Thoughtful and engaged, they amaze me with their distinctive personalities, their passions and opinions, and their curiosity. Their lives are shaped not just by their family but by their community, and I'm grateful that they're growing up and attending public school in Evanston, a community that, in its own messy and conflicted ways, is determined to confront our era's pressing questions of inequality and injustice. Lucky for all of us, my own mother, Ann Masur, has been a constant in our lives—a devoted teacher, protester, grandmother, and bringer of dinner. Finally, and humbly, I thank Peter Slevin, my partner, booster, and co-conspirator. During these years, we both worked demanding but gratifying jobs while raising our kids and contending with the ailments and deaths of several beloved elders. Through it all, Peter urged me to dream big and work less hard. Reconciling those two injunctions is my next and recurring challenge.

As I finished this book, my thoughts returned to Ira Berlin and his contributions to our collective understanding of US history. Ira helped me personally: He read my dissertation when I was an assistant editor at the Freedmen and Southern Society Project, which he had founded years earlier, and he wrote letters on my behalf. He occasionally asked me to read his work, which made me feel like a bona fide historian. Ira's final book, *The Long Emancipation,* published in 2015, framed the end of slavery as a decades-long process and highlighted the struggle for racial equality as an integral part of it. We all work within intellectual lineages, conscious or not. I identify mine with Ira and the larger traditions within which he worked—traditions that merge social history with the history of governing and that place slavery and emancipation at the center of the American story. My gratitude to him and his legacy is immeasurable.

NOTE ON HISTORIOGRAPHY

I BEGAN THIS BOOK wondering about the history of the ideas contained in the Civil Rights Act of 1866 and Section 1 of the Fourteenth Amendment—ideas about race, rights, citizenship, equality, and federalism. How did it come to pass that, in a moment of national crisis, lawmakers turned to some ideas and not others, adopted measures designed to address particular challenges but left others aside? The question seemed interesting as a historical matter but also important for deepening our understanding of a text—Section 1 of the Fourteenth Amendment—that has been at the heart of struggles over rights and power in the United States since its inception.

It turned out that few historians had asked the question and that the answers were more complicated than they might at first appear. Historians of Reconstruction policy have tended to portray the Civil Rights Act and the Fourteenth Amendment as the hasty results of emergency lawmaking, their provisions founded in the exigencies of ending the Civil War and beginning to reconstruct the nation. These historians rarely asked about the ideas legislators already harbored, before the war, concerning how to move from ending slavery to ensuring racial equality in civil rights. Some constitutional historians probed deeper into the past, typically by exploring the court cases and legal treatises cited by Republican lawmakers in 1866, or, in a few instances, by connecting the Fourteenth Amendment to a genealogy of ideas expressed in abolitionist tracts and sermons. Beyond legal scholars, historians of the abolitionist movement have sometimes insisted in a general sense that it was abolitionists who ensured that the idea of racial equality found its way into federal policy; some have argued that African American activists in particular were the measures' progenitors.[1]

In this book, my goal was to create a more precise account of how the ideas of race, rights, citizenship, and federalism that are crystallized in those monumental measures of 1866 made their way into the mainstream of northern politics and then into federal policy. I wondered how those ideas were connected to northerners' own struggle to create and define a post-slavery society, a struggle that began immediately after the American Revolution and was in full swing when the Civil War began. I also wanted to know how northern views about the relative power of the states and the federal government shaped antebellum debates about race and rights and, in turn, structured the choices Republicans made when they reformed the Constitution after the war. This, then, was a project that needed to cross traditional chronological and methodological boundaries.

I saw little advantage in parsing my study into conventional historians' categories of social, political, and legal realms. My central question touched all those areas, and the people I studied readily thought across them too. In this respect, my approach reflects the pursuit of what Hendrik Hartog in 1987 called the "constitutional rights consciousness" of everyday people.[2] The men and women who populate this book developed their constitutional principles in Black churches and conventions, in white-led and racially mixed abolitionist societies, by giving lectures and listening to them, and by writing and reading newspapers. They pressed their points in the courts where they could, but more often they tried to make their influence felt in the political sphere. They petitioned and lobbied legislators, extracted pledges from candidates, built dissident political parties, and pushed at the local and state levels even when their goals were not represented in national party platforms. In a social movement that morphed into a political movement, Americans advanced their own interpretations

of the US Constitution, the Declaration of Independence, and state constitutions, as well as the Bible and natural law. My concern in this book
was not to document *all* the ideas at play but rather to chart the ones that
found their way into federal policy during Reconstruction.

I am certainly not the first historian to write about race and politics
in the antebellum North. An important early answer to my central question came in Jacobus tenBroek's 1951 book, *The Anti-Slavery Origins of the
Fourteenth Amendment*. In work commissioned to support the litigation
associated with *Brown v. Board of Education*, tenBroek and his colleague
Howard J. Graham focused on the original meanings of the Fourteenth
Amendment, particularly the equal protection clause. Sympathetic to the
plaintiffs who sought an end to the doctrine of "separate but equal," they
argued that the amendment's progenitors harbored a sweeping vision of
racial equality. Yet Graham and tenBroek were mainly interested in abolitionist treatises, and they were not particular about distinguishing which
abolitionist ideas became part of a meaningful political movement and
which were quite marginal. Examining ideas largely abstracted from their
context, they mixed together activists who insisted, improbably, that Congress could abolish slavery immediately, with those such as William Jay
and Salmon Chase, whose more carefully calibrated ideas were ultimately
adopted by the Republican Party and channeled into public policy. Graham and tenBroek's work provided important background for subsequent
historians, including William M. Wiecek in his crucial 1977 book on the
history of antislavery constitutional thought, *The Sources of Antislavery
Constitutionalism in America*. But they did not explain how social movements and politics worked, or how once-marginal ideas made their way
into the mainstream of public life. Indeed, they did not even ask.[3]

Even as Graham and tenBroek linked the Fourteenth Amendment
with abolitionist thought, another body of scholarship in social and political history—extremely influential to this day—emphasized the racism
of the white North to the exclusion of almost all else. Leon F. Litwack's
1961 *North of Slavery* was critical here. Focusing on the antebellum era,

Litwack emphasized white northerners' grinding racism and described African Americans in the North largely as victims. Pockets of Black resistance to white supremacy came across as surprising and out of synch with the book's overall tenor. Five years after Litwack's book was released, C. Vann Woodward published an article on Reconstruction called "Seeds of Failure in Radical Race Policy." Drawing almost entirely on Litwack's book for his depiction of the antebellum period, Woodward declared: "The constituency on which the Republican congressmen relied in the North was a race-conscious, segregated society devoted to the doctrine of white supremacy and Negro inferiority." In books published the following year, historians V. Jacque Voegeli and Eugene Berwanger elaborated on the same theme, giving special weight to the racism of whites in the Midwest.[4] Much of the literature seemed to suggest, as James Oakes has written of the early national period, a "racial consensus." Except for "a tiny handful of visionary radicals," the literature suggested, northern whites were monolithically antiblack.[5]

Studies of northern Black communities published since the 1970s have revealed a far more nuanced—and ambitious—picture of African American life than one might have imagined from reading Litwack. Led by the work of James and Lois Horton on Black Bostonians, these studies affirmed that African Americans suffered from institutional racism and white people's quotidian and deeply entrenched prejudices. Yet they also showed how African Americans created vibrant communities, developed independent institutions, and argued over issues of class, gender, and politics. They emphasized African Americans' centrality to the abolitionist movement, showing how Black activists advanced unstintingly radical critiques of American racism that often pushed whites to examine their own prejudices.[6] And yet Litwack's overall interpretation lived on, in part because it was not inherently incompatible with such studies. It was possible to envision a largely repressive white North that permitted pockets of Black advancement.

Meanwhile, few historians took up an insight offered by Eric Foner in 1970, when he observed that when Congress debated the admission of Oregon in 1859, "a distinctive Republican position on the rights of free Negroes finally became clear." The Republicans generally agreed, he wrote, that free African Americans "were human beings and citizens of the United States, entitled to the natural rights of humanity and to such civil rights as would protect the natural rights of life, liberty, and property." Where did that consensus come from if, as Litwack reported, white northerners were so uniformly racist and abolitionists so marginal? I was surprised to discover that few historians had investigated that question. In 1988, legal historian Paul Finkelman, prompted by renewed debates about the outlook of the framers of the Fourteenth Amendment, supplemented Foner's perspective in a thorough law review article that challenged the narratives offered by Litwack, Woodward, and others. Finkelman showed that legislatures in many free states repealed their black laws before the Civil War, that the issue became partisan over time, and that Republican politicians who openly advocated repeal were often powerful and widely respected within the party.[7]

Studies of the political antislavery movement also suggested some answers to the question of where the ideas in those 1866 federal measures came from. Political historians explored how, beginning in the late 1830s, a subset of abolitionists moved their efforts decisively into formal politics. Those activists believed that an independent antislavery political party could reshape American politics by keeping questions of slavery and racial equality on the public agenda and thereby stoking tensions within the two major parties, the Whigs and the Democrats. As Corey M. Brooks has recently shown, third-party activists effectively mobilized the idea that an unrepublican "Slave Power" dominated American politics. In the 1850s, as the Whig Party foundered and pro-slavery elements in the Democratic Party proved ever more rapacious in their demands, growing numbers of free-state voters were willing to join a new party pledged to stopping the spread of slavery.[8]

But what about people who organized for racial equality in civil rights?

We know that during Reconstruction, the nation was preoccupied with navigating questions associated with the end of racial slavery. Were former slaves citizens? Should states be permitted to adopt racially discriminatory laws? What, if any, basic rights would the US government now guarantee to all free people? Much of the existing scholarship suggests that such questions were almost never discussed before 1865. Yet the antebellum North was a post-slavery society too, and well before the Thirteenth Amendment formalized the end of slavery, each of these questions inspired fierce debate in locales as disparate as Massachusetts, Ohio, and Illinois—debate that presaged the efforts in Congress during and after the war. Previous historians have paid considerable attention to the colonization movement, which was founded on the idea that people of different races could not live together on terms of equality. But the more daring proposition that freedom could be accompanied by some form of racial equality has gone largely unexplored. Some studies of the Liberty and Free Soil Parties mention campaigns against the black laws of the Midwest. They show that African American political activists participated in third-party organizing, even in places where Black men were not permitted to vote. Demands to protect the rights of Black sailors in the South occasionally come into view, particularly because of an 1843 report of the House of Representatives.[9] Yet few works of history have given sustained focus to how antebellum northerners, Black and white, came together to demand racial equality before the law: the strategies they employed, the struggles they engaged in, and how their movement shaped formal politics and, eventually, federal policy.

Recent scholarship has made inroads into such questions. Historians have begun to reveal how African Americans grabbed hold of the rhetoric of rights and citizenship—and took advantage of openings offered by law and the courts—to claim freedom itself and to defend their property and their communities. Addressing and expanding on earlier work in social history, historians have shown how, even where no African Americans could vote, Black men and women engaged with politics and law in their everyday activities, by making claims in court, and by publicizing their views in print. They met in church-affiliated groups and local and national conventions, mobilized to petition legislatures, and stumped for political candidates.[10] This book builds on the insights of these scholars, including Martha S. Jones and Stephen Kantrowitz, in emphasizing how African American activists fueled the first civil rights movement and how they engaged with potential white allies, many of whom were not radical abolitionists but nevertheless saw the injustice of racist policies.[11]

In conceptualizing this book, I wanted to focus not only on the coalition that drove the effort to repeal racist laws but also on the opposition it faced, which I viewed as rooted not simply in racism but in a variety of interlocking and widely accepted structures of inequality. To grasp what these activists were up against, I turned to recent scholarship in legal history, written by Laura F. Edwards, William J. Novak, Kunal Parker, and others, that has drawn attention to the formidable nature of the police powers of the states and to the significance of ideas about the "people's welfare" and the public peace in nineteenth-century American governance.[12] This perspective allowed me to consider not just the ideas expressed by the actors I was studying but also the political structures in which they operated.

Legal history scholarship that emphasizes the profoundly hierarchical nature of life in the nineteenth-century United States also helps us understand the achievements of the first civil rights movement. Historians have emphasized how state and local governments, in the name of protecting the public good, classified and regulated residents according to a range of categories, including race, sex, age, marital status, disability, and economic dependency. Amid that welter of inequalities, it becomes clear that the movement's greatest innovation was to insist that race was an inappropriate basis on which to make distinctions in civil rights. It has been easy for historians to speed past that achievement, particularly because the right to vote loomed so large on the other side. Yet the duration and bitterness of the struggle to repeal explicitly racist laws that denied people rights that many people considered fundamental and founded in common law suggests that we ought to pay attention.

Indeed, one of the central challenges of writing history is setting aside our own assumptions about the past and trying to see the world as the people we study saw it. Earlier Americans talked regularly about *state* citizenship under the original privileges and immunities clause. They also self-consciously mobilized the more universal language of personhood characteristic of the Declaration of Independence and the federal Bill of Rights, as well as rights declarations in the states. This made for an antebellum conversation that was divided into two broad strands—one about citizenship and one about personhood—and those strands were reflected in the language of Section 1 of the Fourteenth Amendment itself. The amendment's authors likely could not have foreseen how future judges and scholars would take those strands apart again, parsing each word as if it had been included for its own independent meaning as opposed to forming part of a broader, culture-wide conversation.

My research was enriched by access to the stunning resources for nineteenth-century US history that have now been digitized, including state session laws and law reporters, newspapers, minutes and reports from Black conventions, and published books. This trove of sources, previously accessible only through time-consuming and expensive trips to archives but now available to those with internet access and an affiliation with a research library, make it possible to answer historical questions in new ways. My hope is that by listening to my sources—and by trying to take full measure of the challenges the first civil rights movement faced—I have added something to our collective knowledge of the American past. The people represented in this book bravely insisted that a more just racial order was possible. They labored across generations, most of the time unable to predict when and how their goals might be realized. That the policies they ultimately pursued did not resolve all the problems they saw—much less those they could not see—says more about the magnitude of the challenge than the significance of their efforts.

NOTES

ABBREVIATIONS

Annals	*Annals of Congress*
BAP	C. Peter Ripley, ed., *The Black Abolitionist Papers*, 5 vols. (Chapel Hill: University of North Carolina Press, 1985–1992).
BPL	Boston Public Library
CG	*Congressional Globe*
CHM	Chicago History Museum, Chicago
CN	Arthur Charles Cole Notes, 1912–1920, MS 549, Illinois History and Lincoln Collections, University of Illinois Library, Urbana
CWAL	Roy P. Basler, ed., *Collected Works of Abraham Lincoln*. New Brunswick, NJ: Rutgers University Press, 1953–1955.
FSC	Francis Newton Thorpe, ed. *The Federal and State Constitutions, Colonial Charters, and Other Organic Laws*. Washington, DC: GPO, 1909.
HJ	*Journal of the House of Representatives of the United States*
HRep. 80	"Free Colored Seamen—Majority and Minority Reports," Jan. 20, 1843, 27 Cong., 3d sess., 1843, House Rep. No. 80.
JJP	John Jay Papers, Columbia University, New York, NY
LDD	Paul M. Angle, ed., *Created Equal? The Complete Lincoln-Douglas Debates of 1858*. Chicago: University of Chicago Press, 1958.
MDLC	Manuscript Division, Library of Congress
MHS	Massachusetts Historical Society, Boston
MSA	Massachusetts State Archives, Boston
NARA	US National Archives and Records Administration, Washington, DC
NASS	*National Anti-Slavery Standard*
NST	Norton Strange Townshend Papers, Clements Library, University of Michigan, Ann Arbor
OR	*The War of the Rebellion: A Compilation of the Official Records of the*

	War of the Union and Confederate Armies. Washington, DC: Government Printing Office, 1880–1901.
PAJ	Paul H. Bergeron, ed., *The Papers of Andrew Johnson*, 16 vols. Knoxville: University of Tennessee Press, 1967–2000.
RCR	Ross County Register, *Register of Blacks in Ohio Counties, 1804-1861*. Microfilm. Columbus: Ohio Historical Society, 1971.
Register	*Register of Debates*
SCP	John Niven ed., *The Salmon P. Chase Papers*, 5 vols. Kent, OH: Kent State University Press, 1993–1998.
SCPHSP	Salmon P. Chase Papers, Historical Society of Pennsylvania, Philadelphia
SCW	*Charles Sumner, His Complete Works*, intro. by George Frisbie Hoar, Statesman Edition, 1900. Reprint: New York: Negro Universities Press, 1969.
SLCS	Beverly Wilson Palmer, ed., *The Selected Letters of Charles Sumner*, 2 vols. Boston: Northeastern University Press, 1990.
Stat.	*U.S. Statutes at Large*
Weld-Grimké	Gilbert H. Barnes and Dwight L. Dumond, eds., *Letters of Theodore Dwight Weld, Angelina Grimké Weld and Sarah Grimké, 1822–1844*, 2 vols., 1934. Reprint: Gloucester, MA: P. Smith, 1965.
WFMHS	Winthrop Family Papers, Massachusetts Historical Society, Boston
WMQ	*William & Mary Quarterly*
WNI	*National Intelligencer*, Washington, DC
WWS	George E. Baker, *The Works of William H. Seward*, 3 vols. New York: Redfield, 1853.

PREFACE

1. "Address to the Citizens of Ohio," *Palladium of Liberty*, Dec. 27, 1843.
2. "Whig Consistency upon the Black Laws," *Cincinnati Daily Enquirer*, Oct. 6, 1846.
3. *Annals*, 16 Cong., 2d sess., 546.

CHAPTER 1: "ON THE GROUNDS OF EXPEDIENCY AND GOOD POLICY"

1. RCR, 34–35.
2. Eva Sheppard Wolf, *Race and Liberty in the New Nation: Emancipation in Virginia from the Revolution to Nat Turner's Rebellion* (Baton Rouge: Louisiana State University Press, 2006), 117–18; Ira Berlin, *Slaves Without Masters: The Free Negro in the Antebellum South* (New York: Pantheon, 1974), 79–107. US Bureau of the Census, *Negro Population, 1790–1915*, 1918 (New York: Kraus Reprint Co., 1969), 57.
3. Kunal Parker, *Making Foreigners: Immigration and Citizenship Law in America, 1600–2000* (New York: Cambridge University Press, 2015); Gerald Neuman, "The Lost Century of American Immigration Law (1776–1875)," *Columbia Law*

Review 93 (December 1993): 1833–1901; Stefan A. Riesenfeld, "The Formative Era of American Public Assistance Law," *California Law Review* 43, no. 2 (May 1955): 175–233; Douglas Lamar Jones, "The Strolling Poor: Transiency in Eighteenth-Century Massachusetts," *Journal of Social History* 8, no. 3 (Spring 1975), esp. 43–48; William P. Quigley, "The Quicksands of the Poor Law: Poor Relief Legislation in a Growing Nation, 1790–1820," *Northern Illinois University Law Review* 18 (1997): 52; Aileen Elizabeth Kennedy, *The Ohio Poor Law and Its Administration* (Chicago: University of Chicago Press, 1934); Robert W. Kelso, *The History of Public Poor Relief in Massachusetts, 1620–1920* (Boston and New York: Houghton Mifflin, 1922); Barry Levy, *Town Born: The Political Economy of New England from Its Founding to the Revolution* (Philadelphia: University of Pennsylvania Press, 2009); Kristin O'Brassill-Kulfan, *Vagrants and Vagabonds: Poverty and Mobility in the Early American Republic* (New York: New York University Press, 2019); Barbara Young Welke, *Law and the Borders of Belonging in the Long Nineteenth Century United States* (New York: Cambridge University Press, 2010).

4. William Clinton Heffner, *History of Poor Relief in Pennsylvania, 1682–1913* (Cleona, PA: Holzapfel, 1913), 95.

5. Articles of Confederation. Madison quoted in William J. Novak, "The Legal Transformation of Citizenship in Nineteenth-Century America," in Meg Jacobs, William J. Novak, and Julian E. Zelizer, eds., *The Democratic Experiment: New Directions in American Political History* (Princeton, NJ: Princeton University Press, 2003), 88.

6. *Journals of the Continental Congress, 1774–1789, vol. XI, May 2–Sept. 1, 1778* (Washington, DC: Government Printing Office, 1908), 652.

7. *Federalist Paper No. 17* (emphasis added). Hamilton also used the phrase "mere domestic police" in *Federalist Paper No. 34*.

8. My understanding of "police" is particularly influenced by William J. Novak, *The People's Welfare: Law and Regulation in Nineteenth-Century America* (Chapel Hill: University of North Carolina Press, 1996); Christopher Tomlins, *Law, Labor, and Ideology in the Early American Republic* (New York: Cambridge University Press, 1993); and Harry N. Scheiber, "Public Rights and the Rule of Law in American Legal History," *California Law Review* 72 (1984): 217–51. See also Kate Masur, "State Sovereignty and Migration before Reconstruction," *Journal of the Civil War Era* 9, no. 4 (Dec. 2019): 588–611; Masur, " 'The People's Welfare,' Police Powers, and the Rights of Free People of African Descent," *American Journal of Legal History* 57, no. 2 (2017): 238–42.

9. *Negro Population, 1790–1915*, 57.

10. Leslie M. Harris, *In the Shadow of Slavery: African Americans in New York City, 1626–1863* (Chicago: University of Chicago Press, 2003); Richard S. Newman, *The Transformation of American Abolitionism: Fighting Slavery in the Early Republic* (Chapel Hill: University of North Carolina Press, 2002), 42–43; Gary B. Nash, *Forging Freedom: The Formation of Philadelphia's Black Community,*

1720–1840 (Cambridge: Harvard University Press, 1988), esp. 104–6; Patrick Rael, *Eighty-Eight Years: The Long Death of Slavery in the United States, 1777–1865* (Athens: University of Georgia Press, 2015), 126–59; Manisha Sinha, *The Slave's Cause: A History of Abolition* (New Haven, CT: Yale University Press, 2016), 65–159; Paul J. Polgar, *Standard-Bearers of Equality: America's First Abolition Movement* (Chapel Hill: University of North Carolina Press, 2019).

11. Harris, *In the Shadow of Slavery*, 33, 39; Lorenzo Johnston Greene, *The Negro in Colonial New England, 1620–1776* (New York: Columbia University Press, 1942), 129, 140–41; Joanne Pope Melish, *Disowning Slavery: Gradual Emancipation and "Race" in New England, 1780–1860* (Ithaca, NY: Cornell University Press, 1998).

12. "An Act for the Gradual Abolition of Slavery," March 1, 1780, *Acts of the General Assembly of the Commonwealth of Pennsylvania* (Philadelphia: Francis Bailey, 1782), 282–87. Benjamin Joseph Klebaner, "American Manumission Laws and the Responsibility for Supporting Slaves," *Virginia Magazine of History and Biography* 63, no. 4 (Oct. 1955): 443–53; Harris, *In the Shadow of Slavery*; David N. Gellman, *Emancipating New York: The Politics of Slavery and Freedom, 1777–1827* (Baton Rouge: Louisiana State University Press, 2006); O'Brassill-Kulfan, *Vagrants and Vagabonds*, 105–9.

13. "An Act Concerning Indian, Molatto, and Negro Servants and Slaves," *Acts and Laws of the State of Connecticut, in America* (New-London: Timothy Green, 1784), 233–35.

14. "An Act for suppressing and punishing of Rogues, Vagabonds, common Beggars and Other Idle, Disorderly and Lewd Persons," *General Laws of Massachusetts from the Adoption of the Constitution*, 2 vols. (Boston, 1823), I, 324–25; George H. Moore, *Notes on the History of Slavery in Massachusetts* (New York: Appleton, 1866), 224–37. For enforcement of such provisions: Ruth Wallis Herndon, *Unwelcome Americans: Living on the Margin in Early New England* (Philadelphia: University of Pennsylvania Press, 2001), 1–22; Melish, *Disowning Slavery*, 190–92. One study that compared enforcement of settlement laws against Blacks and whites in New York City and Westchester County from the 1790s to about 1810 found that officials applied the law vigorously to both groups. Robert E. Cray Jr., "White Welfare and Black Strategies: The Dynamics of Race and Poor Relief in Early New York, 1700-1825," *Slavery and Abolition* 7, no. 3 (Dec. 1986): 273–89. Priscilla H. Roberts and James N. Tull, "Moroccan Sultan Sidi Muhammad Ibn Abdallah's Diplomatic Initiatives Toward the United States, 1777–1786," *Proceedings of the American Philosophical Society* 143, no. 2 (June 1999): 233–65.

15. Heffner, *History of Poor Relief*, 111. See also Parker, *Making Foreigners*, 73–77; Jones, "Strolling Poor."

16. Peter S. Onuf, *Statehood and Union: A History of the Northwest Ordinance* (Bloomington: Indiana University Press, 1987); John Craig Hammond, *Slavery, Freedom, and Expansion in the Early American West* (Charlottesville: University of Virginia Press, 2007); Richard Frederick O'Dell, "The Early Anti-Slavery

Movement in Ohio" (PhD diss., University of Michigan, 1948), 23–29; M. Scott Heerman, *The Alchemy of Slavery: Human Bondage and Emancipation in the Illinois Country, 1730–1865* (Philadelphia: University of Pennsylvania Press, 2018).

17. Gregory Evans Dowd, *A Spirited Resistance: The North American Indian Struggle for Unity, 1745–1815* (Baltimore: Johns Hopkins University Press, 1992), 85–89, 103–13; John P. Bowes, *Land Too Good for Indians: Northern Indian Removal* (Norman: University of Oklahoma Press, 2016), 23–25; Bethel Saler, *The Settlers' Empire: Colonialism and State Formation in America's Old Northwest* (Philadelphia: University of Pennsylvania Press, 2015), 13–82; Wiley Sword, *President Washington's Indian War: The Struggle for the Old Northwest, 1790–1795* (Norman: University of Oklahoma Press, 1985); Kristopher Maulden, *The Federalist Frontier: Settler Politics in the Old Northwest, 1783–1840* (Columbia: University of Missouri Press, 2019), 37–61; Michael Witgen, "A Nation of Settlers: The Early American Republic and the Colonization of the Northwest Territory," *WMQ* 76, no. 3, 3d ser. (July 2019): 396–97.

18. William Birney, *James G. Birney and His Times* (New York: D. Appleton, 1890), 431–35. O'Dell, "Early Anti-Slavery Movement," 44–65, 181–90; Hammond, *Slavery, Freedom, and Expansion,* esp. 124–49; Matthew Mason, *Slavery and Politics in the Early American Republic* (Chapel Hill: University of North Carolina Press, 2006), esp. 149–56; Matthew Salafia, *Slavery's Borderland: Freedom and Bondage Along the Ohio River* (Philadelphia: University of Pennsylvania Press, 2013).

19. "A Law for the Relief of the Poor," June 19, 1795, *Laws of the Territory of the United States North-West of the Ohio* (Cincinnati: W. Maxwell, 1796), 127. Bowes, *Land Too Good for Indians,* 25.

20. Ohio Const. of 1803, Art. VIII, §1, in *FSC,* V, 2909. Charles Jay Wilson, "The Negro in Early Ohio," *Ohio Archaeological and Historical Quarterly* 39 (1930), esp. 750–61; O'Dell, "Early Anti-Slavery Movement," 97–127; Hammond, *Slavery, Freedom, and Expansion,* 76–95, 124–49; Donald J. Ratcliffe, *Party Spirit in a Frontier Republic: Democratic Politics in Ohio, 1793–1821* (Columbus: Ohio State University Press, 1998), 44–74.

21. Wolf, *Race and Liberty,* 109–17; Berlin, *Slaves Without Masters,* 41–42, 92; Julius S. Scott, *The Common Wind: Afro-American Currents in the Age of the Haitian Revolution* (New York: Verso, 2018), 199–201; Alejandro de la Fuente and Ariela J. Gross, *Becoming Free, Becoming Black: Race, Freedom, and the Law in Cuba, Virginia, and Louisiana* (New York: Cambridge University Press, 2020), 79–100.

22. Wilson, "The Negro in Early Ohio"; Richard C. Wade, "The Negro in Cincinnati, 1800–1830," *Journal of Negro History* 39, no. 1 (Jan. 1954): 49.

23. "An act, to regulate black and mulatto persons," Jan. 5, 1804, *Acts of the State of Ohio, Second Session of the General Assembly,* 1804 (Reprint: Norwalk, OH: Laning, 1901), 63–66.

24. "An act, for the relief of the poor," Feb. 22, 1805, *Acts of the State of Ohio, Passed and Revised, First Session of the Third General Assembly,* 1805 (Reprint: Norwalk, OH: Laning, 1901), 272–78. "An act to amend the act, entitled 'An

act regulating black and mulatto persons," Jan. 25, 1807, *Acts Passed at the First Session of the Fifth General Assembly of the State of Ohio*, 1807 (Reprint: Norwalk, OH: Laning, 1901), 53–55. Wolf, *Race and Liberty*, 121–27. Paul Finkelman, "Before the Fourteenth Amendment: Black Legal Rights in the Antebellum North," *Rutgers Law Journal* 17 (1985–1986): 435–36.

25. John Craig Hammond, " 'The Most Free of Free States': Politics, Slavery, Race, and Regional Identity in Early Ohio, 1790–1820," *Ohio History* 121 (2014): 46.

26. Stephen Middleton, ed., *The Black Laws in the Old Northwest: A Documentary History* (Westport, CT: Greenwood Press, 1993), 187, 202; Norman Dwight Harris, *The History of Negro Servitude in Illinois, and of the Slavery Agitation in that State, 1719–1864* (Chicago: A. C. McClurg, 1904); Heerman, *Alchemy of Slavery*; Mason, *Slavery and Politics*, 153–54.

27. *Journal of the Twenty-Third House of Representatives of the Commonwealth of Pennsylvania, 1812–13* (Harrisburg, PA: J. Peacock, 1812), 417, 481. Nash, *Forging Freedom*, 177–81. "An Act to Prohibit the Emigration of Free Negroes into this State," Jan. 3, 1807, *At a Session of the General Assembly of Maryland . . .* (Nov. 3, 1806, to Jan. 5, 1807), n.p., n.d.

28. Nicholas P. Wood, "A 'class of Citizens': The Earliest Black Petitioners to Congress and Their Quaker Allies," *WMQ*, 3d ser., 74 (Jan. 2017): 118–20; Erica Armstrong Dunbar, *A Fragile Freedom: African American Women and Emancipation in the Antebellum City* (New Haven, CT: Yale University Press, 2008), 58–60; Nash, *Forging Freedom*, 118–33.

29. Newman, *Transformation*; Polgar, *Standard-Bearers*; Peter P. Hinks, *To Awaken My Afflicted Brethren: David Walker and the Problem of Antebellum Slave Resistance* (University Park: Pennsylvania State University Press, 1997), 70–72, 96–98; Wood, "A 'class of Citizens,' " 118–20. For the argument that from the mid-1780s onward, white Americans largely saw free African Americans as "denizens" rather than citizens, see Douglas Bradburn, *The Citizenship Revolution: Politics and the Creation of the American Union, 1774–1804* (Charlottesville: University of Virginia Press, 2009), 235–71.

30. Petition published in Sidney Kaplan and Emma Nogrady Kaplan, *The Black Presence in the Era of the American Revolution*, rev. ed. (Amherst: University of Massachusetts Press, 1989), 273–76 (emphasis in the original). Forten quoted in Wood, "A 'class of Citizens,' " 138.

31. *Journal of the Twenty-Third House*, 566–67, 588–89. For Forten and his broadside, see Newman, *Transformation*, 94–95; Julie Winch, *A Gentleman of Color: The Life of James Forten* (New York: Oxford University Press, 2002), 11–13, 18–27, 37–52, 169–74; Winch, "The Making and Meaning of James Forten's Letters from a Man of Colour," *WMQ*, 3d ser., 64, no. 1 (Jan. 2007), 129–38.

32. [James Forten], *Letters from a Man of Colour, on a Late Bill before the Senate of Pennsylvania* (n.p., [1813]), 1.

33. Forten, *Letters from a Man of Colour*, 5–6, 9–10.

34. *Journal of the Twenty-Fourth House of Representatives of the Commonwealth of Pennsylvania, 1813-14* (Harrisburg, PA: J. Peacock, 1813), 101, 264, 448, 493-94.

35. *Journal of the Twenty-Fourth House*, 494, 495.

36. *Journal of the Twenty-Fourth House*, 495, 498; *Journal of the Senate of the Commonwealth of Pennsylvania*, 1813–14 (Harrisburg, PA: Christian Cleim, 1813), 504.

37. *Negro Population*, 45, 51; Daniel Drake, *Natural and Statistical View, or Picture of Cincinnati* (Cincinnati, OH: Looker and Wallace, 1815), 171; John W. Blassingame, *Slave Testimony: Two Centuries of Letters, Speeches, and Autobiography* (Baton Rouge: Louisiana State University Press, 1977), 483; *Journal of the Senate of the State of Ohio*, 36th General Assembly, 1837–38, 564. Hammond, "Most Free of the Free," 51. For a recent study of rural Black communities in the Old Northwest, see Anna-Lisa Cox, *The Bone and Sinew of the Land: America's Forgotten Black Pioneers and the Struggle for Equality* (New York: PublicAffairs, 2018). For a helpful discussion of Black migrations in the context of settler colonialism, see Tiya Miles, "Beyond a Boundary: Black Lives and the Settler–Native Divide," *WMQ* 76, no. 3 (July 2019): 417–26.

38. RCR; Ellen Eslinger, "The Evolution of Racial Politics in Early Ohio," in Andrew R. L. Cayton and Stuart D. Hobbs, eds., *The Center of a Great Empire: The Ohio Country and the Early American Republic* (Athens: Ohio University Press, 2005), 87–91.

39. RCR, 17; Evans Family Manumission Papers, VFM5314, Ohio History Connection.

40. RCR, 21. For a person's "credit" in a community context, see Laura F. Edwards, *The People and Their Peace: Legal Culture and the Transformation of Inequality in the Post-Revolutionary South* (Chapel Hill: University of North Carolina Press, 2009).

41. RCR, 38–39.

42. David Blackmore, "Effect of Prejudice," *Philanthropist*, Nov. 28, 1817. Wade, "Negro in Cincinnati," 49.

43. Blackmore, "Effect of Prejudice." For similar accounts of how white Ohioans took advantage of African Americans who were not protected by the law, see E. S. Abdy, *Journal of a Residence and Tour in the United States of North America, April, 1833, to October, 1834*, 3 vols. (London: Murray, 1835), III, 85–86.

44. Blassingame, *Slave Testimony*, 194. For enforcement in 1818, see Andrew Feight, " 'Black Friday': Enforcing Ohio's 'Black Laws' in Portsmouth, Ohio," Scioto Historical, https://sciotohistorical.org/items/show/108. For a broader theory of "republican" law enforcement, see Jonathan Obert, *The Six-Shooter State: Public and Private Violence in American Politics* (New York: Cambridge University Press, 2018).

45. Nathan Guilford to Thomas Rotch, July 16, 1817, Massillon Memory Collection, https://ohiomemory.org/digital/collection/p15005coll39. Philip J. Schwarz, *Migrants against Slavery: Virginians and the Nation* (Charlottesville: University of Virginia Press, 2001), 130–33; O'Dell, "Early Anti-Slavery Movement," 156–59, 223.

46. Untitled, *Scioto Gazette*, June 16, 1819.

47. "An Address," *Philanthropist*, March 11, 1820; "The Black Settlers in Brown Co.," *Philanthropist*, May 27, 1820; "The Black People in Brown County," *Philanthropist*, June 2, 1821; Abdy, *Journal of a Residence*, III, 71. Schwarz, *Migrants against Slavery*, 136–40.

48. Abdy, *Journal of a Residence*, III, 36–37, 49, 73. *Proceedings of the Ohio Anti-Slavery Convention, Held at Putnam, on the Twenty-Second, Twenty-Third, and Twenty-Fourth of April, 1835* (n.p.: Beaumont and Wallace, 1835), 17; "The Black People in Brown County," *Philanthropist*, June 2, 1821.

49. John Malvin, *North Into Freedom, The Autobiography of John Malvin, Free Negro, 1795–1880*, ed. and intro. by Allan Peskin (Cleveland, OH: Press of Western Reserve University, 1966), 40. For free papers as a manifestation of Black vulnerability, see also Elizabeth Stordeur Pryor, *Colored Travelers: Mobility and the Fight for Citizenship before the Civil War* (Chapel Hill: University of North Carolina Press, 2016), 111–14.

50. The literature is extensive, but for a recent treatment of early colonization that examines policies directed at both African Americans and Indigenous people, see Nicholas Guyatt, *Bind Us Apart: How Enlightened Americans Invented Racial Segregation* (New York: Basic Books, 2016). For Black activists, slightly later, pointing out the hypocrisy of people who opposed Indian removal but supported Black colonization, see Natalie Joy, "The Indian's Cause: Abolitionists and Native American Rights," *Journal of the Civil War Era* 8, no. 2 (June 2018): 215–42.

51. Letter of Abraham Camp, July 13, 1818, in *Third Annual Report of the American Society for Colonizing the Free People of Colour of the United States* (Washington, DC: Davis and Force, 1820), 124. Rosalind Cobb Wiggins, *Captain Paul Cuffe's Logs and Letters, 1808–1817: A Black Quaker's "Voice from within the Veil"* (Washington, DC: Howard University Press, 1996), 46–69; Guyatt, *Bind Us Apart*, 260–63; Floyd J. Miller, *The Search for a Black Nationality: Black Emigration and Colonization, 1787–1863* (Urbana: University of Illinois Press, 1975), 3–20, 25–27, 33–43; Richard S. Newman, *Freedom's Prophet: Bishop Richard Allen, the AME Church, and the Black Founding Fathers* (New York: New York University Press, 2008), 186, 195; Nash, *Forging Freedom*, 184–85; Polgar, *Standard-Bearers*, 261–73.

52. Thomas Jefferson to John Lynd, Jan. 21, 1811, in *First Annual Report of the American Society for Colonizing the Free People of Color of the United States* (Washington, DC: D. Rapine, 1818), 13; *Fourth Annual Report of the American Society for Colonizing the Free People of Color of the United States* (Washington, DC: Davis and Force, 1821), 24.

53. *First Annual Report of the American Society,* 8. By 1820, the American Colonization Society claimed branches throughout the Upper South and across the Northeast—for example, in New York City; New Haven and Hartford, Connecticut; Philadelphia and York, Pennsylvania; Providence, Rhode Island; Portland, Maine; and Newburyport, Massachusetts. *Third Annual Report of the American Society,* 136–45. The ACS acknowledged in January 1818 that the plan

was not popular among African Americans, though it expressed hope that people could be persuaded. *First Annual Report of the American Society,* 10–11. Henry Noble Sherwood, "Formation of the American Colonization Society," *Journal of Negro History* 2, no. 3 (July 1917): 209–28. For an effort to separate class-based from race-based concerns in the thought of early colonizationist Charles Fenton Mercer, see Douglas R. Egerton, "'Its Origin Is Not a Little Curious': A New Look at the American Colonization Society," *Journal of the Early Republic* 5, no. 4 (Winter 1985): 463–80.

54. Printed in William Lloyd Garrison, *Thoughts on African Colonization,* 1832, with Introduction by William Loren Katz (New York: Arno Press, 1968), part II, 9, 62–63. Katz in Garrison, *Thoughts,* vii–x; Newman, *Freedom's Prophet,* 183, 189–91, 205–7; Polgar, *Standard-Bearers,* 275–77; Nash, *Forging Freedom,* 238; Winch, *Gentleman of Color,* 190–93; Miller, *Search for a Black Nationality,* 48; Andrew K. Diemer, *The Politics of Black Citizenship: Free African Americans in the Mid-Atlantic Borderland, 1817–1863* (Athens: University of Georgia Press, 2016), 11–30.

55. "Speech of a Colored Brother," *Liberator,* Oct. 13, 1837; Resolution of Jan. 29, 1818, *Acts Passed at the First Session of the Sixteenth General Assembly of the State of Ohio* (Columbus: P. H. Olmsted, 1818), 198–99; *First Annual Report of the American Society,* 9. Middleton, *Black Laws in the Old Northwest,* 19–20.

56. Birney, *James G. Birney,* 390; Ruth Ketring Nuermberger, *Charles Osborn in the Anti-Slavery Movement* (Columbus: The Ohio State Archaeological and Historical Society, 1937), 34–35; O'Dell, "Early Anti-Slavery Movement," 191–96.

57. Excerpts printed in George W. Julian, *The Rank of Charles Osborn as an Anti-Slavery Pioneer* (Indianapolis: Bowen-Merrill, 1891), 19, 21. Randall M. Miller, "The Union Humane Society," *Quaker History* 61, no. 2 (Autumn 1972): 96.

58. Julian, *Charles Osborn,* 23.

59. Blackmore, "Effect of Prejudice." Quaker Thomas Rotch also wanted to see the laws repealed. Thomas Rotch to Benjamin Ladd, June 28, 1817, Massillon Memory Collection, https://ohiomemory.org/digital/collection/p15005coll39.

60. "An Address," *Philanthropist,* June 17, 1820; Thomas Hedges Genin, *Selections from the Writings of the Late Thomas Genin* (New York: E. O. Jenkins, 1869), 13–14, 18–20; *The Life, Travels and Opinions of Benjamin Lundy* (Philadelphia: William D. Parrish, 1847), 17–20; *Minutes of the Proceedings of a Special Meeting of the Fifteenth American Convention for Promoting the Abolition of Slavery* (Philadelphia: Hall & Atkinson, 1818), 42. Miller, "The Union Humane Society"; Merton L. Dillon, *Benjamin Lundy and the Struggle for Negro Freedom* (Urbana: University of Illinois Press, 1966).

61. "Abolition of Slavery. No. 1," *Genius of Universal Emancipation,* Sept. 1821; Dillon, *Benjamin Lundy,* esp. 56–57.

62. Drake, *Natural and Statistical View,* 171; Hammond, "Most Free of the Free," 51–57; O'Dell, "Early Anti-Slavery Movement," 201–6, 230.

63. *Ohio v. Carneal* (1817), in Ervin H. Pollack, ed., *Ohio Unreported Judicial Decisions Prior to 1823* (Indianapolis: Allen Smith Co., 1952), 136, 141.

64. William M. Wiecek, *The Sources of Antislavery Constitutionalism in America, 1760–1848* (Ithaca, NY: Cornell University Press, 1977), 20–39; Derek A. Webb, "The *Somerset* Effect: Parsing Lord Mansfield's Words on Slavery in Nineteenth Century America," *Law and History Review* 32, no. 3 (August 2014): 455–90; Sue Peabody and Keila Grinberg, "Free Soil: The Generation and Circulation of an Atlantic Legal Principle," in Peabody and Grinberg, eds., *Free Soil in the Atlantic World* (New York: Routledge, 2015); Paul Finkelman, *An Imperfect Union: Slavery, Federalism, and Comity* (Chapel Hill: University of North Carolina Press, 1981).

65. "Important Law Decision," *Genius of Universal Emancipation,* Nov. 1821.

66. Ibid; *Polly Gray vs. State*, 4 Ohio 353, 354 (1831); "Address of the State Convention," *Palladium of Liberty,* Nov. 13, 1844. An 1838 Ohio Senate report cited the "humiliating spectacle of a score of witnesses, of various shades of color, before our judges, to ascertain whether they are white enough to testify." *Journal of the Senate of the State of Ohio*, 36th General Assembly, 1837–38 (Columbus, OH: Samuel Medary, 1837–38), 565.

67. "Abolition of Slavery. No. 1," *Genius of Universal Emancipation,* Sept. 1821; Dillon, *Benjamin Lundy*, esp. 56–57.

CHAPTER 2: "A FREE MAN OF COLOUR, AND A CITIZEN OF THIS STATE"

1. Untitled, *Commercial Advertiser,* Aug. 25, 1826.

2. *Free Negroes—District of Columbia*, 19 Cong., 2d sess., House Rep. No. 43, 5; Untitled advertisement, Aug. 1, 1826, *WNI*.

3. "The Case of Horton," *Commercial Advertiser,* Sept. 28, 1826.

4. On the complexities of citizenship as a local, state, and national status in this period, see, for example, Novak, "Legal Transformation of Citizenship"; James H. Kettner, *Development of American Citizenship, 1608–1870* (Chapel Hill: University of North Carolina Press, 1978); Nancy Isenberg, *Sex and Citizenship in Antebellum America* (Chapel Hill: University of North Carolina Press, 1998), esp. 28–39, 147–54; Michael Les Benedict, "'Membership of a Nation, and Nothing More': The Civil Rights Act of 1866 and the Narrowing of Citizenship in the Civil War Era," in Christian G. Samito, ed., *The Greatest and the Grandest Act: The Civil Rights Act of 1866 from Reconstruction to Today* (Carbondale: Southern Illinois University Press, 2018).

5. Kettner, *Development of American Citizenship*, 255–61; Kurt T. Lash, *The Fourteenth Amendment and the Privileges and Immunities of American Citizenship* (New York: Cambridge University Press, 2014), 20–30; Maeve Glass, "Citizens of the State," *University of Chicago Law Review* 85, no. 4 (June 2018): 889n109.

6. *Annals*, 15 Cong., 1 sess., 840. Thomas D. Morris, *Free Men All: The Personal Liberty Laws of the North, 1780–1861* (Baltimore, MD: Johns Hopkins University Press, 1974), 31–41; Wood, "A 'class of Citizens,'" 109–44; Padraig Riley,

Slavery and the Democratic Conscience: Political Life in Jeffersonian America (Philadelphia: University of Pennsylvania Press, 2016), 211–12.

7. Glover Moore, *The Missouri Controversy, 1819–1821* ([Lexington]: University of Kentucky Press, 1953); Robert Pierce Forbes, *The Missouri Compromise and Its Aftermath: Slavery and the Meaning of America* (Chapel Hill: University of North Carolina Press, 2007); Hammond, *Slavery, Freedom, and Expansion*, 57–74, 150–68. On the growth of restrictionist sentiment in the years preceding the Missouri crisis, see, for example, Wiecek, *Sources of Anti-Slavery Constitutionalism*, 84–105; Mason, *Slavery and Politics*; Riley, *Slavery and the Democratic Conscience*; Donald J. Ratcliffe, "The Decline of Anti-Slavery Politics, 1815-1840," in John Craig Hammond and Matthew Mason, eds., *Contesting Slavery: The Politics of Bondage and Freedom in the New American Nation* (Charlottesville: University of Virginia Press, 2011), esp. 270–72; John Craig Hammond, "President, Planter, Politician: James Monroe, the Missouri Crisis, and the Politics of Slavery, *Journal of American History* 105, no. 4 (2019): 843–67.

8. Mo. Const. of 1820, art. 3, §26, in *FSC*, IV, 2154. For Virginia's law of 1783 and Georgia's of 1818, see John Codman Hurd, *Law of Freedom and Bondage in the United States*, 2 vols. (Boston: Little, Brown, 1858), II, 5, 103–4. More generally, Henry W. Farnam, *Chapters in the History of Social Legislation in the United States to 1860* (Washington, DC: Carnegie Institution, 1938), 200–201; Berlin, *Slaves Without Masters*, 89–99.

9. "The Next Session of Congress," *Niles' Weekly Register*, Oct. 21, 1820. Historians have not generally explored the issue of state citizenship and police powers in this critical debate. See, for example, Kettner, *Development of American Citizenship*, 312–15; Lash, *Fourteenth Amendment*; Mason, *Slavery and Politics*, 210–11; Riley, *Slavery and the Democratic Conscience*; Moore, *Missouri Controversy*, 164–69; Rogers M. Smith, *Civic Ideals: Conflicting Visions of Citizenship in U.S. History* (New Haven, CT: Yale University Press, 1997), 175– 77. For a brief treatment, see James Oakes, *The Scorpion's Sting: Antislavery and the Coming of the Civil War* (New York: W. W. Norton, 2014), 90–94. For a recent claim that it was not until the mid-1830s that antislavery people began talking about African Americans' state citizenship under Article IV, Section 2, see Glass, "Citizens of the State."

10. *Annals*, 16 Cong., 2d sess., 85, 549, 557. Archer of Virginia likewise insisted that states were entitled to exclude people—even citizens—they believed threatening to public peace or health. He acknowledged, however, that it might not be "fair" to exclude Black people as a class, since that would be "for a cause not personal, that is to say, accidental to the excluded object" (ibid., 583). For a careful study of Holmes and the Maine context, see Matthew Mason, "Maine and Missouri: Competing Priorities and Northern Slavery Politics in the Early Republic," *Journal of the Early Republic* 33, no. 4 (Winter 2013): 675–700.

11. *Annals*, 16 Cong., 2d sess., 547, 1136, 616.

12. *Annals*, 16 Cong., 2d sess., 556–57, 545–47, 614–15, 618–19.

13. *Annals*, 16 Cong., 2d sess., 566, 601.

14. *Annals,* 16 Cong., 2d sess., 638, 111.

15. *Annals,* 16 Cong., 2d sess., 530, 570-71.

16. *Annals,* 16 Cong., 2d sess., 114, 530.

17. *Annals,* 16 Cong., 2d sess., 100, 116, 119; 3 Stat. 641.

18. *Annals,* 16 Cong., 2d sess., 1079. It had been conventional since the 1787 Northwest Ordinance to specify that new states entered the Union "on an equal footing with the original states."

19. "An Act Concerning Negroes and Mulattoes," *Laws of the State of Missouri* (St. Louis: E. Charles, 1825), II, 600-602 (emphasis added); "An Act Respecting Free Negroes and Mulattoes, Servants and Slaves," Jan. 17, 1829, *Revised Code of Laws, of Illinois* (Shawneetown, IL: Alexander F. Grant, 1829), 129.

20. Wm. Wirt to the Secretary of the Treasury, Nov. 7, 1821, *Opinions of the Attorneys General of the United States, from the Beginning of the Government to March 1st, 1841* (Washington, DC: Blair and Rives, 1841), 383.

21. See note 4, above, and for recent scholarship that emphasizes African Americans' citizenship claims as claims to belonging, see, for example, Christopher James Bonner, *Remaking the Republic: Black Politics and the Creation of American Citizenship* (Philadelphia: University of Pennsylvania Press, 2020); Martha S. Jones, *Birthright Citizens: A History of Race and Rights in Antebellum America* (New York: Cambridge University Press, 2018); Stephen Kantrowitz, *More Than Freedom: Fighting for Black Citizenship in a White Republic, 1829-1889* (New York: Penguin, 2012); Margot Minardi, *Making Slavery History: Abolitionism and the Politics of Memory in Massachusetts* (New York: Oxford University Press, 2010), esp. 132-72; Polgar, *Standard-Bearers.*

22. *Annals,* 16 Cong., 1 sess., 66-67, 83-84.

23. "Massachusetts State Legislature," *Commercial Gazette* (Boston), June 11, 1821; "Legislature of Massachusetts," *Niles' Weekly Register,* July 14, 1821; "Legislature of Massachusetts," *Genius of Universal Emancipation,* Aug. 1821; "The 'Missouri Question' in Massachusetts," *St. Louis Enquirer,* July 28, 1821.

24. "Free Negroes and Mulattos," [Massachusetts] House of Representatives, Jan. 16, 1822, 2, 15. Finkelman, "Before the Fourteenth Amendment," 433; Minardi, *Making Slavery History,* 28-33.

25. Harris, *In the Shadow of Slavery,* 72-133; Gellman, *Emancipating New York,* 189-206; Paul J. Polgar, "'Whenever They Judge it Expedient': The Politics of Partisanship and Free Black Voting Rights in Early National New York," *American Nineteenth Century History* 12, no. 1 (March 2011): 1-23; Sarah L. H. Gronningsater, "'Expressly Recognized by Our Election Laws': Certificates of Freedom and the Multiple Fates of Black Citizenship in the Early Republic," *WMQ,* 3d ser., 75, no. 3 (July 2018): 465-506.

26. *Journal of the Assembly of the State of New York at their Forty-Fourth Session* (Albany, NY: J. Buel, 1820), 45. Legislator quoted in Gronningsater, "Expressly Recognized," 500.

27. *Reports of the Proceedings and Debates of the Convention of 1821, Assembled for the Purpose of Amending the Constitution of the State of New-York* (Albany, NY:

E. and E. Hosford, 1821), 134, 184. Peter Jay argued that "right of suffrage" was "a privilege" of citizenship; thinking about citizenship as a state-level status, he floated the possibility that a Black citizen of Pennsylvania, where Black men could vote, might come to New York, meet all other qualifications for voting, but be disenfranchised merely because "he is of a dark complexion."

28. The relevant clause read, ". . . but no man of color, unless he shall have been for three years a citizen of this State." N.Y. Const. of 1821, art. II, §1, in *FSC*, V, 2642. As Peter Jay's brother William wrote to a colleague in 1827, the citizenship of "free blacks" in New York was "most unquestionable." William Jay to Aaron Ward, Jan. 9, 1827, Aaron Ward Papers, BPL.

29. Unless otherwise noted, the details provided below are based on the following sources: "Text," *New York Daily Advertiser*, Aug. 15, 1826; "Case of Gilbert Horton," Aug. 23, 1826, Untitled, Aug. 26, 1826, "The Case of Horton," Aug. 26, 1826, "The Case of Gilbert Horton," Sept. 2, 1826, all in *Commercial Advertiser*; "The Case of Gilbert Horton," *New York Spectator*, Sept. 5, 1826. Aspects of Horton's story are described in Jones, *Birthright Citizens*, 30–34.

30. Steven Deyle, *Carry Me Back: The Domestic Slave Trade in American Life* (New York: Oxford University Press, 2005); Don E. Fehrenbacher, *The Slaveholding Republic: An Account of the United States Government's Relations to Slavery* (New York: Oxford University Press, 2001), 66–67; Newman, *Transformation*, 50–51.

31. *Negro Population*, 57.

32. Donald Ratcliffe, *The One-Party Presidential Contest: Adams, Jackson, and 1824's Five-Horse Race* (Lawrence: University Press of Kansas, 2015); Daniel Walker Howe, *What Hath God Wrought: The Transformation of America, 1815–1848* (New York: Oxford University Press, 2007), 207–11, 244–60, 275–84; Fehrenbacher, *Slaveholding Republic*, 68–72; Ratcliffe, "Decline of Anti-Slavery Politics," 272–77; Birney, *James G. Birney*, 409.

33. Bayard Tuckerman, *William Jay and the Constitutional Movement for the Abolition of Slavery* (New York: Dodd, Mead, 1893), 29–30.

34. James Franklin Beard, ed., *The Letters and Journals of James Fenimore Cooper*, 6 vols. (Cambridge: Belknap Press of Harvard University Press, 1960), I, 30; Tuckerman, *William Jay*, 14. For William Jay and the Missouri debate, see also John W. Blassingame, ed., *The Frederick Douglass Papers: Series One: Speeches, Debates, and Interviews, Vol. 3: 1855–63* (New Haven, CT: Yale University Press, 1985), 270.

35. Untitled, *Genius of Universal Emancipation*, March 4, 1826; Fehrenbacher, *Slaveholding Republic*, 68. That vision of federalism became what historian William Wiecek called the "federal consensus." Wiecek, *Sources of Anti-Slavery Constitutionalism*, 15–16. Newman, *Transformation*, 46–55; Dillon, *Benjamin Lundy*, 80–85.

36. "Extract of a Letter from a Gentleman in Washington City to his Friend in Philadelphia, dated Saturday, May 13, 1826," *National Gazette* (Philadelphia), May 18, 1826; "Nineteenth Congress, First Session," *Niles' Weekly Register*, May

20, 1826; Charles Francis Richardson and Elizabeth Miner (Thomas) Richardson, *Charles Miner, A Pennsylvania Pioneer* (n.p.: Wilkes-Barre, 1916), 91–94; *HJ*, 19 Cong, 1 sess., May 13, 1826, 559. Newman, *Transformation*, 30, 51–52. The *National Gazette* letter may have been written by Miner himself, since it included testimonials about the Washington jail very similar to those Miner would offer in the winter of 1829.

37. Richardson and Richardson, *Charles Miner*, 93–94; Tuckerman, *William Jay*, 32–33.

38. Letter of DeWitt Clinton to the President of the United States, Sept. 4, 1826, quoted in "Case of Horton," *Commercial Advertiser*, Sept. 28, 1826.

39. "Text," *New York Daily Advertiser*, Aug. 15, 1826. Forbes, *The Missouri Compromise and Its Aftermath*, 51, 56.

40. Granville Ganter, "Stone, William Leete (1792–1844)," *American National Biography*, Feb. 1, 2000, accessed online, Sep. 28, 2020; William L. Stone, *The Life and Times of Sa-go-ye-wat-ha, or Red-Jacket; with a Memoir of the Author, by His Son* (Albany, NY: J. Munsell, 1866), 21, 40. *New York Daily Advertiser*, Aug. 25, 1826; *New York Spectator*, Aug. 25, 1826; *Boston Daily Advertiser*, Aug. 28, 1826; *American* (New York), Aug. 29, 1826; *Hampshire Gazette* (Northampton, MA), Aug. 30, 1826; *The Cabinet* (Schenectady, NY), Aug. 30, 1826; *Vermont Gazette*, Sept. 5, 1826; *Berks and Schuylkill Journal* (Reading, PA), Sept. 2, 1826. *Baltimore Patriot*, Aug. 29, 1826; *Sentinel of Freedom* (Newark, NJ), Aug. 29, 1826; *American Traveler* (Boston), Sept. 1, 1826; *Baltimore Patriot*, Aug. 29, 1826; *Niles' Weekly Register*, Sept. 2, 1826, Sept. 9, 1826, Oct. 7, 1826.

41. "The Good People of Washington," *WNI*, Sept. 2, 1826. The history of the antiquated law is given in *Register*, 19 Cong., 2d sess., 559–60. See also George M. Stroud, *A Sketch of the Laws Relating to Slavery in the Several States of the United States of America* (Philadelphia: Kimber and Sharpless, 1827), 87–88.

42. Editorial, *WNI*, Sept. 2, 1826.

43. Editorial, *Richmond Enquirer*, Sept. 12, 1826.

44. Untitled, *WNI*, Sept. 1, 1826; "Case of Horton," Sept. 10, 1826, and "The Case of Horton," Sept. 28, 1826, *Commercial Advertiser*. The House report said Horton was arrested on July 22 and released on August 28, but it inexplicably also stated that his incarceration lasted twenty-six days. *Free Negroes—District of Columbia*, 5.

45. Editorial, *New York Daily Advertiser*, Sept. 6, 1826; "The Case of Horton," *Commercial Advertiser*, Sept. 10, 1826. *Niles' Weekly Register*, Oct. 7, 1826; *New-York Spectator*, Oct. 2, 1826; *The Cabinet* (Schenectady), Oct. 4, 1826; *Hampshire Gazette* (Northampton, MA), Oct. 4, 1826; *New York American*, Oct. 6, 1826; *Nantucket Inquirer*, Oct. 7, 1826; Untitled, *Genius of Universal Emancipation*, Oct. 24, 1826.

46. Editorial, *New York Daily Advertiser*, Sept. 6, 1826; Untitled, *New York American*, Sept. 15, 1826; "The Next Session of Congress," *Niles' Weekly Register*, Oct. 21, 1820. See also *New Hampshire Republican*, Sept. 19, 1826; "Case of Gilbert Horton," *Rhode-Island American*, Sept. 15, 1826.

47. Editorial, *WNI*, Sept. 2, 1826.
48. *Annals,* 16 Cong., 1 sess., 601. Strong of New York had acknowledged that "aliens, lunatics, vagabonds, and criminals" were not generally considered citizens. Ibid., 570. Novak, *People's Welfare,* 167–71; O'Brassill-Kulfan, *Vagrants and Vagabonds,* 62–71.
49. Editorial, *WNI,* Oct. 5, 1826.
50. *Register,* 19 Cong., 2d sess., 555–56. Ward named the privileges and immunities clause, the promise of a right to a jury trial, and the Fourth, Fifth, and Sixth Amendments. He did not say whether he thought the Constitution protected the same rights in the states, but his allusion to "absolute rights" suggests that he might have.
51. "An Act to prescribe the terms and conditions upon which free negroes and mulattoes may reside in the city of Washington, and for other purposes," April 14, 1821, Chap. 133, *Laws Passed by the Eighteenth Council of the City of Washington,* 109–12.
52. *Costin v. Corporation of Washington,* 6 F. Cas. 612, 613 (C.C.DC. 1821).
53. *Register,* 19 Cong., 2d sess., 556.
54. Richardson and Richardson, *Charles Miner,* 196; *Register,* 19 Cong., 2d sess., 557, 559–60, 558, 562.
55. *Register,* 19 Cong., 2d sess., 567, 562, 565–66, 568.
56. *Register,* 19 Cong., 2d sess., 566. The *Register* did not provide the vote total but stated that Ward's resolution carried "by a large majority." William Jay to Aaron Ward, Jan. 9, 1827, Aaron Ward Papers, BPL; Jay to James Fenimore Cooper, Jan. 5, 1827, in James Fenimore Cooper, ed., *Correspondence of James Fenimore-Cooper,* 2 vols. (New Haven, CT: Yale University Press, 1922), I, 114; Tuckerman, *William Jay,* 33.
57. *Free Negroes—District of Columbia,* 1, 2–3, 4; *Register,* 19 Cong., 2d sess., 562.
58. *Free Negroes—District of Columbia,* 5.
59. *Register,* 19 Cong., 2d sess., 654; *HJ,* 19 Cong., 2d sess., Feb. 1, 1827, 228; *Representation and Resolution of the Mayor and Council of Georgetown, in the District of Columbia,* 19 Cong., 2d sess., House Doc. 71, 4–5. "An Act Concerning Free Negroes, Mulattoes, and Slaves," May 31, 1827, *Laws of the Corporation of the City of Washington, Passed by the Twenty-Fourth Council* (Washington, DC: Way & Gideon, 1827); "City of Washington," *Freedom's Journal,* Nov. 16, 1827.
60. "Speech of a Colored Brother," *Liberator,* Oct. 13, 1837; Hinks, *To Awaken,* 102; Harris, *In the Shadow of Slavery,* 140–41; Polgar, *Standard-Bearers,* 250–53, 302–3.
61. David E. Swift, "Black Presbyterian Attacks on Racism: Samuel Cornish, Theodore Wright and Their Contemporaries," *Journal of Presbyterian History* 51, no. 4 (Winter 1973): 435. David E. Swift, *Black Prophets of Justice: Activist Clergy before the Civil War* (Baton Rouge: Louisiana State University Press, 1989), 19–46; Hinks, *To Awaken,* 101–2; Jones, *Birthright Citizens,* 18–19, 22–23; Bonner, *Remaking the Republic,* 11–33.
62. Untitled, *Freedom's Journal,* Feb. 28, 1828; "Address Delivered before the

General Colored Association at Boston, by David Walker," *Freedom's Journal,*
Dec. 19, 1828; "Speech of a Colored Brother"; William B. Davidson to Ralph
Gurley, Feb. 6, 1827, ACS Papers, MDLC, access via Fold3; Hinks, *To Awaken,*
70, 75, 105.

63. "City of Washington," *Freedom's Journal,* Nov. 16, 1827.

64. "Circular from the Corresponding Committee of the Manumission Society of
New York," *Genius of Universal Emancipation,* March 15, 1828; *Speech of Mr.
Miner, of Pennsylvania, Delivered in the House of Representatives, on Tuesday and
Wednesday, January 6 and 7, 1829* (Washington, DC: Gales & Seaton, 1829);
Slavery—Dist. of Columbia, 20 Cong., 2d sess., House Rept. 60; "District of
Columbia," *Genius of Universal Emancipation,* Jan. 3, 1829; Newman, *Transfor-
mation,* 51–53; Mary Tremain, *Slavery in the District of Columbia: The Policy of
Congress and the Struggle for Abolition* (New York: G. P. Putnam, 1892), 61–69.

CHAPTER 3: "THE SACRED DOCTRINE OF EQUAL RIGHTS"

1. *Proceedings of the Ohio Anti-Slavery Convention, Held at Putnam, on the Twenty-
Second, Twenty-Third, and Twenty-Fourth of April, 1835* (n.p.: Beaumont and
Wallace, 1835), 34; Nikki M. Taylor, *Frontiers of Freedom: Cincinnati's Black
Community, 1802-1868* (Athens: Ohio University Press, 2005), 37–48, 51;
Wade, "The Negro in Cincinnati," 44–46; Bridget Ford, *Bonds of Union: Reli-
gion, Race, and Politics in a Civil War Borderland* (Chapel Hill: University of
North Carolina Press, 2016), 10, 93.

2. Wade, "Negro in Cincinnati," 49–50; Taylor, *Frontiers of Freedom,* 51–57.

3. "From the Cincinnati Centinel [*sic*] of Aug. 20," *Rights of All,* Sept. 18, 1829;
"Colored People in Ohio," *Ohio State Journal,* July 16, 1829. Taylor, *Frontiers of
Freedom,* 50–65; Wade, "Negro in Cincinnati," 50–56. On African Americans'
alliances with the British Empire, see Van Gosse, " 'As a Nation, the English Are
Our Friends': The Emergence of African American Politics in the British Atlantic
World 1772-1861," *American Historical Review* 113, no. 4 (Oct. 2008): 1003–28.

4. "Two Important Inquiries," *Rights of All,* Sept. 18, 1829.

5. *Constitution of the American Society of Free Persons of Colour, for improving their
condition in the United States; for purchasing lands; and for the establishment of
a settlement in upper Canada, also, The Proceedings of the Convention with their
Address to Free Persons of Colour in the United States* (Philadelphia: J. W. Allen,
1831), 9–10.

6. Historians have long understood the significance of petitioning for radical abolitionism, but they have largely focused on petitions to the US Congress and
southerners' efforts to ignore and silence them. For women and petitioning, see,
for example, Susan Zaeske, *Signatures of Citizenship: Petitioning, Antislavery,
& Women's Political Identity* (Chapel Hill: University of North Carolina Press,
2003); and Beth A. Salerno, *Sister Societies: Women's Antislavery Organizations
in Antebellum America* (DeKalb: Northern Illinois University Press, 2005), 63–
68. For African Americans as petitioners, see, for example, Wood, "A 'class of

Citizens,'" and Sarah L. H. Gronningsater, "Practicing Formal Politics Without the Vote: Black New Yorkers in the Aftermath of 1821," in Van Gosse and David Waldstreicher, eds., *Revolutions and Reconstructions: Black Politics in the Long Nineteenth Century* (Philadelphia: University of Pennsylvania Press, 2020).

7. "An Act to Establish a Fund for the Support of Common Schools," March 10, 1831 (emphasis added), and "An Act for the Relief of the Poor," March 14, 1831, in *Acts of the Twenty-Ninth General Assembly of the State of Ohio* (Columbus: Olmsted & Bailhache, 1831). For uprisings of whites in small Ohio towns, see *History of Lower Scioto Valley, Ohio* (Chicago: Inter-State Publishing, 1884), 736 (town of Waverly); Feight, "'Black Friday'"; Abdy, *Journal of a Residence*, III, 38–39, 48–49.

8. *Journal of the House of Representatives of the State of Ohio*, 30th General Assembly, 1831–32 (Columbus, OH: David Smith, 1831), 10–11. Legislative sessions opened in December and mostly met in the first few months of the following year. Berlin, *Slaves Without Masters*, 188–89, 202–3; Wolf, *Race and Liberty*, 202–6, 229–33.

9. *House Journal*, 30th Gen. Assem., 1831-32, 232, 235. Burgoyne later aligned with the Whigs and was a close ally of William Henry Harrison. S. B. Nelson, *History of Cincinnati and Hamilton County, Ohio* (Cincinnati, OH: S. B. Nelson, 1894), 560.

10. *House Journal*, 30th Gen. Assem., 1831-32, 233.

11. *House Journal*, 30th Gen. Assem., 1831-32, 234–35.

12. *Journal of the Senate of the State of Ohio*, 30th General Assembly, 1831–32 (Columbus, OH: David Smith, 1831), 402–3. B. F. Morris, ed. *The Life of Senator Thomas Morris: Pioneer and Long a Legislator of Ohio, and U.S. Senator from 1833 to 1839* (Cincinnati: Moore, Wilstach, Keys & Overend, 1856), 55. For Worthington, *Eleventh Annual Report of the American Society for Colonizing the Free People of Color of the United States* (Washington, DC: James C. Dunn, 1828), 113. On Morris as an antislavery Democrat and his significance for the development of political antislavery, see Sean Wilentz, "Slavery, Antislavery, and Jacksonian Democracy," in Melvyn Stokes and Stephen Conway, eds., *The Market Revolution in America: Social, Political, and Religious Expressions, 1800–1880* (Charlottesville: University Press of Virginia, 1996); Jonathan H. Earle, *Jacksonian Antislavery & the Politics of Free Soil, 1824–1854* (Chapel Hill: University of North Carolina Press, 2004), 37–48.

13. Katz in Garrison, *Thoughts on African Colonization*, part II, 5. Sinha, *Slave's Cause*, 214–27; Mary Hershberger, "Mobilizing Women, Anticipating Abolitionism: The Struggle against Indian Removal in the 1830s," *Journal of American History* 86, no. 1 (June 1999): 15–40.

14. *Constitution of the New-England Anti-Slavery Society* (Boston: Garrison and Knapp, 1832), 3. The New England Anti-Slavery Society also promised to "improve the character and condition of the free people of color . . . and to obtain for them equal civil and political rights and privileges with the whites"

(4). Elisha Whittelsey to John W. Taylor, Sept. 16, 1833, John W. Taylor Papers, box 3, New-York Historical Society, New York. James Brewer Stewart, *Joshua R. Giddings and the Tactics of Radical Politics* (Cleveland: Press of Case Western Reserve University, 1970), 27–33; Chris Padgett, "Evangelicals Divided: Abolition and the Plan of Union's Demise in Ohio's Western Reserve," in John R. McKivigan and Mitchell Snay, eds., *Religion and the Antebellum Debate over Slavery* (Athens: University of Georgia Press, 1998).

15. *Weld-Grimké*, I, xvii, 132–33. *Proceedings of the Ohio Anti-Slavery Convention*, 21–22; Taylor, *Frontiers of Freedom*, 46–49; J. Brent Morris, *Oberlin, Hotbed of Abolitionism: College, Community, and the Fight for Freedom and Equality in Antebellum America* (Chapel Hill: University of North Carolina Press, 2014), 27–35; Kabria Baumgartner, "Building the Future: White Women, Black Education, and Civic Inclusion in Antebellum Ohio," *Journal of the Early Republic* 37 (Spring 2017): 117–45.

16. Sister to Wright, Feb. 3, 1835, Elizur Wright Papers, MDLC; *Weld-Grimké*, I, 273. *A Statement of the Reasons which Induced the Students of Lane Seminary to Dissolve Their Connection with That Institution* (Cincinnati, 1834), 24–26. Gilbert Hobbs Barnes, *The Anti-Slavery Impulse, 1830–1844* (New York: D. Appleton, 1933), 70–71.

17. *Weld-Grimké*, I, 163; *Letters of James Gillespie Birney, 1831–1857*, ed. Dwight L. Dumond, 2 vols. (New York: D. Appleton, 1938), I, 128. Barnes, *Anti-Slavery Impulse*, 69–70; Betty Fladeland, *James Gillespie Birney: Slaveholder to Abolitionist* (Ithaca, NY: Cornell University Press, 1955), 80–89.

18. Barnes, *Anti-Slavery Impulse*, 77, 81–84; Fladeland, *James Gillespie Birney*, 125–36.

19. *Proceedings of the Ohio Anti-Slavery Convention*, 8 (emphasis in the original). Birney, *James G. Birney*, 432–34; Eslinger, "The Evolution of Racial Politics," 94–95.

20. *Proceedings of the Ohio Anti-Slavery Convention*, 21–22.

21. *Proceedings of the Ohio Anti-Slavery Convention*, 34. Modern historians have often criticized such language as patronizing, but it is worth noting that African American activists often adopted similar language and also that because people so often used poor-law language to justify antiblack measures, these arguments for Black self-sufficiency and industriousness had significant legal and political resonance.

22. *Proceedings of the Ohio Anti-Slavery Convention*, 13, 14, 15. Other appeals to ministers struck similar notes. See John Rankin, "An Address to the Churches on Prejudice against People of Color," in *Report of the Third Anniversary of the Ohio Anti-Slavery Society, Held in Granville, Licking County, Ohio, on the 30th of May, 1838* (Cincinnati: Samuel A. Alley, 1838).

23. *Proceedings of the Ohio Anti-Slavery Convention*, 36–37.

24. *Proceedings of the Ohio Anti-Slavery Convention*, 37–38.

25. The literature describing the second party system is extensive. See, for example,

Howe, *What Hath God Wrought*; Sean Wilentz, *The Rise of American Democracy* (New York: W. W. Norton, 2005).

26. John Hutchins, "The Underground Railroad," *Magazine of Western History* 5 (Nov. 1886–April 1887): 680–82; *Proceedings of the Ohio Anti-Slavery Convention*; Samuel A. Lane, *Fifty Years and Over of Akron and Summit County* (Akron, OH: Beacon, 1892), 557.

27. This analysis is particularly indebted to Maggie McKinley, "Petitioning and the Making of the Administrative State," *Yale Law Journal* 127 (2018): 1560–62. See also Gregory A. Mark, "The Vestigial Constitution: The History and Significance of the Right to Petition," *Fordham Law Review* 66 (1998): 2153–2231; Daniel Carpenter and Colin D. Moore, "When Canvassers Became Activists: Antislavery Petitioning and the Political Mobilization of American Women," *American Political Science Review* 108, no. 3 (August 2014): 479–98.

28. *Journal of the House of Representatives of the State of Ohio*, 33rd General Assembly, 1834-35 (Columbus, OH: James M. Gardiner, 1834), 435, 791–92; *Proceedings of the Ohio Anti-Slavery Convention*, 40; *Journal of the House of Representatives of the State of Ohio*, 35th General Assembly, 1836–37 (Columbus, OH: James B. Gardiner, 1836), 696.

29. "Refuge of Oppression. Black Laws of Ohio," *Liberator*, April 4, 1835.

30. A. G. Riddle, "Rise of the Antislavery Sentiment on the Western Reserve," *Magazine of Western History* 6, no. 2 (June 1887): 154; David Smith, *Biography of Rev. David Smith of the A.M.E. Church* (Xenia, OH, 1881), 74, *Documenting the American South*, University Library, University of North Carolina at Chapel Hill, 1999, https://docsouth.unc.edu/neh/dsmith/dsmith.html; *Memorial of the Ohio Anti-Slavery Society, to the General Assembly of the State of Ohio* (Cincinnati: Pugh & Dodd, 1838), 4–26.

31. *Weld-Grimké*, I, 271. Abdy, *Journal of a Residence*, 3, 89–90.

32. *Weld-Grimké*, I, 271–72.

33. *Weld-Grimké*, I, 273–74.

34. Smith, *Biography of Rev. David Smith*, 69–73; Daniel A. Payne, *History of the African Methodist Episcopal Church* (Nashville, TN: A.M.E. Sunday School Union, 1891), 98; "Chillicothe Anti-Slavery Society," *Scioto Gazette*, Aug. 6, 1834. Keith P. Griffler, *Front Line of Freedom: African Americans and the Forging of the Underground Railroad in the Ohio Valley* (Lexington: University Press of Kentucky, 2004), 38–51; Taylor, *Frontiers of Freedom*, 111–13; Stephen Middleton, *Ohio and the Antislavery Activities of Attorney Salmon Portland Chase, 1830–1849* (New York: Garland, 1990), 54–57.

35. Malvin, *North Into Freedom*, 9, 56–57; Richard Albert Folk, "Black Man's Burden in Ohio, 1849–1863" (PhD diss., University of Toledo, 1973), 63–65.

36. *Minutes of the Fifth Annual Convention for the Improvement of the Free People of Colour in the United States; Held by Adjournments, in the Wesley Church, Philadelphia; from the first to the fifth of June, inclusive* (Philadelphia: William P. Gibbons, 1835), 2. "Meeting of the Colored People—Petitions to Legislature,"

Philanthropist, Jan. 20, 1837. Malvin, *North Into Freedom,* 42–44, 65. Garrison encouraged free African Americans to petition as well. "To the Free Colored Population of the U.S.–No. II," *Liberator,* Feb. 5, 1831. Malvin was also involved when, in December 1838, Black activists convened in Cleveland to condemn the American Colonization Society and called on African Americans nationwide to form societies and take action in their own interests. "Resolutions of the People of Color of Cleveland, on the Subject of African Colonization," *Colored American,* March 2, 1839.

37. "Meeting of the Colored People—Petitions to Legislature," *Philanthropist,* Jan. 20, 1837; Malvin, *North Into Freedom,* 65. Clark was a Delaware native. For his background, see Martin Delany, *Official Report of Niger Valley Exploring Party* (New York: Thomas Hamilton, 1861), 31; Smith, *Biography of Rev. David Smith,* 75; *BAP,* vol. 1, *The British Isles, 1830–1865,* 140–41n4. Some of Clark's notes on Black communities are published in *Memorial of the Ohio Anti-Slavery Society,* 18–19.

38. "The Laws of Ohio," *Colored American,* July 22, 1837. *House Journal,* 1836–37, 695–96; "Letter from Columbus," *Philanthropist,* Jan. 30, 1838.

39. "Convention of Colored People," *Philanthropist,* Oct. 17, 1837. For a preliminary report, see "Convention of Colored People of Ohio," *Philanthropist,* Sept. 8, 1837 (excerpted from *Ohio Political Register*). "The Laws of Ohio," *Colored American,* July 22, 1837.

40. "Convention of Colored People," *Philanthropist,* Oct. 17, 1837.

41. Zaeske, *Signatures of Citizenship,* 71–72; Nicholas Wood, " 'A Sacrifice on the Altar of Slavery': Doughface Politics and Black Disenfranchisement in Pennsylvania, 1837–1838," *Journal of the Early Republic* 31 (Spring 2011): 87–89.

42. "Interesting Intelligence," *Philanthropist,* Jan. 23, 1838. *Journal of the Senate of the State of Ohio,* 36th General Assembly, 1837-38 (Columbus, OH: Samuel Medary, 1837–38), 246.

43. "Letter from Columbus," *Philanthropist,* Jan. 30, 1838. "The merits of the petition are not now open for discussion," the future Republican congressman Wade told the House, "and, sir, the *right* of petition I scorn to debate." He threatened that the people were entitled to rise up if their petition was not appropriately dealt with: "The people have the right, and if needs be, they will enforce it at the point of the bayonet." For context, see Frederick J. Blue, "The Plight of Slavery Will Cover the Land: Benjamin and Edward Wade, Brothers in Antislavery Politics," in Blue, *No Taint of Compromise: Crusaders in Antislavery Politics* (Baton Rouge: Louisiana State University Press, 2005).

44. *Senate Journal,* 36th Gen. Assem., 1837–38, 246. "Letter from Columbus."

45. "Letter from Columbus." Smith made a similar argument the next year. "Senate of the State of Ohio," *Philanthropist,* Feb. 5, 1839.

46. *Senate Journal,* 36th Gen. Assem., 1837-38, 563.

47. *Senate Journal,* 36th Gen. Assem., 1837-38, 566, 586.

48. *House Journal,* 36th Gen. Assem., 1837-38, 434–37; *Report of the Third*

Anniversary, 17–18; "Dying Away." King's report was published as *Report of the Select Committee of the Senate, on the Petitions of Sundry Citizens, Praying the Repeal of Certain Laws Restricting the Rights of Persons of Color* [n.p., n.d.].

49. *Report of the Third Anniversary,* 8, 16–19; "Dying Away," *Philanthropist,* March 27, 1838. That session, abolitionist petitions also generated debates or reports concerning rejecting the annexation of Texas, ending the congressional gag rule, asserting Congress's power to abolish slavery in the District of Columbia, advocating jury trials for fugitive slaves, reclaiming Eliza S. Johnson from slavery in Kentucky, and passing laws making towns and citizens liable for damage by mobs. The society noted that in the state Senate, petitions were mostly referred to select committees, while in the House this "courtesy" was generally denied. *Report of the Third Anniversary,* 16.

50. *Report of the Third Anniversary,* 5.

51. Vernon L. Volpe, "The Ohio Election of 1838: A Study in the Historical Method?" *Ohio History* 95 (Winter/Spring 1985): 85–100; Earle, *Jacksonian Antislavery,* 149–50; Stanley Harrold, *Gamaliel Bailey and Antislavery Union* (Kent, OH: Kent State University Press, 1986), 28–31. For the broader debate among abolitionists, see chapter 5.

52. Gamaliel Bailey to Birney, Oct. 28, 1838, in *Birney Letters,* I, 473. "The Fall Elections," *Philanthropist,* July 23, 1839; "Legislative," *Cleveland Daily Herald and Gazette,* Jan. 21, 1839; "Senate of the State of Ohio," *Philanthropist,* Feb. 5, 1839.

53. C. B. Galbreath, "Ohio's Fugitive Slave Law," *Ohio Archaeological and Historical Quarterly* 34 (April 1925): 227–29; Diemer, *Politics of Black Citizenship,* 57–60; William R. Leslie, "The Pennsylvania Fugitive Slave Act of 1826," *Journal of Southern History* 18, no. 4 (Nov. 1952): 435–39.

54. "Ohio Legislature," *Emancipator,* Feb. 7, 1839; "An Act Relating to Fugitives from Labor or Service in Other States," Feb. 26, 1839, in J. R. Swan, ed., *Statutes of the State of Ohio, of a General Nature, in Force December 7, 1840* (Columbus, OH: Samuel Medary, 1841), 595–600. Hyun Hur, "Radical Antislavery and Personal Liberty Laws in Antebellum Ohio, 1803–1857" (PhD diss., University of Wisconsin–Madison, 2012), 102–16.

55. Elliott Cresson to Rev. R. R. Gurley, Aug. 3, 1829, ACS Papers, MDLC. "Colonization Meetings," *African Repository, and Colonial Journal,* May 1839, 130; "Report from Mr. Gurley," ibid., March 1839, 65; "Mr. Gurley in Ohio," ibid., 129; "The Colonization Debate," *Philanthropist,* March 12, 1839. For growing strength of antiabolitionism in Ohio starting in 1839, in part a response to abolitionist successes, see Volpe, "Ohio Election of 1838," 100.

56. James Brewer Stewart, *Joshua R. Giddings* (Cleveland, OH: Press of Case Western Reserve University, 1970), 16, 29–31; George W. Julian, *The Life of Joshua R. Giddings* (Chicago: A. C. McClurg, 1892), 44–45, 52; A. G. Riddle, Unpublished memoir, 92–93, 98–99, box 2, A. G. Riddle Papers, Western Reserve Historical Society.

57. Morris, ed., *Life of Senator Morris,* quotation on 129. See also ibid., 117, 119, 121.

CG, 25 Cong. 3d sess., 104; "Senator Morris's Speech," *Colored American*, March 2, 1839; "Speech of Mr. Morris," *The Emancipator*, March 7, 1839. For Morris's response to Clay and sources of the Slave Power concept, see Earle, *Jacksonian Antislavery*, 46–47; Harrold, *Gamaliel Bailey*, 29–30. For the broader context: Wood, "Sacrifice on the Altar of Slavery"; William G. Shade, " 'The Most Delicate and Exciting Topics': Van Buren, Slavery, and the Election of 1836," *Journal of the Early Republic* 18, no. 3 (Autumn 1998): 459–84.

58. *Journal of the House of Representatives of the State of Michigan, 1838* (Detroit: John S. Bagg, 1838), 120; Augustus Seymour Porter to Jacob Howard, Jan. 4, 184[1], Jacob Merritt Howard Papers, box 1, Burton Historical Collection, Detroit Public Library. Elsa Holderried, "Public Life of Jacob Merritt Howard" (master's thesis, Wayne University, 1950), 28–29; Hamilton Gay Howard, *Civil-War Echoes: Character Sketches and State Secrets by a United States Senator's Son and Secretary* (Washington, DC: Howard Publishing Co., 1907), 270. Arthur Raymond Kooker, "The Antislavery Movement in Michigan, 1796–1840: A Study in Humanitarianism on an American Frontier" (PhD diss., University of Michigan, 1941), 59–61; Roy Finkenbine, "A Beacon of Liberty on the Great Lakes," in Paul Finkelman and Martin J. Hershock, eds., *The History of Michigan Law* (Athens: Ohio University Press, 2006), 85. Many of the antiblack laws of the Old Northwest are excerpted in Middleton, *Black Laws in the Old Northwest*. For protests in Indiana and Illinois, see Thomas D. Hamm et al., " 'A Great and Good People': Midwestern Quakers and the Struggle against Slavery," *Indiana Magazine of History* 100 (March 2004): 8–9; Merton L. Dillon, "The Anti-Slavery Movement in Illinois, 1809–1844" (PhD diss., University of Michigan, 1951), 294–96.

59. "Speech of a Colored Brother," *Liberator,* Oct. 13, 1837; Samuel Cornish to William Jay, Nov. 3, 1838, box 7, JJP; Swift, "Black Presbyterian Attacks on Racism," 433–70.

60. Jay to Gerrit Smith [draft], Oct. 1, 1839, box 38; Gerrit Smith to William Jay, Oct. 9, 1839, box 50, JJP; "The General Theological Seminary of the Protestant Episcopal Church in the U.S.," *Colored American,* Sept. 7, 1839. William Jay, *A View of the Action of the Federal Government, in Behalf of Slavery* (New York: J. S. Taylor, 1839), 34.

61. Birney to Tappan, June 3, 1839, in *Birney Letters,* I, 491; "Home Department," *Colored American,* Sept. 28, 1839. For Jay reading and subscribing to the *Philanthropist,* see William Jay to Ellis Gray Loring, March 5, 1838, box 38; William Jay to Gamaliel Bailey, Sept. 1, 1838, box 38; William Jay to Gamaliel Bailey, Sept. 29, 1838, box 38; Gamaliel Bailey to Wm. Jay, Cincinnati, Sept. 10, 1838, box 2, JJP.

62. "On the Condition of the Free People of Color in the United States," *Anti-Slavery Examiner*, no. 13 (New York: American Anti-Slavery Society, 1839), 12. Jay also lamented that Black northerners were frequently denied access to education, including religious instruction. The pamphlet was first published by the

American Anti-Slavery Society and then reprinted in a compendium of Jay's work. William Jay, *Miscellaneous Writings on Slavery* (Boston: John P. Jewett & Co., 1853). The citations here correspond to the original pamphlet.

63. Jay, "On the Condition," 7.

64. "A New Pamphlet," *Philanthropist*, Dec. 10, 1839. William Jay to the Exec. Committee of the American Anti-Slavery Society, Nov. 27, 1839, and William Jay to Thomas Pyne, Dec. 10, 1839, box 38, JJP. "Condition of the Free People of Color," *Emancipator*, Dec. 26, 1839; "A New Pamphlet," *Philanthropist*, Dec. 10, 1839.

65. *Slave Code of the State of Illinois* (Chicago: Will County Anti-Slavery Society, 1840), 11.

66. Wood, "Sacrifice on the Altar of Slavery"; Diemer, *Politics of Black Citizenship*, 96–101.

CHAPTER 4: "THE RIGHTS OF THE CITIZENS OF MASSACHUSETTS"

1. David L. Child, *The Despotism of Freedom; or the Tyranny and Cruelty of the American Republican Slave-Masters, Shown to be the Worst in the World, in a Speech, Delivered at the First Anniversary of the New England Anti-Slavery Society, 1833* (Boston: Young Men's Anti-Slavery Association, 1833), 70.

2. Child, *Despotism of Freedom*, 70.

3. By one estimate, some 10,000 free African Americans were jailed under the Negro Seamen Laws of the southern states from the 1820s to the Civil War. W. Jeffrey Bolster, *Black Jacks: African American Seamen in the Age of Sail* (Cambridge: Harvard University Press, 1997), 206. Another historian estimates more than 20,000. Michael A. Schoeppner, *Moral Contagion: Black Atlantic Sailors, Citizenship, and Diplomacy in Antebellum America* (New York: Cambridge University Press, 2018), 228. See also Philip M. Hamer, "Great Britain, the United States, and the Negro Seamen Acts, 1822–1848," *Journal of Southern History* 1, no. 1 (Feb. 1935): 3–28; Hamer, "British Consuls and the Negro Seamen Acts, 1850-1860," *Journal of Southern History* 1, no. 2 (May 1935): 138–68; Neuman, "Lost Century of American Immigration Law"; Wiecek, *Sources of Anti-Slavery Constitutionalism*, 130–40; Edlie L. Wong, *Neither Fugitive nor Free: Atlantic Slavery, Freedom Suits, and the Legal Culture of Travel* (New York: New York University Press, 2009), 183–239.

4. Bolster, *Black Jacks*, 191–95; Schoeppner, *Moral Contagion*, 20–24; Scott, *Common Wind*.

5. *Several Late Acts of the Legislature of the State of South-Carolina, Passed at the Session in December, 1822* (Charleston, SC: A. E. Miller, 1823), 4, in HR17A-F7.2, Records of the US House of Representatives, Record Group 233, NARA (hereafter, RG233).

6. "Free People of Color: Memorial of Sundry Masters of American Vessels Lying in the Port of Charleston, S.C.," *Niles' Register*, March 15, 1823, 31–32. The original petition is located in HR17A-F7.2, RG233.

7. Nathan Perl-Rosenthal, *Citizen Sailors: Becoming American in the Age of Revolution* (Cambridge: Harvard University Press, 2015), 177–90, 224–25; Martha S. Putney, *Black Sailors: Afro-American Merchant Seamen and Whalemen Prior to the Civil War* (New York: Greenwood Press, 1987), 11–41.

8. HRep. 80, 27–34.

9. US Constitution, Article I, Section 8; *Gibbons v. Ogden*, 22 U.S. 1, 203 (1824); *New York v. Miln*, 36 U.S. 102, 114–115 (1837).

10. B. F. H., "To the Editors of the *Charleston Courier*," pub'd in *Charleston Mercury*, Nov. 21, 1843.

11. *Elkison v. Deliesseline*, 8 F. Cas. 493 (C.C.D.S.C. 1823); HRep. 80, 15; Marshall quoted in Charles Warren, *The Supreme Court in United States History*, 2 vols., rev. ed. (Boston: Little, Brown, 1932), II, 626. Since Elkison was British, Johnson did not take up the relevance of the US Constitution's privileges and immunities clause. Johnson was a Jefferson appointee and a native South Carolinian, but as a judge he consistently took nationalist positions. Warren, *Supreme Court*, II, 324–41, 624–26; Wiecek, *Sources of Anti-Slavery*, 133–38; Donald G. Morgan, *Justice William Johnson, The First Dissenter: The Career and Constitutional Philosophy of a Jeffersonian Judge* (Columbia: University of South Carolina Press, 1954), 192–202. See also Schoeppner, *Moral Contagion*, 14–63; William W. Freehling, *Prelude to Civil War: The Nullification Controversy in South Carolina, 1816–1836* (1965; New York: Harper Torchbooks, 1968), 97–116.

12. Herman V. Ames, *State Documents on Federal Relations: The States and the United States*, V, *Slavery and the Constitution* (Philadelphia: University of Pennsylvania Department of History, 1904), 12–13; HRep. 80, 9, 35–36. See also Herman V. Ames, *The Proposed Amendments to the Constitution of the United States during the First Century of Its History* (Washington, DC: Government Printing Office, 1897), 210, 339.

13. HRep. 80, 49, 54–55 (emphasis in original). See also Wiecek, *Sources of Anti-Slavery Constitutionalism*, 138; Warren, *Supreme Court*, II, 627. Taney succeeded Berrien as attorney general and drafted his own opinion on the controversial South Carolina law. The opinion was never published, but it rehearsed many of the arguments Taney later made in his *Dred Scott* decision. See Carl Brent Swisher, "Mr. Chief Justice Taney," in Allison Dunham and Philip B. Kurland, eds., *Mr. Justice* (Chicago: University of Chicago Press, 1956), 210–14; Schoeppner, *Moral Contagion*, 84–90.

14. Novak, *People's Welfare*; Kyle G. Volk, *Moral Minorities and the Making of American Democracy* (New York: Oxford University Press, 2014); Masur, "State Sovereignty and Migration."

15. Hinks, *To Awaken*, 76n33, 78, 92–93, 147–49; William Cooper Nell, *The Colored Patriots of the American Revolution, with Sketches of Several Distinguished Colored Persons: To Which Is Added a Brief Survey of the Condition and Prospects of Colored Americans* (Boston: Robert F. Wallcut, 1855), 232, Documenting the

American South. Oliver Johnson, *William Lloyd Garrison and His Times* (Boston: B. B. Russell, 1880), 71–72.

16. Nell, *Colored Patriots,* 344, 346; *Report on the Deliverance of Citizens, Liable To Be Held as Slaves,* Mass. House No. 38, March 1839, 12–13; Jones, *Birthright Citizens,* 37–39; Sinha, *Slave's Cause,* 215.

17. Carolyn L. Karcher, *The First Woman in the Republic: A Cultural Biography of Lydia Maria Child* (Durham, NC: Duke University Press, 1994), 48–49, 81, 181–82, 187.

18. Child, *Despotism of Freedom,* 54–55, 59 (italics in the original).

19. Child, *Despotism of Freedom,* 69. For Roberts's family, see George R. Price and James Brewer Stewart, "The Roberts Case, the Easton Family, and the Dynamics of the Abolitionist Movement in Massachusetts, 1776–1870," *Massachusetts Historical Review* 4 (2002): 105–6; Graham Russell Hodges, "Editor's Introduction," in Robert Roberts, *The House Servant's Directory,* 1827 (Reprint: Armonk, NY: M. E. Sharpe, 1998).

20. Louis Ruchames, ed., *The Letters of William Lloyd Garrison, vol. 2, A House Dividing Against Itself, 1836–1840* (Cambridge: Harvard University Press, 1971), 2; Leonard L. Richards, *"Gentlemen of Property and Standing": Anti-Abolition Mobs in Jacksonian America* (New York: Oxford University Press, 1970), 47–81; David Grimsted, *American Mobbing, 1828–1861* (New York: Oxford University Press, 1998), 3–32; Matthew Mason, *Apostle of Union: A Political Biography of Edward Everett* (Chapel Hill: University of North Carolina Press, 2016), 94–106; Sinha, *Slave's Cause,* 233–39.

21. Petition of Joseph Southwick and Henry C. Benson, and accompanying materials, March 9, 1836, Senate Unpassed 1836, Docket 9865, MSA; *Letters of William Lloyd Garrison, vol. 2,* 56; *William Lloyd Garrison: The Story of His Life, Told By His Children,* 4 vols. (New York: The Century Co., 1885), I, 494–522; II, 1–72; Richards, *Gentlemen of Property and Standing,* 58–59; Salerno, *Sister Societies,* 42–45.

22. James Creighton Odiorne, *Genealogy of the Odiorne Family, with Notices of Other Families Connected Therewith* (Boston: Rand, Avery, & Co., 1875), 75–80; Petition of George Odiorne and twelve others, March [n.d.], 1836, Senate Unpassed 1836, Docket 9863, MSA.

23. Petition of George Odiorne and twelve others.

24. Petition of George Odiorne and twelve others.

25. Summaries of the testimony were provided in the minority report, dated April 12, 1836, which was published as "Report on the Petition of George Odiorne and Others, Relative to Certain Laws of Several of the Southern States," *Liberator,* April 23, 1836.

26. "Report on the Petition of George Odiorne and Others."

27. "Report on the Petition of George Odiorne and Others."

28. For conflicts over slaveholders' rights when traveling in free states, see Finkelman, *Imperfect Union.*

29. "Report on the Petition of George Odiorne and Others."

30. *Report on the Petition of George Odiorne and Others, Relative to Certain Laws of Several of the Southern States,* Mass. Senate No. 90, 1836 (emphasis in the original); *Case of the Slave-Child, Med. Report of the Arguments of Counsel and of the Opinion of the Court, in the Case of Commonwealth vs. Aves* (Boston: Isaac Knapp, 1836), 15.

31. "The Domestic Slave Trade," *Colored American,* Nov. 25, 1837; Lydia Maria Child, *An Appeal in Favor of that Class of Americans Called Africans,* intro. by Carolyn L. Karcher (Amherst: University of Massachusetts Press, 1996), 64.

32. *Report on the Deliverance of Citizens,* 21.

33. *Report on the Deliverance of Citizens,* 20–21.

34. Child, *The Despotism of Freedom,* 59; *Report on the Deliverance of Citizens,* 12–13.

35. Ellis Gray Loring to Mayor of New Orleans, Boston, July 27, 1840, Letterpress book, 1837 to 1841, Ellis Gray Loring Papers, MS Am 1554, Houghton Library, Harvard University. Loring referred the mayor, whose name he did not seem to know, to someone living in the city who would attest to Loring's "personal standing & character" so the mayor would know the request was serious.

36. "An Act to prevent free persons of colour from entering into this State, and for other purposes," March 16, 1830, *Acts Passed at the Second Session of the Ninth Legislature of the State of Louisiana* (Donaldsonville, LA: C. W. Duhy, 1830), 90–94; "An Act More Effectually to Prevent Free Persons of Color from Entering into This State, and For Other Purposes," March 16, 1842, *Acts Passed at the Second Session of the Fifteenth Legislature of the State of Louisiana* (New Orleans: J. C. De St. Romes, 1842), 308–18; [William Powell], "Colored Seamen— Their Character and Condition," *NASS,* Oct. 8, 1846; Loring to Mayor of New Orleans, July 27, 1840; "Kidnapped Freemen—High Handed Cruelty," *Colored American,* Jan. 2, 1841. "Hazard, Hon. Rowland Gibson, L.L.D.," *Biographical Cyclopedia of Representative Men of Rhode Island* (Providence: National Biographical Publishing Co., 1881), 269; *Report on the Deliverance of Citizens,* 18.

37. Jacob Barker, *Incidents in the life of Jacob Barker, of New Orleans, Louisiana, with historical facts, his financial transactions with the government, and his course on important political questions: from 1800 to 1855* (Washington, DC: n.p., 1855), 5–6, 219–20. Barker had supported DeWitt Clinton over Martin Van Buren in the 1810s. For whaling and communities of color on Nantucket, see Justin Andrew Pariseau, "Sea of Change: Race, Abolitionism, and Reform in the New England Whale Fishery" (PhD diss., College of William and Mary, 2015); Isabel Kaldenbach-Montemayor, "Absalom Boston and the Development of Nantucket's African-American Community," in Robert Johnson Jr., ed., *Nantucket's Free People of Color: Essays on History, Politics and Community* (Lanham, MD: University Press of America, 2006).

38. "Colored Freemen," [Letter of Jacob Barker], *Nantucket Inquirer,* Sept. 12, 1837.

39. "Colored Freemen." For merchants seeking lax enforcement of antiblack laws to encourage business, see Richard Tansey, "Out-of-State Free Blacks in Late Antebellum New Orleans," *Louisiana History* 22, no. 4 (Autumn 1981): 372.

40. "Colored Freemen"; Barker, *Incidents in the Life*, 221.

41. *Biographical Cyclopedia of Representative Men of Rhode Island*, 267–71. "Prisons of New Orleans," *NASS*, March 17, 1842. The *National Anti-Slavery Standard* published the grand jury report without mentioning Hazard and Barker.

42. *Biographical Cyclopedia of Representative Men of Rhode Island*, 270; W. H. Channing, *Memoir of William Ellery Channing*, 3 vols. (Boston: W. Crosby and H. P. Nichols, 1848), III, 240. Christy Clark-Pujara, "The Business of Slavery and Antislavery Sentiment: The Case of Rowland Gibson Hazard—An Antislavery 'Negro Cloth' Dealer," *Rhode Island History* 71, no. 2 (Summer/Fall 2013): 35–55.

43. Samuel T. Pickard, *Life and Letters of John Greenleaf Whittier*, 2 vols. (Boston: Houghton, Mifflin, 1899), I, 199–200, quotation on 199. Shade, "Most Delicate and Exciting Topics"; Mason, *Apostle of Union*, 106–7, 109; Morris, *Free Men All*, 73–79.

44. Bruce Laurie, *Beyond Garrison: Antislavery and Social Reform* (New York: Cambridge University Press, 2005), 108–10. For the long struggle against the antiblack militia law, see Kantrowitz, *More Than Freedom*, 2012.

45. [Frances Bradburn], *A Memorial of George Bradburn, By His Wife* (Boston: Cupples, Upham & Co, 1883), 4, 19–20, 93. Writing in the *Anti-Slavery Standard*, Lydia Maria Child praised Bradburn's "amusing style of speaking" and the "half-suppressed mirth that mantles all over his fine countenance." Ibid., 21. Pariseau, "Sea of Change," 137–41, 153–54. For Bradburn, see also Dictionary of Unitarian and Universalist Biography, http://uudb.org/articles/georgebradburn.html.

46. "Letter from the Editor," Boston, *Pennsylvania Freeman*, Feb. 14, 1839; "Massachusetts Legislature," *Boston Courier*, March 11, 1839; *Memorial of George Bradburn*, 5; *Report on the Deliverance of Citizens*, 12–13, 18, 25, 27, 30–31.

47. "Report on the Petition of George Odiorne and Others"; *Report on the Deliverance of Citizens*, 9, 32, 36.

48. *Corfield v. Coryell*, 6 F. Cas. 546, 552 (C.C.E.D. Pa. 1825); Joseph Story, *Commentaries on the Constitution of the United States: With a Preliminary Review of the Constitutional History of the Colonies and States, before the Adoption of the Constitution*, 3 vols. (Boston: Hilliard, Gray, 1833), III, 675.

49. *Corfield v. Coryell*, 552. Gerard N. Magliocca, "Rediscovering *Corfield v. Coryell*," *Notre Dame Law Review* 95, vol. 2 (2019), 712, 718–20.

50. James Kent, *Commentaries on American Law*, 4 vols. (New York: O. Halsted, 1826–27), II, 61–62. Kent, *Commentaries on American Law*, 4 vols., 3d ed. (New York: Clayton & Norden, 1836), II, 258, and, more generally, 70–71, 258–59. In 1833, Connecticut judge David Daggett drew on Kent to argue that free Black people were not citizens under the privileges and immunities clause and therefore had no right to enter Connecticut to attend school. The decision was associated with a school for African American girls established by white abolitionist Prudence Crandall. A lawyer in Pennsylvania wrote a pamphlet extending Daggett's argument, and Chief Justice John Marshall praised the pamphlet as "perfectly sound," saying he was pleased "that in the Northern and middle States, the

opinion of the intelligent on this delicate subject, on which the Slaveholding States are so sensitive, accords so entirely with that of the South." J. Marshall to John F. Denny, Oct. 24, 1834, in Charles F. Hobson, ed., *The Papers of John Marshall*, 12 vols. (Chapel Hill: University of North Carolina, 2006), XII, 427. Meanwhile, William Jay insisted that the Connecticut case was wrongly decided and that free African Americans were clearly citizens of the United States under the Constitution. William Jay, *An Inquiry into the Character and Tendency of the American Colonization, and American Anti-Slavery Societies* (New York: Leavitt, Lord, & Co., 1835), 40–44. In 1839, the Connecticut Supreme Court of Errors held that freedpeople were citizens of the state. Kettner, *Development of American Citizenship*, 316.

51. *Memorial of George Bradburn*, 5; "Massachusetts Legislature," *Boston Courier*, March 11, 1839.

52. *Memorial of George Bradburn*, 5–6; "Massachusetts Legislature"; "Resolves Concerning Certain Laws of Other States which Affect the Rights of Citizens of Massachusetts," Ch. 66, Approved April 8, 1839, MSA.

53. "Report on the Deliverance of Citizens Liable to be Held as Slaves," *Liberator*, March 29, 1839; "The Legislature of Massachusetts," *Emancipator*, April 4, 1839; "Important Resolutions," *Philanthropist*, May 7, 1839.

54. Unidentified newspaper, in *Memorial of George Bradburn*, 23; Samuel J. May to Francis Jackson, March 5, 1839, BPL; "George Bradburn," *Liberator*, May 10, 1839.

55. "More Kidnapping," [Letter of George Bradburn to Wm. Jno. Clarke, Oct. 1, 1839], *Boston Courier*, Oct. 3, 1839; *Memorial of George Bradburn*, 140–41.

56. Seward to Charles Marriott, Jan. 29, 1839, *WWS*, II, 590; "The Worcester Kidnappings," *Emancipator*, Oct. 10, 1839. Paul Finkelman, "The Protection of Black Rights in Seward's New York," *Civil War History* 34, no. 3 (Sept. 1988): 215. A week earlier, the New York legislature had passed a law requiring a jury trial for accused runaways from slavery. Ibid, 221.

57. Seward to Marriott.

CHAPTER 5: "SELF-PRESERVATION IS THE FIRST LAW OF NATURE"

1. G. Bailey to Giddings, Feb. 17, 1839, Giddings-Julian Papers, MDLC.

2. Carpenter and Moore, "When Canvassers Became Activists," 483.

3. Julian, *Life of Joshua R. Giddings*, 48, quotation on 110–11. More generally for Adams's attack on the gag rule and strategy for broadening the antislavery coalition, see Samuel Flagg Bemis, *John Quincy Adams and the Union* (New York: Knopf, 1956), esp. 416–31.

4. For the effectiveness of the "Slave Power" argument for generating northern support for political antislavery, see Corey M. Brooks, *Liberty Power: Antislavery Third Parties and the Transformation of American Politics* (Chicago: University of Chicago Press, 2016). See also Leonard L. Richards, *The Slave Power: The Free North and Southern Domination, 1780–1860* (Baton Rouge: Louisiana State University Press, 2000).

5. Joshua Giddings to Laura, Feb. 18, 1842, Joshua Giddings Papers, Microfilm, reel 1; Charles Francis Adams, ed., *Memoirs of John Quincy Adams, Comprising Portions of his Diary from 1795 to 1848*, 12 vols. (Philadelphia: J. B. Lippincott, 1874–77), XI, 61, 68. Stanley Harrold, *American Abolitionism: Its Direct Political Impact from Colonial Times into Reconstruction* (Charlottesville: University of Virginia Press, 2019), 74–89; James M. McPherson, "The Fight against the Gag Rule: Joshua Leavitt and Antislavery Insurgency in the Whig Party, 1839–1842," *Journal of Negro History* 40, no. 3 (July 1963): 187–94; Brooks, *Liberty Power,* 64–66; Barnes, *Anti-Slavery Impulse*, 178–83; Bemis, *John Quincy Adams*, 423–25; Eric Foner, *The Fiery Trial: Abraham Lincoln and American Slavery* (New York: W. W. Norton, 2010), 55–56.

6. *HJ*, 27 Cong., 2d sess., Jan. 21, 1842, 257–58; Giddings to Daughter, Feb. 8, 1842; Giddings to My Dear Girl, March 2, 1842, Giddings-Julian Papers, MDLC. Schoeppner, *Moral Contagion*, 107–22.

7. *HJ*, 27 Cong., 2d sess., Jan. 24, 1842, 272; Giddings in Julian, *Life of Joshua R. Giddings*, 110; Adams, *Memoirs*, XI, 75, 76. Brooks, *Liberty Power*, 66–67; Bemis, *John Quincy Adams,* 427–37; Barnes, *Anti-Slavery Impulse*, 184–87.

8. *HJ*, 27 Cong., 2d sess., Feb. 2, 1842, 298; Glass, "Citizens of the State," 905. Schoeppner, *Moral Contagion*, 66–75, 101,

9. "Petition of 220 colored seamen citizens of U. States for Protection in the ports . . . ," New York, Feb. 16, 1842, HR 27A-H1.8; Petition of Victor W. Barker and others, n.d., HR 27A-G4.10, RG233.

10. Petition of Daniel Pratt and other masters and owners of vessels, Jan. 23, 1842, HR 27A-H1.8; Petition of Francis F. Hussey and 48 others, Nantucket, ref'd Feb. 14, 1842, HR 27A-G4.10, RG233.

11. *Proceedings of the Ohio Anti-Slavery Convention*, 28; William H. Gibson, "Semi-Centennial of the Public Career of William H. Gibson, Sr.," in Gibson, *History of the United Brothers of Friendship and Sisters of the Mysterious Ten* (Louisville, KY: Bradley & Gilbert, 1897), 30.

12. Petition of Samuel Wiggins and 76 others, Feb. 11, 1843, HR 27A-H1.8, RG233; Chase to Lewis Tappan, Feb. 15, 1843, *SCP*, 2, 101. For context, see Thomas C. Buchanan, *Black Life on the Mississippi: Slaves, Free Blacks, and the Western Steamboat World* (Chapel Hill: University of North Carolina Press, 2004), esp. 23–25.

13. Adams, *Memoirs*, XI, 281. The Massachusetts Anti-Slavery Society identified the petitioners as "many of the principal merchants and other gentlemen of Boston." *Twelfth Annual Report presented to the Massachusetts Anti-Slavery Society, by its Board of Managers, February 24, 1844* (Boston: Oliver Johnson, 1844), 8. Schoeppner, *Moral Contagion*, 140.

14. HRep. 80, 7. Fragment in J. Ingersoll Bowditch Papers II, Ms.S-468, MHS. For Henry Bowditch, Kantrowitz, *More Than Freedom*, 77–83; Laurie, *Beyond Garrison*, 79.

15. *Memorial of George Bradburn*, 7; Robert C. Winthrop Jr., *A Memoir of Robert C. Winthrop* (Boston: Little, Brown, 1897), 19. Known as a "Cotton Whig,"

Winthrop opposed the Massachusetts antislavery political coalition led by Henry Wilson, and he supported the Mexican War. Yet Winthrop was evidently a principled (if paternalistic) supporter of racial equality before the law. Winthrop also helped end the state's ban on interracial marriage, and his son noted in his biography that between 1840 and 1860, Winthrop actively—if quietly—helped African Americans secure free papers for themselves and their families. Ibid., 309.

16. Robert Winthrop to J. Ingersoll Bowditch, Dec. 21, 1842, J. Ingersoll Bowditch Papers II, Ms.S-468, MHS; Adams, *Memoirs*, XI, 281. *HJ*, 27 Cong., 3d sess., Dec. 27, 1842, 103.

17. *Gibbons v. Ogden*, 22 U.S. 1 (1824), 218.

18. Parker, *Making Foreigners*, 41–45; Hidetaka Hirota, *Expelling the Poor: Atlantic Seaboard States and the Nineteenth-Century Origins of American Immigration Policy* (New York: Oxford University Press, 2017), 46–47; Neuman, "Lost Century of American Immigration Law."

19. *NY v. Miln*, 36 U.S. 102, 136–37, 141 (1837). R. Kent Newmyer, *The Supreme Court under Marshall and Taney* (Arlington Heights, IL: Harlan Davidson, 1968), 92–93; Howe, *What Hath God Wrought*, 440–41.

20. *Miln*, 111, 139 (emphasis in original). For the interstate slave trade and the commerce power in this period, see David L. Lightner, *Slavery and the Commerce Power: How the Struggle Against the Interstate Slave Trade Led to the Civil War* (New Haven, CT: Yale University Press, 2006), 69–85.

21. The 1789 Judiciary Act, sec. 14, read, "*Provided,* That writs of *habeas corpus* shall in no case extend to prisoners in jail, unless where they are in custody under or by color of the authority of the United States, or are committed for trial before some court of the same, or are necessary to be brought into some court to testify."

22. "Resolves relating to the Imprisonment of Citizens of this Commonwealth in other States," approved March 3, 1842, Chap. 82, *Acts and Resolves Passed by the Legislature of Massachusetts in the Year 1842 (Winter Session)* (Boston: Dutton and Wentworth, 1842).

23. HRep. 80, 3–4; Adams, *Memoirs*, XI, 298. President Tyler had claimed he could not locate the Johnson decision, but Adams found it in his son's study. Adams wrote that he had been looking for it for two years. On finding it in the library of his son, Charles, he took it to the editor of the *Boston Atlas* and requested that he publish it together with the documents forwarded by the president. *Memoirs*, XI, 271.

24. HRep. 80, 6. Directly addressing Justice Johnson's dilemma, Bowditch also suggested language for a federal law that would permit the judges of the federal circuit and district court to issue writs of habeas corpus "to hear and determine all cases of imprisonment under any proceeding or colour of authority contrary to the Constitution or laws of the United States, and all acts or parts of acts inconsistent with this act are hereby repealed." Bowditch to Winthrop, undated draft, J. Ingersoll Bowditch Papers II, Ms.S-468, MHS. No such law passed until Reconstruction.

25. HRep. 80, 37, 38–39 (emphasis in the original).

26. HRep. 80, 40.

27. *CG,* 27 Cong., 3d sess., 384.

28. Adams said opposition to printing the report was an attempt by the "Jackson jackals" to "suppress circulation among the people." *Memoirs,* XI, 314. For Adams mailing out the report, see ibid., 338. Bowditch had wanted the report printed, including the petition, and had offered that his group would pay for a thousand copies. In the end, that wasn't necessary, since the House voted to print five thousand. Bowditch to Winthrop (draft), Feb. 5, 1843, J. Ingersoll Bowditch Papers II, Ms.S-468, MHS.

29. *William Lloyd Garrison, the Story of His Life, Told by His Children,* 4 vols. (New York: Century, 1889), III, 58–60; Walter M. Merrill, ed., *The Letters of William Lloyd Garrison,* vol. 3, *No Union with Slaveholders, 1841–1849* (Cambridge: Harvard University Press, 1973), 266. For the lesser-known rift in women's organizations, as well as women's Liberty Party–related organizing, see Julie Roy Jeffrey, "The Liberty Women of Boston: Evangelicalism and Anti-Slavery Politics," *New England Quarterly* 85, no. 1 (March 2012): 38–77.

30. Laurie, *Beyond Garrison,* 78–83, 111–19, 121–24; Volk, *Moral Minorities,* 101–16; Kantrowitz, *More Than Freedom,* 70–74. See also Earle, *Jacksonian Antislavery,* 103–22; Brooks, *Liberty Power,* 90–93.

31. See, for example, Fehrenbacher, *Slaveholding Republic,* 29–33, 40–41; Sean Wilentz, *No Property in Man: Slavery and Antislavery at the Nation's Founding* (Cambridge: Harvard University Press, 2018), 60–70.

32. Ames, *Proposed Amendments*; Mason, *Slavery and Politics,* esp. 51–62, 214–19; Michael Vorenberg, *Final Freedom: The Civil War, the Abolition of Slavery, and the Thirteenth Amendment* (New York: Cambridge University Press, 2001), 15–35, 51.

33. *Proceedings of the Ohio Anti-Slavery Convention,* 11; William Jay, *A View of the Action of the Federal Government in Behalf of Slavery,* 184; "To the people of the state of Ohio," *Philanthropist,* March 2, 1842. For Adams's relationship with abolitionists and the schism over whether the Constitution already permitted Congress to abolish slavery in the states, see, for example, Harrold, *American Abolitionism,* 66–72. Constitutional scholar Akhil Amar described as "Barron contrarians" those who insisted that the Bill of Rights was "declaratory" of common-law rights to which everyone was already entitled. His reference was to the 1833 Supreme Court case of *Barron v. Baltimore,* which held that the Bill of Rights protected people's rights against infringement by the federal government, not the states. Abolitionists who adopted that view, and therefore believed Congress already had the constitutional power to abolish slavery in the states, feature prominently in the work of constitutional scholars Jacobus tenBroek and Howard Jay Graham. Akhil Reed Amar, *The Bill of Rights* (New Haven, CT: Yale University Press, 1998); Howard Jay Graham, *Everyman's Constitution: Historical Essays on the Fourteenth Amendment, the "Conspiracy Theory," and American Constitutionalism* (Madison: State Historical Society of Wisconsin, 1968), esp. 295–336; Jacobus tenBroek, *The Antislavery Origins of the Fourteenth Amendment* (Berkeley: University of California Press, 1951).

34. John Quincy Adams, "To the Citizens of the United States," *WNI*, May 28, 1839 (emphasis in the original); *CG*, 25 Cong., 3d sess., 18. Bemis, *John Quincy Adams*, 381–82.

35. *CG*, 28 Cong., 1 sess., 62; Petition of Citizens of LaPorte County, Indiana, Jan. 3, 1845, HR28A-G10.13; Petition of Citizens of Ashtabula County, Ohio, Dec. 26, 1843; Memorial from a Meeting at Brooklyn, N.Y., Dec. 25, 1843, all in RG233; "Constitutional Question," *Niles' National Register*, March 3, 1844, 67. Ames, *Proposed Amendments*, 47–48. Many more petitions for repeal are filed in HR28A-G10.13, RG233.

36. *CG*, 28 Cong., 1 sess., 432, 176. *Massachusetts Resolutions*, 28 Cong., 1 sess., 1844, House Rep. No. 404, 2.

37. Seward to Salmon Chase, Samuel Lewis, and Others, May 26, 1845, *WWS*, III, 441.

38. Seward to Chase, March 24, 1847, *SCP*, 2

39. Speech in Cleveland, Ohio, Oct. 26, 1848, *WWS*, III, 301, 302.

40. *Eleventh Annual Report, Presented to the Massachusetts Anti-Slavery Society, by its Board of Managers* (Boston: Oliver Johnson, 1843), 17–18. Finkelman, "Protection of Black Rights in Seward's New York" ; Finkelman, "States' Rights North and South in Antebellum America," in Kermit L. Hall and James W. Ely Jr., eds., *An Uncertain Tradition: Constitutionalism and the History of the South* (Athens: University of Georgia Press, 1989), 137–44. For earlier conflicts between Virginia and Kentucky on the one side, and Ohio on the other, see Hammond, "Most Free of the Free," 55; and herein, chapter 3.

41. Petition of Victor W. Barker et al., House unpassed 1843, docket 1289, MSA (among the signers were William Cooper Nell, Frederick Douglass, C. Lenox Remond, and other notables); Petition of J. Ingersoll Bowditch et al., n.d., House unpassed 1843, docket 1289A, MSA; "Resolves relating to the Imprisonment of Citizens of this Commonwealth in other States," March 24, 1843, *Acts and Resolves Passed by the Legislature of Massachusetts in the Year 1843* (Boston: Dutton and Wentworth, 1843). For the legislature's growing willingness to confront the Slave Power, see Martin Duberman, *Charles Francis Adams, 1807–1886* (Stanford, CA: Stanford University Press, 1960), 81–96.

42. "Protection of Colored Seamen," *Baltimore Sun*, Nov. 8, 1843; "Hunt, Benjamin Faneuil," *Appleton's Cyclopedia of American Biography* (New York: D. Appleton, 1888), III, 315; B. F. H., "To the Editors of the *Charleston Courier*," pub'd in *Charleston Mercury*, Nov. 21, 1843; *Twelfth Annual Report*, 9.

43. *Journal of the Senate of the Commonwealth of Kentucky* (Frankfort: A. G. Hodges, 1842), 165; *Journal of the Proceedings of the Legislative Council of the Territory of Florida at its Fourth Session* (Tallahassee: Knowles, 1843), 80.

44. "House of Representatives," *Niles' National Register*, March 9, 1844, 31; "Constitutional Question," *Niles' National Register*, March 30, 1844, 67.

45. "Resolves Concerning the Treatment of Samuel Hoar by the State of South Carolina," March 24, 1845, Chap. 111, *Acts and Resolves Passed by the General*

Court of Massachusetts in the Year 1845 (Boston: Dutton and Wentworth, 1845), 640–41; *Message of George N. Briggs, Jan. 6, 1845, with Accompanying Documents*, Mass. Senate No. 4, 17, MSA; *Memoirs of Members of the Social Circle in Concord*, 3d series (Cambridge, MA: Riverside Press, 1907), 37; George F. Hoar, *Autobiography of Seventy Years* (New York: Charles Scribner's Sons, 1903), 24–27. See also Schoeppner, *Moral Contagion*, 144–58.

46. *Message of George N. Briggs*, esp. 23; *Memoirs of Members of the Social Circle*, 39–44.

47. *Journal of the House of Representatives of the State of South Carolina, being the Annual Session of 1844* (Columbia, SC: A. H. Pemberton, 1844), 65.

48. "An Act to Amend An Act Entitled 'An Act More Effectually to Prevent Free Negroes and Other Persons of Color from Entering into this State, and for Other Purposes,'" Dec. 19, 1844, *Acts of the General Assembly of the State of South Carolina, passed in December, 1844* (Columbia, SC: A. H. Pemberton, 1845), 293–94. Loren Schweninger, *Appealing for Liberty: Freedom Suits in the South* (New York: Oxford University Press, 2018), 194–95, 198–200.

49. "Legislative," *Liberator*, Feb. 14, 1845. Scott P. Marler, *The Merchants' Capital: New Orleans and the Political Economy of the Nineteenth-Century South* (New York: Cambridge University Press, 2013).

50. *Resolutions of the Legislature of Alabama*, Feb. 15, 1845, 28 Cong., 2d sess., House doc. 123, 2, 3 (emphasis in the original); *Groves v. Slaughter*, 40 U.S. 441, 508 (1849).

51. "Coloured Seamen—Their Character and Condition. No. V," *NASS*, Nov. 12, 1846, 94. Philip S. Foner, "William P. Powell: Militant Champion of Black Seamen," in Foner, *Essays in Afro-American History* (Philadelphia: Temple University Press, 1978); *BAP*, vol. 3, *The United States, 1830–1846*, 302–3.

52. "Coloured Seamen—Their Character and Condition, No. II," *NASS*, Sept. 17, 1846, 62; "Coloured Seamen—Their Character and Condition. Statistics of Coloured Seamen Imprisoned in Southern and Foreign Ports. No. III," *NASS*, Oct. 1, 1846, 69; "Coloured Seamen—Their Character and Condition. No. III," *NASS*, Oct. 15, 1846, 78.

53. Woodbury Davis to John P. Hale, May 4, 1848, box 7, John P. Hale Papers, New Hampshire Historical Society; John G. Palfrey, *Papers on the Slave Power, First Published in the "Boston Whig"* (Boston: Merrill, Cobb, 1846), 46–47, 50.

54. Henry Wilson, *The History of the Rise and Fall of the Slave Power in America*, 3 vols. (Boston: James R. Osgood, 1877), I, 582, 585–86.

CHAPTER 6: "THAT ALL MEN ARE CREATED FREE AND EQUAL"

1. Norton S. Townshend, "Salmon P. Chase," *Ohio Archaeological and Historical Publications* 1 (June 1887–March 1888), 115. Undated mss., box 13; Samuel G. McClure, "A Romance," *Cleveland Leader*, Sept. 2, 1894, box 20, NST; Chase to John T. Trowbridge, March 16, 1864, box 14, SCPHSP.

2. Historians have focused more on the vicissitudes of party realignment and

antislavery politicians' views on slavery than on the efforts to repeal racist state laws and secure the right to vote for Black men. Richard H. Sewell, *Ballots for Freedom: Antislavery Politics in the United States, 1837–1860* (New York: Oxford University Press, 1976); Theodore Clarke Smith, *The Liberty and Free Soil Parties in the Northwest* (New York: Longmans, Green, 1897); Reinhard O. Johnson, *The Liberty Party, 1840–1848: Antislavery Third-Party Politics in the United States* (Baton Rouge: Louisiana State University Press, 2009); Frederick J. Blue, *The Free Soilers: Third Party Politics, 1848–54* (Urbana: University of Illinois Press, 1973); Blue, *Salmon P. Chase: A Life in Politics* (Kent, OH: Kent State University Press, 1987). For the third-party background of many prominent Republicans, see Eric Foner, *Free Soil, Free Labor, Free Men: The Ideology of the Republican Party before the Civil War,* 1970 (New York: Oxford University Press, 1995), esp. 105–6.

3. Augustine, "The West—No. VII," *Colored American,* Aug. 31, 1839. The rest of the series was published in *Colored American* between February and July 1839.

4. *Minutes of the National Convention of Colored Citizens: Held at Buffalo* (New York: Piercy & Reed, 1843), 35 (hereafter, *Buffalo Convention*). "Population of Ohio—Facts for Our Legislators," *Philanthropist,* Dec. 30, 1840. J. D. B. DeBow, *Statistical View of the United States . . . being a Compendium of the Seventh Census* (Washington, DC, 1854), IV, 40, 63, 97.

5. *Proceedings of the Ohio Anti-Slavery Convention,* 24; "Ohio—No. 1," *Colored American,* Oct. 12, 1839; *Buffalo Convention,* 38; Eddie Mabry, *The History of Wood River Baptist District Association* (St. Louis: John S. Swift, 1996), 5; Smith, *Biography of Rev. David Smith,* 69–73; Carter G. Woodson, "The Negroes of Cincinnati Prior to the Civil War," *Journal of Negro History* 1, no. 1 (Jan. 1916), esp. 7–13; Taylor, *Frontiers of Freedom,* 102–4; William Cheek and Aimee Lee Cheek, *John Mercer Langston and the Fight for Black Freedom, 1829-65* (Urbana: University of Illinois Press, 1989), 51–58.

6. Steven J. Ross, *Workers on the Edge: Work, Leisure, and Politics in Industrializing Cincinnati, 1788–1890* (New York: Columbia University Press, 1985), 47–54; Bruce Levine, "Community Divided: German Immigrants, Social Class, and Political Conflict in Antebellum Cincinnati," in Henry D. Shapiro and Jonathan D. Sarna, eds., *Ethnic Diversity and Civic Identity: Patterns of Conflict and Cohesion in Cincinnati since 1820* (Urbana: University of Illinois Press, 1992), 42–54.

7. Quotations in Finkelman, *Imperfect Union,* 165, 166. See also Finkelman, "Race, Slavery, and Law in Antebellum Ohio," in Michael Les Benedict and John F. Winkler, eds., *The History of Ohio Law,* 2 vols. (Athens: Ohio University Press, 2004), 1, 766. Chase to Charles D. Cleveland, May 18, 1841, in *SCP,* 2, 75–76.

8. *Tenth Annual Report of the Board of Managers of the Massachusetts Anti-Slavery Society* (Boston: Dow & Jackson, 1842), 99–103. Untitled, *Cincinnati Enquirer,* Aug. 10, 1841; Taylor, *Frontiers of Freedom,* 118–19; Julie A. Mujic, "A Border Community's Unfulfilled Appeals: The Rise and Fall of the 1840s Anti-Abolitionist Movement in Cincinnati," *Ohio Valley History* 7, no. 2 (Summer

2007): 54–57. For rising racial tensions, see also Cheek and Cheek, *John Mercer Langston*, 59–62.

9. "Report of the Committee of Public Safety," and "The Late Disturbances," *Cincinnati Enquirer*, Sept. 10, 1841; Flamen Ball to Chase, Sept. 4, 1841, *SCP*, 2, 78; *Tenth Annual Report*, 99–103. Taylor, *Frontiers of Freedom*, 122–24; Cheek and Cheek, *John Mercer Langston*, 62–65; Harrold, *Gamaliel Bailey*, 42–43; Richards, *Gentlemen of Property and Standing*, 123–29.

10. John Mercer Langston, *From the Virginia Plantation to the National Capitol*, 1894 (Reprint: New York: Johnson Reprint, 1968), 65–67. Flamen Ball to Chase, Sept. 4, 1841, *SCP*, 2, 78.

11. "Petitions," *Philanthropist*, Nov. 3, 1841; *Tenth Annual Report*, 103; Harrold, *Gamaliel Bailey*, 43.

12. "Proceedings of the Liberty Convention of the State of Ohio," *Philanthropist*, Jan. 5, 1842; "Proceedings," *Philanthropist*, Jan. 12, 1842; "For Governor, Leicester King," *Philanthropist*, Feb. 16, 1842.

13. Blue, *Salmon P. Chase*, esp. 27–31, 41–46; Harrold, *Gamaliel Bailey*, 28–51. For Chase's law practice: Matthew A. Axtell, "What Is Still 'Radical' in the Antislavery Legal Practice of Salmon P. Chase," *Hastings Race and Poverty Law Journal* 11 (2014): 269–320.

14. Chase to Charles D. Cleveland, Oct. 22, 1841, *SCP*, 2, 80. See also Chase to Wm. Ellery Channing, May 3, 1842, *SCP*, 2, 94–95; *The Address and Reply on the Presentation of a Testimonial to S. P. Chase, by the Colored People of Cincinnati* (Cincinnati: Henry W. Derby & Co., 1845), 27–32. Harrold, *Gamaliel Bailey*, 28–51; Sewell, *Ballots for Freedom*, 92–93; Michael Les Benedict, "Salmon P. Chase and Constitutional Politics," in Benedict, *Preserving the Constitution: Essays on Politics and the Constitution in the Reconstruction Era* (New York: Fordham University Press, 2006), esp. 134–37; Foner, *Free Soil, Free Labor, Free Men*, 73–102; Wiecek, *Sources of Antislavery Constitutionalism*, 202–19; James Oakes, *Freedom National: The Destruction of Slavery in the United States* (New York: W. W. Norton, 2013), 17–21, 26–28.

15. Chase to Wm. Ellery Channing, May 3, 1842, *SPC*, 2, 95; Minutes and Address of the Lorain County [OH] Liberty Convention, held at Elyria, Sept. 27, 1841 (broadside), box 24, NST. "Population of Ohio—Facts for Our Legislators," *Philanthropist*, Dec. 30, 1840.

16. "Interrogatories propounded to Judge King at Cincinnati," Aug. 22, 1842, box 7, SCPHSP. King received between 5,100 and 5,400 votes, a significant increase in the number of Liberty Party votes cast and about 2 percent of the vote statewide. Harrold, *Gamaliel Bailey*, 51; Johnson, *Liberty Party*, 180–81.

17. Harrold, *Gamaliel Bailey*, 42, 46–48; Earle, *Jacksonian Antislavery*, 144–57.

18. Chase to Giddings, Jan. 21, 1842, *SCP*, 2, 85–86; Giddings to Chase, Jan. 4, 1842, box 5, SCPHSP. For later Liberty Party debates about making an alliance with the Whigs versus emphasizing an independent third party, see Brooks, *Liberty Power*, 130–37.

19. "Colored People of Columbus," *Philanthropist,* March 29, 1843. Cheek and Cheek, *John Mercer Langston,* 149–50; *Report of the Proceedings of the Colored National Convention, Held at Cleveland, Ohio, on Wednesday September 6, 1848* (Rochester, NY: John Dick, 1848), 6. In 1843, about 1,000 African Americans lived in Columbus (as compared with 4,500 in Cincinnati). Members of Columbus's Black community owned real estate worth $35,000 and counted two churches, three schools, a temperance society, a literary society, two female benevolent societies, five "agriculturalists," and twelve mechanics. *Buffalo Convention,* 38. In 1850, according to the US Census, Columbus was home to 1,277 people of color, while 3,237 resided in Cincinnati. Cincinnati was far larger overall, with 115,435 total inhabitants, compared with Columbus's 17,882. DeBow, *Statistical View . . . Seventh Census,* IV, 395.

20. Letter of William H. Yancy, "Convention of Colored People at Columbus," *Philanthropist,* July 26, 1843. *Buffalo Convention,* 3; "Proceedings of the Colored Convention," *Philanthropist,* Oct. 4, 1843.

21. *Buffalo Convention,* 15–16, 26. Johnson, *The Liberty Party,* 242–49; Kantrowitz, *More Than Freedom,* 101–8; Sinha, *Slave's Cause,* 418–19; Bonner, *Remaking the Republic,* 57–62.

22. *Buffalo Convention,* 18, 35.

23. Kirk H. Porter, comp., *National Party Platforms* (New York: Macmillan, 1924), 7, 13 (emphasis added). "Buffalo Convention," *Emancipator and Free American,* Sept. 7, 1843. Blue, *Salmon P. Chase,* 49–50; Harrold, *Gamaliel Bailey,* 62–66; Charles H. Wesley, "The Participation of Negroes in Anti-Slavery Political Parties," *Journal of Negro History* 29, no. 1 (Jan. 1944): 44–45.

24. "Address to the Citizens of Ohio," *Palladium of Liberty,* Dec. 27, 1843; *Buffalo Convention,* 27–30.

25. "Address of the State Convention," *Palladium of Liberty,* Nov. 13, 1844.

26. Stephen E. Maizlish, *The Triumph of Sectionalism: The Transformation of Ohio Politics, 1844–1856* (Kent, OH: Kent State University Press, 1983), 27–39; Johnson, *Liberty Party,* 310; Blue, *Salmon P. Chase,* 50.

27. Joshua Giddings to David Lee Child, April 6, 1845 [Ms. A. 4.2. p. 12], BPL. "Report of the Select Committee," Dec. 14, 1844, *Journal of the Senate of the State of Ohio,* 43rd General Assembly, 1844–45 (Columbus: Samuel Medary, 1845); "Report of a Majority of the Select Committee," and "Report of the Minority of the Select Committee," Jan. 18, 1845, *Journal of the House of Representatives of the State of Ohio,* 43rd General Assembly, 1844–45 (Columbus: Samuel Medary, 1844). Stephen Middleton, *The Black Laws: Race and the Legal Process in Early Ohio* (Athens: Ohio University Press, 2005), 136–38; Leonard Erickson, "Politics and Repeal of Ohio's Black Laws, 1837–1849," *Ohio History* 82, nos. 3, 4 (Summer/Autumn 1973): 156–57.

28. "Letter from Horace Greeley to the Anti-Slavery Convention at Cincinnati," June 3, 1845, in *New-York Tribune,* June 20, 1845; "The New York Tribune, and the Recent Anti-Slavery Convention in Cincinnati," *Cincinnati Weekly Herald*

and Philanthropist, July 2, 1845. Blue, *Salmon P. Chase,* 50–51; Harrold, *Gamaliel Bailey,* 73–74.

29. John A. Bingham to Salmon Chase et al., Aug. 6, 1845, SCPHSP. Richard L. Aynes, "The Antislavery and Abolitionist Background of John A. Bingham," *Catholic University Law Review* 37 (Summer 1988): 881–933; Gerard N. Magliocca, *American Founding Son: John Bingham and the Invention of the Fourteenth Amendment* (New York: New York University Press, 2013), 13–16, 18–19.

30. "The Parties and the Black Laws," *Cincinnati Weekly Herald and Philanthropist,* Aug. 5, 1846. William G. W. Lewis, *Biography of Samuel Lewis, the First Superintendent of Common Schools for the State of Ohio* (Cincinnati: Methodist Book Concern, 1857), 367; "Ohio—Her Election—The Black Laws," *New York Tribune,* Oct. 22, 1846; Erickson, "Politics and Repeal," esp. 156–59; Vernon L. Volpe, *Forlorn Hope of Freedom: The Liberty Party in the Old Northwest* (Kent, OH: Kent State University Press, 1990), 103–6; Smith, *Liberty and Free Soil Parties,* 91. In late 1846, at the urging of Cincinnati's African American Union Baptist Church, the Miami Baptist Association—a regional organization that represented almost two thousand members, most of them white—condemned the Ohio black laws and called on "all christians and philanthropists" to petition for their repeal. Ford, *Bonds of Union,* 218–19.

31. "The Parties and the Black Laws"; Edwin Stanton to Chase, Nov. 30, 1846, box 10, SCPHSP. Benjamin P. Thomas and Harold Hyman, *Stanton: The Life and Times of Lincoln's Secretary of War* (New York: Knopf, 1962), 11, 42–43; William Marvel, *Lincoln's Autocrat: The Life of Edwin Stanton* (Chapel Hill: University of North Carolina Press, 2015), 47–52; Smith, *Liberty and Free Soil,* 92.

32. Edwin Stanton to Chase, Aug. 1846 [undated], box 10, SCPHSP; Chase to Joshua Giddings, Oct. 20, 1846, *SCP,* 2, 134; Joshua Giddings to J. A. Giddings, June 28, 1846, Giddings Papers, reel 1. "Ohio—The Political Prospect," *New York Tribune,* Oct. 13, 1846; "The Black Laws of Ohio," *Cincinnati Daily Enquirer,* Sept. 8, 1846. Smith, *Liberty and Free Soil,* 93.

33. "The Black Laws of Ohio," *Cincinnati Daily Enquirer,* Sept. 8, 1846; "Whig Consistency upon the Black Laws," ibid., Oct. 6, 1846 (emphases in the original).

34. "Whig Consistency upon the Black Laws," *Cincinnati Daily Enquirer,* Oct. 6, 1846. "An Act to Prevent the Bringing into the State of Ohio, Paupers, Having no Settlement Therein," March 12, 1845, *Acts of a General Nature Passed by the 43rd General Assembly of the State of Ohio* (Columbus, OH: Samuel Medary, 1845). Ray Allen Billington, *The Protestant Crusade, 1800–1860: A Study of the Origins of American Nativism* (New York: Macmillan, 1938), 194–234; Hirota, *Expelling the Poor,* 46–48, 55–57.

35. "The Cincinnati Gazette, and the Black Laws of Ohio," *Cincinnati Weekly Herald and Philanthropist,* Jan. 7, 1846.

36. Swift, "Black Presbyterian Attacks on Racism," 454–55, 464–67; Salerno, *Sister Societies,* 92–111; Sinha, *Slave's Cause,* 278–88.

37. "Records of the Henry County Female Anti-Slavery Society" (typescript), 25, Henry County, 1830–1847, Manuscripts and Rare Books Division, Indiana State Library. Stacey M. Robertson, *Hearts Beating for Liberty: Women Abolitionists in the Old Northwest* (Chapel Hill: University of North Carolina Press, 2010), esp. 37–66; Dana Elizabeth Weiner, *Race and Rights: Fighting Slavery and Prejudice in the Old Northwest, 1830–1870* (DeKalb: Northern Illinois University Press, 2013), esp. 26–28, 87–96; Baumgartner, "Building the Future"; Salerno, *Sister Societies,* 142–48.

38. Henry Bibb, *Narrative of the Life and Adventures of Henry Bibb, An American Slave, Written by Himself,* 178–82. Johnson, *Liberty Party,* 246–48, 250–53; Kantrowitz, *More Than Freedom,* 103–8; Harris, *History of Negro Servitude in Illinois,* 154; Cheek and Cheek, *John Mercer Langston,* 45n13.

39. Robert R. Dykstra, "White Men, Black Laws: Territorial Iowans and Civil Rights, 1883 [*sic*]–1843," *Annals of Iowa* 46, no. 6 (1982): 438.

40. Z. Eastman, "History of the Anti-Slavery Agitation, and the Growth of the Liberty and Republican Parties in the State of Illinois," in Rufus Blanchard, ed., *Discovery and Conquests of the Northwest with the History of Chicago,* 2 vols. (Chicago: R. Blanchard, 1900), II, 124, 135, 137–41; "The Abolitionists," *Chicago Tribune,* June 11, 1874; Paula Glasman, "Zebina Eastman: Chicago Abolitionist" (master's thesis, University of Chicago, 1968), 2–9; Harris, *History of Negro Servitude in Illinois,* 138, 148, 152, 157, 162, 233–34, 439–40; Johnson, *Liberty Party,* 254–55. For the fight against the black laws across the Old Northwest, see also Weiner, *Race and Rights,* 55–75.

41. Lori D. Ginzberg, "'Moral Suasion is Moral Balderdash': Women, Politics, and Social Activism in the 1850s," *Journal of American History* 73, no. 3 (Dec. 1986): 601–22; Ginzberg, *Untidy Origins: A Story of Women's Rights in Antebellum New York* (Chapel Hill: University of North Carolina Press, 2005); Faye E. Dudden, *Fighting Chance: The Struggle over Woman Suffrage and Black Suffrage in Reconstruction America* (New York: Oxford University Press, 2011), 13–38; Isenberg, *Sex and Citizenship,* 15–20; Laura E. Free, *Suffrage Reconsidered: Gender, Race, and Voting Rights in the Civil War Era* (Ithaca, NY: Cornell University Press, 2015), 9–49.

42. "Reply to the Colored Citizens of Albany," Jan. 10, 1843, *WWS,* III, 438; Phyllis F. Field, *The Politics of Race in New York: The Struggle for Black Suffrage in the Civil War Era* (Ithaca, NY: Cornell University Press, 1982), 45–52, quotation on 48; William Seward to S. P. Chase, Samuel Lewis, and others, May 26, 1845, *WWS,* III, 442. Wesley, "Participation of Negroes," 40–42; Swift, *Black Prophets of Justice,* 132–35; Gronningsater, "Practicing Formal Politics Without the Vote."

43. *Jeffries v. Ankeny,* 11 Ohio 372 (1842); *Thacker v. Hawk,* 11 Ohio 376 (1842). Kenneth J. Winkle, "Ohio's Informal Polling Place: Nineteenth-Century Suffrage in Theory and Practice," in Jeffrey P. Brown and Andrew R. L. Cayton, eds., *The Pursuit of Public Power: Political Culture in Ohio, 1787–1861* (Kent, OH:

Kent State University Press, 1994), 172–74, 81; Alexander Keyssar, *The Right to Vote: The Contested History of Democracy in the United States* (New York: Basic Books, 2000), 32–33, table A.9; R. J. M. Blackett, *Beating Against the Barriers: Biographical Essays in Nineteenth-Century Afro-American History* (Baton Rouge: Louisiana State University Press, 1986), 297. The 1848 Wisconsin Constitution and the 1850 Michigan Constitution granted suffrage to Native American male inhabitants who were "civilized" and not members of a tribe. Saler, *Settlers' Empire*, 274, Theodore J. Karamanski, "State Citizenship as a Tool of Indian Persistence: A Case Study of the Anishinaabeg of Michigan," *Michigan Historical Review* 37, no. 1 (Spring 2011): 119–38.

44. *Address and Reply*, 22; "Address of the State Convention," *Palladium of Liberty*, Nov. 13, 1844. For the meeting, see Ford, *Bonds of Union*, 137–41.

45. Emil Olbrich, *The Development of Sentiment on Negro Suffrage to 1860*, Bulletin of the University of Wisconsin, no. 477 ([Madison]: The University of Wisconsin, 1912), 77, 79–85; J. Stanley Lemons and Michael A. McKenna, "Re-Enfranchisement of Rhode Island Negroes," *Rhode Island History* 30, no. 1 (Feb. 1971): 2–13; Leslie H. Fischel Jr., "Wisconsin and Negro Suffrage," *Wisconsin Magazine of History* 46, no. 3 (Spring 1963): 184–85; Michael J. McManus, *Political Abolitionism in Wisconsin, 1840–1861* (Kent, OH: Kent State University Press, 1998); James Connor, "The Anti-Slavery Movement in Iowa," *Annals of Iowa* 40, no. 5 (Summer 1970): esp. 357–58; David M. Katzman, *Before the Ghetto: Black Detroit in the Nineteenth Century* (Urbana: University of Illinois Press, 1973), 33–35, 38–39; Ronald P. Formisano, "The Edge of Caste: Colored Suffrage in Michigan, 1827-1861," *Michigan History* 56, no. 1 (Spring 1972): 24–27, 28–34; Sewell, *Ballots for Freedom*, 97–98, 178–79; Keyssar, *Right to Vote*, 57–59; Silvana R. Siddali, *Frontier Democracy: Constitutional Conventions in the Old Northwest* (New York: Cambridge University Press, 2016).

46. Fischel, "Wisconsin and Negro Suffrage," 189; Olbrich, *Development of Sentiment*, 127–28; Leon F. Litwack, *North of Slavery: The Negro in the Free States, 1790–1860* (Chicago: University of Chicago Press, 1961), 74–93; Keyssar, *Right to Vote*, 71–76, Table A.9.

47. Samuel Gridley Howe to Charles Sumner, Jan. 30, 1842, Howe Family Papers, MS Am 2119, Houghton Library, Harvard University. *Minutes and Address of the State Convention of the Colored Citizens of Ohio, Convened at Columbus, Jan. 10th, 11th, 12th, & 13th, 1849* (Oberlin, OH: J. M. Fitch, 1849), 19.

48. *Argument of Charles Sumner, Esq. against the Constitutionality of Separate Colored Schools* (Boston: B. F. Roberts, 1849), 21; *Roberts v. City of Boston*, 59 Mass. 198 (1849). Price and Stewart, "The Roberts Case"; Kantrowitz, *More Than Freedom*, 124–33, 138–39; Volk, *Moral Minorities*, 116–31; Laurie, *Beyond Garrison*, 113–16, 119–21, 172–73.

49. Sewell, *Ballots for Freedom*, 127–29; Richard H. Sewell, *John P. Hale and the Politics of Abolition* (Cambridge: Harvard University Press, 1965), 52–85. For the Liberty Party's growing appeal to Democratic voters—and some antislavery

Whigs' commitment to sticking with the party—see Johnson, *Liberty Party*, 272–76; Brooks, *Liberty Power*, 98–100.

50. *Herkimer Convention. The Voice of New York!* (Albany, NY: Albany Atlas, 1847), 8. David M. Potter, *The Impending Crisis, 1848–1861* (New York: Harper & Row, 1976), 77–81; Foner, *Free Soil, Free Labor, Free Men*, 152–53; Brooks, *Liberty Power*, 107–19, 123–24, 139–40.

51. Chase to Charles Sumner, published in the *National Era*, May 3, 1849, *SPC*, 2, 237.

52. Stewart, *Joshua Giddings*, 141–54; Sewell, *Ballots for Freedom*, 139–41, 166; Laurie, *Beyond Garrison*, 153–60; Elias Nason and Thomas Russell, *The Life and Public Service of Henry Wilson, Late Vice-President of the United States* (Boston: B. B. Russell, 1876), 89–91.

53. Foner, *Free Soil, Free Labor, Free Men*, 267; Porter, *National Party Platforms*, 22–25.

54. NST to "Friend West," *Courier* (Elyria, OH), Sept. 12, 1848, clipping in box 19, NST. Sewell, *Ballots for Freedom*, esp. 175; Maizlish, *Triumph of Sectionalism*, 110–11; Johnson, *Liberty Party*, 86. For Massachusetts, see Laurie, *Beyond Garrison*, 170–73.

55. Speech in Cleveland, Ohio, Oct. 26, 1848, *WWS*, III, 293, 300, 301. Stewart, *Joshua Giddings*, 158–59.

56. NST to "Friend West"; "Col. John Flavet Morse," unidentified clipping, box 24, NST. See also "To Editor of the Herald," Sept. 6, 1848, and "Ishmael," clippings in ibid; Frederick J. Blue and Robert McCormick, "Norton S. Townshend: A Reformer for All Seasons," in Brown and Cayton, eds., *Pursuit of Public Power*; Robert W. McCormick, *Norton S. Townshend, M.D., Antislavery Politician and Agricultural Educator* (Worthington, OH: n.p., 1988). The Free Soilers had sent three men to the Senate and eight to the House. Maizlish, *Triumph of Sectionalism*, 124.

57. NST Memoranda Book, 1848–1853, entry for Dec. 4, 1841, box 11, NST; "Dr. Townshend's Letter," and "Ohio—Narrative of the Late Dispute on Organizing Its Legislature," clippings in box 24, NST; Salmon Chase to Sara Bella D. L. Chase, Dec. 20, 1848, *SCP*, 2, 204–7; Chase to Stanley Matthews, Dec. 23, 1848, ibid., 211. See also Sewell, *Ballots for Freedom*, 206–9; Maizlish, *Triumph of Sectionalism*, 121–46; Stewart, *Joshua Giddings*, 172–75.

58. "Convention of Colored Citizens," *North Star*, Dec. 8, 1848. *Minutes and Address . . . 1849*, 15. For the broader context, see Martha S. Jones, *All Bound Up Together: The Woman Question in African American Public Culture, 1830–1900* (Chapel Hill: University of North Carolina Press, 2007), 59–82; Salerno, *Sister Societies*, 140–42.

59. *Minutes and Address . . . 1849*, 6, 27–28. William J. Simmons, *Men of Mark: Eminent, Progressive and Rising* (Cleveland: George M. Rewell, 1887), 979; Cheek and Cheek, *John Mercer Langston*, 137, 142, 148; Blackett, *Beating Against the Barriers*, 388–94.

60. Entry of Dec. 7, John Niven et al., *SCP*, 1, 201; "Dr. Townshend's Letter," Dec. 7, 1848, clipping in box 24, NST. See also NST to Editor of the *True Democrat*, Jan. 15, 1849, and J. F. Morse to H. C. Gray, Esq., Jan. 18, 1849, clippings in box 24, NST; Townshend, "Salmon P. Chase," 115–18.

61. Salmon Chase to NST, Jan. 23, 1849, box 1, NST. See also Chase to John F. Morse, Jan. 19, 1849, *SCP*, 2, 216–19; Chase to Stanley Matthews, Jan. 27, 1849, ibid., 221; Chase to Hamlin, Jan. 17, 1849, ibid., 214. Thomas J. Clemens to Norton Townshend, Feb. 4, 1848 [1849]; William Patterson et al. to Norton Townshend, Jan. 26, 1849; H. C. Taylor to Norton Townshend, Jan. 30, 1849, all in box 1, NST.

62. "An Act to Authorize the Establishment of Separate Schools for the Education of Colored Children, and for Other Purposes," Feb. 10, 1849, *Acts of a General Nature Passed by the Forty-Seventh General Assembly* (Columbus, OH: Chas. Scott, 1849), 17–18 (emphasis added). "Ohio Black Laws," *North Star*, March 9, 1849; "Communication: Meeting at Columbus," *North Star*, March 23, 1849; "Black Laws of Ohio," *Oberlin Evangelist*, Feb. 28, 1849.

63. "An Act to Authorize the Establishment of Separate Schools." Erickson, "Politics and Repeal," 172–73.

64. A. J. Anderson, "Colored Citizenship in Ohio," *North Star*, March 23, 1849; *Minutes of the State Convention, of the Colored Citizens of Ohio* (Columbus, OH: Gale & Cleveland, 1850); Blackett, *Beating Against the Barriers*, 296–97; Cheek and Cheek, *John Mercer Langston*, 136, 138, 344n18.

65. "Rights of the African Race—Colonization—Popular Votes," *New York Tribune*, Aug. 28, 1851. McClure, "A Romance"; Townshend, "Salmon P. Chase"; A. G. Riddle, "Recollections of the Forty-Seventh General Assembly of Ohio, 1847–48 [*sic*]" *Magazine of Western History* 6 (May–Oct. 1887): 341–51.

66. A. G. Riddle, "Recollections," 341, 350. For later historians who echoed Greeley, see Frank Uriah Quillin, *The Color Line in Ohio* (Ann Arbor, MI: G. Wahr, 1913), 43; Malvin, *North Into Freedom*, 67n7.

CHAPTER 7: "INJUSTICE AND OPPRESSION INCARNATE"

1. Charles A. Gliozzo, "John Jones: A Study of a Black Chicagoan," *Illinois Historical Journal* 80, no. 3 (Autumn 1987): 177–78; *History of Madison County, Illinois* (Edwardsville, IL: W. R. Brink, 1882), 472.

2. "Meeting of the Colored People," *Western Citizen*, Sept. 23, 1848; "New Movement," *Illinois State Register*, Sept. 29, 1848; John Jones Obituary, *Chicago Tribune*, May 22, 1879. Gliozzo, "John Jones," 178–79, 183; Eastman, "History of the Anti-Slavery Agitation," 139. Perry J. Stackhouse, *Chicago and the Baptists* (Chicago: University of Chicago Press, 1933), 30–32; Richard Junger, "'Thinking Men and Women, Who Desire to Improve Our Condition': Henry O. Wagoner, Civil Rights, and Black Economic Opportunity in Frontier Chicago and Denver, 1846–1887," in William H. Alexander et al., eds., *Voices from within the*

Veil: African Americans and the Experience of Democracy (Newcastle upon Tyne, UK: Cambridge Scholars, 2008); Jennifer R. Harbour, *Organizing Freedom: Black Emancipation Activism in the Civil War Midwest* (Carbondale: Southern Illinois University Press, 2020).

3. "Free Colored Men.—No. 2," *Western Citizen,* Sept. 28, 1847; "Pleading their Own Cause," [Letter of J. J.], *Western Citizen,* Sept. 21, 1847.

4. "An Act Respecting Slaves, Free Negroes, and Mulattoes," Feb. 16, 1847, *Laws of the State of Missouri Passed at the First Session of the Fourteenth General Assembly* (Jefferson, MO: James Lusk, 1847), 103–4.

5. *The Constitutional Debates of 1847,* ed. Arthur Charles Cole (Springfield: Illinois State Historical Library, 1919), 202, 208, 213, 216–19, 224, 861 (hereafter, *CD 1847*). On "upland southerners" and cultural differences in the Midwest, see Nicole Etcheson, *The Emerging Midwest: Upland Southerners and the Political Culture of the Old Northwest, 1787-1861* (Bloomington: Indiana University Press, 1995).

6. *CD 1847,* 860, 212, 221.

7. *CD 1847,* 210, 213, 204. See also 206, 215, 858.

8. *CD 1847,* 855, 863, 858, 860, 861. An even more restrictive proposal—which provided that "no negro or mulatto shall hereafter be permitted to acquire and exercise any civil or political rights, or residence within this state"—was overwhelmingly defeated. Ibid., 856, 863. Ameda Ruth King, "The Last Years of the Whig Party in Illinois—1847 to 1856," *Transactions of the Illinois State Historical Society for the Year 1925* ([Springfield]: Board of Trustees of the Illinois State Historical Society, [1925]), 118.

9. Quintard Taylor, "Slaves and Free Men: Blacks in the Oregon Country, 1840-1860," *Oregon Historical Quarterly* 83, no. 2 (Summer 1982): 155–58; Ky. Const. of 1850, art. X, §2, in *FSC,* III, 1310; Emma Lou Thornbrough, *The Negro in Indiana: A Study of a Minority* (Indianapolis: Indiana Historical Bureau, 1957), 55–68; Finkelman, "Before the Fourteenth Amendment," 438.

10. *Journal of the House of Representatives of the Sixteenth General Assembly of the State of Illinois* (Springfield, IL: Charles H. Lanphier, 1849), 510; *Message of His Excellency, Richard Yates, Governor of Illinois, to the General Assembly* (Springfield, IL: Baker & Phillips, 1865), 23. *Report of the Debates and Proceedings of the Convention for the Revision of the Constitution of the State of Indiana, 1850,* 2 vols. (Indianapolis: A. H. Brown, 1850), I, 616. Frederick J. Blue, "Black Men Have No Rights Which White Men are Bound to Respect: Charles Langston and the Drive for Equality," in *No Taint of Compromise,* 72; "Ohio Legislature," *Ohio Statesman,* Feb. 11, 1851.

11. Morris, *Free Men All,* 71–129; Wilentz, *Rise of American Democracy,* 637–53.

12. *CG,* 31 Cong., 1 sess., appendix, 421–22, 1625.

13. *CG,* 31 Cong., 1 sess., appendix, 1628–29. "I entered the Senate," WFMHS.

14. "An Act to Amend, and Supplementary to, the Act entitled 'An Act Respecting Fugitives from Justice, and Persons Escaping from the Service of their Masters,'

approved February twelfth, one thousand seven hundred and ninety-three," 9 Stat. 462–65.

15. Samuel Ringgold Ward, *Autobiography of a Fugitive Negro*, 1855 (New York: Arno and the New York Times, 1968), 117. The literature on responses to the Fugitive Slave Act is extensive. See, for example, R. J. M. Blackett, *The Captive's Quest for Freedom: Fugitive Slaves, the 1850 Fugitive Slave Law, and the Politics of Slavery* (New York: Cambridge University Press, 2018); Sinha, *Slave's Cause*, 500–542; Kantrowitz, *More Than Freedom*, 175–214; Kellie Carter Jackson, *Force and Freedom: Black Abolitionists and the Politics of Violence* (Philadelphia: University of Pennsylvania Press, 2019), 48–79.

16. *CG*, 31 Cong., 2d sess., 246–47; "African Colonization," *African Repository*, Jan. 1851, 22; Blackett, *Captive's Quest for Freedom*, 88–134; Daniel Walker Howe, *The Political Culture of the American Whigs* (Chicago: University of Chicago Press, 1979), 135–37; P. J. Staudenraus, *The African Colonization Movement, 1816-1865* (New York: Columbia University Press, 1961), 244–46.

17. "Benevolence to the African Race," *African Repository*, July 1851, 209; Rights of the African Race—Colonization—Popular Votes," *New-York Tribune*, Aug. 28, 1851; "Extract from the Message of Governor Hunt," *African Repository*, Feb. 1852, 34–37.

18. "Address to the People of the State of New York," *Frederick Douglass' Paper*, Feb. 5, 1852.

19. "Mr. Birney on Colonization," *Frederick Douglass' Paper*, Feb. 12, 1852. David W. Blight, *Frederick Douglass: Prophet of Freedom* (New York: Simon & Schuster, 2018), esp. 189–92, 215–21, 238–40.

20. Blackett, *Captive's Quest for Freedom*, 47; Gosse, "As a Nation, the English Are Our Friends."

21. Charles W. Mann, *The Chicago Common Council and the Fugitive Slave Law of 1850* (Chicago: Chicago Historical Society, 1903); Potter, *Impending Crisis*, 108–16.

22. "Meeting of the Colored People," *Western Citizen*, Oct. 8, 1850; Mann, *Chicago Common Council*, 70–75, 85. Christopher Robert Reed, *Black Chicago's First Century, vol. 1, 1833–1900* (Columbia: University of Missouri Press, 2005), 49, 91–92. DeBow, *Statistical View*, IV, 395.

23. Eastman, "History of the Anti-Slavery Agitation," 144; Zebina Eastman, "Founding a Party: The Origin and Growth of the Republican Party in Illinois," *Chicago Times*, Nov. 18, 1882, clipping in Zebina Eastman Papers, CHM; Arthur Charles Cole, *The Era of the Civil War, vol. 3, Centennial History of Illinois* (Chicago: A. C. McClurg & Co., 1922), 108–11. James P. Jones, *"Black Jack": John A. Logan and Southern Illinois in the Civil War Era* (Tallahassee: Florida State University, 1967), 14.

24. H. O. Wagoner to Friend Douglass, Dec. 28, 1852, *Frederick Douglass' Paper*, Jan. 14, 1853; John J. Halsey, *A History of Lake County, Illinois* (Chicago: Harmegnies & Howell, 1912), 93–94, 96, 121, 132. Pamela R. Peters, *The*

Underground Railroad in Floyd County, Indiana (Jefferson, NC: McFarland & Co., 2001), 71–72.

25. "The Legislature," *Illinois Daily Journal*, Jan. 21, 1853. Jones, *"Black Jack,"* 2–13; Darrel Dexter, *Bondage in Egypt: Slavery in Southern Illinois* (Cape Girardeau: Center for Regional History, Southeast Missouri State University, 2011), 287.

26. *Moore v. Illinois*, 55 U.S. 13 (1852), 15–16, 18; *Eells v. People*, 5 Ill. 498 (1843). Cole, *Era of the Civil War*, 112; Jones, *"Black Jack,"* 15, 17–19.

27. "An Act to Prevent the Immigration of Free Negroes into this State," Feb. 12, 1853, *General Laws of the State of Illinois Passed by the Eighteenth General Assembly* (Springfield, IL: Lanphier and Walker, 1853), 57–60.

28. "Illinois Legislature," *Illinois Daily Journal*, Feb. 4, 1853. Halsey, *History of Lake County*, 96.

29. Undated speech by John A. Logan, box 55, John A. Logan Papers, MDLC. "Illinois Legislature," *Illinois Daily Journal*, Feb. 4, 1853; "The Negro Law," *Illinois Daily Journal*, Feb. 17, 1853; Ch. 30, §149, *Compilation of the Statutes of the State of Illinois, of a General Nature, in Force January 1, 1856* (Chicago: Keen & Lee, 1856), I, 386.

30. Brent M. S. Campney, " 'The Peculiar Climate of this Region': The 1854 Cairo Lynching and the Historiography of Racist Violence against Blacks in Illinois," *Journal of the Illinois State Historical Society* 107, no. 2 (Summer 2014): 143–44, 154–55; Dexter, *Bondage in Egypt*, 390–93.

31. "Free Colored Men.—No. 2," *Western Citizen*, Sept. 28, 1847; Eric Foner, "Politics and Prejudice: The Free Soil Party and the Negro, 1849–1852," *Journal of Negro History* 50, no. 4 (Oct. 1965): 250–53; Wesley, "Participation of Negroes," 64; Blight, *Frederick Douglass*, 268–70; Edward Magdol, *Owen Lovejoy, Abolitionist in Congress* (New Brunswick, NJ: Rutgers University Press, 1967), 97–100; Jane Ann Moore and William F. Moore, *Owen Lovejoy and the Coalition for Equality: Clergy, African Americans, and Women United for Abolition* (Urbana: University of Illinois Press, 2020), esp. 78–83.

32. "The Illinois Press on the Black Law," *Western Citizen*, March 8, 1853; "The Black Law," *Western Citizen*, March 22, 1853; "Infamous," *National Era*, March 10, 1853. See also "Illinois Slave Law," *Springfield Journal*, April 2, 1853; "Egypt Not All Darkness," *National Era*, Aug. 4, 1853; "The Illinois Black Law," *Massachusetts Spy*, March 23, 1853.

33. "Colored Tea Party," *Daily Democrat Press* (Chicago), March 11, 1853, CN, box 7; "The African Methodist Church," *Western Citizen*, April 5, 1853; "Organization of a Colored Baptist Church in Chicago," and "Meeting of the Colored People," *Western Citizen*, May 3, 1853.

34. Miller, *Search for a Black Nationality*, 115–69; Cheek and Cheek, *John Mercer Langston*, 172–73, 188–93; Jones, *Birthright Citizens*, 95–96; Ford, *Bonds of Union*, 117–20; Nikki M. Taylor, *America's First Black Socialist: The Radical Life of Peter H. Clark* (Louisville: University Press of Kentucky, 2013), 46–60.

35. *Proceedings of the Colored National Convention, Held in Rochester, July 6th, 7th, and 8th, 1853* (Rochester, NY: Frederick Douglass' Paper, 1853), 8–10.
36. *Proceedings of the Colored National Convention . . . 1853*, 11–13, 15–16.
37. *Proceedings of the First Convention of Colored Citizens of the State of Illinois*, 13, CHM; "Address of the Colored State Convention to the People of the State of Illinois," *Frederick Douglass' Paper*, Oct. 28, 1853. See also Roger D. Bridges, "Antebellum Struggle for Citizenship," *Journal of the Illinois State Historical Society* 108 (Fall–Winter 2015): 296–321.
38. John Jones to Frederick Douglass, *Frederick Douglass' Paper*, Nov. 18, 1853. "State Convention," *Western Citizen*, Oct. 18, 1853.
39. "The Press of Chicago and Mr. Douglass' Meetings," *Western Citizen*, Oct. 18, 1853. Potter, *Impending Crisis*, 155–76. Michael F. Holt, *The Fate of Their Country: Politicians, Slavery Extension, and the Coming of the Civil War* (New York: Hill & Wang, 2004), 92–110.
40. The literature on party realignment is voluminous. For Illinois, see, for example, Cole, *Era of the Civil War*, 128–29, 143–45, 207–11; James L. Huston, "The Illinois Political Realignment of 1844-1860: Revisiting the Analysis," *Journal of the Civil War Era* 1, no. 4 (Dec. 2011): 506–636; Stanley Harrold, *Lincoln and the Abolitionists* (Carbondale: Southern Illinois University Press, 2018), 33–40, 49–59. For the national scene, see Foner, *Free Soil, Free Labor, Free Men*, 124–48; Brooks, *Liberty Power*, 195–206; William E. Gienapp, *The Origins of the Republican Party, 1852-1856* (New York: Oxford University Press, 1987); Potter, *Impending Crisis*, 225–66; Wilentz, *Rise of American Democracy*, 672–706; Adam I. P. Smith, *The Stormy Present: Conservatism and the Problem of Slavery in Northern Politics, 1846–1865* (Chapel Hill: University of North Carolina Press, 2017), esp. 68–80. For a recent argument that Harriet Beecher Stowe's *Uncle Tom's Cabin* was central to this process, see John L. Brooke, *"There Is A North": Fugitive Slaves, Political Crisis, and Cultural Transformation in the Coming of the Civil War* (Amherst: University of Massachusetts Press, 2019).
41. Treaty of Guadeloupe Hidalgo (1848), 9 Stat. 929. For the distinction between state and national citizenship before the Fourteenth Amendment, see Lash, *Fourteenth Amendment*, 47–65; Parker, *Marking Foreigners*, 63–65; Kettner, *Development of American Citizenship*.
42. "Secretary Clayton's Law of Passports," *North Star*, Aug. 24, 1849; "Letter from William W. Brown," *North Star*, Dec. 14, 1849. Craig Robertson, *The Passport in America: The History of a Document* (New York: Oxford University Press, 2010), 131–34, 143–48; Pryor, *Colored Travelers*, 114–23; Litwack, *North of Slavery*, 54–56.
43. *CG*, 33 Cong., 1 sess., 1744.
44. Allison Brownwell Tirres, "Ownership without Citizenship: The Creation of Noncitizen Property Rights," *Michigan Journal of Race & Law* 19 (Fall 2013): 23–24.
45. "Pre-emption Rights of Colored Persons," *Opinions of the Attorney General* 4:148

(emphasis in the original); *Buffalo Convention*, 35. A longer tradition held that "denizens" were exempted from anti-alien property laws. Tirres, "Ownership without Citizenship," 12.

46. *CG*, 33 Cong., 1 sess., 1073, 1072. In 1850, a federal law providing land for settlers in Oregon had made only white people eligible, despite protests by anti-slavery congressmen. James M. Bergquist, "The Oregon Donation Act and the National Land Policy," *Oregon Historical Quarterly* 58, no. 1 (March 1957): 17–35. Roy M. Robbins, *Our Landed Heritage: The Public Domain, 1776–1936* (Princeton, NJ: Princeton University Press, 1942); Mark A. Lause, *Young America: Land, Labor, and the Republican Community* (Urbana: University of Illinois Press, 2005).

47. *CG*, 33 Cong., 1 sess., 1072.

48. *CG*, 33 Cong., 1 sess., 529, 504.

49. "Relation of Indians to Citizenship," *Opinions of the Attorney General* 7:747, 751, 753.

50. Don E. Fehrenbacher, *The Dred Scott Case: Its Significance in American Law and Politics* (New York: Oxford University Press, 1978), 256–65, 276–80. See also Kenneth C. Kaufman, *Dred Scott's Advocate: A Biography of Roswell M. Field* (Columbia: University of Missouri Press, 1996); Lea Vandervelde, *Redemption Songs: Suing for Freedom before Dred Scott* (New York: Oxford University Press, 2014); Kelly M. Kennington, *In the Shadow of Dred Scott: St. Louis Freedom Suits and the Legal Culture of Slavery in Antebellum America* (Athens: University of Georgia Press, 2017); Twitty, *Before Dred Scott.*

51. *Dred Scott v. Sanford*, 60 U.S. 393, 451 (1857). Fehrenbacher, *Dred Scott Case*, 288; and, for the deeper history of slaveholders' arguments, see Wilentz, *No Property in Man*, esp. 191–98, 214–15, 233–34.

52. *Dred Scott*, 407.

53. *CG*, 31 Cong., 1 sess., appendix, 1664.

54. Fehrenbacher, *Dred Scott Case*, 267–78, 281–82; William Ernest Smith, *The Francis Preston Blair Family in Politics*, 2 vols. (New York: Macmillan, 1933), I, 380–96.

55. "John Mercer Langston," *Frederick Douglass' Paper*, June 16, 1854; "Address to the Citizens of Ohio," *Palladium of Liberty*, Dec. 27, 1843. Cheek and Cheek, *John Mercer Langston*, 208–10, 226–27.

56. *Argument of Montgomery Blair, of Counsel for the Plaintiff in Error* (no publication information), 13.

57. *Dred Scott*, 409, 416, 404.

58. *Dred Scott*, 405, 416–17, 422.

59. "Advice Which No Black Man Is Bound to Respect," *Frederick Douglass' Paper*, March 27, 1853. Fehrenbacher, *Dred Scott Case*, 417–48; Jones, *Birthright Citizens*, 132–43; Sarah L. H. Gronningsater, "'On Behalf of His Race and the Lemmon Slaves': Louis Napoleon, Northern Black Legal Culture, and the Politics of Sectional Crisis," *Journal of the Civil War Era* 7, no. 2 (June 2017):

220–28; Millington Bergeson-Lockwood, "'In Accordance with the Spirit of the Times': African American Citizenship and the Civil Rights Act of 1866 in New England Law and Politics," in Samito, ed., *Greatest and the Grandest Act* (Carbondale: Southern Illinois University Press, 2018), 89–99; Bonner, *Remaking the Republic*, 126–48.

60. Wilson, *Rise and Fall*, I, 488. Nason and Russell, *Life and Public Service of Henry Wilson*, 30–31, 48–50; Ernest McKay, *Henry Wilson: Practical Radical* (Port Washington, NY: Kennikat Press, 1971), 93, 112–15.

61. *CG*, 36 Cong., 1 sess., 60; Charles S. Wilson to Lyman Trumbull, May 12, 1858, CN, box 10. Mark M. Krug, *Lyman Trumbull, Conservative Radical* (New York: A. S. Barnes, 1965), 61–62, 96–111.

62. "Negro Equality in Illinois," *Springfield State Register*, May 19, 1857, CN, box 7; *Remarks of the Hon. Stephen A. Douglas on Kansas, Utah, and the Dred Scott Decision* (Chicago: Daily Times, 1857), 7–9; *CG*, 31 Cong., 1 sess., appendix, 1664. Cole, *Era of the Civil War*, 153–54.

63. "Speech at Springfield, Illinois," June 26, 1857, *CWAL*, II, 406; *LDD*, 42.

64. *LDD*, 19–20, 111.

65. *LDD*, 235, 82. "The Real Issue," *Chicago Press and Tribune*, July 16, 1858, CN, box 10. See also "Negro Equality," *Alton* [IL] *Daily Courier*, July 22, 1858, ibid. For further context, see Foner, *Fiery Trial*, 102–10, 117–23.

66. *Proceedings of the State Convention of Colored Citizens of the State of Illinois, Held in the City of Alton, Nov. 13th, 14th and 15th, 1854* (Chicago: Hays & Thompson, 1856), 18; "Sunday Morning Session," *Anti-Slavery Bugle*, Oct. 6, 1860. See also "Speech of H. Ford Douglass," *Liberator*, July 13, 1860. Robert L. Harris, Jr., "H. Ford Douglas: Afro-American Antislavery Emigrationist," *Journal of Negro History* 62, no. 3 (July 1977): 217–34.

67. Ore. Const. of 1857, art. 1, §36, art. 15, §8, in *FSC*, V, 3000, 3015. Foner, *Free Soil, Free Labor, Free Men*, 284–98; Finkelman, "Before the Fourteenth Amendment," 429–30.

68. *CG*, 35 Cong., 2d sess., 1967, 979.

69. *CG*, 35 Cong., 2d sess., 1965, 976.

70. *CG*, 35 Cong., 2d sess., 982–85. Julian, *Life of Joshua R. Giddings*, 398–99; Magliocca, *Bingham*, 42.

CHAPTER 8: "ESTABLISHING ONE LAW FOR THE WHITE AND COLORED PEOPLE ALIKE"

1. Letter printed in Nason and Russell, *Life and Public Service of Henry Wilson*, 318. For John Jay II's work on his father's biography, see Tuckerman, *William Jay*, iii.

2. The issues discussed in this chapter have often been written about individually but rarely if ever discussed as part of a coherent agenda to promote racial equality in civil rights.

3. James M. McPherson, *Battle Cry of Freedom: The Civil War Era* (New York: Oxford University Press, 1988), 264–75; Oakes, *Freedom National*, 110–44.

4. *OR*, ser. 1, vol. 2, 40–42, 60. *The Civil War Defenses of Washington: Historic Resources Study*, United States Department of the Interior, National Park Service, National Capital Region, Washington, DC, ch. 4, https://www.nps.gov/parkhistory/online_books/civilwar/hrst.htm.

5. "Chronicles of the War," *NASS*, May 4, 1861; *OR*, ser. 1, vol. 2, 299–300, 759; *Eighth Annual Report of William J. Mullen, Prison Agent, to the Philadelphia Society, for Alleviating the Miseries of Public Prisons, Jan. 1, 1862* (Philadelphia: Familton & Chemin, 1862), 14. Northern Virginia was less dense with plantations and slaves than the state's southeastern counties near Union-occupied Fort Monroe. Still, enslaved people comprised between 26 percent and 30 percent of the population in Fairfax, Loudon, and Prince William Counties, according to the 1860 US Census.

6. Ira Berlin et al., eds., *Freedom: A Documentary History of Emancipation*, ser. 1, vol. 1, *The Destruction of Slavery* (New York: Cambridge University Press, 1985), 168.

7. *Report of William J. Mullen*, 13–14; "A Visit to Washington Jail," *Liberator*, Dec. 13, 1861; "Virtual Emancipation," *New York Evening Post*, Oct. 21, 1861.

8. Grimes and Cameron quoted in William Salter, *The Life of James W. Grimes* (New York: D. Appleton, 1876), 142, 143. See also ibid., 53–55, 68–69, 70–71, 75–76, 115, 99, 118–19, 128. *SCP*, 2, 387–88; Morton M. Rosenberg, *Iowa on the Eve of the Civil War: A Decade of Frontier Politics* (Norman: University of Oklahoma Press, 1972), 90–109; Dykstra, *Bright Radical Star*, 116–17, 126–27, 149–50.

9. "Our Washington Letter," *Chicago Tribune*, Dec. 5, 1861.

10. "Imprisoning Slaves at Washington," *Bangor Daily Whig and Courier*, Oct. 7, 1861. See also *Liberator*, Oct. 18, 1861; "From Washington," *North American and United States Gazette*, Nov. 18, 1861; Untitled, *Douglass' Monthly*, Nov. 1861, 557; "Notes from the Capital," *Independent*, Oct. 10, 1861.

11. For the suggestion that the instructions to Pinkerton originated in Seward's State Department, which discovered alleged fugitive slaves in the jail while looking for state prisoners, see "News from Washington," *New York Times*, Dec. 8, 1861. Pinkerton letters to McClellan in vols. 31, 32 of George Brinton McClellan Papers, MDLC. On Pinkerton: "Death Comes at Last," *Chicago Herald*, July 2, 1884, clipping in Pinkerton Papers, CHM; Allen [*sic*] Pinkerton, "To the Liberty Friends," *Western Citizen*, Oct. 29, 1850; *History of Johnson County, Iowa, Containing a History of the County and its Townships, Cities and Villages from 1836 to 1882* (Iowa City, 1883), 475–76; James D. Horan, *The Pinkertons: The Detective Dynasty That Made History* (New York: Crown, 1967), 19–23, 31, 36.

12. *CG*, 37 Cong., 2d sess., 10–11.

13. *CG*, 37 Cong., 2d sess., 10. For Hale's 1848 "riot bill," see John Parker Hale Papers, box 7, New Hampshire Historical Society, and Stanley C. Harrold, Jr., "The Pearl Affair: The Washington Riot of 1848," *Records of the Columbia Historical Society* 50 (1980): 140–60.

14. *OR*, ser. 2, vol. 1, 782. James M. McPherson, *The Struggle for Equality: Abolitionists and the Negro in the Civil War and Reconstruction* (Princeton, NJ: Princeton University Press, 1964), 72–81.

15. *OR*, ser. 2, vol. 1, 783. Amon Duvall to Henry Wilson, Dec. 6, 1861, William Seward Papers, MDLC.

16. *Report of William J. Mullen*, 14; "A Visit to Washington Jail," *Liberator*, Dec. 13, 1861; "Persecution of Negroes in the Capitol [*sic*]: Astounding Revelations," *Frank Leslie's Illustrated Weekly*, Dec. 28, 1861, 82.

17. "Erroneous Statement," *Washington Evening Star*, Dec. 11, 1861; "Political Experimentation," *WNI*, April 4, 1862.

18. The Republican majority had beaten back an effort, led by Democrats, to require all persons liberated by the act to be "colonized" outside the United States. *CG*, 37 Cong., 2d sess., 1191, 1333. Leonard P. Curry, *Blueprint for Modern America: Non-Military Legislation of the First Civil War Congress* (Nashville, TN: Vanderbilt University Press, 1968), 36–43.

19. "Message to Congress," April 16, 1862, *CWAL*, 5, 192; Doolittle quoted in Curry, *Blueprint*, 43.

20. *CG*, 37 Cong., 2d sess., 917–18.

21. *CG*, 37 Cong., 2d sess., 1350, 1351; *SCW*, VIII, 305.

22. "An Act Providing for the Education of Colored Children in the Cities of Washington and Georgetown, District of Columbia, and for Other Purposes," 12 Stat. 407; *CG*, 37 Cong., 2d sess., 1518, 3138. The *Congressional Globe* published Senate votes for the bills on DC emancipation, public schools and repeal of the black laws, Sumner's equal testimony amendment, and the larger bill that included that amendment; House vote totals are available for the emancipation bill and the larger bill that contained Sumner's testimony provision. Among all the votes provided, only two Republicans, Edgar Cowan of Pennsylvania and Orville Browning of Illinois, recorded votes in opposition. Both men voted against the equal testimony amendment but went on to support the larger law of which it was part. *CG*, 37 Cong., 2d sess., 1526, 1648–49, 2037, 2157, 3138, 3215–16. Kate Masur, *An Example for All the Land: Emancipation and the Struggle over Equality in Washington, D.C.* (Chapel Hill: University of North Carolina Press, 2010), 25, 27.

23. Testimony of George E. H. Day, Esq., [March 1863,] American Freedmen's Inquiry Commission Records, file 1, (National Archives Microfilm Publication M619, roll 200), NARA.

24. "First Inaugural Address—Final Text," March 4, 1861, in Basler, ed., *CWAL*, 4, 264.

25. Sumner to Francis W. Bird, March 12, 1862, *SLCS*, II, 104; Sumner to Horace Gray Jr., April 5, 1862, ibid., 108–9.

26. "Circumventing the Dred Scott Decision," 280–81, 286, 287.

27. Marvin R. Cain, *Lincoln's Attorney General Edward Bates of Missouri* (Columbia: University of Missouri Press, 1965), 46, 78, 79; Smith, *Francis Preston Blair*

Family, I, 461–69; Anne Twitty, *Before Dred Scott: Slavery and Legal Culture in the American Confluence, 1787–1857* (New York: Cambridge University Press, 2016), 111–12. Don Fehrenbacher speculated that the case influenced Bates's decision to become a Republican. Fehrenbacher, *Dred Scott Case,* 565.

28. Memorandum read by E. Bates (in C.C.), Sept. 25, 1862, box 1, Edward Bates Papers, MDLC. Bates's biographer wrote that Bates favored "forcible deportation," but there is no evidence for that. Cain, *Lincoln's Attorney General,* 221.

29. James P. McClure et al., "Circumventing the Dred Scott Decision: Edward Bates, Salmon P. Chase, and the Citizenship of African Americans," *Civil War History* 43, no. 4 (Dec. 1997): 288.

30. Edward Bates to Francis Lieber, Oct. 21, 1862, box 2, Francis Lieber Papers, Huntington Library, San Marino, CA. See also Bates to Lieber, Nov. 22, 1862, Dec. 1, 1862, ibid.; Lieber to Bates, Oct. 25, 1862, Nov. 21, 1862, Nov. 25, 1862, Nov. 29, 1862, box 23, Lieber Papers. Entry of Sept. 15, 1862, *SCP,* 1, 287; "Circumventing the Dred Scott Decision," 280, 282. Frank Freidel, *Francis Lieber: Nineteenth-Century Liberal* (Baton Rouge: Louisiana State University Press, 1947), 309, 314–15.

31. *Opinion of Attorney General Bates on Citizenship* (Washington, DC: Government Printing Office, 1862), 15, 26–27.

32. Bates to Winthrop, Jan. 5, 1863, WFMHS. Bates added that if states could "exclude for color, then why not for race, religion, nativity, or any other discretionary cause?"

33. Bates to Winthrop, Jan. 5, 1863; Bates to Winthrop, Jan. 12, 1863, WFMHS.

34. "Dred Scott Redivivus," *Milwaukee Daily Sentinel,* Dec. 22, 1862.

35. Charles Sumner to Lord Wharncliffe, Dec. 19 and 24, 1852, in *SLCS,* I, 379. Fehrenbacher, *Slaveholding Republic,* 116–18.

36. "Annual Message to Congress," Dec. 3, 1861, *CWAL,* 5, 39; Sumner to John Andrew, April 22, 1862, *SLCS,* II, 109; *SCW,* VIII, 310, 328; "The Recognition of Negro Hayti and Negro Liberia,—Negro Equality Proclaimed," *Cincinnati Daily Enquirer,* June 6, 1862. For Lincoln's motivations for recognizing Haiti at this time, including the possibility that he may have seen it as a destination for Black emigration, see Rayford W. Logan, *The Diplomatic Relations of the United States with Haiti, 1776–1891* (Chapel Hill: University of North Carolina Press, 1941), 296–303; Foner, *Fiery Trial,* 186, 222.

37. "Arrival of the Haytian Minister," *New York Times,* Feb. 18, 1863; "The Minister from Hayti," *New York Times,* March 2, 1863; "Gentlemen of Color," *Cincinnati Daily Enquirer,* May 7, 1863.

38. "The Manhood of the Negro," *Independent,* Oct. 24, 1861, reprinted with transcription of the passport in *Douglass' Monthly,* Nov. 1861, 557. The department also provided a passport to Robert Morris Jr., the son of an African American lawyer from Boston with whom Sumner worked closely. *SCW,* VII, 229–30.

39. "A Striking Conjunction," *Detroit Free Press,* March 15, 1863. "Great Honors to a Negro," *Cincinnati Daily Enquirer,* March 21, 1863; George Lawrence, Jr., to the Editor of the New York Sunday *Mercury, Liberator,* March 13, 1863; "The

Diplomatic Dinner," ibid., March 27, 1863; Untitled, *Newport Mercury*, March 21, 1863.

40. "Speech of Frederick Douglass," *Liberator*, July 24, 1863.

41. Ira Berlin et al., eds., *Freedom: A Documentary History of Emancipation*, ser. 2, *The Black Military Experience* (New York: Cambridge University Press, 1982), 370–71. For an overview of the conflict and resolution: ibid., 362–68; McPherson, *Struggle for Equality*, 212–17.

42. *Black Military Experience*, 436; *Proceedings of the National Convention of Colored Men, Held in the City of Syracuse, N.Y., October 4, 5, 6, and 7, 1864* (Boston: J. S. Rock and Geo. L. Ruffin, 1864), 23. The Republican platform, released in May ·1864, demanded equal pay for Black soldiers, stating: "That the Government owes to all men employed in its armies, without regard to distinction of color, the full protection of the laws of war." Porter, comp., *National Party Platforms*, 62. Herman Belz, *A New Birth of Freedom: The Republican Party and Freedmen's Rights, 1861 to 1866* (Westport, CT: Greenwood Press, 1976), 22–25.

43. *Constitutional Union*, June 22, 1863; James J. Ferree to Gen. Martindale, July 20, 1863, Letters Received, ser. 646, Department of Washington, Records of the United States Army Continental Commands, 1828-1920, Record Group 393, pt. 2, NARA.

44. *Washington Evening Star*, June 10, 1863; *Anglo-African*, Aug. 1, 1863; *Christian Recorder*, June 20, 1863, July 4, 1863, July 11, 1863, Oct. 3, 1863.

45. *Anglo-African*, November 7, 1863.

46. *SCW*, VIII, 6, 247; ibid., XI, 2–42, 389–96. The mail bill did not pass until the spring of 1865. 13 Stat. 515. Alfred Avins, "The Right to Be a Witness and the Fourteenth Amendment," *Missouri Law Review* 31, no. 4 (Fall 1966): 484–88. In the spring of 1862, Sumner also oversaw the addition of a measure barring racial discrimination in legal proceedings associated with the Second Confiscation Act. Curry, *Blueprint for Modern America*, 92.

47. *CG*, 38 Cong., 1 sess., 1706, 1844, 2350.

48. In December 1863, Congressman James Ashley of Ohio proposed that rebel states be readmitted with Black men enfranchised. After the proposal was hashed over in committee, it emerged as the Wade-Davis bill without a provision for Black men's enfranchisement. Belz, *New Birth of Freedom*, 57–59; Vorenberg, *Final Freedom*, 49–50.

49. *CG*, 38 Cong., 1 sess., 1346.

50. *CG*, 38 Cong., 1 sess., 1746, 1844, 2348. See also ibid., 1705–6, 1744–45, 1842–46, 2347–48. Quintard Taylor, *In Search of the Racial Frontier: African Americans in the American West, 1528–1990* (New York: W. W. Norton, 1998), 121; Michael Les Benedict, *A Compromise of Principle: Congressional Republicans and Reconstruction, 1863–1869* (New York: W. W. Norton, 1974), 78–79.

51. For the origin of the bill, see *CG*, 38 Cong., 1 sess., 631; *The Charter of the City of Washington . . . Passed by the Congress of the United States* (Washington, DC: John T. Towers, 1848), 21; C. A. Stewart et al. to the U.S. Senate and House of Representatives, [April 1864], 38A-J4, Records of the US Senate, Record Group

46, NARA. "Our Washington Correspondence," *Anglo-African,* February 13, 1864; "The Suffrage at the Capitol," ibid., June 4, 1864.

52. *CG,* 38 Cong., 1 sess., 2239–49, 2140, 2512; "The District before Congress," *WNI,* March 24, 1864; "Corporation of Washington," *WNI,* March 25, 1864; "A Resolution to Amend the Charter of the City of Washington," 13 Stat. 407.

53. James M. McPherson, *The Negro's Civil War: How American Negroes Felt and Acted during the War for the Union* (New York: Vintage, 1965), 275–79; David S. Cecelski, *The Fire of Freedom: Abraham Galloway & the Slaves' Civil War* (Chapel Hill: University of North Carolina Press, 2012), 115–17.

54. *Anderson v. Milliken,* 9 Ohio St. 568 (1859); Winkle, "Ohio's Informal Polling Place," 181–82; "An Act to repeal section two of an act entitled 'an act for the relief of the poor,' passed March 14, 1853," *General and Local Laws . . . Passed at the Fifty-Sixth General Assembly of the State of Ohio* (Columbus: Richard Nevins, 1865), 62, 133. *The Code of Civil Procedure and Other General Statutes of Oregon . . . 1862* (n.p., OR: Asahel Bush, 1863), 174–76. Finkelman, "Before the Fourteenth Amendment," 422, 437; Stacey L. Smith, *Freedom's Frontier: California and the Struggle over Unfree Labor, Emancipation, and Reconstruction* (Chapel Hill: University of North Carolina Press, 2013), 180–81. Oregon did not repeal its constitutional ban on Black settlement until 1926, though it was not legally enforceable after the 1866 Civil Rights Act and ratification of the Fourteenth Amendment.

55. Nathan E. Coffin, "The Case of Archie P. Webb, A Free Negro," *Annals of Iowa,* ser. 3, vol. 11 (Apr. 1913–Jan. 1915): 200–214; Leslie Schwalm, *Emancipation's Diaspora: Race and Reconstruction in the Upper Midwest* (Chapel Hill: University of North Carolina Press, 2009), 102–4.

56. "Barbarism in Illinois," *Liberator,* March 27, 1863; *Nelson v. Illinois,* 33 Ill. 390, 396 (1864).

57. "The News," *Chicago Tribune,* Jan. 6, 1865; John Jones, *The Black Laws of Illinois, and a Few Reasons Why They Should Be Repealed* (Chicago: Tribune, 1864), 13; "The 'Black Laws' of Illinois," *Liberator,* Dec. 9, 1864; "Illinois Legislature," *Chicago Tribune,* Jan. 6, 1865.

58. *Proceedings . . . 1864,* 51–52. Vorenberg, *Final Freedom,* 148–57. Garrison had also said that summer that he did not favor Black men's immediate enfranchisement. McPherson, *Struggle for Equality,* 294–95.

59. *Proceedings . . . 1864;* Jones, *All Bound Up Together*; Dudden, *Fighting Chance,* 18–19.

60. *Proceedings . . . 1864,* 49, 50, 56, 60.

61. *Proceedings . . . 1864,* 36–37, quotation on 36.

CHAPTER 9: "TO RESTRAIN THE POWER OF THE STATES"

1. "The Anniversaries," *New York Times,* May 10, 1865; "Thirty-Second Anniversary of the American Anti-Slavery Society," *NASS,* May 20, 1865.

2. Frederick Douglass, "In What New Skin Will the Old Snake Come Forth? An

Address Delivered in New York, New York, on 10 May 1865," in John W. Blassingame and John R. McKivigan, eds., *The Frederick Douglass Papers: Series One: Speeches, Debates, and Interviews, Vol. 4: 1864–80* (New Haven: Yale University Press, 1991), 81.

3. Douglass, "In What New Skin," 82.

4. Belz, *New Birth of Freedom*, 38–48; Vorenberg, *Final Freedom*, esp. 109–10; Leonard L. Richards, *Who Freed the Slaves? The Fight over the Thirteenth Amendment* (Chicago: University of Chicago Press, 2015); Amy Dru Stanley, "Instead of Waiting for the Thirteenth Amendment: The War Power, Slave Marriage, and Inviolate Human Rights," *American Historical Review* 115, no. 3 (June 2010): 733n3, 740, 744–47; Laura F. Edwards, *A Legal History of the Civil War and Reconstruction: A Nation of Rights* (New York: Cambridge University Press, 2015), 79–89.

5. "Proclamation Establishing Government for North Carolina," May 29, 1865, in *PAJ*, vol. 8, *May–August 1865*, 136–38. Johnson twice stated publicly that he favored the right to vote for African Americans who were literate or wealthy taxpayers, but he never required a state government to implement Black men's enfranchisement in any form. Benedict, *Compromise of Principle*, 107–8; Brooks D. Simpson, *The Reconstruction Presidents* (Lawrence: University Press of Kansas, 1998), 78–80.

6. Brooks D. Simpson, Leroy P. Graf, and John Muldowny, eds., *Advice After Appomattox: Letters to Andrew Johnson, 1865–1866* (Knoxville: University of Tennessee Press, 1987), 90, 100. See also essays and documents in Steven Hahn et al., eds., *Freedom: A Documentary History of Emancipation, 1861–1867,* ser. 3, vol. 1, *Land and Labor, 1865* (Chapel Hill: University of North Carolina Press, 2008).

7. *Land and Labor, 1865*, 187.

8. General Orders 77, *OR,* ser. 1, vol. 46, pt. 3, 1293. See also *Land and Labor, 1865*, 205–14, 339–40.

9. *Land and Labor, 1865*, 221, 259, 957. The army remained consistent, at least at the level of top brass. See, for example, ibid., 189–92.

10. Simpson, *Reconstruction Presidents,* 80–89; Eric Foner, *Reconstruction: America's Unfinished Revolution, 1863–1877* (New York: Harper & Row, 1988), 199–200; Vorenberg, *Final Freedom,* 228–33.

11. Edward McPherson, *Political History of the United States of America during the Period of Reconstruction* (Washington, DC: Solomons & Chapman, 1875), 29–32.

12. Johnson to Benjamin Humphreys, Nov. 17, 1865, in *PAJ*, vol. 9, *September 1865–January 1866,* 397. Benedict, *Compromise of Principle*, 128–31; *Land and Labor, 1865*, 291, 910–11; Gregory P. Downs, *After Appomattox: Military Occupation and the Ends of War* (Cambridge: Harvard University Press, 2015), 104–11; Donald G. Nieman, *To Set the Law in Motion: The Freedmen's Bureau and the Legal Rights of Blacks, 1865–1868* (Millwood, NY: KTO Press, 1979), 7, 17–23.

13. "Address from the Colored Citizens of Norfolk, Va., to the People of the

United States," in Philip S. Foner and George E. Walker, *Proceedings of the Black National and State Conventions, 1865–1900* (Philadelphia: Temple University Press, 1986), 84; "An Address to the Loyal Citizens and Congress of the United States of America," in Philip S. Foner and George E. Walker, *Proceedings of the Black State Conventions, 1840–1865*, 2 vols. (Philadelphia: Temple University Press, 1979–1980), II, 271; "Memorial to the Senate and House of Representatives of the United States, in Congress Assembled," in ibid., 302. *Land and Labor, 1865*, 195–96; Simpson, *Reconstruction Presidents*, 83–84.

14. *Anglo-African*, Nov. 11, 1865 (letter of Oct. 20, 1865); *Land and Labor, 1865*, 457; *BAP*, vol. 5, *The United States, 1859–1865*, 372–73; *Proceedings of the First Annual Meeting of the Equal Rights League* (Philadelphia: E. C. Markle and Son, 1865), 47; "An Address to the Colored People of the United States by William Nesbit, Esq.," in Foner and Walker, *Proceedings of the Black National and State Conventions*, 66; "Convention of Colored Citizens," *Boston Advertiser*, Dec. 2, 1865. The *Anglo-African* endorsed the plan in its issues of Nov. 11, 1865, and Dec. 23, 1865. For additional meetings to select delegates, see *San Francisco Daily Evening Bulletin*, Jan. 3, 1866; *Bangor Daily Whig & Courier*, Dec. 18, 1865; *New Hampshire Statesman*, Jan. 5, 1866.

15. Benedict, *Compromise of Principle*, 121–26, 134–61; Simpson, *Reconstruction Presidents*, 85–92; Foner, *Reconstruction*, 224–27, 239; Downs, *After Appomattox*, 115–19.

16. "Message to Congress," Dec. 4, 1865, in *PAJ*, vol. 9, *September 1865–January 1866*, 474.

17. *CG*, 39 Cong., 1 sess., 39–43.

18. McPherson, *Political History*, 6, 72–74. Downs, *After Appomattox*, 114, 121–22.

19. "An Act to Protect All Persons in the United States in their Civil Rights, and to Furnish the Means of their Vindication," S. 61, 39 Cong., 1 sess., passed by the Senate, Feb. 2, 1866. For Trumbull's many modifications of the bill, see Benedict, *Compromise of Principle*, 147–49.

20. *CG*, 39 Cong., 1 sess., 474, 1292. Many historians have failed to recognize that the Senate passed the Civil Rights Bill with the "inhabitants" language intact, nor have they connected that move to the fact that in the antebellum United States, people not recognized as citizens (including immigrant aliens and, in many cases, free African Americans) regularly exercised what people commonly understood as civil rights. See, for example, George Rutherglen, *Civil Rights in the Shadow of Slavery: The Constitution, Common Law, and the Civil Rights Act of 1866* (New York: Oxford University Press, 2013), esp. 29, 51; Lash, *Fourteenth Amendment*, 114–18. For an exception, however, see Benedict, "Membership of a Nation."

21. William Horatio Barnes, *History of the Thirty-ninth Congress of the United States* (New York: Harper & Bros., 1868), 190. Robert J. Kaczorowski, "The Inverted Constitution: Enforcing Constitutional Rights in the Nineteenth Century," in Sandra F. VanBurkleo, Kermit L. Hall, and Kaczorowski, eds., *Constitutionalism*

and American Culture: Writing the New Constitutional History (Lawrence: University Press of Kansas, 2002).

22. CG, 39 Cong., 1 sess., 474–75.

23. Benedict, "Salmon P. Chase and Constitutional Politics," 136–37; Richard L. Aynes, "On Misreading John Bingham and the Fourteenth Amendment," Yale Law Journal 103 (1993): 74–78.

24. CG, 39 Cong., 1 sess., 474, 322. Senator Jacob Howard, who had served on the Judiciary Committee that drafted the Thirteenth Amendment, attested that the committee had sought to give to Congress "precisely the power over the subject of slavery and the freedmen which is proposed to be exercised by the bill." CG, 39 Cong., 1 sess., 503. Belz, New Birth of Freedom, 117–28, 159; Vorenberg, Final Freedom, 55–56; Edwards, Legal History of the Civil War and Reconstruction, 98–110.

25. CG, 39 Cong., 1 sess., 504, 1118.

26. CG, 39 Cong., 1 sess., 505. Johnson warned that any law, imposed from above, that was out of step with local sentiment would be vehemently opposed, as the Fugitive Slave Act had been in the free states. Congress would be moving toward a situation in which enforcement would necessarily be "by bayonet."

27. CG, 39 Cong., 1 sess., 498.

28. CG, 39 Cong., 1 sess., 1122.

29. Boston Daily Advertiser, Jan. 17, 1866, Jan. 24, 1866; "General Howard and the Colored Delegation," National Republican, Jan. 24, 1866; O. O. Howard, Autobiography. 2 vols. (New York: Baker and Taylor, 1907), II, 317; Chicago Tribune, Feb. 1, 1866; "Appeal of the Representative Colored Men to Congress," National Republican, Jan. 18, 1866.

30. "The Claims of Our Race: An Interview with President Andrew Johnson in Washington, D.C., on 7 February 1866," in Frederick Douglass Papers: Series One . . . Vol. 4: 1864-80, 98. See also "The President and a Colored Deputation," WNI, Feb. 8, 1866.

31. "The Claims of Our Race," 99–103, 106. Like so many of his allies—including Andrew Jackson Rogers—Johnson said he wanted the best for Black people. For example: "God knows that anything I can do I will do. In the mighty process by which the great end is to be reached, anything I can do to elevate the races. . . ." (104).

32. "The Claims of Our Race," 612–13.

33. "Speech to First Regiment, USCT," Oct. 10, 1865, in PAJ, vol. 9, September 1865–January 1866, 219–23. Eric L. McKitrick, Andrew Johnson and Reconstruction (Chicago: University of Chicago Press, 1960), 292–95; Benedict, Compromise of Principle, 155–56; Simpson, Reconstruction Presidents, 94–95; Benjamin B. Kendrick, The Journal of the Joint Committee of Fifteen on Reconstruction (New York: Columbia University Press, 1914), 225–34, 239–50.

34. CG, 39 Cong., 1 sess., 505, 500, 497. On Johnson's veto influencing the House debate, see Lash, Fourteenth Amendment, 97, 119.

35. *CG*, 39 Cong., 1 sess., 1293. Wilson's changes are printed in "An Act to Protect All Persons in the United States in their Civil Rights, and to Furnish the Means of their Vindication," S. 61, 39 Cong., 1 sess., March 13, 1866, 10–11, A Century of Lawmaking for a New Nation, Library of Congress, https://memory.loc.gov/ammem/amlaw/.

36. *CG*, 39 Cong., 1 sess., 1291, 1034. Bingham might have been influenced by Chase in his view that the Constitution had not empowered Congress to enforce Article IV, §2. In the Civil Rights Act debate, Bingham also argued that a clause that banned discrimination in "civil rights and immunities" was too general and might be construed as including voting rights, which he did not favor. The House removed the clause, but Bingham continued to oppose the bill. Benedict, *Compromise of Principle*, 158–60; 162–64.

37. "Veto of Civil Rights Bill," in *PAJ*, vol. 10, *February–July 1866*, 313–14, 319–20. Johnson also said the Civil Rights Act, by allowing special recourse for people who believed they had been discriminated against, would "operate in favor of the colored and against the white race" (319).

38. René Hayden et al., eds., *Freedom: A Documentary History of Emancipation, 1861–1867*, ser. 3, vol. 2, *Land and Labor, 1866–1867* (Chapel Hill: University of North Carolina Press, 2013), 20–21. McKitrick, *Andrew Johnson*, esp. 364–420; Simpson, *Reconstruction Presidents*, 100–130.

39. Stephen Kantrowitz, " 'Not Quite Constitutionalized': The Meanings of 'Civilization' and the Limits of Native American Citizenship," in Gregory P. Downs and Kate Masur, eds., *The World the Civil War Made* (Chapel Hill: University of North Carolina Press, 2015); Earl M. Maltz, "The Fourteenth Amendment and Native American Citizenship," *Constitutional Commentary* 17, no. 3 (Winter 2000): 555–73; Najia Aarim-Heriot, *Chinese Immigrants, African Americans, and Racial Anxiety in the United States, 1848–82* (Urbana: University of Illinois Press, 2003), 84–90, 140–44; Charles J. McClain, *In Search of Equality: The Chinese Struggle against Discrimination in Nineteenth-Century America* (Berkeley: University of California Press, 1994), 36–40; Masur, *An Example for All the Land*, 141–45, 178–88; Dudden, *Fighting Chance*, esp. 70–80.

40. "The Civil Rights Bill," *Daily Cleveland Herald*, April 17 and 19, 1866; "The Civil Rights Bill," *New York Times*, April 8, 1866; "Fort Monroe: The Civil Rights Bill and the Freedmen," *New York Times*, April 15, 1866; "The Civil Rights Bill," *Boston Daily Advertiser*, April 13, 1866; "The Civil Rights Bill: Mass Meeting of the Colored People," *Chicago Tribune*, April 13, 1866; "The Emancipation Celebration," *WNI*, April 20, 1866.

41. "Disturbance in Norfolk—One White Man Killed and Two Mortally Wounded by the Negroes," *WNI*, April 17, 1866; Memphis *Bulletin*, quoted in "From Memphis," ibid., May 8, 1866. John Hammond Moore, "The Norfolk Riot, 16 April 1866," *Virginia Magazine of History and Biography* 90, no. 2 (April 1982): 155–64.

42. "The Beginning of the Test," *North American Gazette*, April 20, 1866; *Richmond*

Palladium (Wayne Co., IN), April 26, 1866; "The First Case," *Chicago Republican,* April 17, 1866; "Supreme Court of Indiana," *Cincinnati Gazette,* Nov. 2, 1866; *Smith v. Moody,* 26 Ind. 299 (1866). An Indianapolis judge also formally recognized the binding force of the Civil Rights Act when he admitted an African American person's testimony. "Indianapolis Local Elections." *WNI,* April 27, 1866.

43. "Spirit of the Southern Press," *Chicago Tribune,* April 13, 1866; "Colored Witness in a MD Court," *New York Times,* April 20, 1866; Unidentified, Scrapbook on Civil Rights Bill, 1866, 109, Edward McPherson Papers, MDLC; "Civil Rights Bill Enforced in Louisiana," *New York Tribune,* May 2, 1866; "By Telegraph," Boston *Daily Advertiser,* May 2, 1866. "The Civil Rights Bill," date unident., McPherson Scrapbook, 92–93; "The Validity of the Civil Rights Bill—Interesting Case in a Memphis Court," *Detroit Free Press,* April 20, 1866; "Legal Intelligence," *Memphis Daily Advertiser,* April 16, 1866.

44. "An Act to Protect All Persons in the United States in their Civil Rights, and Furnish the Means of their Vindication," 14 Stat. 27.

45. "Civil Rights in Tennessee," *Daily News and Herald* (Savannah, GA), May 7, 1866; "Civil Rights," *Detroit Post,* McPherson Scrapbook, 120; "The Civil Rights Law a Source of Wholesale Litigation," *WNI,* April 24, 1866; *Baltimore Gazette,* date unident., McPherson Scrapbook, 107; "Another Civil Rights Case in Baltimore," date unident., McPherson Scrapbook, 109; Untitled, *WNI,* May 8, 1866.

46. "Case Under the Civil Rights Law in Baltimore," *Baltimore Gazette,* May 25, 1866, McPherson Scrapbook, 111; Joseph P. Reidy, "Bradley, Aaron Alpeora (1815?–October 1882)," *American National Biography,* Feb. 1, 2000, accessed online, Sept. 28, 2020. Joseph William Singer, "No Right to Exclude: Public Accommodations and Private Property," *Northwestern University Law Review* 90, no. 4 (1995–96): esp. 1337–40, 1342–44.

47. *CG,* 39 Cong., 1 sess., 1034.

48. *CG,* 39 Cong., 1 sess., 1063–64, 1066, 1089, 1094.

49. *CG,* 39 Cong., 1 sess., 1095.

50. *CG,* 39 Cong., 1 sess., 2286. For committee deliberations, see Kendrick, *Journal,* 213–16, 292–306. For a good recent overview, see Eric Foner, *The Second Founding: How the Civil War and Reconstruction Remade the Constitution* (New York: W. W. Norton, 2019), 68–80. For evolving understandings of what constituted the American "Bill of Rights," see Gerard N. Magliocca, *The Heart of the Constitution: How the Bill of Rights Became the Bill of Rights* (New York: Oxford University Press, 2018).

51. *CG,* 39 Cong., 1 sess., 1034.

52. *CG,* 39 Cong., 1 sess., 1292. By the late nineteenth century, many argued that the Republicans of 1866 had intended the amendment's personhood language to include corporations and thus to establish expansive rights that corporations could claim against state regulation. That vision of a hidden agenda has been debunked: Graham, *Everyman's Constitution,* 23–97; Adam Winkler, *We the*

Corporations: How American Businesses Won Their Civil Rights (New York: Liveright, 2018), 113–60.

53. Quotations in Stanley, "Instead of Waiting," 742, 743. See also Nancy F. Cott, *Public Vows: A History of Marriage and the Nation* (Cambridge, MA: Harvard University Press, 2000), 82, 94–101.

54. Kettner, *Development of American Citizenship*, esp. 311–23. See also Belz, *New Birth of Freedom*, 163.

55. *CG*, 39 Cong., 1 sess., 2769.

56. *SCW*, XVIII, 144–68; Jones, *Birthright Citizens*; Aarim-Heriot, *Chinese Immigrants*, 144–53; Moon-Ho Jung, *Coolies and Cane: Race, Labor, and Sugar in the Age of Emancipation* (Baltimore: Johns Hopkins University Press, 2006), 136–45.

57. *The Civil Rights Cases*, 109 U.S. 3 (1883). For a brief discussion of these well-known cases, see Foner, *Second Founding*, 144–48, 154–57.

58. *CG*, 39 Cong., 1 sess., 2766.

59. *CG*, 39 Cong., 1 sess., 2459.

60. Salter, *Life of Grimes*, 292. Simpson, *Reconstruction Presidents*, 102–3; Kendrick, *Journal*, 304–19; Foner, *Reconstruction*, 222–24; Benedict, *Compromise of Principle*, 115–16.

61. "The Emancipation Celebration," *WNI*, April 20, 1866. Blackett, *Beating Against the Barriers*, 312–23. Dudden, *Fighting Chance*, 67–68, 70–80; Free, *Suffrage Reconsidered*, 109–32; Benedict, *Compromise of Principle*, 182–84.

EPILOGUE

1. Jane Rhodes, *Mary Ann Shadd Cary: The Black Press and Protest in the Nineteenth Century* (Bloomington: Indiana University Press, 1998), 10–14, 20–21, 82–88, 91–93.

2. M. A. Shadd, "Correspondence for the Provincial Freeman," *Provincial Freeman*, Feb. 2, 1856.

3. Frederick Douglass, "Reconstruction," *Atlantic Monthly*, Dec. 1866, 761–62.

4. *Slaughter-House Cases*, 83 U.S. 36, 71, 79, 78 (1873).

5. *Slaughter-House*, 125, 129, 89, 116.

6. *Argument of Charles Sumner*, 20; Peggy Pascoe, *What Comes Naturally: Miscegenation Law and the Making of Race in America* (New York: Oxford University Press, 2009), 40–45.

7. *Pace v. Alabama*, 106 U.S. 583, 585 (1883). Pascoe, *What Comes Naturally*, 47, 55–64.

8. *Roberts v. Boston*, 209; *Plessy v. Ferguson*, 163 U.S. 537 (1896).

9. "Remarks of Charles Lenox Remond," *Liberator*, Feb. 25, 1842.

10. *Land and Labor, 1865*, 12, 277. Amy Dru Stanley, *From Bondage to Contract: Wage Labor, Marriage, and the Market in the Age of Slave Emancipation* (New York: Cambridge University Press, 1998), 123–27; David Montgomery, *Beyond Equality: Labor and the Radical Republicans* (New York: Knopf, 1967), esp. x, 78–84; Foner, *Reconstruction*, 200, 372–73, 363, 593.

11. Foner, *Reconstruction*, 519; Stanley, *From Bondage to Contract*, 108–11, 116–18; Novak, *People's Welfare*, 170; Clare Pastore, "When Paupers Became People: *Edwards v. California*, (1941)," in Marie A. Failinger and Ezra Rosser, eds., *The Poverty Law Canon: Exploring the Major Cases* (Ann Arbor: University of Michigan Press, 2016), 13–31; Risa Goluboff, *Vagrant Nation: Police Power, Constitutional Change, and the Making of the 1960s* (New York: Oxford University Press, 2016).

12. Litwack, *North of Slavery*; C. Vann Woodward, "Seeds of Failure in Radical Race Policy," *Proceedings of the American Philosophical Society* 110, no. 1 (1966): 1–9; Eugene H. Berwanger, *The Frontier against Slavery: Western Anti-Negro Prejudice and the Slavery Extension Controversy* (Urbana: University of Illinois Press, 1967); V. Jacque Voegeli, *Free but Not Equal: The Midwest and the Negro during the Civil War* (Chicago: University of Chicago Press, 1967).

13. In 1865 and 1866, referenda for Black men's enfranchisement failed in several states, including Wisconsin, Connecticut, Ohio, and New York. Foner, *Reconstruction*, 223; Blackett, *Beating Against the Barriers*, 343–55.

14. J. Morgan Kousser, *Dead End: The Development of Nineteenth-Century Litigation on Racial Discrimination in Schools* (Oxford, UK: Clarendon Press, 1986); Hugh Davis, *"We Will Be Satisfied With Nothing Less": The African American Struggle for Equal Rights in the North during Reconstruction* (Ithaca, NY: Cornell University Press, 2011), 48, 72–96; Foner, *Reconstruction*, 471–72.

15. *CG*, 41 Cong., 2d sess., 3434; *Civil Rights Cases*. Gilbert Thomas Stephenson, *Race Distinctions in American Law* (New York: D. Appleton, 1910), 112, 114–115. Masur, *Example for All the Land*, 224–31; James M. McPherson, "Abolitionists and the Civil Rights Act of 1875," *Journal of American History* 52, no. 3 (Dec. 1965): 493–510.

16. Stephenson, *Race Distinctions*, 113–14, 116–18, 120–21, 216–17; David A. Joens, *From Slave to State Legislator: John W. E. Thomas, Illinois' First African American Lawmaker* (Carbondale: Southern Illinois University Press, 2012), 113–14.

17. *To Secure These Rights: The Report of the President's Committee on Civil Rights*, 1947, https://www.trumanlibrary.gov/library/to-secure-these-rights; Risa L. Goluboff, *The Lost Promise of Civil Rights* (Cambridge: Harvard University Press, 2007), esp. 115–17; *Brown v. Board of Education*, 347 U.S. 483 (1954).

18. "Address by the Reverend Dr. Martin Luther King," Oct. 15, 1962, Cornell College News Center, https://news.cornellcollege.edu/dr-martin-luther-kings-visit-to-cornell-college/. See also Martin Luther King Jr., "Recognition and Opportunity," *New York Amsterdam News*, June 6, 1964.

NOTE ON HISTORIOGRAPHY

1. The literature is voluminous, so I cite just a few examples here. Eric Foner, *Reconstruction: America's Unfinished Revolution, 1863-1877* (New York: Harper & Row, 1988); Michael Les Benedict, *A Compromise of Principle: Congressional Republicans and Reconstruction, 1863–1869* (New York: W. W. Norton, 1974); Michael Kent Curtis, *No State Shall Abridge: The Fourteenth Amendment and the*

Bill of Rights (Durham, NC: Duke University Press, 1986); Akhil Reed Amar, *The Bill of Rights* (New Haven, CT: Yale University Press, 1998); Kurt T. Lash, *The Fourteenth Amendment and the Privileges and Immunities of American Citizenship* (New York: Cambridge University Press, 2014); Manisha Sinha, *The Slave's Cause: A History of Abolition* (New Haven, CT: Yale University Press, 2016); Martha S. Jones, *Birthright Citizens: A History of Race and Rights in Antebellum America* (New York: Cambridge University Press, 2018); Michael A. Schoeppner, *Moral Contagion: Black Atlantic Sailors, Citizenship, and Diplomacy in Antebellum America* (New York: Cambridge University Press, 2018).

2. Hendrik Hartog, "The Constitution of Aspiration and 'The Rights That Belong to Us All,'" *Journal of American History* 74, no. 3 (Dec. 1987): 1013–34.

3. Graham's essays, written over two decades, are compiled in Howard Jay Graham, *Everyman's Constitution: Historical Essays on the Fourteenth Amendment, the 'Conspiracy Theory,' and American Constitutionalism* (Madison: State Historical Society of Wisconsin, 1968); Jacobus tenBroek, *The Antislavery Origins of the Fourteenth Amendment* (Berkeley: University of California Press, 1951); William M. Wiecek, *The Sources of Antislavery Constitutionalism in America, 1760–1848* (Ithaca, NY: Cornell University Press, 1977).

4. Leon F. Litwack, *North of Slavery: The Negro in the Free States, 1790–1860* (Chicago: University of Chicago Press, 1961); C. Vann Woodward, "Seeds of Failure in Radical Race Policy," *Proceedings of the American Philosophical Society* 110, no. 1 (1966): 1. Eugene H. Berwanger, *The Frontier against Slavery: Western Anti-Negro Prejudice and the Slavery Extension Controversy* (Urbana: University of Illinois Press, 1967); V. Jacque Voegeli, *Free but Not Equal: The Midwest and the Negro during the Civil War* (Chicago: University of Chicago Press, 1967).

5. James Oakes, "Conflict vs. Racial Consensus in the History of Antislavery Politics," in John Craig Hammond and Matthew Mason, eds., *Contesting Slavery: The Politics of Bondage and Freedom in the New American Nation* (Charlottesville: University of Virginia Press, 2011), 299.

6. This is a large literature that includes Benjamin Quarles, *Black Abolitionists* (New York: Oxford University Press, 1969); James Oliver Horton and Lois E. Horton, *Black Bostonians: Family Life and Community Struggle in the Antebellum North,* 1979 (Reprint: New York: Holmes & Meier, 1999); Gary B. Nash, *Forging Freedom: The Formation of Philadelphia's Black Community, 1720–1840* (Cambridge: Harvard University Press, 1988); Patrick Rael, *Black Identity and Black Protest in the Antebellum North* (Chapel Hill: University of North Carolina Press, 2002); Leslie M. Harris, *In the Shadow of Slavery: African Americans in New York City, 1626–1863* (Chicago: University of Chicago Press, 2003); Nikki M. Taylor, *Frontiers of Freedom: Cincinnati's Black Community, 1802–1868* (Athens: Ohio University Press, 2005); Erica Ball, *To Live an Antislavery Life: Personal Politics and the Antebellum Black Middle Class* (Athens: University of Georgia Press, 2012).

7. Eric Foner, *Free Soil, Free Labor, Free Men: The Ideology of the Republican Party*

before the Civil War, 1970 (Reprint: New York: Oxford University Press, 1995), 290; Paul Finkelman, "Before the Fourteenth Amendment: Black Legal Rights in the Antebellum North," *Rutgers Law Journal* 17 (1985–86): 415–82.

8. Corey M. Brooks, "Reconsidering Politics in the Study of American Abolitionists," *Journal of the Civil War Era* 8, no. 2 (June 2018): 291–317; Brooks, *Liberty Power: Antislavery Third Parties and the Transformation of American Politics* (Chicago: University of Chicago Press, 2016). Charles H. Wesley, "The Participation of Negroes in Anti-Slavery Political Parties," *Journal of Negro History* 29, no. 1 (Jan. 1944); Richard H. Sewell, *Ballots for Freedom: Antislavery Politics in the United States, 1837–1860* (New York: Oxford University Press, 1976); Reinhard O. Johnson, *The Liberty Party, 1840–1848: Antislavery Third-Party Politics in the United States* (Baton Rouge: Louisiana State University Press, 2009), as well as state studies such as Stephen E. Maizlish, *The Triumph of Sectionalism: The Transformation of Ohio Politics, 1844–1856* (Kent, OH: Kent State University Press, 1983), Phyllis F. Field, *The Politics of Race in New York: The Struggle for Black Suffrage in the Civil War Era* (Ithaca, NY: Cornell University Press, 1982), and Bruce Laurie, *Beyond Garrison: Antislavery and Social Reform* (New York: Cambridge University Press, 2005). There are also good biographies of some prominent editors and politicians in the political antislavery movement, including Gamaliel Bailey, Benjamin Lundy, James Birney, Salmon Chase, and Owen Lovejoy.

9. Stephen Middleton, *The Black Laws: Race and the Legal Process in Early Ohio* (Athens: Ohio University Press, 2005).

10. Stephen Kantrowitz, *More Than Freedom: Fighting for Black Citizenship in a White Republic, 1829–1889* (New York: Penguin, 2012); Anne Twitty, *Before Dred Scott: Slavery and Legal Culture in the American Confluence, 1787–1857* (New York: Cambridge University Press, 2016); Kelly M. Kennington, *In the Shadow of Dred Scott: St. Louis Freedom Suits and the Legal Culture of Slavery in Antebellum America* (Athens: University of Georgia Press, 2017); Kimberly M. Welch, *Black Litigants in the Antebellum American South* (Chapel Hill: University of North Carolina Press, 2018); Christopher James Bonner, *Remaking the Republic: Black Politics and the Creation of American Citizenship* (Philadelphia: University of Pennsylvania Press, 2020); Jones, *Birthright Citizens*; Sarah L. H. Gronningsater, *The Arc of Abolition: The Children of Gradual Emancipation and the Origins of National Freedom* (Philadelphia: University of Pennsylvania Press, forthcoming).

11. The better-known Republican politicians discussed in this book have often been the subject of biographies, including by historians interested in the sources of their thinking about rights and equality. These include Rebecca E. Zietlow, *The Forgotten Emancipator: James Mitchell Ashley and the Ideological Origins of Reconstruction* (New York: Cambridge University Press, 2018); Gerard N. Magliocca, *American Founding Son: John Bingham and the Invention of the Fourteenth Amendment* (New York: New York University Press, 2013); Richard

L. Aynes, "The Antislavery and Abolitionist Background of John A. Bingham," *Catholic University Law Review* 37, no. 4 (Summer 1998): 881–933; Lea VanderVelde, "Henry Wilson: Cobbler of the Frayed Constitution: Strategist of the Thirteenth Amendment," *Georgetown Journal of Law and Public Policy* 15 (2017): 173–264.

12. Laura F. Edwards, *The People and Their Peace: Legal Culture and the Transformation of Inequality in the Post-Revolutionary South* (Chapel Hill: University of North Carolina Press, 2009); Kunal Parker, *Making Foreigners: Immigration and Citizenship Law in America, 1600–2000* (New York: Cambridge University Press, 2015); William J. Novak, *The People's Welfare: Law and Regulation in Nineteenth-Century America* (Chapel Hill: University of North Carolina Press, 1996); Harry N. Scheiber, "Public Rights and the Rule of Law in American Legal History," *California Law Review* 72 (1984): 217–51; Christopher Tomlins, *Law, Labor, and Ideology in the Early American Republic* (New York: Cambridge University Press, 1993).

INDEX